Thomas More

Utopia

Latin text and English translation

Thomas More

UTOPIA

LATIN TEXT AND
ENGLISH TRANSLATION

EDITED BY
GEORGE M. LOGAN
ROBERT M. ADAMS
AND
CLARENCE H. MILLER

CAMBRIDGE
UNIVERSITY PRESS

CAMBRIDGE UNIVERSITY PRESS
Cambridge, New York, Melbourne, Madrid, Cape Town, Singapore, São Paulo

Cambridge University Press
The Edinburgh Building, Cambridge CB2 2RU, UK

Published in the United States of America by Cambridge University Press, New York

www.cambridge.org
Information on this title: www.cambridge.org/9780521403184

First published 1995
This digitally printed first paperback version 2006

A catalogue record for this publication is available from the British Library

Library of Congress Cataloguing in Publication data

More, Thomas, Sir, Saint, 1478–1535.
[Utopia, English & Latin]
Utopia: a reading text and an English translation / Thomas More:
edited by George M. Logan, Robert M. Adams, and Clarence H. Miller.
p.   cm.
Latin text based on the Froben edition of March 1518, but spelling
and punctuation have been regularized in accordance with modern
practices.
Includes bibliographical references and index.
ISBN 0 521 40318 9 (hard)
1. Utopias   I. Logan, George M., 1941–   .   II. Adams, Robert
Martin, 1915–   .   III. Miller, Clarence H.   IV. Title.
HX810.5.E54   1994
321′.07–dc20   93–42534   CIP

ISBN-13 978-0-521-40318-4 hardback
ISBN-10 0-521-40318-9 hardback

ISBN-13 978-0-521-02497-6 paperback
ISBN-10 0-521-02497-8 paperback

First published in Latin in 1516, Thomas More's *Utopia* is one of the most influential books in the Western philosophical and literary tradition and one of the supreme achievements of Renaissance humanism. This is the first edition of *Utopia* since 1965 (the Yale edition) to combine More's Latin text with an English translation, and also the first edition to provide a Latin text that is at once accurate and readable. The text is based on the early editions (with the Froben edition of March 1518 as copy-text), but spelling and punctuation have been regularised in accordance with modern practices. The translation is a revised version of the acclaimed Adams translation, which also appears in Cambridge Texts in the History of Political Thought. The edition, which incorporates the results of recent Utopian scholarship, includes an introduction, textual apparatus, a full commentary and a guide to the voluminous scholarly and critical literature on *Utopia*.

Germano Marc'hadour
Amabili et eximio amico Mori
et
Amicorum Mori

CONTENTS

PREFACE

This edition of *Utopia* is a revised and expanded version of the one that Robert M. Adams and I prepared for the Cambridge Texts in the History of Political Thought (1989). That edition printed More's book only in translation; this one adds a redaction of the Latin text, together with a textual introduction and notes, and an appendix on the choice of copy-text. It also incorporates changes to the introductory materials and annotations of the earlier edition, prompted by the addition of the text and apparatus and the attendant redirection of the edition to a partly different readership from the undergraduate students to whom the Cambridge Texts series is primarily directed. The present edition also incorporates corrections of some errors in the earlier edition, as well as many revisions to its translation.

In presenting the Latin text, the readers we have had primarily in mind are specialists in fields such as English literature or the history of political thought; that is, readers who have some Latin but are not Neo-Latin scholars. With such an audience in view, we have – as the textual introduction explains in detail – modernised our copy-text (the Froben edition of March 1518) in three respects. First, we have regularised spellings to conform to standard modern orthography for Latin. Second, we have divided the text into paragraphs. Third, we have thoroughly repunctuated it. Punctuation in the early editions of *Utopia* is (as with other early books) based on principles partly different from those underlying modern punctuation, employs a partly different set of marks, and is, moreover, erratic. Repunctuation is not nearly as simple as it may sound. Having undertaken it, we have constantly had to confront problems of syntax and meaning that Father Surtz (as editor of the conservative reprint in the Yale edition) generally passed over in silence. We hope that our solutions to these problems will meet with approval; at the least, the discussion of them in the apparatus may direct attention to matters that have not previously received as much of it as they deserve.

I should explain how the Cambridge Texts pair of editors came

to be expanded into a trio. When the present edition was in what I took to be nearly final form, I asked Clarence Miller if he would give it a critical reading. With no expectation of recompense beyond the usual acknowledgement in the Preface, he agreed to do so. But when he returned the manuscript, the quantity and quality of his annotations on all parts of it were such that it seemed obvious that he should be named (if indeed he were *willing* to be named) as one of the editors. To my great satisfaction, he agreed to be associated with the edition in this way, and also to perform various tasks in its completion. I was, too, particularly eager to have him join the project because other commitments had forced Adams to withdraw from further participation in the preparation of the edition, just after he had examined the same version of it that I had sent to Miller.

The division of labour in this edition and its Cambridge Texts predecessor, then, is as follows. For the Cambridge Texts edition, Adams revised the translation he had previously published with W. W. Norton & Company and made new translations of some of the ancillary letters and poems that buttress More's text in the early editions; for the present edition, he prepared the Latin text and the textual introduction and notes. For both editions, I provided the other introductory materials and the commentary; and for this one I added the appendix on copy-text. Adams and I thoroughly vetted each other's contributions; and, as I noted above, Miller subsequently vetted all parts of the edition, correcting errors in the text and making suggestions for changes in the apparatus and in the translation and commentary. As coordinator of the project, I was finally responsible for accepting, rejecting or modifying suggestions made by my co-editors – and I am therefore wholly responsible for all remaining errors and infelicities.

On my own and Adams's behalf, I take this opportunity to record again our gratitude to Quentin Skinner and Richard Tuck for their valuable comments on the introductory materials in their earlier form, and to Ruth Sharman, whose reading of the Cambridge Texts edition on behalf of the Press prompted many improvements. Skinner also vetted the introductory materials of the present edition. We are indebted to the late, and greatly lamented, John Benedict, Vice President and Editor of W. W. Norton, for securing Norton's acquiescence in our publication of a revised version of Adams's translation. For the new edition as for its predecessor, Karen Donnelly provided indispensable help of several kinds.

Mike Smith solved many computer problems – a few of them tricky even for him. Virginia Catmur, the Press's editor for the new edition, ideally combined care, erudition and patience.

Our greatest debt – one both general and particular – is reflected in the dedication of the edition to Father Germain Marc'hadour. As a More scholar of unmatched breadth and intensity, and as paterfamilias of the international community of those who study and admire More and his works, Father Marc'hadour merits acknowledgement in *every* piece of More scholarship. But he also performed a particular service for this one. Shortly after the publication of the Cambridge Texts edition, I asked him if he would read through it, with a view to identifying flaws that should be avoided in the new edition. In his usual thorough and precise fashion, Father Marc'hadour voluminously annotated the book from front to back, suggesting many changes that have been incorporated into the introduction, translation and commentary of the present edition.

G.M.L.

TEXTUAL PRACTICES

(1) *References.* CW = Yale *Complete Works of St Thomas More*; *Selected Letters* = St Thomas More: *Selected Letters*, ed. Elizabeth F. Rogers; *CWE* =Toronto *Collected Works of Erasmus*. References to the Bible are to the Authorised ('King James') Version – except for the Apocrypha, where references are to the Vulgate. Except where otherwise specified, references to Greek and Roman classics are to the editions of the Loeb Classical Library. Three important exceptions are Aristotle's *Politics*, which we quote from the edition of Sir Ernest Barker, and Plato's *Republic* and *Laws*, quoted from the Penguin editions by, respectively, H. D. P. Lee and Trevor J. Saunders. For all other works, initial references include publication data; place of publication is London unless otherwise specified. Subsequent references are made as brief as is compatible with clarity. Publication data are repeated in 'Works cited', which also gives these data for the Loeb Classical Library editions quoted.

(2) *Names.* Names of historical figures of More's era are spelled as in *Contemporaries of Erasmus: A Biographical Register of the Renaissance and Reformation* (ed. Peter G. Bietenholz and Thomas B. Deutscher). The sole exception is Pieter Gillis, for whom we use the familiar anglicised form Peter Giles.

(3) *Modernisation.* Whenever sixteenth-century English is quoted, spelling (and sometimes punctuation) is silently modernised. Spelling and punctuation in the Latin text are also modernised: for specifics, see the textual introduction. Greek words appearing in the commentary are given in transliterated form.

(4) *Gendered language.* Where More uses nouns or pronouns that can, in classical Latin, encompass not just males but human beings of either sex (for example, *homo*, *puer* and *nemo*), we have employed similarly inclusive English equivalents in the translation. We have also avoided gendered pronouns in passages where the Latin permits us to do so, and where More may plausibly be thought not to have intended to restrict his reference to males. But *Utopia* – like all other Renaissance

works, and despite the fact that one of its notable features is
the nearly equal treatment that the Utopian republic accords to
women and men in education, work and military training and
service – is the product of a culture in which intellectual and
political life were generally regarded as almost exclusively male
domains; and the truth is that we have probably translated into
gender-neutral language some passages where More had in mind
only males.

INTRODUCTION

PART I: INTERPRETATIVE CONTEXTS

Utopia treats fundamental issues of human nature and society, and brings to bear on them a seldom-matched combination of classical learning, practical experience and depth and complexity of mind. Richly allusive and endlessly enigmatic, intriguing to scholars in several disciplines and inspiring to reformers and revolutionaries, More's little book has spawned an unusually varied interpretative tradition. As editors, we are not called upon to promulgate a comprehensive interpretation of our own – even if we could agree on one. We do, though, believe that any interpretation needs to take into account certain fundamental facts about *Utopia* and its background, and that it is our role to provide the necessary starting points for interpretation, by setting the book in its contexts in More's life and times, and in the history of political thought. In this process, Part I of the Introduction provides the broad outlines, and the annotations to the text fill in details; in turn, these annotations, together with the 'Brief guide to scholarship', point the reader to the most important texts on which a fuller and deeper understanding of *Utopia* and its critical tradition depends.

More to Utopia

Thomas More was born in London on 7 February 1478, or possibly 1477.[1] His father, John More, was determined that his eldest son should follow him into the legal profession. Thomas spent a few years at St Anthony's School, learning the fundamentals of Latin grammar and composition. At the age of about twelve, he was placed as a page in the household of Henry VII's Lord Chancellor, John Morton. (Morton was also Archbishop of Canterbury and, from 1493, a cardinal.) This placement was ideally suited to expos-

---

[1] See the most recent biography: Richard Marius, *Thomas More* (New York, 1984), p. 7.

ing More to the ways of public life, and to securing him a powerful patron. After two years at Morton's, the boy was sent to Oxford, presumably to sharpen the skills in rhetoric and logic that would be important to a legal career. He was then, at about sixteen, brought back to London to begin legal training in the Inns of Court.

During his years as a law student, however, More came increasingly under the influence of a group of literary scholars, central figures of the emerging tradition of humanism in England. As Paul Oskar Kristeller has taught us, Renaissance humanism was not a philosophical position but a particular scholarly orientation. The term 'humanist' derives from *studia humanitatis*, a Ciceronian phrase that came to designate a family of disciplines: grammar, rhetoric, history, poetry and moral philosophy.[2] In the Renaissance as in the Middle Ages, Latin was the normal language of learning. Beginning in the fourteenth century, humanists like Petrarch attempted to revive the classical form of that language; by the early fifteenth century, they had undertaken a parallel attempt for classical Greek. More studied Latin composition with the grammarian John Holt, and Greek under William Grocyn. He also fell strongly under the influence of John Colet. Like Grocyn, Colet had studied in Italy, the centre of humanist learning. After his return to England in 1496, he gave several series of lectures at Oxford on the epistles of St Paul, lectures that constituted the earliest English application of some of the exegetical and historiographical techniques of Italian humanism; later he became Dean of St Paul's Cathedral, and founded there the first of the humanist grammar schools in England. And in 1499, More made the acquaintance of the great Dutch humanist Erasmus, who in that year first visited England.

Indeed, at this period More seems to have been at least as intent on the pursuit of literary scholarship as of the law. He also seriously considered becoming a priest – doubtless in part because scholarship was almost exclusively the province of clerics. According to a biographical sketch of More that Erasmus wrote in 1519, for a time 'he applied his whole mind to the pursuit of piety, with vigils and fasts and prayer and similar exercises preparing himself for the priesthood' (*CWE*, VII, 21). In fact More seems to have tested his vocation not merely for the priesthood – a calling that, as Morton's example shows, need not have precluded a legal career – but also for a life of religious withdrawal. The biography by his son-in-law

[2] Kristeller, *Renaissance Thought: The Classic, Scholastic, and Humanist Strains* (New York, 1961), pp. 8–23.

William Roper says that at about this time More lived four years with the Carthusians, the strictest of the monastic orders.[3]

Eventually More made his choices. In late 1504 or early 1505, he closed the door to the priesthood and monasticism by marrying Joan Colt;[4] nor is there any sign, in the years following his marriage, that he thought of abandoning the law. Given the necessity of supporting a growing family – Joan bore him four children before her death in 1511, after which More married a middle-aged widow, Alice Middleton – he could scarcely afford to entertain such thoughts.

In the decade following his first marriage, More rose rapidly in the legal profession. Roper says that he was a member of the Parliament of 1504, and he almost certainly represented the City of London in that of 1510. In the same year, he began to act as a city judge, having been appointed an undersheriff of London. Increasingly he won assignments that drew on his literary and rhetorical as well as his legal skills. By August 1517, and perhaps somewhat earlier, he had entered Henry VIII's council.[5] His first conciliar assignment was as a diplomat, in a trade mission to Calais. And though his subsequent tasks spanned a broad range of activities, his main employment, before he became Lord Chancellor in 1529, was as secretary to the king. He also served frequently as the king's orator. And when Henry decided to write against Martin Luther (in 1520), More acted as his literary adviser and editor.

In the earlier part of his professional life, More also managed to carry out a substantial amount of independent scholarship and writing. It is striking how precisely his works of this period conform to the five associated disciplines of the *studia humanitatis*.[6] As grammarian (in the Renaissance understanding of the term), he translated Greek poems and four short works by the Greek ironist Lucian. As rhetorician, he wrote a declamation in reply to Lucian's *Tyrannicide*. (The declamation was a standard rhetorical exercise, a speech on a paradoxical or otherwise ingenious topic, often involving the impersonation of some historical or mythical figure.)

[3] *The Life of Sir Thomas More*, in *Two Early Tudor Lives*, ed. Richard S. Sylvester and Davis P. Harding (New Haven and London, 1962), p. 198.

[4] On her given name, see Germain Marc'hadour, 'More's first wife . . . Jane? or Joan?', *Moreana*, 29, No. 109 (1992), 3–22.

[5] J. A. Guy, *The Public Career of Sir Thomas More* (New Haven and London, 1980), pp. 6–7.

[6] See Kristeller, 'Thomas More as a Renaissance Humanist', *Moreana*, No. 65–6 (1980), 5–22.

Erasmus reports a lost dialogue, evidently in the spirit of a declamation, defending the community of wives advocated in Plato's *Republic*. Several of More's longer, polemical letters of these years belong to the rhetorical subgenre of invective. As poet, he wrote, in addition to a few English poems, a large number of Latin epigrams. As historian, he practised the humanist genre of historical biography, in Latin and English versions of his unfinished *History of King Richard III* (a splendid, sardonic work that, having been incorporated into the chronicle histories, became the main source of Shakespeare's play) and in his translation of a biography of the fifteenth-century Italian philosopher Pico della Mirandola. As moral and political philosopher, he wrote *Utopia*. The publication of *Utopia* came near the end of this phase of More's literary career. Apart from three long polemical letters in defence of Erasmus and humanist learning, for several years after 1516 he wrote little other than what was required of him in his profession; and when he resumed writing books in the 1520s – works opposing the Lutheran 'heresy', and a series of devotional works – they no longer fitted the humanist categories.

The composition of Utopia

Utopia was conceived in the summer of 1515. In May of that year, More left England for Flanders, as a member of a royal trade commission. The negotiations conducted by this commission and its Flemish counterpart at Bruges were suspended by 21 July, but More did not return to England until 25 October. In the three months from late July to late October, he enjoyed a rare period of leisure; it was during this period that *Utopia* began to take shape.

At some point in the summer More visited Antwerp, where he met Peter Giles, to whom Erasmus had recommended him. Giles was a man after More's own heart. He was a classical scholar and an intimate of Erasmus and his circle; he was also a man of practical affairs, city clerk of Antwerp and as such deeply involved in the business of that cosmopolitan shipping and commercial centre. Book I of *Utopia* opens with a brief account of the trade mission, which leads into an account of More's acquaintance with Giles. At this point, the work glides from fact into fiction. More says he encountered Giles after Mass one day, and Giles introduced him to Raphael Hythloday, with whom they proceeded to have the conversation that is recorded in *Utopia*. This fictional conversation is presumably the transformation and expansion of actual conversa-

tions between More and Giles.[7] Be that as it may, More's visit to Antwerp served to crystallise and fuse a range of concerns most of which had (on the evidence of his earlier writings) been in his mind for years.

We have no direct information as to when More began drafting *Utopia*. In his biographical sketch, Erasmus reported that More wrote the second book 'earlier, when at leisure; at a later opportunity he added the first in the heat of the moment' (*CWE*, VII, 24). As J. H. Hexter argues, if More wrote Book II first, it seems very likely that he initially regarded it as a complete work; probably this version of *Utopia* was well in hand by the time he returned to England.[8] Back in London, though, he found reason to add the dialogue of Book I.[9]

Hexter points out that the first version of *Utopia* must have included not only the account of Utopia that now occupies all but the last few pages of Book II but also an introduction something like the opening of the present Book I. Otherwise it would not be clear who is speaking in the monologue on Utopia, and under what circumstances. The second phase of composition must have begun, then, not with the embassy to Bruges and the diversion to Antwerp but with the dialogue of Book I. Indeed the precise point where More, as Hexter says, 'opened a seam' in the first version of *Utopia* to insert the dialogue can be identified with some confidence (see below, p. 49n). After writing the dialogue, More must also have revised the conclusion of the work as a whole. In the final paragraph of Book II, as Hexter points out, the narrator recalls that Hythloday 'had reproached certain people who were afraid they might not appear knowing enough unless they found something to criticise in the ideas of others'. But Hythloday's censures occur in the dialogue of Book I (p. 53), so that this allusion to them must have been written after the dialogue.

The fact that *Utopia* was composed in this odd sequence presumably has implications for its interpretation. As with many other facts about the book, though, this one cuts two ways. On the one

---

[7] Giles seems to hint as much in the commendatory letter he wrote for the first edition of *Utopia*: see below, p. 25.

[8] See *More's 'Utopia': The Biography of an Idea* (Princeton, 1952; rpt with an epilogue, New York, 1965), pp. 15–30; *CW*, IV (*Utopia*), xv–xxiii.

[9] Hythloday's narrative of an imaginary meeting of the French privy council includes (pp. 83–5) references to Milan as under French control (it was recaptured by France in September 1515) and to Ferdinand II of Aragon as a force to be reckoned with (he died in January 1516). These allusions suggest a time-frame for the composition of Book I that is consistent with Erasmus' claim.

hand, it may suggest that More split open a complete, unified book to insert a dialogue which, though interesting in itself, doesn't really belong with the original material – that *Utopia* is really *two* books. Or it may suggest that More had second thoughts about the account of Utopia and saw a need to insert a new section which would be in effect an introduction to it. In any event, the dialogue affects our view of Utopia. For one thing, it gives us a much sharper sense of Hythloday, who is both our only source of information about the island commonwealth and its foremost enthusiast.

Shaping forces

More's book benefited greatly both from his experience in law and politics and from his humanist learning. Though the social problems *Utopia* addresses are perennial, the particular formulations of them, and the data of recent and contemporary English and European life that the book deploys, reflect More's personal and professional experience. But the intellectual paradigms that he brings to bear on the understanding of these problems, and the form and style of his book, derive primarily from his literary humanism.

The most obvious relation between *Utopia* and More's humanist learning is that with the central Greek works of political philosophy. The full title of More's book – *De optimo reipublicae statu deque nova insula Utopia* – identifies it as belonging to the oldest genre of political writing, the discourse on the ideal commonwealth initiated by Plato's *Republic* and *Laws* and continued in Aristotle's *Politics* – and subsequently in many other works. Plato's and Aristotle's discussions of the ideal commonwealth are, however, purely argumentative, whereas the Utopian part of More's book consists of Hythloday's fictional travelogue. The decision to present his imaginary society in the form of a long speech by a fictional personage is responsible both for much of the book's interest and for much of its enigmatic quality. Fictions are attractive, but in their very nature they are unapt to resolve into unambiguous meanings.[10]

For the debate of Book I, the primary formal models are the dialogues of Plato – and, perhaps even more, those of Cicero. Like

---

[10] More's decision to present Utopia as a fiction has also been responsible for much of his book's influence: the literary genre of the utopia, which *Utopia* initiated, differs from the philosophical discourse *de optimo reipublicae statu* precisely in that it offers a fictionalised account of the ideal commonwealth as if it already existed. In the second of the two letters on *Utopia* that More addressed to Giles, he commented obliquely on the advantage of this way of proceeding. See p. 269.

Utopia and unlike the Platonic dialogues, Cicero's dialogues consist mainly of long speeches punctuated by brief interruptions; like *Utopia*, too (and like other humanist dialogues and again unlike Plato's), Cicero's dialogues are more concerned with expounding alternative positions than with reaching definite and prescriptive conclusions. There are also precedents for the main *topic* of More's debate, in humanist as well as classical literature. Arguing about whether Hythloday should join a king's council is a way of getting at the general, and very frequently discussed, problem of 'counsel': the problem of ensuring that rulers get – and take – appropriate advice. As Quentin Skinner observes, this problem could be approached either from the point of view of the ruler, in which case the focus is on 'the importance of choosing good councillors and learning to distinguish between true and false friends', or from the point of view of the prospective councillor, when the focus is on the question of whether a scholar should commit himself to practical politics.[11] Viewed in this second perspective, the problem amounts to one formulation of the ancient question of the relative merits of the active and contemplative lives.[12] Since, as Skinner says, 'humanists tended to see themselves essentially as political advisers', counsel was the political topic that most intrigued them. More himself had special reason to be intrigued: he had been edging closer to full-time royal service, and, in the period when he wrote the dialogue of Book I, seems to have been pondering a first invitation to join Henry's council.[13] This would be a professional move toward which all his training and experience as lawyer and diplomat pointed, and yet contemplating it would have prompted some anxiety in a man who was also imbued with the ideals of scholarly and religious detachment.

Though the topic of counsel is commonplace, More's treatment of it is distinctive. This is also the case with his treatment (in Hythloday's account (pp. 55–77) of a debate he had taken part in at John Morton's table) of the problem of theft, which expands into

[11] *The Foundations of Modern Political Thought*, 2 vols. (Cambridge, 1978), I, 216–17.

[12] Influential – and durably interesting – treatments of this issue are found in Plato (*Republic* VI.496C–497B and Epistle VII) and Seneca ('On leisure' and 'On tranquillity of mind', in *Dialogi*), who make the case for non-involvement, and in one of Plutarch's *Moralia*, 'That a Philosopher ought to converse especially with men in power'. Cicero sees merit in both courses (*De officiis* I.xx.69–xxi.72, xliii.153–xliv.156).

[13] See Jerry Mermel, 'Preparations for a politic life: Sir Thomas More's entry into the king's service', *The Journal of Medieval and Renaissance Studies*, 7 (1977), 53–66.

a general analysis of the condition of England. More's handling of these matters differs from that of most other social or political writers of the period in what we may call its systemic or holistic approach. As Hexter puts it, More sees 'in depth, in perspective, and in mutual relation problems which his contemporaries saw in the flat and as a disjointed series' (*CW*, IV, ci). He understands that the problem of counsel cannot be solved by sending a few wise men to court, because, in the existing structure of society, most of the people they would encounter there – including especially the rulers – are motivated by blinkered self-interest. Similarly, the problem of theft cannot be solved by punishing thieves, because theft stems primarily from poverty, which is in turn the product of a number of social factors. The polity as a whole is a complex network of reciprocally-affecting parts.

The social analysis of Book I is also distinguished by its passionate intensity, its pervasive moral outrage at the status quo. The analysis of the problem of theft constitutes a scathing indictment of a system of 'justice' in which the poor are 'driven to the awful necessity of stealing and then dying for it' (p. 57). The root cause of this situation lies in the pride, sloth and greed of the upper classes. Noblemen live idly off others' labour, and also 'drag around with them a great train of idle servants' (p. 59), who, when they are later dismissed, know no honest way of making a living. The practice of enclosure (fencing common land as pasturage for sheep) deprives farm labourers of their livelihood and sets them to wander and beg – or to steal and be hanged.

Though it is Hythloday who delivers this indictment, one can hardly doubt that it embodies More's own views; and in fact More portrays himself as concurring in Hythloday's analysis (p. 81). In the debate on counsel, however, More portrays Hythloday and himself as taking opposite positions, with Hythloday opposing involvement and More favouring it. Both positions are powerfully argued, and they are never bridged: at the end of Book I, the disputants simply drop the topic and go on to another – the desirability of abolishing private property – about which they also never reach agreement.

These facts suggest another aspect of the relation between *Utopia* and its author's character and experience: that the personality and views of More's two main characters project his own persistent dividedness of mind. That 'More' closely resembles the author is clear. Yet it is equally clear that this cautious, practical lawyer and family man is More without his passion and vision, a More who

could not have written *Utopia*, nor ever have chosen martyrdom. The most obvious literary models for Hythloday – notwithstanding that his name is a Greek coinage that means something like 'nonsense peddler'[14] – are the stern experts on comparative politics of Plato's political dialogues. In the book's generic economy, Hythloday corresponds to the austere Stranger of the *Statesman* or the Old Athenian of the *Laws*, whose detachment from practical affairs enables them to see and speak the truth. But this is as much as to say that Hythloday is to some extent More's fantasy – partly wistful, partly critical – of what he himself might have been, had he made different choices a decade earlier; even as 'More' is his slightly deprecating representation of the practical man he had become.[15]

More's dividedness of mind is also related, via his humanist learning, to the seriocomic mode of *Utopia*. Here the key author is Lucian, four of whose works, as we noted above, More had translated. (These were published in 1506, together with some additional translations by Erasmus.)

A Syrian sophist of the second century AD, Lucian was one of the last writers of classical Greek. In a series of dialogues and other short prose pieces, he played a key part in the development of a tradition of making serious points under the guise of jokes, other examples of which are the *Golden Ass* of Apuleius, numerous mock orations and festive treatises (like those listed as precedents in Erasmus' preface to *The Praise of Folly*), and works of later writers like Rabelais and Swift. This tradition is sometimes characterised by the phrase *serio ludere* – 'to play seriously'.[16]

As More says in his preface to the translations of Lucian, this kind of writing satisfies the Horatian injunction that literature should combine delight with instruction (CW, III, Part I, 3); in his second letter to Giles, he indicates that this was why he chose a seriocomic mode for *Utopia*. But More was also attracted to the tradition of *serio ludere* for another, deeper reason. The divided, complex mind, capable of seeing more than one side of a question and reluctant to make a definite commitment to any single position,

---

[14] On the derivation, see below, p. 35n. Dominic Baker-Smith points out that Socrates is accused of peddling nonsense (Greek *hythlos*) in the *Republic*. See *More's 'Utopia'* (London and New York, 1991), p. 83.

[15] Hythloday also recalls Pico della Mirandola, who was to More a particularly intriguing modern exemplar of philosophic *otium*. On Pico and *Utopia*, see Baker-Smith, pp. 15–21.

[16] See, for example, Edgar Wind, *Pagan Mysteries in the Renaissance*, rev. edn (New York, 1968), esp. pp. 236–7, and Rosalie L. Colie, *Paradoxia Epidemica: The Renaissance Tradition of Paradox* (Princeton, 1966).

has a proclivity for ironic discourse; and *serio ludere* – in which the play can serve to qualify or undercut any statement – is one of the great vehicles of irony. The first major humanist work in the Lucianic tradition is *The Praise of Folly* (written in More's house in 1509). This is a declamation of bewilderingly complex irony, in which Erasmus has Folly (supposed to be a goddess) praise folly, thus setting up a sort of verbal hall of mirrors. The situation in *Utopia* is equally complex: a 'nonsense peddler' condemns Europe and praises Noplace (the meaning of the Greek nonce word 'Utopia');[17] and his views – many of which are clearly not nonsense – are reported by a character who bears the author's name, and who dissociates himself from most of them.

Book I

The dialogue of Book I constitutes a debate on a course of action: should Hythloday join a royal council? Moreover, this debate encompasses several others, on questions of public policy. At Morton's table, the topic is that of the best policy for dealing with the problem of theft; and, after recounting this debate, Hythloday goes on to describe imaginary meetings of two royal councils, debating respectively policy choices in foreign and domestic affairs. Finally, the book concludes with an exchange on the merits of communism.

For a Renaissance humanist like More, steeped in the tradition of classical rhetoric, debates on policy questions could scarcely fail to be conceived and developed in accordance with the theory of deliberative oratory, the oratory of persuasion and dissuasion. (Deliberative is one of the three *genera* of classical rhetoric, along with the demonstrative genre and the judicial.) A fundamentally important consequence of the affinity of Book I with deliberative oratory is that the arguments of the book are uniformly structured by the central *topoi* of the deliberative genre. The *topoi* (of which rhetorical manuals, like textbooks of logic, provided long lists) are the catalysts of *inventio*, subject-matter categories that suggest apposite arguments for the different genres; in the deliberative genre, invention is channelled by two paired, dominant topics, *honestas* and *utilitas* – honour and expediency.[18] The deliberative orator

---

[17] See below, p. 31n.
[18] On the key role of these topics, see, for example, Cicero, *De inventione* II.li.156–8, or Quintilian, *Institutio oratoria* III.viii.1–3, 22–5.

　　The fact that *Utopia* is closely akin to oratory in *inventio* (and in *dispositio* or arrangement) should not be taken to mean that its *style* is also oratorical. More's book exemplifies the *genus humile*, the so-called 'plain' or 'Attic' style (see below, p. 31 and note). As Cicero explains in the *Orator* (XIX.63–4), the plain style is

normally argues that a particular course of action is advisable on the ground that it is honourable, or on the ground that it is expedient – or argues that it is *in*advisable, as being either dishonourable or inexpedient. Naturally, the strongest case is made when it can be shown that considerations of honour and expediency point in the same direction.

This turns out to be the nature of Hythloday's argument not only on the problem of theft but on all the questions he addresses. The discussion of theft opens with the question of why this problem continues unabated despite the execution of so many thieves. Hythloday's response begins with, and is organised by, the contention that executing thieves is neither moral nor practical: 'The penalty is too harsh in itself, yet it isn't an effective deterrent. Simple theft is not so great a crime that it ought to cost a man his head, yet no punishment however severe can restrain those from robbery who have no other way to make a living' (p. 57). By contrast, Hythloday argues that the milder punishment he recommends is both just and expedient. Similarly, to 'More' and Giles he argues that joining a king's council would be neither honourable nor useful, since kings use councillors only to tell them how best to accomplish dishonourable and destructive ends. In his two narratives of imaginary privy council meetings, Hythloday portrays himself as arguing that the supposedly expedient courses recommended by the other councillors are both immoral and self-defeating. When 'More', at the climax of the debate on counsel, argues for an 'indirect', temporising approach, in which the councillor, knowing that he cannot turn all to good, will at least try to make things as little bad as possible, Hythloday responds that such a strategy is neither practical nor consistent with Christian morality. Indeed, we get the strong impression that he would say that the moral and the expedient *never* truly conflict, that correct analysis will always show that a dishonourable course is also impractical. This position links him with the Stoics, for whom (as Cicero explains in *De officiis*) the identity of the moral and the expedient is a key doctrine.

characteristic of philosophical writing; the correct term for this species of eloquence is *sermo* ('conversation') rather than *oratio*. The comparative simplicity of the plain style should not, however, be confused with artlessness. The Attic stylist, Cicero observes, cultivates the 'non ingratam neglegentiam de re hominis magis quam de verbis laborantis' (77: 'not unpleasant carelessness on the part of a man who is paying more attention to thought than to words'). Cf. More on Hythloday's 'neglecta simplicitas' (30:11–12). More's observation that Hythloday's 'sermo' was 'subitarius atque extemporalis' (30:8–9) may be intended to recall another standard authority, Demetrius' *On Style*, where we read that the style of dialogue 'reproduces an extemporary utterance' (IV.224).

Evidently the question of the relation of the moral and the expedient interested More deeply, as it did other humanists. The claim that the two are identical was a standard theme of early humanist political thought, which is permeated by Stoicism; but in the fifteenth century, some Italian humanists began to assert that *honestas* is *not* always the same as *utilitas*. In 1513, Machiavelli produced, in *The Prince*, the most famous of all statements of this position. More could not have known Machiavelli's book (it wasn't published until 1532), but he certainly knew the tradition of thought that it crystallised.

It is also evident that the question of the relation of *honestas* and *utilitas* is linked with the subject of the best condition of the commonwealth. If the moral and the expedient – the practical – are ultimately identical, then it is theoretically possible to design a viable commonwealth that would always act morally. But if the moral and the expedient cannot be fully reconciled, then this ideal could never be achieved, even in theory.

That More recognised the importance of this issue to the theory of the ideal commonwealth seems clear from what follows the exchange about the indirect approach to counsel. The question of the validity of this approach is never resolved – surely because More was of two minds about it. In More's *fiction*, though, the question is left unresolved because it is sidetracked by Hythloday's sudden confession that he thinks the abolition of private property offers the only route to social justice. 'More' disputes this claim, not on the ground that communism is unjust, but on the basis of arguments (derived from Aristotle's critique of the *Republic*) that it is impractical. The commonwealth cannot be stable, prosperous and happy without private property and the inequality that goes with it. Hythloday counters that More would think differently if he had seen Utopia: for that commonwealth embodies the equality that More thinks impractical, and yet it is uniquely happy and well-governed, with institutions that are both 'wise and sacred' (p. 101). This, then, is the context that More provided for the account of Utopia: a dispute about the degree of compatibility of the moral and the expedient in political life, and in particular whether the ideal of equality is compatible with stability and prosperity.

Book II

If Book I of *Utopia* is affiliated with deliberative oratory, Book II has an equally clear connection with the demonstrative or epideictic genre, the oratory of praise or blame. Whatever More's readers (or

More himself) might think of Utopia, for Hythloday it is 'that commonwealth which I consider not only the best but indeed the only one that can rightfully claim that name' (p. 241). Praise of a polis or *civitas* was a recognised subgenre of demonstrative oratory, and a perusal either of Quintilian's discussion of the praise of a city or of the list of *topoi* for this subgenre in Menander Rhetor's treatise on epideictic raises the question of whether such passages may not have suggested some features of the order of topics treated, and perhaps a few of the topics themselves, in Hythloday's long speech.[19]

If the order and selection of topics in the account of Utopia to some extent reflect the dicta of rhetorical theory, though, the structure of the commonwealth itself certainly derives from *political* theory. First, More took many of the institutional arrangements of Utopia from the discussions of the ideal commonwealth by Plato and Aristotle, and from idealised accounts of historical polities and their lawgivers by such authors as Tacitus and, especially, Plutarch. These appropriations range from small (but often striking) items such as the Utopians' custom of having wives stand 'shoulder to shoulder' (p. 211) with their husbands in battle (which seems to have been inspired or authorised by a passage in Plato's *Republic*: see p. 213n) to fundamental features of Utopian life such as the restrictions on property and privacy, the institution of the common tables, and the heavy use, in the inculcation of desirable behaviour, of what we should call positive and negative reinforcement.[20]

Second (and even more important), the structure into which the

---

[19] Quintilian III.vii.26–7. Menander's treatise (without translation) can be found in *Rhetores Graeci*, ed. Christianus Walz, 9 vols. (Osnabrück, 1968; originally published 1832–6), IX, 127–330; for a summary, see Theodore C. Burgess, 'Epideictic literature', *University of Chicago Studies in Classical Philology*, 3 (1902), 109–12.

[20] Our notes to the translation call attention to many of these appropriations; fuller treatments of the subject are found in the commentary in the Yale edition, and in several monographs: Edward L. Surtz, SJ, *The Praise of Pleasure* (Cambridge, Mass., 1957) and *The Praise of Wisdom* (Chicago, 1957); Thomas I. White, 'Aristotle and *Utopia*', *Renaissance Quarterly*, 29 (1976), 635–75; and George M. Logan, *The Meaning of More's 'Utopia'* (Princeton, 1983).

An interesting question is whether More also borrowed from Renaissance discussions of the best commonwealth, especially those by Platina, Beroaldo and Francesco Patrizi of Siena. More never mentions any modern work; but since an aversion to mentioning modern works (however much one may happen to be indebted to them) is a convention of humanist discourse, the absence of allusions does not imply that he did not profit from such books. As the Yale commentary makes abundantly clear, there are many parallels between the account of Utopia and writings of these moderns, especially Patrizi. But it seems to be impossible to say whether the parallels represent borrowings, or simply the fact that More and the Italians read the same classical books.

borrowed institutions are fitted appears to have been constructed by applying the method for designing an ideal commonwealth devised by Plato and Aristotle. In this method, creating such a commonwealth is not simply a matter of piling together all the desirable features one can think of. On the contrary, the design premise is the principle of *autarkeia*, self-sufficiency: the best commonwealth will be one that includes everything that is necessary to the happiness of its citizens, and nothing else. Starting from this economical premise, Plato developed, and Aristotle refined, a four-step procedure for constructing an ideal commonwealth.[21] First, one must determine what constitutes the happiest life for the individual. This is the central question of ethical theory, and, as Aristotle explains at the beginning of Book VII of the *Politics*, its answer constitutes the starting point of political theory. Second, from these conclusions about the most desirable life, the theorist derives the communal goals whose attainment will result in the happiness of the citizens. Third, it is necessary to form a sort of checklist of the physical and institutional components that the commonwealth must include: a certain size of population will be required, and a certain kind and extent of territory; certain occupational functions will have to be performed; and so on. Finally, the theorist determines the particular form that each of these components should be given in order to assure that, collectively, they will constitute the best commonwealth. For More, most of these forms are (as we noted above) appropriated from Plato's and Aristotle's discussions of the ideal commonwealth and from idealised accounts of actual commonwealths.

Though there are many other useful things to say about Book II of *Utopia*, it seems beyond dispute, and fundamental, that the book presents the results of a best-commonwealth exercise performed according to the Greek rules. This fact is obscured by More's decision to present his results in the form of a speech in praise of a supposedly existing commonwealth – the decision, as it were, to invent the genre of the utopia instead of writing a work of political theory. This decision entailed suppressing or disguising the various components of the dialectical substructure of his model. But once we recognise that Book II of *Utopia* embodies a best-commonwealth exercise, some mystifying aspects of the work begin to make sense. In particular, this recognition tells us how to take the lengthy account of Utopian moral philosophy (pp. 159–79);

---

[21] See Plato, *Republic* II.369B–372E; Aristotle, *Politics* VII.i–viii.

and it suggests an answer to a key question about the book: why did More create an imaginary commonwealth that seems (*pace* Hythloday) so clearly *not* ideal in some respects?

The passage on moral philosophy is in fact the cornerstone of the Utopian edifice: it constitutes the first step of the best-commonwealth exercise, the determination of the happiest life for the individual. The Utopians (who take it for granted that self-interest is the basic fact about human nature) maintain that pleasure is the goal of life, but they find that the most pleasurable life is the life of virtue. This is also the conclusion of Plato and Aristotle, but for them the virtuous life is that of contemplative leisure, made possible by the labour of slaves and artisans whose happiness is not a goal of the commonwealth. By contrast, the Utopians conclude that individual felicity is incompatible with special privilege, and think that the foremost pleasure 'arises from practice of the virtues and consciousness of a good life' (p. 175). Thus, though the Utopians are not Christians and their arguments consider only self-interest, they conclude that the best life for the individual is one lived in accordance with the moral norms of Christianity. Moreover, parallels between their arguments and passages in others of More's works confirm that he thought these arguments valid – though many readers have found them convoluted and strained.

But even if we grant that, for each individual, morality is always expedient, is this also true for the commonwealth as a whole? For the most part, Utopia supports this view. If, as the Utopians conclude, one's happiness is incompatible with spoiling the happiness of others, then it follows that the institutions of the commonwealth, whose goal is to maximise the happiness of its citizens, must be structured so as to implement the Golden Rule. Indeed, the institutions and policies of Utopia (many of which, as noted above, derive from previous treatments of the ideal commonwealth) are on the whole much preferable to those of European nations and are in many respects completely consistent with Christian standards, as those are interpreted in the writings of More and his associates.

Yet some Utopian practices are incompatible with these standards, and would seem to be justifiable only on grounds of expediency. To take the most disturbing examples, there is, first, the severe restriction of personal freedom. In Book I, Hythloday criticises repressive policies on the ground that 'it's an incompetent monarch who knows no other way to reform his people than by depriving them of all life's benefits' (p. 93), and this attitude harmonises with many passages in the writings of More's humanist

circle. The Utopians themselves believe that 'no kind of pleasure is forbidden, provided harm does not come of it' (p. 143). But in fact their lives are hedged round with numerous prohibitions: many activities are either forbidden, stigmatised or rigidly channelled – even the use of leisure time is limited to a few approved activities.

Then there are the troubling aspects of Utopian foreign policy. For the most part, the Utopians are generous toward their neighbours. They distribute their surplus commodities among them 'at moderate prices', and they are always happy to provide them with skilful and honest administrators (pp. 147, 197). They detest war, and, whenever it cannot be avoided, go to great lengths to minimise its destructiveness. Yet it turns out that they will go to war for a good many reasons – including to obtain territory for colonisation, whenever the Utopian population exceeds the optimum number. Furthermore, some of their military tactics are of very dubious morality. They offer rewards for the assassination of enemy leaders. They employ mercenaries to do as much of their fighting as possible – and the mercenaries they prefer are the savage Zapoletes, whose use is hard to reconcile with the aim of minimising war's destructiveness. Moreover, despite their compassion for the common citizens of enemy nations, the Utopians enslave the prisoners taken in wars in which they have employed their own forces.[22]

The explanation of these discrepancies between Utopian practices and More's own ideals would seem to lie in his recognition of the fact that even in the best commonwealth there will always be conflicts between valid goals – a problem that occurs but rarely to theorists of the ideal commonwealth or writers of utopias. More's awareness of the conflict of goals is first apparent in the section on moral philosophy. Utopian ethics is a strange fusion of Stoicism and Epicureanism. One feature of Epicureanism that would seem to have interested More greatly is the so-called 'hedonic calculus', Epicurus' rule that, in choosing among pleasures, one should always choose a greater pleasure over a lesser, and should reject any pleasure that will eventually result in pain: this formula occurs three times in one form or another in the passage on moral philosophy. Presumably More thought that similar principles should be applied

---

[22] Robert P. Adams shows that many of the 'antichivalric' Utopian military practices are consonant with Stoic and Erasmian humanist ideas (*The Better Part of Valor* (Seattle, 1962), pp. 152–4). But this argument cannot account for the particular practices mentioned here.

to resolving conflicts between goals at the political level; and it is possible to understand most of the unattractive features of Utopia in terms of such principles.

More was evidently impressed by the Aristotelian objections to egalitarianism that he has 'More' voice near the end of Book I. If Utopia does not manifest the chaos that 'More' had claimed would be inevitable in a communist society, the explanation would seem to lie in the elaborate system of constraints that More has built into it. Apparently he believed that too much freedom would threaten the stability and security of the commonwealth – which, in the nature of things, has to be the political goal of highest priority.

The same line of explanation can be applied to the disturbing Utopian practices in foreign policy. It is impossible to believe that More approved of all these practices; yet apparently he thought them necessary. The internal arrangements of Utopia or any other commonwealth will not really matter unless the commonwealth can be made externally secure; and as long as other commonwealths are not utopian, it is hard to see how to secure it without indulging in some practices that are expedient but certainly not moral.

Despite its abundant wit, *Utopia* is in fact a rather melancholy book. More evidently shared with St Augustine (whose *City of God* he had expounded in a series of lectures about 1501) the conviction that no human society could be wholly attractive; and he seems to have thought, too, that even the attractive arrangements that are theoretically possible are in practice very difficult to achieve. Is there any reason not to take at face value the final judgement of 'More' that Utopia includes 'many features that in our own societies I would wish rather than expect to see'? Yet 'More' also insists, in the debate on the 'indirect approach' to counsel, that things can be made at least a little less bad, by working tactfully on rulers and their councillors. Here as in other ways history has generally borne him out. Many of the reforms proposed in *Utopia* have been effected in the centuries since it was written – though not always by peaceful means, and not always resulting in clear net improvements.

PART II: THE LATIN TEXT

There is no holograph or other manuscript of *Utopia*. The first four printed editions, in which More or his direct agents might conceivably have had a hand – though in fact he was in England,

and all four printings were made on the continent – are dated 1516
(Louvain), 1517 (Paris), and March and November 1518 (both
Basel, in the shop of Johann Froben). For various reasons (set forth
in the Appendix), our copy-text has been 1518 March, which we
accordingly follow except in places where there is compelling
reason to follow another text, or to depart from the texts altogether
in favour of an emendation. We have footnoted all alternate readings that seemed potentially moot; but we have silently ignored the
great mass of variants, patently erroneous and/or trivial in themselves. Our controlling principle has been to produce a Latin text
that could be used by a reader with even the rudiments of the
tongue to check the English version across the page.

All the editions abound in mechanical errors. An occasional letter
may be dropped out, as when 1517 prints *Cuhberti* for *Cuthberti*
(40:13); a *u* or an *n* may be mistakenly printed upside down, as
when 1517 gives *inventa* for *iuventa* (54:23); or an *e* may be picked
up in error for a *c*, as when 1517 prints *eum* for *cum* (56:12). These
errors are understandable when one thinks, not of keyboarding a
manuscript, but of lifting tiny bits of lead from the type-boxes into
which they had been distributed by busy and not always attentive
boys. More had friends, or friends of friends, at the three printing
establishments that worked on *Utopia*, but he could not exercise
close control. The range of variants that resulted may be studied in
the edition of André Prévost, or in the Yale edition of Surtz and
Hexter.[23] In the present version, most are silently disregarded, along
with variants from editions later than 1518N, when they contribute
nothing to an understanding of the text.[24]

Certain conventions of sixteenth-century printers, perfectly
unremarkable in that age and understood without effort by readers,
have become obsolete over the centuries and look exceedingly
strange today. Following scribal practice, early printers made free
use of abbreviations, especially in Latin texts, where standardised
case endings and enclitic formations made the practice easy. In the
light of our controlling principle, and following the example of

---

[23] Neither edition records every variant spelling, abbreviation, or detail of punctuation, though Prévost records more of them than Yale.

[24] Odd variants, mentioned here only so readers will see the kind of thing they do
not have to cope with, are the fondness of 1518N for printing all forms of Rome
with an *h* (*Rhomani, Rhomanorum*, etc.); the pleasant error of 1517 in making
Cardinal Morton dismiss the parasite with a *nuptu* (marriage) instead of a *nutu*
(nod) (80:11); and 1516's alternative to having the Utopians collect rain, *pluvia*
(118:2), in cisterns. They collect instead *plunia* – rare objects indeed, unknown
to any dictionary.

most modern editions, we have silently expanded all these abbreviations. We should add, though, that the abbreviations are not always free from ambiguities. The most common one, a superior bar (‾), may stand either for an omitted *m* or an omitted *n*; it may refer to a previously as well as a subsequently omitted letter – *em̄* (where *i* is also omitted) stands for *enim*, as *nō* stands for *non*. In general, the printer's marks were but crude and limited imitations of the much greater variety of marks used by medieval scribes, the all-but-infinite range of which may be explored in Adriano Cappelli's *Dizionario di abbreviature latine ed italiane*.[25]

Aiming at ease of comprehension, we have paragraphed the Latin text, as the original typesetters did not; by making Latin paragraphs correspond with English paragraphs, we hope to have made equivalent passages easier to locate. (In passing, we note that our paragraphing of the text, though executed without any such deliberate intent, brings out a frequent function of the marginal glosses, in marking transitions to new topics.)[26]

Early printers had no quotation marks, and we have not introduced them into the Latin, feeling that their presence in the English suffices. Again, early fonts did not include the exclamation mark. The question mark doubled for interrogatories and exclamations; and sometimes we have replaced a question mark in the copy-text by an exclamation mark. Sometimes, too, we have cut a sentence in the middle with a question mark, when the question seemed to be over, but then allowed some subordinate clauses to trail on in declarative form, without the formality of a separate sentence. This practice is not alien to More's style: he does not always cut off his sentences crisply or start new ones decisively. Parentheses also called for frequent adjustment, to keep the parenthetical unit from gobbling up some essential unit of the surrounding sentence.

The early printings of *Utopia* do not employ the semicolon; but it occasionally seems an indispensable aid in clarifying More's syntax, and we have therefore not scrupled to use it. Similarly, we

---

[25] 6th edn, Milan, 1961. Cappelli's prefatory treatise has been translated by David Heimann and Richard Kay, as *The Elements of Abbreviation in Medieval Latin Paleography* (Lawrence, Kansas, 1982). A brief treatment of 'Abbreviations and contractions in early printed books' constitutes Appendix IV (pp. 319–24) in Ronald B. McKerrow's *An Introduction to Bibliography for Literary Students* (Oxford, 1927). The Latin text in Prévost's edition is a photographic facsimile of 1518N, and his Introduction includes a guide to expanding the abbreviations in that text (pp. 268–9).

[26] Sometimes the 1518M printer failed to place a gloss precisely opposite the passage to which it refers: in such cases we have silently repositioned the gloss.

have sometimes used the untextual dash (–). It is an inauthentic
mark of punctuation; but when the flow of a sentence is sharply
interrupted by an inner irony (62:27), an outer breach (66:28), or
an uncommonly long suspension, from which the reader must be
rescued with a visible effort (124:15–18) – under these circumstances we have introduced the dash.

The printer of 1518M did not carefully distinguish between the
three major marks of punctuation at his disposal, period, colon and
comma; he did not use them consistently to bring out the grammatical relations of his text. Not infrequently he put a period at either
end of a subordinate clause, thereby cutting it off from the principal
clause on which it must depend. In several notable passages, he
indulged in a profusion of unnecessary colons that radically interfere, not only with the flow of sentences, but with their syntax:

Quo enim pacto falleret ac tegeret fugam: homo nulla vestium parte
populo similis: nisi abeat nudus? (74:14–15; sig. f₄v)

Or:

Quae tantum absunt a facultate conspirandi: ut ne convenire quidem: et
colloqui aut salutare se mutuo liceat: ut credantur interim id consilium
intrepide credituri suis: quod reticentibus periculosum, prodentibus
maximo esse bono sciant. (74:19–23; sigs. f₄v–g₁)

In a single passage of about a page in length (194:23–196:19; sigs.
q₃–q₃v), we count twenty-eight unnecessary and frequently
obstructive colons, as well as two periods disjoining elements of a
sentence that make sense only when connected.

No less erratic was the printer's use of commas. He printed, for
example, a needless spate of them at 116:20–4 (sig. k₂). He often
divided the two parts of a compound subject, or of a joint direct
object. He regularly laid a comma between the two terms of a
comparison, and broke up with a comma the two parts of a *vel* . . .
vel or an *aut* . . . *aut* construction. He did not, on the other hand,
regularly set off parenthetical interjections or divide the elements
of a quotation, as for example:

Profecto mi Raphael inquam magna me affecisti voluptate . . . (80:24;
sig. g₃)

The effect of these disconcerting oddities in the punctuation of
Utopia is magnified by an erratic pattern of capitalisation. About
half the time the printer capitalised the first word of a new sentence
(the first word after a period), half the time he did not. Occasionally
he capitalised the first word after a comma, the first word after a

colon, or the first word of a parenthesis in the middle of a sentence. Still, the trouble these vagaries cause is limited: they are obvious to modern readers, and, once accustomed to them, they are easy to disregard. More insidious is a hidden effect of that prevalent overpunctuation which is the Froben printer's major fault. It encourages modern readers, who are perhaps not too confident of their Latinity in the first place, to take the text a phrase at a time, and thus to lose sight of the parallel and antithetical constructions in which Latin, even when as un-Ciceronian as More's, abounds. Bearing in mind the controlling principle of our text, and given the ready availability of two facsimiles (1516 by Scolar Press, 1518N by Prévost), not to mention Yale's very conservative reprint of 1518M, we have chosen to repunctuate and recapitalise the text to encourage rather than impede comprehension.[27]

Other sixteenth-century conventions of styling, which distract the modern eye without adding anything to the significance or sound of the text, include the use of *u* for *v*, as in *octauus*, for which we substitute *octavus*, or *uirtus*, which we replace with *virtus*. In capital letters the process is inverted, with *V* often but not invariably substituting for *U*; we print *Utopia* not *Vtopia*, *Ulysses* not *Vlysses*. When two *i*'s fall together, Renaissance printers, including Froben's 1518M man, commonly printed the second one as a *j*; we have altered to modern practice, as by printing *scriniis* rather than *scrinijs*.

The decision to modernise spelling in these particulars is easy; but other aspects of the orthography of 1518M pose more difficult questions. As is generally true of books printed before the advent of the copy-editor, Froben's *Utopia* spells the same word differently in different passages. The genitive of the Latin word for 'Castile' is *Castellae* when it first appears (40:10); when it recurs, it is *Castelliae* (84:5). There are twelve passages using *affectus* or variations, two using *adfectus*; there are nine *affero* formations, two *adfero* ones; there are two uses of *cerimonia*, one of *ceremonia*; and so on.[28]

[27] We follow in this respect the example set by the first of the 'modern' texts, the edition of J. H. Lupton (Oxford, 1895), and also by the edition of Marie Delcourt (Paris, 1936).

[28] These and the statistics in following paragraphs are based on Books I and II and the prefatory letter to Giles. They do not take into account the other preliminary and appended materials in 1518M, or More's second letter to Giles (which was included only in the 1517 edition), or the marginal glosses to the text (which are not by More). Note that Ladislaus J. Bolchazy's concordance to *Utopia* (which is based on the Yale edition) also excludes the *first* letter to Giles: *A Concordance to the 'Utopia' of St. Thomas More and A Frequency Word List* (Hildesheim and New York, 1978).

Variations such as these appear to be random. In other cases, there would seem to be a rationale of some kind at work, if sporadically. The word for 'only' – *dumtaxat* or *duntaxat* – occurs thirteen times: four times as *dum-*, nine as *dun-*. But three of the *duntaxat's* in 1518M were changed from an earlier *dumtaxat*, none the other way; and two of the four *dumtaxat's* were changed to *dun-* in 1518N. *Cum* in the text of *Utopia* often takes the form *quum*. There is a general tendency, though far from an invariable rule, to use *quum* as the conjunction (with the force of 'when' or 'while', sometimes in the causal relation implied by 'since') and *cum* as the preposition ('with') – but occasionally *cum* is used as the conjunction. *Carus* in the sense of 'expensive' occurs three times (64:5, 17, 23), but there are eleven occurrences of *charus* (including derivants such as *charitas*), all of them implying love and affection.[29] In seven passages an accusative plural is given the ending *-eis*: *forenseis, tutioreis, rebelleis, taleis, Ultra-aequinoctiales* and *omneis* (twice). These are but seven instances of several hundred; they may reflect an exceedingly fitful impulse to distinguish the accusative from the nominative.[30]

For a few special groups of words, someone charged with preparing copy for early editions of *Utopia* clearly had a distinct preference in spelling. The words *ocium* and *precium* are consistently printed instead of the forms (current over the last couple of centuries) *otium* and *pretium*; and *negocium* predominates over *negotium* by a margin of sixteen to five – but all five *t* forms (as well as *Negotiatio* in a marginal gloss (146:12)) are changed to *c* in 1518N. (Add also a solitary occurrence of *mundicies*.) To be sure, a number of similar words, such as *vitium, gratia, servitium, silentium* and *solatium* are spelled with a *t* throughout. *Spacium/spatium* is spelled now one way, now the other, as is *delicium/delitium*; and on at least one occasion a word that should be spelled with a *c* is spelled with a *t*: *discrutiet* (186:12; we have changed it to the *c* spelling).

With regard to the use of *i* or *y* in one set of words, we have a small bit of external evidence that More himself may have expressed a preference. In a jocose dialogue by More's friend Richard Pace (*De Fructu Qui Ex Doctrina Percipitur*, published by Froben in

---

[29] There is a contrary usage, *annonae charitas*, in 1516, 1517 and 1518N, but it is changed to *caritas* in 1518M (64:28).

[30] Prévost suggests that the archaic *-eis* forms aim at establishing a '*distance esthétique* entre le lecteur et le texte' (p. 249) – a phrase by which, in this context, we are not persuaded.

October 1517), the author's porte-parole is made to say that More 'struck out the *i* and put in the *y* in *considero* when he was correcting the *Utopia* in his own hand'.[31] There are in fact five words in the 1518M *Utopia* where *y* substitutes for *i* contrary to common usage. *Desyderium* is used nine times; *syncerus* four times; *consydero, sydus* and *hyems* twice apiece.[32] In six of these nineteen places *y* required to be changed from a previous *i*; the others had *y* from the beginning. There is no reason to doubt the authenticity of Pace's anecdote. But we cannot think without irony of an author making changes so minute and so imperceptibly significant in a text as carelessly printed as the first two editions of *Utopia*.

Of all these (and other) variant spellings, the only ones that can occasion significant difficulty are the few that are neither immediately recognisable nor easily located in a modern Latin dictionary. But we can eliminate *all* potential difficulties of this kind if we regularise spellings by bringing them into conformity with the preferred spellings in modern dictionaries; and, given the controlling principle of our text and the fact that the semantic loss in regularisation is very close to zero, we have chosen to follow this course. (Like the decision to repunctuate, this one is made easier by the availability of facsimiles of 1516 and 1518N, and Yale's conservative reprint of 1518M.) Our rule, then, has been to regularise all spellings – apart from the exceptions noted below – to the preferred spellings in the standard dictionary of Lewis and Short.[33] Thus, for example, *duntaxat* becomes *dumtaxat*, *affero* becomes *adfero*, *ocium* and *negocium* become *otium* and *negotium*, the seven accusatives in *-eis* are replaced by *-es* forms, and (despite More's reported efforts in the other direction) *consydero* yields to *considero*. We have, however, let stand those variant spellings where the variance may involve a semantic difference: thus *quum* and *charus* are retained. And in cases where 1518M includes not merely alternate spellings but alternate *forms* (*ut/uti, sicut/sicuti, velut/veluti, neu/ nive, seu/sive*) or synonymous but etymologically distinct words

---

[31] Ed. and trans. Frank Manley and Richard S. Sylvester (New York, 1967), p. 69.

[32] In 1516 and 1518M and N, *inclytae* (usually spelled with *u* or *i*) occurs both on the title page and in the heading of Book I; and there are two occurrences of *hystoria* in More's second letter to Giles.

[33] *A Latin Dictionary*, 'Founded on Andrews' Edition of Freund's Latin Dictionary, Revised, Enlarged, and in Great Part Rewritten by' Charlton T. Lewis and Charles Short (Oxford, 1879, with reprintings to 1966). On the rare occasions when a word used in 1518M does not appear in this dictionary – the Latin word for 'Castile', for example, and various other post-classical words – we follow the *Oxford Latin Dictionary* or a dictionary of medieval Latin.

(*musica/musice*), we have preserved both forms. Nor have we tried to impose order on the varied forms of nouns and adjectives denoting places (*Castellae/Castelliae, Londiniensis/Londinensis*).[34]

We have also effected one other kind of regularisation: the many Latin connectives, adverbs and indefinite pronouns that can be fitted out with enclitics or joined with one another to form a symphony of compounds have been fused whenever the sense did not positively forbid it. *Verumetiam, quandoquidem, alteruter, quotusquisque, haudquaquam, usqueadeo, quamobrem* and their many friends have been put or kept together where they did not cry out for separation. One strong reason for doing this is to make the passages stand out where potential combinations are for good and sufficient reason printed as separate words. *Post quam* means 'after which', not 'afterwards' (*postquam*), *qua re* means 'than which', not 'why' (*quare*), and *nihilo minus* means 'in no way less', not 'nonetheless' (*nihilominus*).

More's is an extremely eclectic Latin, bearing with it the mingled aromas of the marketplace, the pulpit, the law court, the classroom, the church fathers, the historians (like Sallust, who was so fond of archaisms) and the familiar letters of Cicero – who was not always as Ciceronian as we think.[35] Though More gives some signs of using Latin as a second language, it was one with which he was joyously familiar; his Latin is full of ellipses, colloquialisms, half-rhymes, neologisms rubbing shoulders with archaisms, locutions drawn from one context and boldly adapted for use in another. He is not always rigidly accurate in coordinating singulars with plurals; he uses a good many pronouns that a classical author would leave implicit in the form of the verb; he uses *ubi* very often in the sense

---

[34] For the occasional bit of Greek – in marginal glosses and in several of the ancillary letters – we have brought the placement of accents and breathings into conformity with modern practice.

[35] On More's Latinity, see R. Monsuez, 'Le latin de Thomas More dans *Utopia*', *Caliban*, 3 (1966), 35–78. Monsuez' study is based in part on Delcourt's discussion in her edition of *Utopia*. Much of the substance of both treatments is reproduced in the section on the Latin of *Utopia* in Prévost's edition (pp. 241–52). See also Surtz, 'Aspects of More's Latin style in *Utopia*', *Studies in the Renaissance*, 14 (1967), 93–109, and Clarence H. Miller, 'Style and meaning in More's *Utopia*: Hythloday's sentences and diction', in *Acta Conventus Neo-Latini Hafniensis: Proceedings*, ed. Rhoda Schnur *et al.* (Binghamton, N.Y., 1994), pp. 675–83. Among contemporaries, More's Latinity was condemned scathingly and at length by his enemy Germain de Brie (whose *Antimorus* is printed in CW, III, Part II, 482–547) and glancingly criticised by his friend Erasmus, who in his biographical sketch of More observes that there is 'a certain unevenness' in the style of *Utopia* (*CWE*, VII, 24). What such criticisms boil down to is the fact that More's Latin did not observe as strict a classical decorum as humanists normally demanded.

of *cum*; he is not above starting a sentence on one grammatical tack and switching abruptly to another. More's fondness for the unanticipated word or construction leads Delcourt to speak of his 'coquetterie' (p. 29); but she also recognises and applauds the fact that his nonchalance about grammar and syntax shows that for him Latin was a living language.

BRIEF GUIDE TO SCHOLARSHIP

The earliest biography of More is the ingenuous and engaging *Life of Sir Thomas More* by his son-in-law William Roper; it is published in *Two Early Tudor Lives*, ed. Richard S. Sylvester and Davis P. Harding (New Haven and London, 1962). The other notable sixteenth-century biographies are Nicholas Harpsfield, *The Life and Death of Sir Thomas Moore*, ed. E. V. Hitchcock (1932), and Thomas Stapleton, *The Life and Illustrious Martyrdom of Sir Thomas More*, trans. Philip E. Hallett, ed. E. E. Reynolds (1966). By far the most influential modern biography is R. W. Chambers' *Thomas More* (1935). The most recent one is Richard Marius, *Thomas More* (New York, 1984), which offers a resolutely unflattering portrait of More, in sharp contrast to its predecessors. Marius' revisionism follows the lead of G. R. Elton, in such studies as 'Thomas More, Councillor (1517–1529)', in *St. Thomas More: Action and Contemplation*, ed. R. S. Sylvester (New Haven and London, 1972), pp. 87–122, and 'The real Thomas More?', in *Reformation Principle and Practice*, ed. Peter N. Brooks (1980), pp. 23–31. With mixed success, Louis L. Martz attempts to correct the revisionist view, in *Thomas More: The Search for the Inner Man* (New Haven and London, 1990). More's professional life is traced by J. A. Guy, *The Public Career of Sir Thomas More* (New Haven and London, 1980). There is an engrossing psychobiographical study in Stephen Greenblatt's *Renaissance Self-fashioning from More to Shakespeare* (Chicago and London, 1980), pp. 11–73. Alistair Fox also interprets More's works in the context of an exploration of his complex psychology, in *Thomas More: History and Providence* (New Haven and London, 1983); his book has affinities with the revisionist view. (See below for Fox's monograph on *Utopia*.) A rich and convenient source of biographical information about More's contemporaries is *Contemporaries of Erasmus: A Biographical Register of the Renaissance and Reformation*, ed. Peter G. Bietenholz and Thomas B. Deutscher, 3 vols. (Toronto, Buffalo and London, 1985–7).

The first four editions of *Utopia* are discussed in our appendix

on the choice of copy-text. Two of them have been republished in photographic facsimile: 1516 by Scolar Press (1966), and 1518 November as the text in André Prévost's edition, *L'Utopie de Thomas More* (Paris, 1978). The earliest English translation is by Ralph Robinson, originally published in 1551 and reprinted many times (including a Scolar facsimile (1970) of the second, 1556 edition), perhaps most usefully as the translation in J. H. Lupton's Latin–English edition of *Utopia* (Oxford, 1895). More's English *Works* were published in 1557 (reproduced in a Scolar facsimile, 1978); the collected Latin works in 1563 (Basel) and 1565–6 (Louvain). The current standard edition for both languages is the fifteen-volume Yale edition of the *Complete Works of St. Thomas More*, launched in 1963 and now nearly complete. A 'Modernized Series' supplement provides translations of forty-four of More's Latin letters and texts of twenty-two English ones: *Selected Letters*, ed. Elizabeth F. Rogers (New Haven and London, 1961); Latin texts are available in Rogers' edition of *The Correspondence of Sir Thomas More* (Princeton, 1947). Some works not yet published in the Yale edition are available in *The English Works of Sir Thomas More*, ed. W. E. Campbell, with notes by A. W. Reed, 2 vols. (London and New York, 1931). Under the auspices of the Yale project, R. W. Gibson and J. Max Patrick published *St. Thomas More: A Preliminary Bibliography of His Works and of Moreana to the Year 1750* (New Haven and London, 1961). This volume lists the libraries where copies of the various items are to be found; for addenda to these lists (together with a few additions to the list of items itself), see Constance Smith, *An Updating of R. W. Gibson's 'St. Thomas More: A Preliminary Bibliography'* (St Louis, 1981), and Ralph Keen and Constance Smith, 'Updating an updating', *Moreana*, 25, No. 97 (1988), 137–40.

Utopia, ed. Edward Surtz, SJ, and J. H. Hexter (1965), is Vol. IV of the Yale edition. The other important modern critical editions are those of Lupton and Prévost (above), and that of Marie Delcourt (Paris, 1936), later reprinted with a French translation (Geneva, 1983). Other editions of *Utopia* referred to in our textual notes include those in the collected Latin works of 1563 and 1565–6, and the edition of V. Michels and T. Ziegler (Berlin, 1895). There is a concordance of *Utopia* by Ladislaus J. Bolchazy (Hildesheim and New York, 1978).

Utopia participates in a sort of dialogue with earlier (and later) works of political thought. The Greek and Roman works in this dialogue, as well as almost all of the other classical works to which

More alludes, are handily available in the bilingual editions of the Loeb Classical Library; these are the editions cited throughout this volume. Three extremely important exceptions, though, are Aristotle's *Politics*, which we quote in the translation by Ernest Barker (Oxford, 1948), and Plato's *Republic* and *Laws*, where we cite the engaging and handy Penguin translations: *The Republic*, trans. H. D. P. Lee, 2nd edn (Harmondsworth, 1974); *The Laws*, trans. Trevor J. Saunders (Harmondsworth, 1970). Passages in the works of More's fellow humanist Erasmus often provide the best gloss on passages of *Utopia*. Many of the major works are now available in the *Collected Works of Erasmus*, issuing from the University of Toronto Press (1974–).

For the context of *Utopia* in Renaissance political thought, see J. W. Allen, *A History of Political Thought in the Sixteenth Century* (1928; rpt with revised bibliographical notes, 1957), Quentin Skinner, *The Foundations of Modern Political Thought*, 2 vols. (Cambridge, 1978) and Skinner's chapter on political philosophy in *The Cambridge History of Renaissance Philosophy*, ed. Charles B. Schmitt *et al.* (Cambridge, 1988), pp. 387–452; for the context in moral philosophy, see Jill Kraye's chapter in the same work, pp. 301–86. *Utopia* participates in the Renaissance revival and extension of classical republicanism. Two major works on this subject are Hans Baron, *The Crisis of the Early Italian Renaissance: Civic Humanism and Republican Liberty in an Age of Classicism and Tyranny*, rev. one-vol. edn (Princeton, 1966), and J. G. A. Pocock, *The Machiavellian Moment: Florentine Political Thought and the Atlantic Republican Tradition* (Princeton, 1975). The history of utopian literature is massively treated by Frank E. and Fritzie P. Manuel, *Utopian Thought in the Western World* (Cambridge, Mass., 1979).

English translations of three early accounts of the New World reflected in *Utopia* are Amerigo Vespucci, *Mundus Novus: Letter to Pietro di Medici*, trans. George Tyler Northup (London and Princeton, 1916); *The Four Voyages of Amerigo Vespucci*, in Martin Walseemüller, *Cosmographiae Introductio* (Ann Arbor, 1966 (University Microfilms); rpt from the US Catholic Historical Society Monograph IV, 1907); and *De Orbe Novo: The Eight Decades of Peter Martyr D'Anghera*, trans. Francis A. MacNutt, 2 vols. (New York and London, 1912; rpt New York, 1970).

Hexter's section of the introduction to the Yale edition constitutes the most challenging and influential recent interpretation of *Utopia*; Surtz' section and his 300-page commentary supply a

wealth of information on the literary and historical contexts of the book. For information on any passage of *Utopia*, Surtz' commentary is the first place to look. Lupton's edition also has a full and interesting commentary; and there is a huge one in Prévost's edition. The most influential books on *Utopia* are Hexter's brilliant little *More's 'Utopia': The Biography of an Idea* (Princeton, 1952; rpt with an epilogue, New York, 1965), and two 1957 books by Surtz: *The Praise of Pleasure: Philosophy, Education, and Communism in More's Utopia* (Cambridge, Mass.) and *The Praise of Wisdom: A Commentary on the Religious and Moral Problems and Backgrounds of St. Thomas More's 'Utopia'* (Chicago). Both contain a wealth of illuminating contextual information – much of which is, however (like much of the substance of Hexter's book), incorporated into the Yale *Utopia*. Karl Kautsky's *Thomas More and His Utopia*, trans. H. J. Stenning (1927; first German edn 1888; rpt with a foreword by Russell Ames, New York, 1959), is largely invalidated by special pleading and anachronism, and is now of only historical interest. A much more sophisticated and plausible Marxist interpretation is Russell Ames's *Citizen Thomas More and His Utopia* (Princeton, 1949). Robert P. Adams, *The Better Part of Valor: More, Erasmus, Colet, and Vives, on Humanism, War, and Peace, 1496–1535* (Seattle, 1962), links *Utopia* to Erasmian pacifism. George M. Logan, *The Meaning of More's 'Utopia'* (Princeton, 1983), is primarily concerned with the relation between *Utopia* and classical and Renaissance political philosophy. This is also the focus of Quentin Skinner, 'Sir Thomas More's *Utopia* and the language of Renaissance humanism', in *The Languages of Political Theory in Early-Modern Europe*, ed. Anthony Pagden (Cambridge, 1987), pp. 123–57. Skinner is primarily concerned with Cicero; two excellent studies by Thomas I. White examine the relation between *Utopia* and Greek ethical and political theory: 'Aristotle and *Utopia*', *Renaissance Quarterly*, 29 (1976), 635–75; 'Pride and the public good: Thomas More's use of Plato in *Utopia*', *Journal of the History of Philosophy*, 20 (1982), 329–54. Timothy Kenyon's *Utopian Communism and Political Thought in Early Modern England* (1989) is half about More and half about Gerrard Winstanley. The book is useful in putting the ideas of *Utopia* and some of More's other writings into their contexts in the history of political and moral ideas, but its value as interpretation is largely vitiated by an unquestioning assumption that Utopia is More's ideal commonwealth. Colin Starnes's *The New Republic: A Commentary on Book I of More's 'Utopia' Showing Its Relation to Plato's 'Republic'*

(Waterloo, Ontario, 1990) has an untenable thesis – that Book I constitutes a systematic 'criticism' of the *Republic* – but includes a good deal of interesting material. Dominic Baker-Smith's *More's 'Utopia'*, for the Unwin Critical Library (London and New York, 1991), adroitly synthesises much recent scholarship and criticism. Alistair Fox, *'Utopia': An Elusive Vision*, Twayne's Masterwork Studies (New York, 1993), includes a survey of the critical tradition and an excellent annotated bibliography. Fox's own reading purports to trace in *Utopia* More's progressive disillusionment with Utopia.

The discussions of the Latin text of *Utopia* in the critical editions listed above are supplemented by two important reviews of the Yale edition: Arthur Barker, '*Clavis Moreana*: The Yale edition of Thomas More', *JEGP*, 65 (1966), 318–30, reprinted in *Essential Articles for the Study of Thomas More* (below) and Clarence H. Miller, in *English Language Notes*, 3 (1965–6), 303–9. Delcourt's treatment of the Latinity of *Utopia* has been influential; subsequent studies are R. Monsuez, 'Le latin de Thomas More dans *Utopia*', *Caliban*, 3 (1966), 35–78, and Surtz, 'Aspects of More's Latin style in *Utopia*', *Studies in the Renaissance*, 14 (1967), 93–109. See also Appendix B in the Yale edition: 'Vocabulary and diction in *Utopia*'. A study by Miller, 'Style and meaning in More's *Utopia*', is published in *Acta Conventus Neo-Latini Hafniensis: Proceedings*, ed. Rhoda Schnur *et al.* (Binghamton, N.Y., 1994), pp. 675–83. There is also a detailed treatment of More's Latin style, and of his habits of composition, in Miller's Introduction to *De Tristitia Christi*, Vol. XIV, Part II (1976) of the Yale *Complete Works*. An excellent study of one characteristic aspect of the style of *Utopia* – ironic understatement – is Elizabeth McCutcheon's 'Denying the contrary: More's use of litotes in the *Utopia*', *Moreana*, No. 31–2 (1971), 107–21 (reprinted in *Essential Articles*). McCutcheon's brief book on More's prefatory letter to Giles further confirms how much *Utopia* yields to close stylistic analysis: see *My Dear Peter: The 'Ars Poetica' and Hermeneutics for More's 'Utopia'* (Angers, 1983). McCutcheon is particularly acute on More's use of the paradoxical tradition of *serio ludere*.

Essential Articles for the Study of Thomas More, ed. R. S. Sylvester and G. P. Marc'hadour (Hamden, Conn., 1977), reprints a number of influential articles on *Utopia*, on other works by More and on facets of More's biography. The journal *Moreana* publishes articles on More, reviews scholarship on him, and reports the many and varied activities of the global circle of More scholars and admirers. Nothing published about *Utopia* will fail to be noticed there.

xlvi

UTOPIA

TEXT AND TRANSLATION

DE OPTIMO
REIPUBLICAE STATU
DEQUE NOVA INSULA
UTOPIA

libellus vere aureus,
nec minus salutaris quam festivus,
clarissimi disertissimique viri
THOMAE MORI
inclutae civitatis Londinensis civis
et Vicecomitis

ON THE BEST
STATE OF A COMMONWEALTH
AND ON THE NEW ISLAND
OF UTOPIA

A Truly Golden Handbook,
No Less Beneficial than Entertaining,
by the Most Distinguished and Eloquent Author
THOMAS MORE
Citizen and Undersheriff of the Famous City
of London

ERASMUS ROTERODAMUS IOANNI FROBENIO COMPATRI SUO CHARISSIMO S.D.[1]

Cum antehac omnia Mori mei mihi supra modum semper placuerint, tamen ipse meo iudicio nonnihil diffidebam ob artissimam inter nos amicitiam. Ceterum ubi video doctos uno ore omnes meo subscribere suffragio ac vehementius etiam divinum hominis ingenium suspicere, non quod plus ament sed quod plus cernant, serio plaudo meae sententiae nec verebor posthac quod sentio palam eloqui. Quid tandem non praestitisset admirabilis ista naturae felicitas si hoc ingenium instituisset Italia? si totum Musarum sacris vacaret, si ad iustam frugem ac velut autumnum suum maturuisset? Epigrammata lusit adolescens admodum ac pleraque puer. Britanniam suam numquam egressus est nisi semel atque iterum, principis sui nomine legatione fungens apud Flandros. Praeter rem uxoriam, praeter curas domesticas, praeter publici muneris functionem et causarum undas, tot tantisque regni negotiis distrahitur, ut mireris esse otium vel cogitandi de libris.

[1] This letter appears in 1518M and N, but not in 1516 or 1517.

4

ERASMUS OF ROTTERDAM TO HIS VERY DEAR FRIEND JOHANN FROBEN, THE FATHER OF HIS GODSON, GREETINGS[1]

While heretofore I have always thought extremely well of all of my friend More's writings, yet I rather mistrusted my own judgement because of the very close friendship between us. But when I see all the learned unanimously subscribe to my opinion, and esteem even more highly than I the divine wit of this man, not because they love him better but because they see more deeply into his merits, I am wholly confirmed in my opinion and no longer shrink from saying openly what I feel. How admirably would his fortunate disposition have stood forth if his genius had been nurtured in Italy![2] If he had devoted his whole energy to the service of the Muses, maturing gradually, as it were, towards his own proper harvest! As a youth, he toyed with epigrams, many written when he was only a lad. He has never left Britain except a couple of times to serve his prince as an ambassador to Flanders.[3] Apart from the cares of a married man and the responsibilities of his household, apart from his official post and floods of legal cases, he is distracted by so many and such important matters of state business that you would marvel he finds any free time at all for books.

---

[1] In a letter of *c.* 20 September 1516, More told Erasmus that he was anxious that *Utopia* 'be handsomely set off with the highest of recommendations, if possible, from several people, both intellectuals and distinguished statesmen' (*Selected Letters*, p. 76). Erasmus complied, in spades. The practice of publishing books with buttressing commendations was common then as now, but the amount of ancillary material in *Utopia* is unusual. The letters and poems are valuable, though, in indicating how *Utopia* struck the humanist readers for whom More appears primarily to have intended it. We print all these items, in the position and order in which they occur in 1518M: this and the following letters, poems and other materials before More's text; three other items after it (pp. 250–7). For Beatus Rhenanus' prefatory remarks about *Utopia*, and for three items that had appeared in previous editions but were not reprinted in 1518M, see pp. 258–69.
  It is interesting that Erasmus' own tribute – which implies some reservations – did not appear until this third edition of the book. The addressee, Johann Froben (*c.* 1460–1527), was the distinguished printer whose Basel shop produced the edition and its November successor.
[2] I.e., in the centre of humanist learning.
[3] Actually More had visited the Universities of Louvain and Paris in 1508 (see *Selected Letters*, p. 17). The Flanders missions were the one during which he began *Utopia* (1515) and another in 1517.

Proinde misimus ad te progymnasmata illius et Utopiam ut (si videtur) tuis excusa typis orbi posteritatique commendentur. Quando ea est tuae officinae auctoritas ut liber vel hoc nomine placeat eruditis si cognitum sit e Frobenianis aedibus prodisse. Bene vale cum optimo socero, coniuge suavissima, ac mellitissimis liberis. 5 Erasmum filiolum mihi tecum communem, inter literas natum, fac optimis literis instituendum cures.

Louanii VIII Cal. Septemb. An. M.D.XVII.

GUILLIELMUS BUDAEUS THOMAE LUPSETO ANGLO S.[2]

10

―――――

Gratiam sane ingentem a nobis iniisti, Lupsete adolescentum doctissime, qui me porrecta mihi UTOPIA THOMAE MORI ad iucundissimae simul et usui futurae lectionis intentionem avertisti. Nam cum a me dudum precibus id contendisses, id quod meapte ipse sponte magnopere exoptaturus eram, ut THOMAE LINACRI 15 medici utraque lingua praestantissimi libros sex de sanitate tuenda legerem, quos ille ex Galeni monumentis latinitate nuper ita donavit, vel quibus ipse potius latinitatem, ut si omnia eius auctoris opera (quae ego instar omnis medicinae esse puto) Latina tandem fiant, non magnopere tum medicorum schola Graecae linguae 20 cognitionem desideratura videatur, eum librum ex schedis

―――――

[2] Budé's letter appears in 1517 and 1518M, N.

For this reason I am sending you his *Exercises*[4] and his *Utopia*, so that, if you think proper, their appearance under your imprint may commend them to the world and to posterity. For the authority of your firm is such that a book is sure of pleasing the learned as soon as it is known to issue from the house of Froben. Farewell to you, to your excellent father-in-law,[5] your dear wife, and your delightful children. Make sure that Erasmus, the little son we share in common, and who was born among books, is educated in the best of them.

Louvain, 25 August 1517

GUILLAUME BUDE TO THOMAS LUPSET OF ENGLAND, GREETINGS[6]

Most learned of young men, Lupset, you have left me enormously in your debt by presenting me with the *Utopia* of Thomas More, and thereby introducing me to an extremely amusing and profitable book. In fact, you had recently asked me to do what on my own account I was more than ready to do – that is, to read over the six books of Galen, *On Protecting One's Health*, which the physician Thomas Linacre, a man equally skilled in both languages, lately translated from the extant originals, endowing them with Latinity – or rather bestowing them on Latinity – in such a way that if all the works of this author (who all by himself, in my view, comprehends the entire science of medicine) were turned into such Latin, the medical profession would then not need to know Greek. I consider

---

[4] The *Exercises* (*Progymnasmata*) were a series of rival translations by More and the grammarian William Lily: both men made Latin versions of the same Greek epigrams. The *Progymnasmata* were bound with *Utopia* in the Froben editions, along with a second series of epigrams by More and a collection of poems by Erasmus.

[5] Wolfgang Lachner, a bookseller who played an important part in Froben's business.

[6] While studying in Paris in 1517, Thomas Lupset (c. 1498–1530) supervised the printing of two of Thomas Linacre's translations of works by Galen (the great medical authority of classical Greece), and of the second edition of *Utopia*. He also made the acquaintance of Budé (1468–1540), the foremost French humanist of the time. Budé's lengthy epistle, which typifies humanist rhetoric at its most florid, was first published in the 1517 edition. Erasmus described the letter as an 'elegant preface' for More's book (*CWE*, V, 326), and he made a point of getting it into the Basel editions. See below, p. 272.

LINACRI tumultuaria lectione ita percurri (quarum mihi usum tantisper a te indultum summi loco beneficii duco) ut ea lectione multum me profecisse existimem, sed ex libri editione quae nunc a te sedulo procuratur in officinis huius urbis, ego maiorem etiam profectum mihi spondeam. Hoc nomine cum me tibi obstrictum 5 esse satis crederem, ecce tu mihi velut prioris beneficii vel appendicem vel auctarium UTOPIAM illam MORI donasti, hominis in primis acris, ingenioque amoeno, et in rerum humanarum aestimatione veteratoris.

Eum librum cum ruri in manibus cursitando, satagendo, operis 10 imperitando haberem (partim enim nosti, partim audisti villaticis me negotiis alterum iam hunc annum multum operae impendisse), usqueadeo eius lectione affectus sum cognitis et perpensis Utopianorum moribus et institutis ut paene rei familiaris procurationem intermiserim atque etiam abiecerim, cum nugas esse viderem artem 15 omnem industriamque oeconomicam, omnemque[3] omnino curam census ampliatricem.

Qua tamen ipsa omne genus mortalium velut oestro quodam intestino et congenito exagitari nemo est qui non videat et intelligat, ut legitimarum prope dixerim et civilium artium ac disciplinarum eum 20 esse scopum fateri necesse sit: ut tam livida quam accurata sollertia alter ab altero, quicum civilitatis ius ei et interdum gentilitatis intercedit, quippiam semper abducat, abstrahat, abradat, abiuret, exprimat, extundat, exsculpat, extorqueat, excutiat, excudat, subducat, suffuretur, suppilet, involet, legibusque partim coniventibus, 25 partim auctoribus, auferat et intervertat.

Id adeo magis in eis gentibus apud quas iura quae civilia et pontificia vocantur amplius in utroque foro valent. Quorum moribus et institutis eam invaluisse opinionem nemo non videt ut homines cautionum prudentes, vel captionum potius, et inconsultorum 30 civium aucupes, et formularum, id est excipularum opifices, ac pactilis iuris callentissimi, et litium concinnatores iurisque controversi, perversi, inversi, consulti, antistites esse iustitiae aequitatisque exsistimentur, solique digni qui de aequo bonoque responsitent, atque etiam (quod maius est multo) qui cum imperio ac potestate statuant 35

---

[3] *omnemque* supplied from 1517; omitted 1518M, N.

your lending to me for so long a time the manuscripts of Linacre an act of the highest generosity; I believe I profited immensely from my first hasty reading of them, and I promise myself even richer rewards from the printed volume which you are just now busily ushering through the presses of this city. For this reason I already thought myself sufficiently in your debt; and now, as an appendix or supplement to your former gift, you send me the *Utopia* of More, a man of the keenest wit, the most agreeable temper and the most profound experience in judging human affairs.

I took his book with me to the country and kept it in my hands as I bustled about, in constant activity, supervising the various workmen (for you no doubt know, or have at least heard, that for two years now I have been absorbed in business connected with my country house); but when I read it I was so fascinated with learning about and reflecting on the customs of the Utopians that I almost forgot and even dismissed entirely the management of my household affairs. What nonsense, I thought, is all this bustle over maintaining a household, this whole business of constantly accumulating more and more!

And yet this appetite, like a hidden parasite rooted in our flesh from birth, preys on the whole human race – there is no one who does not see and understand that fact. I might almost say we are bound to admit that this is the real end of legal training and the profession of the civil law: to make each man act with ingrained and calculated malice towards the neighbour to whom he is linked by ties of citizenship and sometimes of blood. He is always grabbing something, taking it away, extorting it, suing for it, squeezing it out, breaking it loose, gouging it away, twisting it off, snatching it, snitching it, filching it, pinching it, pilfering it, pouncing on it – partly with the tacit complicity of the laws, partly with their direct sanction, he carries off what he wants and makes it his own.

This is particularly frequent in those countries where the two codes of law, called civil and canonical, exercise their double jurisdiction more widely. Everyone knows that through their precedents and institutions the opinion has solidified that only men skilled in the ways – or perhaps just the wiles – of the law, only those who set snares for unwary citizens, artists of the legal phrase or fraud, contrivers of complicated contracts, fosterers of litigation, exponents of a perverse, confused and unjust justice – only such men as these are to be thought the high priests of justice and equity. They only are qualified to say peremptorily what is just and good, they only have the authority and power to decide (a much greater

quid unum quemque habere, quid non habere, quatenus quam-
diuque liceat, alucinantis id utique sensus communis iudicio,
quippe cum plerique hominum crassis ignorantiae lemis caecuti-
entes, tam aequissimam fere causam unum quemque putemus
habere quam maxime ius postulat, aut iure subnixus est.   5

Cum si ad veritatis normam et ad simplicitatis evangelicae praescriptum exigere iura velimus, nemo sit tam stupidus quin intelligat,
nemo tam vecors quin fateatur si urgeas, tam ius et fas hodie ac
iamdiu in sanctionibus pontificiis, et ius atque aequum in legibus
civilibus et principum placitis dissidere, quam CHRISTI rerum   10
humanarum conditoris instituta eiusque discipulorum ritus, ab
eorum decretis et placitis qui Croesi et Midae acervos bonorum
finem esse putant et felicitatis cumulum. Adeo si iustitiam finire
nunc velis quomodo priscis auctoribus placuit, quae ius suum unicuique tribuat, vel nullibi eam in publico invenias, vel (si dicere id   15
mihi permittam) culinariam quandam dispensatricem esse ut fatea-
mur necesse sit, sive nunc imperitantium mores spectes, sive civium
inter se et popularium affectus.

Nisi vero a germana mundique aequali iustitia (quod ius naturale
vocant) manasse ius id contenderint, ut quo quisque plus polleat, eo   20
etiam plus habeat, quo autem plus habeat, eo plus eminere inter cives
debeat. Quo fit ut iam iure gentium receptum esse videamus ut qui
nec arte nec industria memorabili iuvare cives suos et populares possunt, si modo pactiles illos nexus et contractiles nodos teneant, queis[4]
hominum patrimonia obstringuntur (quosque vulgus ignarum,   25

---

[4] An archaic form of *quibus*.

matter) what each and every man should have, what he should not have, how much he can have and how long he can keep it; and all of this is accepted by a public opinion vitiated by illusions. Because they are bleary-eyed almost to the point of blindness, most men tend to think an individual has received full justice to the extent that he has satisfied the requirements of the law or received what the law allots him.

But if we measured our rights by the norm of truth and the prescriptions of evangelical simplicity, nobody is so dull or sense-less as not to recognise, and (if pressed) to admit, that there are enormous differences. Justice is as remote from what is dispensed by papal decrees (both today and for a long time past), and real equity is as distant from what is expressed through civil laws and royal decrees, as the rule, established by Christ, founder of our human condition, and observed by his disciples, is distant from the decrees and regulations of those who think the perfection of human happiness and the ultimate good are to be found in the gold-bags of Croesus and Midas. So much so that if you now mean by justice what it used to mean in days gone by, that is, the power which gives to each his due,[7] you must either conclude it has no public existence at all or else we shall have to confess that it is (excuse the expression) like the servant girl who doles out the kitchen supplies. And this is true whether you regard the behaviour of our modern rulers or the relations between our fellow citizens and fellow countrymen.

Of course some argue that our modern law derives from an ancient and authentic code (which they call the law of nature), according to which the stronger a man is the more goods he should have, and the more goods he has the more authority he should exercise over his fellow citizens.[8] The result of this logic is that it is now an accepted principle of the law of nations that men who are of no practical use whatever to their fellow citizens and country-men – so long as they can keep everyone else tied up in contractual

---

[7] Cf. Cicero, *De finibus* V.xxiii.65; and Justinian, *Digesta seu Pandectae* I.i.10.

[8] The idea that there is an unchanging, universally valid body of natural law, which human beings apprehend by reason and instinct, was a central concept of legal and political theory from classical antiquity to the nineteenth century. Since human equality was normally regarded as a fundamental precept of natural law, the doctrine that might makes right could be derived from it only by a perverse understanding. The 'law of nations' (below) signifies the body of legal principles common to different peoples: what is universally practised, but not necessarily consonant with natural justice. For a clear exposition of the development and relation of these concepts, see R.W. Carlyle and A.J. Carlyle, *A History of Mediaeval Political Theory in the West*, 6 vols. (1903–36), I, especially 33–44.

hominesque literis humanioribus dediti ac procul foro animi
causa aut veritatis indagandae ergo agentes, partim Gordii vincula
esse ducunt, partim circulatoria, nec magnopere miranda) ei mil-
lenorum civium censum et saepe singularum civitatum aut etiam
ampliorem habeant, eidemque tum locupletes, tum frugi homines,   5
tum magnifici conquisitores honorifice vocitentur, quippe eis saeculis, eis institutis, eis moribus, in eis gentibus quae id ius esse
statuerunt ut tam summa fide atque auctoritate quisque sit quam
maximis opibus penates suos architectatus est ipse heredesque eius.
Idque eo magis atque magis quo eorum adnepotes horumque rursus   10
abnepotes patrimonia a maioribus parta luculentis certatim acces-
sionibus cumulaverint, id est quo longius latiusque confines,
adfines, cognatos, consanguineosque summoverint.

   At vero CHRISTUS possessionum conditor et moderator
Pythagoricam communionem et charitatem inter asseclas suos rel-   15
ictam, luculento sanxit exemplo damnato capitis Anania ob temera-
tam communionis legem. Quo certe instituto CHRISTUS omne[5]
iuris istius civilis pontificiique adeo recentioris argumentosa volumina inter suos quidem abrogasse mihi videtur. Quod ipsum ius
hodie arcem tenere prudentiae videmus ac fata nostra regere.   20

   UTOPIA vero insula, quam etiam UDEPOTIAM appellari
audio, mirifica utique sorte (si credimus) Christianos vero ritus ac
germanam ipsam sapientiam publice privatimque hausisse perhib-
etur, intemeratamque ad hunc usque diem servasse, utpote quae tria
divina instituta—hoc est bonorum malorumque inter cives aequalit-   25
atem (seu malis civilitatem numeris omnibus suis absolutam) et
pacis ac tranquillitatis amorem constantem ac pertinacem, et auri
argentique contemptum—consertis (ut aiunt) manibus retinet, tria
(ut ita loquar) everricula[6] omnium fraudum, imposturarum, circum-
scriptionum, versutiarum et planicarum[7] improbitatum. Superi suo   30
numine facerent ut haec tria UTOPIANAE legis capita trabalibus
clavis firmae ac statae persuasionis in sensibus omnium mortalium

---

[5] *omne* should have been corrected to *omnia*, to agree with *volumina* (next line).
[6] The early editions read *everticula*, which cannot be found in classical or medieval
dictionaries. Hence we have emended to *everricula* (*r* and *t* were easily confused).
In *De natura deorum* III.xxx.74, Cicero has the phrase 'everriculum malitiarum
omnium' ('the dragnet of all kinds of wickedness').
[7] This word, which does not appear in classical or medieval dictionaries, is probably
an adjective formed from *planus* ('imposter').

knots and complicated testamentary clauses (matters which appear to the ignorant multitude, no less than to those humanistic scholars who live as retired and disinterested seekers after truth, as a vulgar combination of Gordian-knot tricks and common charlatanry surely not to be admired) – such men, it is now agreed, should have incomes equal to a thousand ordinary citizens, equal to a whole city, or even more. And they also acquire an honourable reputation, as wealthy men, worthy men, magnificent entrepreneurs. This happens in every age, under any customs and institutions and among any peoples who have decided that a man should have supreme power and authority in the degree that he has built up the biggest possible private fortune for himself and his heirs. And the process is cumulative, since his descendants and their descendants strive to build up their inheritance by one gigantic increment after another – meanwhile cutting off stringently all their connections and relatives by marriage, birth or blood.

But the founder and controller of all property, Christ, left his followers a Pythagorean rule of mutual charity and community property; not only so, but he confirmed it unmistakably when Ananias was sentenced to death for violating the rule of community property.[9] By this arrangement, Christ seems to me to have undermined – at least among his own disciples – all that body of civil and the more recent canon law worked out in so many vast volumes. Yet this is the law which we see now holding the fort of wisdom and ruling over our destinies.

The island of Utopia, however, which I hear is also called Udepotia,[10] is said (if the story is to be believed) to have imbibed, by marvellous good fortune, both in its public and its private life, truly Christian customs and authentic wisdom, and to have kept them inviolate even to this day. It has done so by holding tenaciously to three divine institutions: equality of all good and evil things among the citizens (or, if you prefer, full and complete citizenship for all); a fixed and unwavering dedication to peace and tranquillity; and utter contempt for gold and silver. These three principles are the dragnets (so to speak) which sweep up all swindles, impostures, tricks, wiles and underhanded deceptions. Would that the gods, by their divine power, could cause these three pillars of Utopian policy

---

[9] Pythagoras was believed to have instituted a communal life among his followers. On the communism of the early Christians, see Acts 2:44–5. When Ananias sold a possession and 'kept back part of the price', Peter reproached him and he fell dead (Acts 5:1–5).

[10] From Greek *oudepote*, 'never'. On the meaning of 'Utopia', see below, p. 31n.

figerentur. Protinus superbiam, cupiditatem, contentionem vesanam atque alia paene omnia vulnifica Stygii adversarii tela concidere languereque videres, iurisque illam voluminum vim immensam, tot eximia solidaque ingenia ad libitinam usque detinentia[8] ut cassa et vacantia teredinibus permitti aut involucris officinarum dicari.   5

Proh divi immortales, quaenam Utopianorum sanctitas eam divinitus beatitudinem emereri potuit ut avaritia et cupiditas in eam unam insulam irrumpere aut irrepere tot saeculis non potuerint nec inde iustitiam cum pudore protervitate sua impudentiaque explodere et exigere? Deus nunc optimus maximus tam benigne   10 cum eis provinciis egisset quae ab eius sacratissimo nomine cognomentum retinent et amplectuntur. Certe avaritia tot mentes alioquin egregias arduasque depravans et pessumdans semel hinc facesseret et aureum saeculum Saturniumque rediret. Hic enimvero periculum esse quispiam autumarit ne forte Aratus et poetae prisci opinione   15 falsi fuerint qui Iustitiam e terris decedentem in signifero circulo collocaverunt. Restitisse enim eam in Utopia insula necesse est, si Hythlodaeo credimus necdum in caelum pervenisse.

Verum ego Utopiam extra mundi cogniti fines sitam esse percontando comperi, insulam nimirum fortunatam Elysiis fortasse campis   20 proximam (nam Hythlodaeus nondum situm eius finibus certis tradidit, ut Morus ipse testatur), multas quidem ipsam in urbes distractam, sed unam in civitatem coeuntes aut conspirantes, nomine Hagnopolin, suis utique ritibus bonisque acquiescentem, innocentia beatam, caelestem quodammodo vitam agentem, ut infra caelum sic   25 supra mundi huius cogniti colluvionem, quae in tot mortalium

---

[8] *detinentia* should have been corrected to *detinentium* or *detinentiam*, to agree with *voluminum* or *vim*.

to be fixed by the bolts of strong and settled conviction in the minds of all mortals. You would promptly witness the withering away of pride, greed, idiot competition and almost all the other deadly weapons of our hellish adversary. The immense weight of all those legal volumes, which occupy so many brilliant and solid minds for their whole lifetimes, would suddenly turn to empty air, the paper food for worms or used to wrap parcels in shops.

By all the gods above, I wonder what special holiness protected the Utopians, so that their island alone was shielded for so many centuries from the assaults, either stealthy or violent, of avarice and cupidity? What prevented those enemies from driving out justice and modesty under an onslaught of shameless effrontery? Would that almighty God, in his infinite goodness, had dealt as kindly with those regions which embrace and take their title from his most holy name! Surely avarice, the vice which now depraves and debases so many minds which might otherwise have been keen and vigorous, would then depart forever, and the golden age of Saturn[11] would return. One might even assert that Aratus and the other old poets were mistaken when they said Justice had fled the earth, and gave her a place in the zodiac.[12] For if we believe Hythloday, she must have remained on the island of Utopia and not yet have gone to heaven.

In fact, I have discovered, after investigating the matter, that Utopia lies outside the bounds of the known world. Perhaps it is one of the Fortunate Isles,[13] near neighbour to the Elysian Fields. As More himself says, Hythloday has not yet told exactly where it is to be found. Though it is divided into a number of different cities, they are all united or confederated in a single society named Hagnopolis,[14] a nation content with its own customs and possessions, blessedly innocent, leading a celestial life, as it were – lower than heaven, indeed, but far above the smoke and stir of this known world, which – among men's constant squabbles, as violent and

[11] Saturn ruled over the first and best of the mythological Four Ages of Man, an era of peace and happiness that ended when he was deposed by his son Jupiter.
[12] According to the Greek poet Aratus (fl. third century BC), the goddess of Justice, Astraea, who is identified with the constellation Virgo, departed earth in the face of mounting human wickedness.
[13] In classical culture, the Fortunate Isles, or Islands of the Blest, were the eternal paradise of heroes. They were thought to be situated – like Utopia – in the remotest west. The Isles were sometimes loosely identified with the Elysian Fields, that part of Hades where the virtuous pass eternity in the favourite pursuits of their former lives.
[14] Holy City, or City of the Saints.

studiis, ut acribus et incitatis sic inanibus et irritis, turbide et aestuose in praecipitium rapitur.

Eius igitur insulae cognitionem THOMAE MORO debemus, qui beatae vitae exemplar ac vivendi praescriptum aetate nostra promulgavit, ab Hythlodaeo (ut ipse tradit) inventum cui omnia fert 5 accepta. Qui ut Utopianis civitatem architectatus sit, ritusque illis et instituta condiderit, id est beatae vitae argumentum nobis inde mutuatus sit et importarit, MORUS certe insulam et sancta instituta stilo orationeque illustravit ac civitatem ipsam Hagnopolitanorum ad normam regulamque expolivit, omniaque ea addidit unde operi 10 magnifico decor venustasque accedit et auctoritas, etiamsi in ea opera navanda sibi tantum partes structoris vindicavit. Videlicet religio fuit maiores sibi partes in eo opere sumere, ne Hythlodaeus iure queri posset gloriam sibi a MORO praecerptam praeflorat-amque relinqui si quando suos ipse labores literis mandare 15 constituisset, εὐλαβουμένου δῆθεν αὐτοῦ, μὴ Ὑθλόδαιος αὐτὸς ὁ τῇ Ὀυδεποτίᾳγε νήσῳ ἐμφιλοχωρῶν ἐπιφανείς ποτε δυσχεράνειε καὶ βαρύνοιτο ταύτην ἀγνωμοσύνην αὐτοῦ τοῦγε ἐγκαταλι- πόντος αὐτῷ προαπηνθισμένον τὸ κλέος τοῦ εὑρέματος τούτου. Ὀύτω γὰρ πεπεῖσθαι, πρὸς ἀνδρῶν ἐστὶν ἀγαθῶντε καὶ 20 σοφῶν.

MORO autem homini per se gravi et auctoritate magna subnixo, fidem plane ut habeam efficit Petri Aegidii Antverpiensis testimonium, quem virum numquam coram a me cognitum (mitto nunc doctrinae morumque commendationem) eo nomine amo quod 25 ERASMI, clarissimi viri ac de literis sacris, profanis, omneque genus meritissimi, amicus est iuratissimus, quicum etiam ipso iamdiu societatem amicorum contraxi literis ultro citroque obsignatis.

Vale, Lupsete mi dilectissime, et LINACRUM Britannici nominis columen (quod quidem ad literas bonas attinet) non magis iam ves- 30 trum (ut spero) quam nostrum verbis meis saluta vel coram vel epistola internuntia, idque primo quoque tempore. Is enim unus est paucorum quibus me perlibens approbarim si possim, cum et

bitter as they are silly and futile – is being swept down a whirling cataract to the abyss.

Our knowledge of this island we owe to Thomas More, who in our time made known this model of the happy life and rule for living well. The actual discovery he attributes to Hythloday, to whom he assigns the whole thing. Thus, if Hythloday is the architect of the Utopian nation, the founder of its customs and institutions from which he has borrowed and brought home for us the very pattern of a happy life, More certainly is its adorner, who has bestowed on the island and its holy institutions the grace of his style, the polish of his diction. He it is who has shaped the city of the Hagnopolitans to the standard of a model and a general rule, and added all those touches which give beauty, order and authority to a magnificent work. And yet he claims as his part of the task only the role of a humble artisan. Evidently he made scruple of asserting too great a role in the book, lest Hythloday have grounds for complaint that More had prematurely plucked and pre-empted the glory due to him, which he might have had if he himself had chosen to write up his travels. *He feared, of course, that Hythloday, who was living of his own free will on the island of Udepotia, might some day return, and be angry and vexed at More's unfairness in leaving him only the husks of credit for his discovery. Such a conviction is characteristic of wise and virtuous men.*

While More himself is a man of weight whose word carries great authority, I am bound to give him full credit on the word of Peter Giles of Antwerp.[15] Though I do not know Giles personally – apart from commendations that have reached me of his learning and character – I love him because he is the sworn and intimate friend of Erasmus, a most distinguished man who has contributed so much to every sort of literary study, whether sacred or profane. With him I have long been in correspondence, with him I have long been on terms of close friendship.

Farewell, my dearest Lupset, and as soon as you can convey my greetings, whether in person or by letter, to Linacre, that pillar of the British name in all that concerns good learning; by now, I hope, he is no more yours than ours. He is one of the very few men whose good opinion I should be glad, if possible, to earn. When he was here, he made the very deepest and most favourable impres-

---

[15] For Giles, see p. 43, and the Introduction, p. xx.

ipse coram hic agens mihi se summe, Ioannique Ruellio amico meo, studiorumque conscio probaverit, et eius excellentem doctrinam, exactamque diligentiam in primis suspiciam aemularique contendam.

Velim etiam ut MORO salutem unam et alteram mandato meo ₅ vel mittas (ut dixi) vel dicas. Quem virum in Minervae sacratius album iamdiu opinione mea sermoneque meo relatum, de Utopia novi orbis insula summe et amo et veneror. Eius enim historiam aetas nostra posteraeque aetates habebunt velut elegantium utiliumque institutorum seminarium, unde translaticios mores in suam ₁₀ quisque civitatem important et adcommodent. Vale.

Parisiis pridie Cal. August.

HEXASTICHON ANEMOLII POETAE LAUREATI, HYTHLODAEI EX SORORE NEPOTIS IN UTOPIAM INSULAM⁹ ₁₅

Utopia priscis dicta ob infrequentiam,
Nunc civitatis aemula Platonicae,
Fortasse victrix (nam quod illa literis
Delineavit, hoc ego una praestiti
Viris et opibus, optimisque legibus): ₂₀
Eutopia merito sum vocanda nomine.

⁹ The hexastichon appears in all four early editions.

sion on me and on Jean Du Ruel, my friend and fellow student.[16]
His excellent learning and careful diligence I shall always especially
admire and strive to imitate.

Give my best regards also to More, either by letter, as I said
before, or in person. He is a man whose name, in my opinion, and
as I have often said, stands high in the ledgers of Minerva;[17] I
particularly love and revere him for what he has written about this
island of the New World, Utopia. Our own age and ages to come
will discover in his narrative a seedbed, so to speak, of elegant and
useful concepts from which they will be able to borrow practices
to be introduced into their own several nations and adapted for use
there. Farewell.

Paris, 31 July [1517]

SIX LINES ON THE ISLAND OF UTOPIA WRITTEN BY ANEMOLIUS,[18] POET LAUREATE, AND NEPHEW TO HYTHLODAY BY HIS SISTER

'No-Place'[19] was once my name, I lay so far;
But now with Plato's state I can compare,
Perhaps outdo her (for what he only drew
In empty words I have made live anew
In men and wealth, as well as splendid laws):
'The Good Place'[20] they should call me, with good cause.

---

[16] Like Linacre, Du Ruel was a physician and translator.
[17] The Roman goddess of wisdom and the arts, identified with the Greek goddess Athena.
[18] From Greek *anemolios* 'windy'. The real author of the poem is not known.
[19] The meaning of 'Utopia'. See p. 31n.
[20] *Eutopia*, from Greek *eu-* ('happy', 'fortunate') plus *topos* ('place').

UTOPIAE INSULAE TABULA[10]

[10] The map is the work of the Dutch painter Ambrosius Holbein, brother of the much better-known Hans Holbein the Younger. The 1516 edition had a cruder map, by an unknown hand. We reproduce it on the following page.

UTOPIAE INSULAE FIGURA

UTOPIENSIUM ALPHABETUM[11]

a b c d e f g h i k l m n o p q r s t u x y
ObⲰⲐⲐⲐⲐⲐⲐⲐⲐⲐⲐⲐⲐⲐⲐⲐⲐⲐⲐⲐⲐ

TETRASTICHON VERNACULA UTOPIENSIUM
LINGUA

5

Vtopos　ha　　Boccas　　　peula　chama.

polta　　chamaan

Bargol　　he　　maglomi　　　baccan　　10

ſoma　　　gymnoſophaon

Agrama　　gymnoſophon　　　labarem

bacha　　bodamilomin

15

Voluala　　barchin　　　heman　la

lauoluola　　dramme　　pagloni.　　20

HORUM VERSUUM AD VERBUM HAEC EST
SENTENTIA

Utopus me dux ex non insula fecit insulam.
Una ego terrarum omnium absque philosophia　　25
Civitatem philosophicam expressi mortalibus.
Libenter impertio mea, non gravatim accipio meliora.

[11] This page was omitted from 1517.

THE UTOPIAN ALPHABET[21]

---

a b c d e f g h i k l m n o p q r s t u x y

ȮӨⰀⲞⰄⰉⰆϾⰀⱰꙄ⏀ⰈⰋⰃⰂⰄⰃⰁⰅⰍⰄⰊⰄⰃⱰ

A QUATRAIN IN THE UTOPIAN LANGUAGE

Vtopos   ha   Boccas   peula   chama.

polta   chamaan

Bargol   he   maglomi   baccan

foma   gymnofophaon

Agrama   gymnofophon   labarem

bacha   bodamilomin

Voluala   barchin   heman   la

lauoluola   dramme   pagloni.

A LITERAL TRANSLATION OF THESE VERSES

The commander Utopus made me, who was once not an island,
into an island. I alone of all nations, without philosophy, have
portrayed for mortals the philosophical city. Freely I impart my
benefits; not unwillingly I accept whatever is better.

[21] Peter Giles was evidently responsible for this page (see below, p. 27). The sample
of the Utopian language, which reveals affinities with Greek and Latin, has enough
internal consistency to suggest that it was worked out with some care. See the
discussion in CW, IV, 277–8.

CLARISSIMO D. HIERONYMO BUSLIDIO PRAEPOSITO ARIENSI, CATHOLICI REGIS CAROLI A CONSILIIS, PETRUS AEGIDIUS ANTVERPENSIS S.D.[12]

Superioribus hisce diebus, ornatissime Buslidi, misit ad me [5] THOMAS ille MORUS, te quoque teste, cui notissimus est, eximium huius aetatis nostrae decus, Utopiam insulam, paucis adhuc mortalibus cognitam, sed dignam in primis quam ut plusquam Platonicam omnes velint cognoscere, praesertim ab homine facundissimo sic expressam, sic depictam, sic oculis subiectam, ut quoties [10] lego, aliquanto plus mihi videre videar quam cum ipsum Raphaelem Hythlodaeum (nam ei sermoni aeque interfui ac MORUS ipse) sua verba sonantem audirem, etiamsi vir ille haud vulgari praeditus eloquentia sic rem exponeret, ut facile appareret eum non ea referre quae narrantibus aliis didicisset sed quae comminus hausisset oculis [15] et in quibus non exiguum tempus esset versatus, homo mea quidem sententia regionum, hominum, et rerum experientia vel ipso Ulysse superior, et qualem octingentis hisce annis nusquam arbitrer natum, ad quem collatus Vespucius nihil vidisse putetur. Iam praeterquam quod visa quam audita narramus efficacius, aderat homini peculiaris [20] quaedam ad explicandas res dexteritas. Attamen eadem haec quoties MORI penicillo depicta contemplor, sic adficior ut mihi videar nonnumquam in ipsa versari Utopia. Et hercule crediderim Raphaelem

---

[12] Giles's letter appears in all the early editions.

TO THE MOST DISTINGUISHED GENTLEMAN, MASTER JEROME DE BUSLEYDEN, PROVOST OF AIRE AND COUNCILLOR TO THE CATHOLIC KING CHARLES, PETER GILES OF ANTWERP SENDS GREETINGS:[22]

Most eminent Busleyden, the other day Thomas More (who, as you very well know from your intimate acquaintance with him, is one of the great ornaments of our age) sent me his *Island of Utopia*. It is a place known so far to only a few men, but which should be known by everyone, as going far beyond Plato's Republic. It is particularly interesting because it has been so vividly described, so carefully depicted and brought before our very eyes, by a man of such great eloquence. As often as I read it, I seem to see even more than when I heard the actual words of Raphael Hythloday – for I was present at his discourse quite as much as More himself. As a matter of fact, Hythloday himself showed no mean gifts of expression in setting forth his topic; it was perfectly plain that he wasn't just repeating what he had heard from other people but was describing exactly what he had seen close at hand with his own eyes and experienced in his own person, over a long period of time. I consider him a man with more knowledge of nations, peoples and business than even the famous Ulysses. Such a man as this has not, I think, been born in the last eight hundred years; by comparison with him, Vespucci seems to have seen nothing at all. Apart from the fact that we naturally describe what we have seen better than what we have only heard about, the man had a particular skill in explaining things. And yet when I contemplate the same matters as sketched by More's pen, I am so affected by them that I sometimes seem to be living in Utopia itself. I can scarcely believe, by heaven,

[22] This letter dedicates *Utopia* to Busleyden and also gives Giles a chance to talk about the book and his own role in its creation. The Burgundian Busleyden (*c.* 1470–1517) was a prominent statesman and patron of learning. His dignities included the office of Provost of St Peter's Church at Aire and membership in the council of Charles, Prince of Castile, who inherited the title 'the Catholic' (along with the throne of Aragon) at the death of his grandfather Ferdinand II in 1516. More met Busleyden in 1515 and wrote three flattering epigrams about him and his fine house. He was particularly interested in having an opinion about *Utopia* from Busleyden, whom he regarded as ideally combining learning, virtue and practical experience (*Selected Letters*, pp. 80, 76). For Busleyden's commendation of *Utopia*, see pp. 250–5.

ipsum minus in ea insula vidisse per omne quinquennium quod illic
egit, quam in MORI descriptione videri[13] liceat. Tantum hic occurrit
undique miraculorum ut ambigam quid primum aut potissimum
admirer, felicissimae memoriae fidem, quae tot res auditas dumtaxat
paene ad verbum reddere potuerit; an prudentiam, qua[14] vulgo igno- 5
tissimos fontes unde omnia reipublicae vel oriuntur mala vel oriri
possent bona sic animadvertit; an orationis vim ac facultatem qua
tanta sermonis Latini puritate, tantis dicendi nervis, tot res com-
plexus est, praesertim unus in tot publica simul et domestica negotia
distractus. Verum haec omnia tu minus admiraris, doctissime Bus- 10
lidi, qui familiari etiam consuetudine penitus habes cognitum
homine maius ac prope divinum hominis ingenium.

In ceteris igitur nihil est quod illius scriptis queam adicere.
Tantum tetrastichum vernacula Utopiensium lingua scriptum quod
a MORI discessu forte mihi ostendit Hythlodaeus apponendum 15
curavi, praefixo eiusdem gentis alphabeto, tum adiectis ad margines
aliquot annotatiunculis.

Nam quod de insulae situ laborat MORUS, ne id quidem omnino
tacuit Raphael, quamquam paucis admodum ac velut obiter attigit,
velut hoc alii servans loco. Atque id sane nescio quomodo casus 20
quidam malus utrique nostrum invidit. Siquidem cum ea loqueretur
Raphael, adierat MORUM e famulis quispiam, qui illi nescio quid
diceret in aurem; ac mihi quidem tanto attentius auscultanti, com-
itum quispiam clarius ob frigus opinor navigatione collectum tussi-
ens, dicentis voces aliquot intercepit. Verum non conquiescam 25
donec hanc quoque partem ad plenum cognovero adeo ut non
solum situm insulae sed ipsam etiam poli sublationem sim tibi ad
unguem redditurus, si modo incolumis est noster Hythlodaeus.

Nam varius de homine rumor adfertur, alii adfirmant perisse in
itinere, rursum alii reversum in patriam, sed partim suorum mores 30
non ferentem, partim Utopiae desiderio sollicitatum, eo remigrasse.

[13] For *videri*, 1516 and 1517 print *videre*. Both readings are possible, but the passive
infinitive seems to go better with the impersonal verb.

[14] All the early editions except 1518N have *qui*, which requires a rather strained
construction with *illius* understood. Hence we have emended to the *qua* of 1518N,
which can be taken as an ordinary ablative of means, and which is parallel with
qua in line 7.

Raphael saw as much in the five years he lived on the island as can be seen in More's description. That description contains, in every part of it, so many wonders that I don't know what to marvel at first or most. Perhaps it should be the accuracy of his splendid memory, which could recite almost word for word so many different things that he had only heard; or else his good judgement, which traced back to sources of which the common man is completely ignorant the evils that arise in commonwealths and the blessings that could arise in them. Or finally I might marvel at the strength and amplitude of his language, in which he has gathered together so much matter and presented it in a Latin both pure and vigorous. This is all the more remarkable in a man distracted, as he is, by a mass of public business and private concerns. But of course none of this will surprise you, most erudite Busleyden, since you have already learned from your intimate acquaintance with him to appreciate the more-than-human, the almost-divine genius of the man.

For the rest, I can add nothing to what he has written. Only I did see to it that the book included a quatrain written in the Utopian tongue, which Hythloday showed to me after More had gone away. I've prefixed to it the alphabet of the Utopians, and also added to the volume some marginal notes.[23]

As for More's difficulties about locating the island, Raphael did not try in any way to suppress that information, but he mentioned it only briefly and in passing, as if saving it for another occasion. And then an unlucky accident caused both of us to miss what he said. For while Raphael was speaking of it, one of More's servants came in to whisper something in his ear; and though I was listening, for that very reason, more intently than ever, one of the company, who I suppose had caught cold on shipboard, coughed so loudly that some of Raphael's words escaped me. But I will never rest till I have full information on this point and can give you not just the general location of the island but its exact latitude – provided only our friend Hythloday is safe and sound.

For we hear various stories about him, some people asserting that he died on the way home, others that he got home but could not bear the ways of his countrymen, retained his old hankering for Utopia, and so made his way back there.[24]

---

[23] Giles here seems to claim credit for the marginal glosses in *Utopia*. On the title page of the 1517 edition, however, they are attributed to Erasmus. Perhaps both contributed glosses; or perhaps the 1517 edition is wrong.

[24] Cf. More's second letter to Giles (from the 1517 edition), which says (p. 269) that Hythloday is alive and well and living in Portugal.

Nam quod huius insulae nomen nusquam apud cosmographos reperiatur, pulchre dissolvit Hythlodaeus ipse. Siquidem fieri potuit, inquit, ut nomen quo veteres sint usi postea sit commutatum, aut etiam illos haec fugerit insula, quando et hodie complures oriuntur terrae priscis illis geographis intactae. Quamquam quorsum attinet hic argumentis astruere fidem, cum MORUS ille sit auctor?

Ceterum quod is ambigit de editione, equidem laudo et agnosco viri modestiam. At mihi visum est opus modis omnibus indignum quod diu premeretur et cum primis dignum quod exeat in manus hominum, idque tuo potissimum nomine commendatum orbi, vel quod MORI dotes tibi praecipue sint perspectae, vel quod nemo magis idoneus qui rectis consiliis iuvet rempublicam, in qua iam annis compluribus summa cum laude versaris tum prudentiae, tum integritatis. Bene vale, studiorum Maecenas et huius saeculi decus.

Antverpiae An. M.D.XVI. Cal. Novemb.

It's true, of course, that the name of this island is not to be found among the cosmographers, but Hythloday himself had an elegant answer for that. For, he said, either the name that the ancients gave it was later changed, or else they never discovered the island at all. Nowadays we find all sorts of lands turning up that the old geographers never mentioned. But what's the point of piling up these arguments authenticating the story, when we already have it on the word of More himself?

His uncertainty about having the book published I attribute to his modesty, and very creditable it is. But on many scores it seems to me a work that should not be suppressed any longer; on the contrary, it eminently deserves to be sent forth into the hands of men, especially as commended to the world by the patronage of your name. Nobody knows More's good qualities better than you do, and no one is better suited than you to serve the commonwealth with good counsels. At this work you have laboured for many years, earning the highest praise for wisdom as well as integrity. Farewell, then, you Maecenas[25] of learning and ornament of our era.

Antwerp, 1 November 1516

---

[25] Maecenas was the patron of Virgil, Horace and other Roman writers; and is often, as here, the type of the patron.

29

THOMAS MORUS PETRO AEGIDIO S.D.[1]

Pudet me propemodum, charissime Petre Aegidi, libellum hunc de Utopiana republica post annum ferme ad te mittere, quem te non dubito intra sesquimensem expectasse. Quippe quum scires mihi demptum in hoc opere inveniendi laborem, neque de dispositione 5 quicquam fuisse cogitandum, cui tantum erant ea recitanda quae tecum una pariter audivi narrantem Raphaelem. Quare nec erat quod in eloquendo laboraretur, quando nec illius sermo potuit exquisitus esse, quum esset primum subitarius atque extemporalis, deinde hominis, ut scis, non perinde Latine docti quam Graece, et 10 mea oratio quanto accederet propius ad illius neglectam simplicitatem, tanto futura sit propior veritati, cui hac in re soli curam et debeo et habeo.

Fateor, mi Petre, mihi adeo multum laboris his rebus paratis detractum ut paene nihil fuerit relictum. Alioquin huius rei vel 15 excogitatio vel oeconomia potuisset, ab ingenio neque infimo neque prorsus indocto, postulare tum temporis nonnihil, tum studii. Quod si exigeretur ut diserte etiam res non tantum vere scriberetur, id vero a me praestari nullo tempore, nullo studio potuisset. Nunc

---

[1] The letter appears in all of the early editions. The 1516 heading is *PREFATIO in opus de optimo reipublicae statu. THOMAS MORUS PETRO AEGIDIO S.P.D.*

THOMAS MORE TO PETER GILES, GREETINGS[1]

My dear Peter Giles, I am almost ashamed to be sending you after nearly a year this little book about the Utopian[2] commonwealth, which I'm sure you expected in less than six weeks.[3] For, as you were well aware, I faced no problem in finding my materials, and had no reason to ponder the arrangement of them.[4] All I had to do was repeat what you and I together heard Raphael[5] relate. Hence there was no occasion for me to labour over the style, since what he said, being extempore and informal, couldn't be couched in fancy terms.[6] And besides, as you know, he is a man not so well versed in Latin as in Greek;[7] so that my language would be nearer the truth, the closer it approached to his casual simplicity. Truth in fact is the only thing at which I should aim and do aim in writing this book.

I confess, my dear Peter, that having all these materials ready to hand left hardly anything at all for me to do. Otherwise, thinking through this topic from the beginning and disposing it in proper order might have demanded no little time and work, even if one were not entirely deficient in talent and learning. And then if the matter had to be set forth with eloquence, not just factually, there is no way I could have done that, however hard I worked, for

[1] Note that this letter is called the 'preface' in the 1516 edition; this is also its running title in the 1518 editions. On Giles (c. 1486–1533), see p. 43 and, on his role in the genesis of *Utopia*, pp. 25–7 and the Introduction, pp. xx–xxi.
[2] *Utopia* was coined by fusing the Greek adverb *ou* – 'not' – with the noun *topos* – 'place' – and giving the resulting compound a Latin ending. The word puns on another Greek compound, *eutopia* – 'happy' or 'fortunate' place. See the poem on p. 19.
[3] On the chronology, see Introduction, pp. xx–xxi.
[4] Finding materials, disposing them in the proper order and couching them in the appropriate style are the three steps of literary composition (*inventio, dispositio, elocutio*), as that subject is treated in the classical textbooks of rhetoric and their medieval and Renaissance successors.
[5] I.e., Raphael Hythloday. His given name links him with the archangel Raphael, traditionally a guide and healer. (On his surname, see p. 35n.)
[6] Rhetorical theory identified three levels of style: the grand, the middle and the plain. This sentence hints that *Utopia* is written in the plain style – according to theory, the appropriate one for philosophical dialogue. See above, pp. xxvi–xxviin.
[7] Knowledge of Greek was still uncommon among humanists in the early sixteenth century and thus carried considerable prestige in their circles. Greek studies had been More's own preoccupation as a scholar in the decade leading up to *Utopia*.

vero quum, ablatis curis his in quibus tantum fuit sudoris exhauri-
endum, restiterit tantum hoc, uti sic simpliciter scriberentur audita,
nihil erat negotii. Sed huic tamen tam nihilo negotii peragendo,
cetera negotia mea minus fere quam nihil temporis reliquerunt.
Dum causas forenses assidue alias ago, alias audio, alias arbiter finio, 5
alias iudex dirimo, dum hic officii causa visitur, ille negotii, dum
foris totum ferme diem aliis impertior, reliquum meis; relinquo
mihi, hoc est literis, nihil.

Nempe reverso domum, cum uxore fabulandum est, garriendum
cum liberis, colloquendum cum ministris. Quae ego omnia inter 10
negotia numero, quando fieri necesse est (necesse est autem, nisi
velis esse domi tuae peregrinus) et danda omnino opera est, ut quos
vitae tuae comites aut natura providit aut fecit casus aut ipse delegi-
sti, his ut te quam iucundissimum compares, modo ut ne comitate
corrumpas aut indulgentia ex ministris dominos reddas. Inter haec 15
quae dixi elabitur dies, mensis, annus.

Quando ergo scribimus? Nec interim de somno quicquam sum
locutus, ut nec de cibo quidem, qui multis non minus absumit
temporis quam somnus ipse, qui vitae absumit ferme dimidium. At
mihi hoc solum temporis acquiro quod somno ciboque suffuror, 20
quod quoniam parcum est, lente, quia tamen aliquid aliquando per-
feci, atque ad te, mi Petre, transmisi Utopiam ut legeres et si quid
effugisset nos uti tu admoneres. Quamquam enim non hac parte
penitus diffido mihi (qui utinam sic ingenio atque doctrina aliquid
essem, ut memoria non usquequaque destituor), non usqueadeo 25
tamen confido ut credam nihil mihi potuisse excidere.

Nam et Ioannes Clemens puer meus, qui adfuit ut scis una, ut
quem a nullo patior sermone abesse in quo aliquid esse fructus

however long a time. But now when I was relieved of all these concerns, over which I could have sweated forever, there was nothing for me to do but simply write down what I had heard. Well, little as it was, that task was rendered almost impossible by my many other obligations. Most of my day is given to the law – pleading some cases, hearing others, arbitrating others, and deciding still others. I pay a courtesy call to one man and visit another on business; and so almost all day I'm out dealing with other people, and the rest of the day I give over to my family and household; and then for myself – that is, my studies – there's nothing left.

For when I get home, I have to talk with my wife, chatter with my children, and consult with the servants. All these matters I consider part of my business, since they have to be done unless a man wants to be a stranger in his own house. Besides, you are bound to bear yourself as agreeably as you can towards those whom nature or chance or your own choice has made the companions of your life. But of course you mustn't spoil them with your familiarity, or by overindulgence turn the servants into your masters. And so, amid the concerns I have mentioned, the day, the month, the year slips away.

When do I write, then? Especially since I still have said nothing about sleeping or even eating, to which many people devote as much time as to sleep itself, which consumes almost half of our lives. My own time is only what I steal from sleeping and eating.[8] It isn't very much (hence the slow pace), but it's something, and so I've finally finished *Utopia*, and I'm sending it to you now. I hope, my dear Peter, that you'll read it over and let me know if you find anything that I've overlooked. Though on this point I do not lack all confidence in myself – I wish my judgement and learning were up to my memory, which isn't too bad – still, I don't feel so confident that I would swear I've missed nothing.

For my servant John Clement[9] has raised a great doubt in my mind. As you know, he was there with us, for I always want him to be present at conversations where there's profit to be gained.

---

[8] More's sixteenth-century biographer Thomas Stapleton says that he slept four or five hours a night, rising at 2 a.m. See *The Life and Illustrious Martyrdom of Sir Thomas More*, trans. Philip E. Hallett, ed. E.E. Reynolds (1966), p. 28. Claiming that a book was composed in odd hours or inopportune circumstances was conventional, but in More's case there is no reason to doubt that the convention corresponded to fact.

[9] John Clement (d. 1572) was one of the first students of St Paul's School, the humanist grammar school founded by John Colet about 1509. By 1514 he had entered More's household as servant and pupil; in later life he became a respected physician.

potest, quoniam ab hac herba quae² et Latinis literis et Graecis coepit evirescere, egregiam aliquando frugem spero, in magnam me coniecit dubitationem.³ Siquidem quum, quantum ego recordor, Hythlodaeus narraverit Amauroticum illum pontem quo fluvius Anydrus insternitur quingentos habere passus in longum, Ioannes meus ait detrahendos esse ducentos, latitudinem fluminis haud supra trecentos ibi continere. Ego te rogo rem ut revoces in memoriam. Nam si tu cum illo sentis, ego quoque assentiar et me lapsum credam, sin ipse non recolis, scribam ut feci quod ipse recordari videor mihi, nam ut maxime curabo ne quid sit in libro falsi, ita si quid sit in ambiguo, potius mendacium dicam quam mentiar, quod malim bonus esse quam prudens.

Quamquam facile fuerit huic mederi morbo si ex Raphaele ipso aut praesens scisciteris aut per literas: quod necesse est facias vel ob alium scrupulum qui nobis incidit, nescio mea ne culpa magis, an tua, an Raphaelis ipsius. Nam neque nobis in mentem venit quaerere, neque illi dicere, qua in parte novi illius orbis Utopia sita sit. Quod non fuisse praetermissum sic, vellem profecto mediocri pecunia mea redemptum, vel quod suppudet me nescire quo in mari sit insula de qua tam multa recenseam, vel quod sunt apud nos unus et alter, sed unus maxime, vir pius et professione theologus, qui miro flagrat desiderio adeundae Utopiae, non inani et curiosa libidine collustrandi nova, sed uti religionem nostram, feliciter ibi coeptam, foveat atque adaugeat. Quod quo faciat rite, decrevit ante curare ut mittatur a pontifice atque adeo ut creetur Utopiensibus episcopus, nihil eo scrupulo retardatus quod hoc antistitium sit illi precibus impetrandum. Quippe sanctum ducit ambitum, quem non honoris aut quaestus ratio, sed pietatis respectus pepererit.

Quamobrem te oro, mi Petre, uti aut praesens si potes commode,

Nota theologicam differentiam inter mentiri et mendacium dicere

Sanctus ambitus

---

² All the early texts print *qua*; the emendation is Lupton's. *evirescere* (next line): In classical Latin this rare verb meant 'to fade', 'to grow pale'. Surtz points out, though, that in Cooper's *Thesaurus* (1573) the meaning required by the context here is given: 'to become green'. Moreover, R. E. Latham, *Dictionary of Medieval Latin from British Sources*, 4 fasc. to date (1975–), gives the meanings 'to grow green', 'to flourish'.

³ For *in magnam ... dubitationem*, 1516 and 1517 print *in magnum ... dubium*. The balance seems to lie between elegance and energy of expression.

(And one of these days I expect we'll get a fine crop of learning from this young sprout, who has already made excellent progress in Greek as well as Latin.) Anyhow, as I recall matters, Hythloday[10] said the bridge over the Anyder at Amaurot was five hundred yards long; but my John says that is two hundred yards too much – that in fact the river is not more than three hundred yards wide there. So I beg you, consult your memory. If your recollection agrees with his, I'll yield and confess myself mistaken. But if you don't recall the point, I'll follow my own memory and keep my present figure. For, as I've taken particular pains to avoid having anything false in the book, so, if anything is in doubt, I'd rather say something untrue than tell a lie. In short, I'd rather be honest than clever.

Note the theological distinction between a deliberate lie and an untruth[11]

But the difficulty can easily be cleared up if you'll ask Raphael about it – either face-to-face or else by letter. And you must do this anyway, because of another problem that has cropped up – whether through my fault, or yours, or Raphael's, I'm not sure. For it didn't occur to us to ask, nor to him to say, in what part of the New World Utopia is to be found. I would give a sizeable sum of money to remedy this oversight, for I'm rather ashamed not to know the ocean where this island lies about which I've written so much. Besides, there are various people here, and one in particular, a devout man and a professor of theology, who very much wants to go to Utopia.[12] His motive is not by any means idle curiosity, a hankering after new sights, but rather a desire to foster and further the growth of our religion, which has made such a happy start there. To do this properly, he has decided to arrange to be sent there by the pope, and even to be named bishop to the Utopians. He feels no particular scruples about applying for this post, for he considers it a holy ambition, arising not from motives of glory or gain, but from religious zeal.

Office-seeking in a good cause

Therefore I beg you, my dear Peter, to get in touch with Hythlo-

---

[10] From Greek *hythlos* ('idle talk', 'nonsense') plus *daiein* ('to distribute') or perhaps *daios* in the rare sense of 'knowing', 'cunning': hence 'nonsense peddler' or 'expert in nonsense'. See N.G. Wilson, 'The name Hythlodaeus', *Moreana*, 29, No. 110 (1992), 33. Similarly, 'Anyder' and 'Amaurot' are from *anydros*, 'waterless', and *amauroton*, 'made dark or dim'. For the bridge, see p. 117 below.

[11] This distinction has not been located in the theological literature. More's formulation of it echoes a passage in a late classical work well known to humanists, Aulus Gellius' *Noctes Atticae* (XI.xi). The marginal glosses are apparently by Giles, though Erasmus may also have had a hand in them (see p. 27 and note).

[12] A note in a 1624 translation of *Utopia* identifies this learned divine as Rowland Phillips, Warden of Merton College, Oxford. But there is nothing to support the identification, and the passage may simply be one of the book's jokes at the expense of theologians.

aut absens per epistolam, compelles Hythlodaeum atque efficias ne quicquam huic operi meo aut insit falsi aut veri desideretur. Atque haud scio an praestet ipsum ei librum ostendi. Nam neque alius aeque sufficit si quid est erratum corrigere, neque is ipse aliter hoc praestare potest quam si quae sunt a me scripta perlegerit. Ad haec, 5 fiet ut hoc pacto intelligas accipiatne libenter, an gravatim ferat, hoc operis a me conscribi. Nempe si suos labores decrevit ipse mandare literis, nolit fortasse me: neque ego certe velim, Utopiensium per me vulgata republica, florem illi gratiamque novitatis historiae suae praeripere. 10

Quamquam, ut vere dicam, nec ipse mecum satis adhuc constitui an sim omnino editurus. Etenim tam varia sunt palata mortalium, *Ingrata hominum* tam morosa quorundam ingenia, tam ingrati animi, tam absurda *iudicia* iudicia, ut cum his haud paulo felicius agi videatur qui iucundi atque hilares genio indulgent suo, quam qui semet macerant curis ut edant 15 aliquid quod aliis aut fastidientibus aut ingratis vel utilitati possit esse vel voluptati. Plurimi literas nesciunt: multi contemnunt. Barbarus ut durum reicit quicquid non est plane barbarum, scioli aspernantur ut triviale quicquid obsoletis verbis non scatet. Quibusdam solum placent vetera, plerisque tantum sua. Hic tam tetricus est ut 20 *Simos vocat* non admittat iocos, hic tam insulsus ut non ferat sales. Tam simi *homines nullo* quidam sunt ut nasum omnem velut aquam ab rabido morsus cane *naso* reformident. Adeo mobiles alii sunt ut aliud sedentes probent, aliud stantes.

Hi sedent in tabernis, et inter pocula de scriptorum iudicant 25 ingeniis, magnaque cum auctoritate condemnant, utcumque libitum est, suis quemque scriptis, veluti capillicio vellicantes, ipsi interim *Proverbium* tuti, et quod dici solet, ἔξω βέλους. Quippe tam leves et abrasi

36

day – in person if you can, or by letters if he's gone – and make sure that my work contains nothing false and omits nothing true. Perhaps it would be better to show him the book itself. If I've made a mistake, there's nobody better qualified to correct me; but even he cannot do it, unless he reads over my book. Besides, you will be able to discover in this way whether he's pleased or annoyed that I have written the book. If he has decided to write out his own story himself, he may not want me to do so; and I should be sorry, too, if in publicising the commonwealth of Utopia I had robbed him and his story of the flower of novelty.

But, to tell the truth, I'm still of two minds as to whether I should publish the book at all.[13] For men's tastes are so various, the tempers of some are so severe, their minds so ungrateful, their judgements so foolish, that there seems no point in publishing a book that others will receive only with contempt and ingratitude. Better simply to follow one's own natural inclinations, lead a merry life, and avoid the harrowing task of publishing something either useful or pleasant. Most people know nothing of learning; many despise it. The clod rejects as too difficult whatever isn't cloddish. The pedant dismisses as mere trifling anything that isn't stuffed with obsolete words. Some readers approve only of ancient authors; many men like only their own writing. Here's a man so solemn he won't allow a shadow of levity, and there's one so insipid of taste that he can't endure the salt of a little wit. Some are so flat-nosed[14] that they dread satire as a man bitten by a rabid dog dreads water; some are so changeable that they like one thing when they're seated and another when they're standing.[15]

These people lounge around the taverns, and over their cups they pass judgement on the intelligence of writers. With complete assurance they condemn every author by his writings, just as the whim takes them, plucking each one, as it were, by the beard. But they themselves remain safe – 'out of range', so to speak. No use

The ungrateful judgements of men

Men who can't stand satire, he calls 'flat-nosed'

A saying

---

[13] Although More's letters express considerable anxiety about the reception of *Utopia*, the claim that he is ambivalent about publishing it would seem to be largely conventional. In a letter of *c*. 20 September 1516 he told Erasmus (who saw the book through the press), 'I am most anxious to have it published soon', and on 15 December he confided that 'from day to day I look forward to my *Utopia* with the feelings of a mother waiting for her son to return from abroad' (*Selected Letters*, pp. 76, 87).

[14] The nose, traditionally the organ expressive of anger and derision, is the seat of satire. So those who don't relish satire are *homines nullo naso* or *simi* ('flat-nosed').

[15] The last phrase echoes *In M. Tullium Ciceronem* (IV.7), attributed to Sallust; the paragraph as a whole resembles Erasmus' complaints, in his letter to Maarten van Dorp, about ill-natured readers of *The Praise of Folly* (*CWE*, III, 129).

undique ut ne pilum quidem habeant boni viri, quo possint apprehendi.

Sunt praeterea quidam tam ingrati ut quum impense delectentur *Mira collatio* opere, nihilo tamen magis ament auctorem. Non absimiles inhumanis hospitibus, qui quum opiparo convivio prolixe sint excepti, 5 saturi demum discedunt domum, nullis habitis gratiis ei a quo sunt invitati. I nunc et hominibus tam delicati palati, tam varii gustus, animi praeterea tam memoris et grati, tuis impensis epulum instrue.

Sed tamen, mi Petre, tu illud age quod dixi cum Hythlodaeo. Postea tamen integrum erit hac de re consultare⁴ denuo. Quamquam 10 si id ipsius voluntate fiat—quandoquidem scribendi labore defunctus, nunc sero sapio—quod reliquum est de edendo, sequar amicorum consilium, atque in primis tuum. Vale, dulcissime Petre Aegidi cum optima coniuge, ac me ut soles ama, quando ego te amo etiam plus quam soleo. 15

---

⁴ For *consultare* and *voluntate* (next line), 1516 and 1517 print *consulere* and *voluptate*.

38

trying to lay hold of them; these good men are shaved so close, there's not so much as a hair of their heads to catch them by.

Moreover, some people are so ungrateful that even though they're delighted with a work, they don't like the author any better because of it. They are no different from rude guests who, after *A neat comparison* they have been lavishly entertained at a splendid banquet, finally go home stuffed, without a word of thanks to the host who invited them. A fine task, providing at your own expense a banquet for men of such finicky palates and such various tastes, who will remember and reward you with such thanks!

Nevertheless, my dear Peter, raise with Hythloday the points I mentioned. Afterwards I will be free to consider the matter once more. But in fact, if he himself gives his consent – since it is late to be wise now that I have finished all the work – in all other considerations about publishing I will follow the advice of my friends, and especially yours. Farewell, my very dear Peter Giles; my regards to your excellent wife. Love me as you always have; I am more fond of you than I have ever been.

SERMONIS QUEM
RAPHAEL HYTHLODAEUS VIR EXIMIUS
DE OPTIMO REIPUBLICAE STATU HABUIT
LIBER PRIMUS,
PER ILLUSTREM VIRUM THOMAM MORUM
INCLUTAE BRITANNIARUM URBIS LONDINI
ET CIVEM ET VICECOMITEM

Quum non exigui momenti negotia quaedam invictissimus Angliae
Rex HENRICUS eius nominis octavus, omnibus egregii principis
artibus ornatissimus, cum serenissimo Castellae principe CAROLO
controversa nuper habuisset, ad ea tractanda componendaque ora-
torem me legavit in Flandriam, comitem et collegam viri incompara-
bilis Cuthberti Tunstalli, quem sacris scriniis nuper ingenti omnium
gratulatione praefecit. De cuius sane laudibus nihil a me dicetur,
non quod verear ne parum sincerae fidei testis habenda sit amicitia,
sed quod virtus eius ac doctrina maior est quam ut a me praedicari
possit, tum notior ubique atque illustrior quam ut debeat, nisi videri
velim solem lucerna, quod aiunt, ostendere.

Occurrerunt nobis Brugis (sic enim convenerat) hi quibus a principe negotium demandabatur, egregii viri omnes. In his praefectus
Brugensis, vir magnificus, princeps et caput erat, ceterum os et
pectus Georgius Temsicius Cassiletanus Praepositus, non arte
solum verumetiam natura facundus, ad haec iure consultissimus,

Cuthbertus
Tunstallus[1]

Paroemia

---

[1] This gloss first appeared in 1518N.

40

THE BEST STATE OF A COMMONWEALTH, A DISCOURSE BY THE EXTRAORDINARY RAPHAEL HYTHLODAY, AS RECORDED BY THE NOTED THOMAS MORE, CITIZEN AND UNDERSHERIFF[1] OF THE FAMOUS CITY OF BRITAIN, LONDON

BOOK I

The most invincible King of England, Henry, the eighth of that name, a prince adorned with the royal accomplishments beyond any other,[2] had recently some differences of no slight import with Charles, the most serene Prince of Castile,[3] and sent me into Flanders as his spokesman to discuss and settle them. I was companion and associate to that incomparable man Cuthbert Tunstall, whom *Cuthbert Tunstall* the king has recently created Master of the Rolls, to everyone's enormous satisfaction.[4] I will say nothing in praise of this man, not because I fear the judgement of a friend might be questioned, but because his integrity and learning are greater than I can describe and too well known everywhere to need my commendation – unless I would, according to the proverb, 'show the sun with a lantern'. *Adage*

Those appointed by the prince to deal with us, all excellent men, met us at Bruges by pre-arrangement. Their head man and leader was the Mayor of Bruges, a most distinguished person. But their main speaker and guiding spirit was Georges de Themsecke, the Provost of Cassel, a man eloquent by nature as well as by training,

[1] More had been an undersheriff of London since 1510. His principal duty was to act as a judge in the Sheriff's Court (a city court that heard a wide variety of cases).

[2] When he succeeded to the throne in 1509 at the age of seventeen, Henry appeared to be something very close to the humanist ideal of a cultivated, just and peace-loving monarch, and More had enthusiastically heralded his accession in several Latin poems (CW, III, Part II, 101–17). By 1516, however, this view had been considerably undermined, especially by the king's fondness for martial (not yet marital) adventure.

[3] The disputes between the two nations were commercial ones, especially over tariffs. Charles was grandson of the Emperor Maximilian I and Duke of Burgundy after his father's death in 1506. He became, nominally though not formally, Prince of Castile after the death of Ferdinand II (23 January 1516), and Holy Roman Emperor in 1519.

[4] A royal commission of 7 May 1515 appointed five commissioners, including More, with Tunstall as their chief. Tunstall (1474–1559) was created Master of the Rolls (principal clerk of the Chancery Court) and Vice-Chancellor of the realm on 12 May 1516.

tractandi vero negotii cum ingenio tum assiduo rerum usu eximius artifex. Ubi semel atque iterum congressi quibusdam de rebus non satis consentiremus, illi in aliquot dies vale nobis dicto, Bruxellas profecti sunt, principis oraculum sciscitaturi.

Ego me interim (sic enim res ferebat) Antverpiam confero. Ibi 5 dum versor, saepe me inter alios, sed quo non alius gratior, invisit *Petrus Aegidius*[2] Petrus Aegidius Antverpiae natus, magna fide et loco apud suos honesto, dignus honestissimo: quippe iuvenis haud scio doctiorne an moratior. Est enim et optimus et literatissimus, ad haec animo in omnes candido, in amicos vero tam propenso pectore, amore, 10 fide, affectu tam sincero, ut vix unum aut alterum usquam invenias quem illi sentias omnibus amicitiae numeris esse conferendum. Rara illi modestia, nemini longius abest fucus, nulli simplicitas inest prudentior, porro sermone tam lepidus et tam innoxie facetus ut patriae desiderium ac laris domestici, uxoris, et liberorum, quorum studio 15 revisendorum nimis quam anxie tenebar (iam tum enim plus quattuor mensibus afueram domo), magna ex parte mihi dulcissima consuetudine sua et mellitissima confabulatione levaverit.

Hunc quum die quadam in templo divae Mariae, quod et opere pulcherrimum et populo celeberrimum est, rei divinae interfuissem, 20 atque peracto sacro pararem inde in hospitium redire, forte colloquentem video cum hospite quodam, vergentis ad senium aetatis, vultu adusto, promissa barba, paenula neglectim ab humero dependente, qui mihi ex vultu atque habitu nauclerus esse videbatur. At Petrus, ubi me conspexit, adit ac salutat. Respondere conantem sed- 25 ucit paululum, et Vides, inquit, hunc? (Simul designabat eum cum quo loquentem videram.) Eum, inquit, iam hinc ad te recta parabam ducere.

Venisset, inquam, pergratus mihi tua causa.

Immo, inquit ille, si nosses hominem, sua. Nam nemo vivit hodie 30 mortalium omnium qui tantam tibi hominum terrarumque incognitarum narrare possit historiam. Quarum rerum audiendarum scio avidissimum esse te.

Ergo, inquam, non pessime coniectavi. Nam primo aspectu protinus sensi hominem esse nauclerum. 35

Atqui, inquit, aberrasti longissime: navigavit quidem non ut Palinurus, sed ut Ulysses, immo velut Plato. Nempe Raphael iste, sic

---

[2] This gloss also first appeared in 1518N.

also very learned in the law, and most skilful in diplomatic affairs through his ability and long practice. After we had met several times, certain points remained on which we could not come to agreement; so they adjourned the meeting[5] and went to Brussels for some days to learn their prince's pleasure.

Meanwhile, since my business required it, I went to Antwerp. Of those who visited me while I was there, no one was more welcome to me than Peter Giles. He was a native of Antwerp, a man *Peter Giles* of high reputation, already appointed to a good position and worthy of the very best: I hardly know whether the young man is distinguished more in learning or in character. Apart from being cultured, virtuous and courteous to all, with his intimates he is so open-hearted, affectionate, loyal and sincere that you would be hard-pressed to find another man anywhere whom you would think comparable to him in all the points of friendship. No one is more modest or more frank; no one better combines simplicity with wisdom. Besides, his conversation is so pleasant, and so witty without malice, that the ardent desire I felt to see again my native country, my home, my wife and my children (from whom I had been separated more than four months) was much eased by his most agreeable company and delightful talk.

One day after I had heard Mass at Notre Dame, the most beautiful and most popular church in Antwerp, I was about to return to my quarters when I happened to see him talking with a stranger, a man of quite advanced years, with a sunburned face, a long beard, and a cloak hanging loosely from his shoulders; from his face and dress, I took him to be a ship's captain. When Peter saw me, he came up and greeted me. As I was about to reply, he drew me aside and, indicating the man with whom I had seen him talking, said, 'Do you see that fellow? I was just on the point of bringing him straight to you.'

'He would have been very welcome on your behalf', I answered.

'And on his own too, if you knew him', said Peter, 'for there is no mortal alive today can tell you so much about unknown peoples and unexplored lands; and I know that you're always greedy for such information.'

'In that case', said I, 'my guess wasn't a bad one, for at first glance I supposed he was a ship's captain.'

'Then you're far off the mark', he replied, 'for his sailing has not been like that of Palinurus, but more that of Ulysses, or rather

---

[5] On or before 21 July 1515. See Introduction, p. xx.

enim vocatur, gentilicio nomine Hythlodaeus, et Latinae linguae
non indoctus et Graecae doctissimus (cuius ideo studiosior quam
Romanae fuit, quoniam totum se addixerat philosophiae: qua in re
nihil quod alicuius momenti sit, praeter Senecae quaedam ac Cicer-
onis, exstare Latine cognovit), relicto fratribus patrimonio quod ei ₅
domi fuerat (est enim Lusitanus), orbis terrarum contemplandi
studio Americo Vespucio se adiunxit, atque in tribus posterioribus
illarum quattuor navigationum quae passim iam leguntur, perpetuus
eius comes fuit, nisi quod in ultima cum eo non rediit. Curavit
enim atque adeo extorsit ab Americo ut ipse in his XXIIII esset qui ₁₀
ad fines postremae navigationis in castello relinquebantur. Itaque
relictus est, uti obtemperaretur animo eius, peregrinationis magis
Apophthegma quam sepulchri curioso. Quippe cui haec assidue sunt in ore, Caelo
tegitur qui non habet urnam, et Undique ad superos tantundem
esse viae. Quae mens eius, nisi deus ei propitius adfuisset, nimio ₁₅

of Plato.[6] This man, who is named Raphael – his family name is Hythloday – knows a good deal of Latin and is particularly learned in Greek. He studied Greek more than Latin because his main interest is philosophy, and in that field he recognised that the Romans have left us nothing very valuable except certain works of Seneca and Cicero.[7] Being eager to see the world, he left to his brothers the patrimony to which he was entitled at home (he is a Portuguese),[8] and joined Amerigo Vespucci. He was Vespucci's constant companion on the last three of his four voyages, accounts of which are now common reading everywhere,[9] but on the last voyage, he did not return home with him. After much persuasion and expostulation he got Amerigo's permission to be one of the twenty-four men who were left in a garrison at the farthest point of the last voyage. Being left in this way was altogether agreeable to him, as he was more concerned about his travels than his tomb. He would often say, "The man who has no grave is covered by the *Aphorism* sky", and "Wherever you start from, the road to heaven is the same length."[10] Yet this attitude would have cost him dear, if God had

---

[6] Palinurus was Aeneas' pilot: he dozed at the helm and fell overboard (*Aeneid* V. 833–61, VI.337–83). Ulysses' reputation as a man who saw many cities and knew men's minds is based on the opening lines of the *Odyssey*. (But Ulysses could also be regarded – as in the opening of Lucian's 'A True Story' – as a notable liar.) According to the Life of Plato by Diogenes Laertius (fl. third century AD), Plato travelled widely in the Mediterranean world (*Lives of Eminent Philosophers* III.6, 18–19).

[7] This opinion is echoed in More's 1518 Letter to Oxford (*CW*, XV, 143). Seneca was a Stoic; and though Cicero styled himself an adherent of the sceptical philosophy associated with the later phase of the Platonic Academy, his sympathies in ethical and political theory lay mainly with the Stoics, whose views he often rehearsed at length. Hythloday's own views are permeated by Stoic ideas.

[8] Hythloday's nationality links him with several of the great explorers of the period, who were either Portuguese or sponsored by the King of Portugal. His renunciation of his patrimony recalls the Italian philosopher Pico della Mirandola (1463–94), whose biography More had translated, and whom he greatly admired. See Introduction, p. xxvn.

[9] Two Latin accounts (now of disputed authenticity) of the voyages of the Florentine explorer Amerigo Vespucci (1451–1512), who sailed for the King of Portugal, were published about 1504: *Mundus novus* and *Quattuor Americi Vespucci navigationes*. *Utopia* exhibits parallels with both. *Quattuor navigationes* tells that Vespucci left twenty-four men at the farthest point of his fourth voyage. See C. G. Herbermann, ed., *The Cosmographiae Introductio of Martin Walseemüller in Facsimile, Followed by the Four Voyages of Amerigo Vespucci*, trans. Mario E. Cosenza, US Catholic Historical Society Monograph IV (New York, 1907; rpt Ann Arbor, 1966), pp. 149–50. *Mundus novus* has also been translated: *Mundus novus: Letter to Lorenzo Pietro di Medici*, trans. G.T. Northup (Princeton, 1916).

[10] The first of these sayings is quoted from the epic poem by Seneca's nephew Lucan, *Pharsalia* (VII.819); the second is adapted from Cicero (*Tusculanae disputationes* I.xliii.104).

fuerat illi constatura. Ceterum postquam digresso Vespucio multas regiones cum quinque castellanorum comitibus emensus est, mirabili tandem fortuna Taprobanen delatus, inde pervenit in Caliquit, ubi repertis commode Lusitanorum navibus, in patriam denique praeter spem revehitur.

Haec ubi narravit Petrus, actis ei gratiis quod tam officiosus in me fuisset, ut cuius viri colloquium mihi gratum speraret eius uti sermone fruerer tantam rationem habuisset, ad Raphaelem me converto: tum ubi nos mutuo salutassemus atque illa communia dixissemus quae dici in primo hospitum congressu solent, inde domum meam digredimur, ibique in horto considentes in scamno caespitibus herbeis constrato, confabulamur.

Narravit ergo nobis quo pacto posteaquam Vespucius abierat, ipse sociique eius qui in castello remanserant conveniendo atque blandiendo coeperint se paulatim eius terrae gentibus insinuare, iamque non innoxie modo apud eas, sed etiam familiariter versari, tum principi cuidam (cuius et patria mihi et nomen excidit) grati charique esse. Eius liberalitate narrabat commeatum atque viaticum ipsi et quinque eius comitibus affatim fuisse suppeditatum, cum itineris (quod per aquam ratibus, per terram curru peragebant) fidelissimo duce qui eos ad alios principes quos diligenter commendati petebant, adduceret. Nam post multorum itinera dierum, oppida atque urbes aiebat reperisse se, ac non pessime institutas magna populorum frequentia respublicas.

Nempe sub aequatoris linea tum hinc atque inde ab utroque latere quantum fere spatii solis orbita complectitur, vastas obiacere[3] solitudines perpetuo fervore torridas. Squalor undique et tristis rerum facies, horrida atque inculta omnia, feris habitata serpentibusque aut denique hominibus neque minus efferis quam sint beluae neque minus noxiis. Ceterum ubi longius evectus sis, paulatim omnia mansuescere. Caelum minus asperum, solum virore blandum, mitiora animantium ingenia, tandem aperiri populos, urbes, oppida, in his assidua non inter se modo ac finitimos sed procul etiam dissitas gentes terra marique commercia. Inde sibi natam facultatem multas ultro citroque terras invisendi, quod nulla navis ad iter quodlibet

---

[3] *subiacere* (1516, 1517) is an alternative to *obiacere* (1518M, N): 'lie below' instead of 'lie in the way of'.

not been gracious to him. After Vespucci's departure he travelled through many countries with five companions from the garrison. At last, by strange good fortune, he got via Ceylon to Calicut,[11] where he opportunely found some Portuguese ships; and so, beyond all hope, he finally returned to his own country.'[12]

When Peter had told me this, I thanked him for his great kindness in introducing me to a man whose conversation he hoped I would enjoy, and then I turned towards Raphael. After we had greeted each other and exchanged the usual civilities of strangers upon their first meeting, we all went off to my house. There in the garden we sat down on a bench covered with grassy turf[13] to talk together.

He told us how, after Vespucci sailed away, he and his companions who had stayed behind in the garrison met with the people of that land, and by ingratiating speeches gradually made up to them. Before long they came to dwell with them not only safely but even on friendly terms. The prince also gave them his favour (I have forgotten his name and that of his country). He told how this prince generously furnished him and his five companions not only with ample provisions but with means for travelling – rafts when they went by water, wagons when they went by land. In addition, he sent with them a most trusty guide, who was to conduct them to other princes they wanted to visit, and supplied them with strong letters of recommendation. After many days' journey, he said, they found towns and cities, and commonwealths that were both very populous and not badly governed.

To be sure, under the equator and as far on both sides of the line as the sun moves, there lie vast empty deserts, scorched with the perpetual heat. The whole region is desolate and squalid, grim and uncultivated, inhabited by wild beasts and serpents, and by men no less wild and dangerous than the beasts themselves. But as you go on, everything gradually grows milder. The sun is less fierce, the earth greener, the creatures less savage. At last you reach people, cities and towns which not only trade among themselves and with their neighbours but even carry on commerce by sea and land with remote countries. After that, he said, they were able to visit different lands in every direction, for there was no ship readied for a

---

[11] Calicut is a seaport on the west coast of India. Portuguese ships landed there several times in the early sixteenth century.

[12] As G.B. Parks points out, Hythloday was thus the first European to circumnavigate the globe. (Magellan's men completed the trip in 1522.) See 'More's Utopia and geography', *JEGP*, 37 (1938), 226.

[13] The small woodcut of the scene in the 1518 editions shows the bench as a long wooden box filled with earth and covered on top with growing grass.

instruebatur in quam non ille comitesque eius libentissime admittebantur.

Naves quas primis regionibus conspexerunt carina plana fuisse narrabat, vela consutis papyris aut viminibus intendebantur, alibi coriacea. Post vero acuminatas carinas, canabea vela reppererunt, omnia denique nostris similia. Nautae maris ac caeli non imperiti, sed miram se narrabat inisse gratiam, tradito magnetis usu, cuius antea penitus erant ignari. Ideoque timide pelago consuevisse sese, neque alias temere quam aestate credere. Nunc vero eius fiducia lapidis contemnunt hiemem, securi magis quam tuti: ut periculum sit ne quae res magno eis bono futura putabatur, eadem per imprudentiam magnorum causa malorum fiat.

Quid quoque in loco se vidisse narravit et longum fuerit explicare, neque huius est operis institutum: et alio fortasse loco dicetur a nobis, praesertim quicquid ex usu fuerit non ignorari, qualia sunt in primis ea quae apud populos usquam civiliter conviventes animadvertit recte prudenterque provisa. His enim de rebus et nos avidissime rogabamus et ille libentissime disserebat, omissa interim inquisitione monstrorum, quibus nihil est minus novum. Nam Scyllas et Celaenos rapaces et Laestrygonas populivoros,[4] atque eiuscemodi immania portenta, nusquam fere non invenias, at sane ac sapienter institutos cives haud reperias ubilibet. Ceterum ut multa apud novos illos populos adnotavit perperam consulta, sic haud pauca recensuit unde possint exempla sumi corrigendis harum urbium, nationum, gentium ac regnorum erroribus idonea: alio, ut dixi, loco a me commemoranda. Nunc ea tantum referre animus est quae de moribus atque institutis narrabat Utopiensium, praemisso tamen eo sermone quo velut tractu quodam ad eius mentionem

---

[4] On the analogy of 'carnivorous', etc., More constructs the neologism *populivorus*, 'people-eating'. *institutos* (l. 22) follows 1516 and 1517 against the impossible *instituto* of 1518M, N.

journey on which he and his companions were not welcome as passengers.

The vessels they saw in the first regions were flat-bottomed, he said, with sails made of stitched papyrus-reeds or wicker, elsewhere of leather. Farther on they found ships with pointed keels and canvas sails, in every respect like our own. The seamen were not unskilled in managing wind and water; but they were most grateful to him, Raphael said, for showing them the use of the compass, of which they had been entirely ignorant. For that reason they had formerly sailed with great timidity, and only in summer. Now they have such trust in that loadstone that they no longer fear winter at all, and tend to be careless rather than safe. There is some danger that through their imprudence this device, which they thought would be so advantageous to them, may become the cause of much mischief.

It would take too long to repeat all that Raphael told us he had observed in each place, nor would it serve our present purpose. Perhaps on another occasion we shall tell more about these things, especially those that it would be useful not to be ignorant of – above all, the wise and prudent provisions that he observed among the civilised nations. We asked him many eager questions about such things, and he answered us willingly enough. We made no inquiries, however, about monsters, for nothing is less new or strange than they are. There is no place where you will not find Scyllas, ravenous Celaenos, man-eating Laestrygonians[14] and that sort of monstrosity, but well and wisely trained citizens you will hardly find anywhere. While he told us of many ill-considered usages in these new-found nations, he also described quite a few other customs from which our own cities, nations, races and kingdoms might take lessons in order to correct their errors. These I shall discuss in another place, as I said. Now I intend to relate only what he told us about the customs and institutions of the Utopians,[15] but first recounting the conversation that drew him into

[14] Scylla, a six-headed sea monster, appears in both the *Odyssey* (XII.73–100, 234–59) and the *Aeneid* (III.420–32). Celaeno, one of the Harpies (birds with women's faces), appears in the *Aeneid* (III.209–58). The Laestrygonians were gigantic cannibals in the *Odyssey* (X.76–132).

[15] At this point the dialogue suddenly goes off on a different tack. The account of Utopia is postponed; and the ensuing conversation includes, among other things, precisely those matters that More has just said he won't relate: Hythloday's descriptions of the practices of other new-found nations. As Hexter argues (*More's 'Utopia': The Biography of an Idea*, pp. 18–21; *CW*, IV, xviii–xx), it was almost certainly here that More opened a seam in the first version of *Utopia* to insert the additions that constitute the remainder of Book I. See Introduction, p. xxi.

reipublicae deventum est. Nam quum Raphael prudentissime recensuisset alia hic, alia illic errata, utrobique certe plurima, tum quae apud nos quaeve item sunt apud illos cauta sapientius, quum uniuscuiusque populi mores atque instituta sic teneret, tamquam in quemcumque locum divertisset totam ibi vitam vixisse videretur, 5 admiratus hominem Petrus, Miror profecto, mi Raphael, inquit, cur te regi cuipiam non adiungas, quorum neminem esse satis scio cui tu non sis futurus vehementer gratus, utpote quem hac doctrina atque hac locorum hominumque peritia non oblectare solum, sed exemplis quoque instruere atque adiuvare consilio sis idoneus: 10 simul hoc pacto et tuis rebus egregie consulueris et tuorum omnium commodis magno esse adiumento possis.

Quod ad meos attinet, inquit ille, non valde commoveor, nempe in quos mediocriter opinor me officii mei partes implevisse. Nam quibus rebus alii non nisi senes et aegri cedunt, immo tum quoque 15 aegre cedunt quum amplius retinere non possunt, eas res ego non sanus modo ac vegetus sed iuvenis quoque cognatis amicisque dispartivi, quos debere puto hac mea esse benignitate contentos, neque id exigere atque exspectare praeterea ut memet eorum causa regibus in servitium dedam. 20

Bona verba, inquit Petrus, mihi visum est non ut servias regibus, sed ut inservias.

Hoc est, inquit ille, una syllaba plus quam servias.

At ego sic censeo, inquit Petrus, quoquo tu nomine rem appelles, eam tamen ipsam esse viam qua non aliis modo et privatim et pub- 25 lice possis conducere, sed tuam quoque ipsius conditionem reddere feliciorem.

Feliciorem me,[5] inquit Raphael, ea via facerem, a qua abhorret animus? Atqui nunc sic vivo ut volo, quod ego certe suspicor paucissimis purpuratorum contingere. Quin satis est eorum qui 30 potentum amicitias ambiunt, ne magnam putes iacturam fieri, si me atque uno aut altero mei similibus sint carituri.

---

[5] The texts print *Feliciorum ne* (read as one word by Delcourt and Surtz). The emendation provides an object for *facerem*.

speaking of that commonwealth. Raphael had been discoursing very thoughtfully on the faulty arrangements both in that hemisphere and in this (and there are many in both places), and had also spoken of the wiser provisions among us or among them, talking as shrewdly about the customs and institutions of each place he had visited as if he had lived there all his life. Peter was amazed. 'My dear Raphael', he said, 'I'm surprised that you don't enter some king's service; for I don't know of a single prince who wouldn't be very glad to have you. Your learning and your knowledge of various countries and peoples would entertain him while your advice and supply of examples would be helpful at the counsel board. Thus you might admirably advance your own interests and be of great use at the same time to all your relatives and friends.'

'About my relatives and friends', he replied, 'I'm not much concerned, because I consider I've already done my duty by them tolerably well. While still young and healthy, I distributed among my relatives and friends the possessions that most men do not part with till they're old and sick (and then only reluctantly, when they can no longer keep them). I think they should be content with this gift of mine, and not insist, or even expect, that for their sake I should enslave myself to any king whatever.'

'Well said', Peter replied; 'but I do not mean that you should be in servitude to any king, only in his service.'

'The difference is only a matter of one syllable', said Raphael.

'All right', said Peter, 'but whatever you call it, I do not see any other way in which you can be so useful to your friends or to the general public, in addition to making yourself happier.'

'Happier indeed!' said Raphael. 'Would a way of life so absolutely repellent to my spirit make my life happier? As it is now, I live as I please,[16] and I fancy very few courtiers, however splendid, can say that. As a matter of fact, there are so many men soliciting favours from the powerful that you need not think it will be a great loss if they have to do without me and a couple of others like me.'

---

[16] Hythloday paraphrases Cicero's definition of liberty, which occurs in a context similar to the present one (*De officiis* I.xx.69–70). In a letter translated by More and appended to *The Life of John Picus* (1505), Pico also cites the philosopher's love of liberty as his reason for declining royal service. See *The English Works of Sir Thomas More*, ed. W.E. Campbell, annotated by A.W. Reed, 2 vols. (London and New York, 1931), I, 370. As Dominic Baker-Smith points out (*More's 'Utopia'*, pp. 18–21, 99–100), this letter – which gives not only Pico's position but the opposed one of his correspondent, Andrea Corneo – forms a parallel to the debate on counsel in *Utopia* (although the debate in the letter is, by comparison, simplistic and one-sided).

Tum ego, Perspicuum est, inquam, te, mi Raphael, neque opum esse neque potentiae cupidum, atque ego profecto huius tuae mentis hominem non minus veneror ac suspicio quam eorum quemvis qui maxime rerum sunt potentes. Ceterum videberis plane rem te atque istoc animo tuo tam generoso, tam vere philosopho, dignam fac- 5 turus, si te ita compares ut vel cum aliquo privatim incommodo ingenium tuum atque industriam publicis rebus accommodes, quod numquam tanto cum fructu queas quanto si a consiliis fueris magno alicui principi, eique (quod te facturum certe scio) recta atque honesta persuaseris. Nempe a principe bonorum malorumque omnium 10 torrens in totum populum, velut a perenni quodam fonte, promanat. In te vero tam absoluta doctrina est ut vel citra magnum rerum usum, porro tanta rerum peritia ut sine ulla doctrina, egregium consiliarium cuivis regum sis praestaturus.

Bis erras, inquit ille, mi More, primum in me, deinde in re ipsa. 15 Nam neque mihi ea est facultas quam tu tribuis, et si maxime esset, tamen quum otio meo negotium facesserem, publicam rem nihil promoveam. Primum enim principes ipsi plerique omnes militaribus studiis (quorum ego neque peritiam habeo neque desidero) libentius occupantur quam bonis pacis artibus, maiusque multo stu- 20 dium est quibus modis per fas ac nefas nova sibi regna pariant quam uti parta bene administrent. Praeterea quicumque regibus a consilio sunt, eorum nemo est qui non aut vere tantum sapit ut non egeat, aut tantum sibi sapere videtur ut non libeat, alterius probare consilium, nisi quod absurdissimis quibusque dictis assentiuntur et suppa- 25 rasitantur eorum quos, ut maximae[6] apud principem gratiae, student assentatione demereri sibi. Et certe sic est natura comparatum, ut sua cuique inventa blandiantur. Sic et corvo suus arridet pullus, et suus simiae catulus placet.

Quod si quis in illo coetu vel alienis invidentium vel praeferen- 30 tium sua aliquid adferat quod aut aliis temporibus factum legit, aut aliis fieri locis vidit, ibi qui audiunt perinde agunt ac si tota sapientiae suae periclitaretur opinio et post illa pro stultis plane sint habendi, nisi aliquid sufficiant invenire quod in aliorum inventis vertant vitio. Si cetera destituant tum huc confugiunt: haec nostris, 35 inquiunt, placuere maioribus, quorum prudentiam utinam nos aequaremus. Itaque hoc dicto veluti egregie perorata re considunt, tamquam magnum sit periculum si quis ulla in re deprehendatur maioribus suis sapientior, a quibus tamen, ut quicque optime con-

---

[6] The texts read *maxima*; we follow 1563 and some later editions in emending (*maximae* modifying *gratiae*).

Then I said, 'It is clear, my dear Raphael, that you seek neither wealth nor power, and indeed I prize and revere a man of your disposition no less than I do the mightiest persons in the world. Yet I think if you could bring yourself to devote your intelligence and energy to public affairs, you would be doing something worthy of your noble and truly philosophical nature, even if you did not much like it. You could best perform such a service by joining the council of some great prince and inciting him to just and noble actions (as I'm sure you would): for a people's welfare or misery flows in a stream from their prince as from a never-failing spring. Your learning is so full, even if it weren't combined with experience, and your experience is so great, even apart from your learning, that you would be an extraordinary counsellor to any king in the world.'

'You are twice mistaken, my dear More', he said, 'first in me and then in the situation itself. I don't have the capacity you ascribe to me, and if I had it in the highest degree, the public would still not be any better off if I exchanged my contemplative leisure for active endeavour. In the first place, most princes apply themselves to the arts of war, in which I have neither ability nor interest, instead of to the good arts of peace. They are generally more set on acquiring new kingdoms by hook or crook than on governing well those they already have. Moreover, the counsellors of kings are so wise already that they don't need to accept or approve advice from anyone else – or at least they have that opinion of themselves. At the same time they endorse and flatter the most absurd statements of the prince's special favourites, through whose influence they hope to stand well with the prince. It's only natural, of course, that each man should think his own inventions best: the crow loves his fledgling and the ape his cub.

'Now in a court composed of people who envy everyone else and admire only themselves, if a man should suggest something he has read of in other ages or seen in practice elsewhere, those who hear it act as if their whole reputation for wisdom would be endangered, and as if henceforth they would look like simpletons, unless they can find fault with the proposals of others. If all else fails, they take refuge in some remark like this: "The way we're doing it was good enough for our ancestors, and I only wish we were as wise as they were." And with this deep thought they take their seats, as though they have said the last word on the subject – implying, of course, that it would be a very dangerous matter if anyone were found to be wiser on any point than his ancestors. As a matter of

sultum est, ita aequissimo animo valere sinimus. At si qua de re potuit consuli prudentius, eam protinus ansam cupide arreptam mordicus retinemus. Itaque in haec superba, absurda, ac morosa iudicia, cum saepe alibi, tum semel in Anglia quoque, incidi.

Obsecro, inquam, fuisti apud nos?

Fui, inquit, atque aliquot menses ibi sum versatus, non multo post eam cladem qua Anglorum occidentalium civile adversus regem bellum miseranda ipsorum strage compressum est. Interea multum debui reverendissimo patri Ioanni Mortono Cantuariensi Archiepiscopo et Cardinali, ac tum quoque Angliae Cancellario: viro, mi Petre (nam Moro cognita sum narraturus), non auctoritate magis quam prudentia ac virtute venerabili. Etenim statura ei mediocris erat, nec aetati, quamquam serae, cedens. Vultus quem revereare, non horreas. In congressu non difficilis, serius tamen et gravis. Libido erat asperius interdum compellando supplicantes experiri, sed sine noxa, quid ingenii, quam animi praesentiam, quisque prae se ferret: qua velut cognata sibi virtute, modo abesset impudentia, delectabatur, et ut idoneam ad res gerendas amplectebatur. Sermo politus et efficax, iuris magna peritia, ingenium incomparabile, memoria ad prodigium usque excellens. Haec enim natura egregia discendo atque exercendo provexit. Huius consiliis rex plurimum fidere, multum respublica niti (cum ego aderam) videbatur. Quippe qui ab prima fere iuventa protinus a schola coniectus in aulam, maximis in negotiis per omnem versatus aetatem, ac variis fortunae aestibus assidue iactatus, prudentiam rerum (quae sic recepta non facile elabitur) multis magnisque cum periculis didicerat.

De legibus parum aequis Forte fortuna quum die quodam in eius mensa essem, laicus quidam legum vestratium peritus aderat. Is nescio unde nactus occasionem, coepit accurate laudare rigidam illam iustitiam quae tum illic exercebatur in fures, quos passim narrabat nonnumquam sus-

fact, we have no misgivings about neglecting the best examples they have left us; but if on some point their deliberations could have been more prudent, we immediately and eagerly seize the excuse of reverence for times past and cling to it desperately. Such proud, obstinate, ridiculous judgements I have encountered many times, and once even in England.'

'What!' I said, 'Were you ever in my country?'

'Yes', he said, 'I spent several months there. It was not long after the revolt of the west-countrymen against the King had been put down with the lamentable slaughter of the rebels.[17] During my stay I was deeply beholden to the reverend father John Morton, Archbishop of Canterbury and Cardinal, and also at that time Lord Chancellor of England.[18] He was a man, my dear Peter (for More already knows what I'm going to say), as much respected for his wisdom and virtue as for his authority. He was of medium height, not bent over despite his age; his looks inspired respect, not fear. In conversation, he was not forbidding, though serious and grave. When petitioners came to him, he liked to test their spirit and presence of mind by speaking to them sharply, though not maliciously. He liked to uncover these qualities, which were those of his own nature, as long as they were not carried to the point of effrontery; and he thought such men were best qualified to carry on business. His speech was polished and pointed, his knowledge of the law was great, he had an incomparable understanding and a prodigious memory, for he had improved excellent natural abilities by study and practice. At the time when I was in England, the King depended greatly on his advice, and he seemed the mainspring of all public affairs. He had been taken straight from school to court when scarcely more than a boy, had devoted all his life to important business, and had been whirled about by violent changes of fortune so that in the midst of great dangers he had learned practical wisdom, which is not soon lost when so purchased.

'It happened one day when I was dining with him there was present a layman, learned in the laws of your country, who for some reason took occasion to praise the rigid execution of justice *Of unjust laws* then being practised on thieves. They were being executed every-

---

[17] Angered by Henry VII's rapacious taxation, an army of Cornishmen marched on London in 1497. They were defeated at the Battle of Blackheath; estimates of the number killed vary from 200 to ten times that many.

[18] More had deeply admired Morton (1420–1500) since serving as a page in his household. There is a similar portrait of him in *The History of King Richard III* (CW, II, 90–1).

pendi viginti in una cruce, atque eo vehementius dicebat se mirari, cum tam pauci elaberentur supplicio, quo malo fato fieret uti tam multi tamen ubique grassarentur. Tum ego (ausus enim sum libere apud Cardinalem loqui): Nihil mireris, inquam. Nam haec punitio furum et supra iustum est et non ex usu publico. Est enim ad vind- 5
icanda furta nimis atrox, nec tamen ad refrenanda sufficiens. Quippe neque furtum simplex tam ingens facinus est ut capite debeat plecti, neque ulla poena est tanta ut ab latrociniis cohibeat eos qui nullam aliam artem quaerendi victus habent. Itaque hac in re non vos modo sed bona pars huius orbis imitari videtur malos praeceptores, qui 10

Qua ratione fieri discipulos verberant libentius quam docent. Decernuntur enim fur-
possit ne tam anti gravia atque horrenda supplicia, cum potius multo fuerit pro-
multi sint fures videndum uti aliquis esset proventus vitae, ne cuiquam tam dira sit furandi primum dehinc pereundi necessitas.

Est, inquit ille, satis hoc provisum: sunt artes mechanicae, est 15
agricolatio, ex his tueri vitam liceat, ni sponte mali esse mallent.

At non sic evades, inquam. Nam primum omittamus eos qui saepe vel ab externis bellis vel civilibus mutili redeunt domum, ut nuper apud vos e Cornubiensi proelio, et non ita pridem e Gallico, qui vel reipublicae impendunt membra vel regi: quos neque pris- 20
tinas artes exercere debilitas patitur, neque aetas novam discere. Hos (inquam) omittamus, quando bella per intermissas vices com-meant: ea contemplemur quae nullo die non accidunt. Tantus est ergo nobilium numerus qui non ipsi modo degant otiosi tamquam fuci laboribus aliorum, quos, puta suorum praediorum colonos, 25

where, he said, with as many as twenty at a time being hanged on a single gallows.[19] And then he declared he was amazed that so many thieves sprang up everywhere when so few of them escaped hanging. I ventured to speak freely before the Cardinal, and said, "There is no need to wonder: this way of punishing thieves goes beyond the call of justice, and is not in any case for the public good. The penalty is too harsh in itself, yet it isn't an effective deterrent. Simple theft is not so great a crime that it ought to cost a man his head, yet no punishment however severe can restrain those from robbery who have no other way to make a living. In this matter not only you in England but a good part of the world seem to imitate bad schoolmasters, who would rather whip their pupils than teach them. Severe and terrible punishments are enacted for theft, when it would be much better to enable every man to earn his own living, instead of being driven to the awful necessity of stealing and then dying for it."

How to reduce the number of thieves

' "Oh, we've taken care of that", said the fellow. "There are the trades and there is farming by which men may make a living, unless they choose deliberately to do evil."

' "No", I said, "you won't get out of it that way. We may overlook the cripples who come home from foreign and civil wars, as lately from the Cornish battle and not long before that from your wars with France.[20] These men, who have lost limbs in the service of the common good or the king, are too shattered to follow their old trades and too old to learn new ones. But since wars occur only from time to time, let us, I say, overlook these men and consider what happens every day. There are a great many noblemen who live idly like drones off the labour of others,[21] their tenants whom

---

[19] Holinshed reports that, in the reign of Henry VIII alone, 72,000 thieves were hanged (*Holinshed's Chronicles [of] England, Scotland, and Ireland*, 6 vols. (1807; rpt New York, 1965), I, 314).

[20] Since the dramatic date of the conversation is 1497 or shortly thereafter, Hythloday may be referring to the relatively small number of casualties suffered by the English during the sporadic hostilities in France in 1489–92. But More is probably thinking of the heavier casualties of Henry VIII's French excursions of 1512–13.

[21] In the *Republic*, Socrates uses the same metaphor to describe the kind of monied individual who contributes nothing to society: 'Though he may have appeared to belong to the ruling class, surely in fact he was neither ruling, nor serving society in any other way; he was merely a consumer of goods ... Don't you think we can fairly call him a drone?' (VIII.552B–C). In general, Plato's characterisation of oligarchy seems to have provided More with a framework for his observations on the condition of England. An oligarchy is 'a society where it is wealth that counts ... and in which political power is in the hands of the rich and the poor have no share of it' (VIII.550C). The 'worst defect' of such a society is that it generates functionless people (552A).

augendis reditibus ad vivum usque radunt (nam eam solam frugalit-
atem novere, homines alioquin ad mendicitatem usque prodigi),
verum immensam quoque otiosorum stipatorum turbam circum-
ferunt, qui nullam umquam quaerendi victus artem didicere. Hi
simul atque erus obierit aut ipsi aegrotaverint eiciuntur ilico. Nam 5
et otiosos libentius quam aegrotos alunt, et saepe morientis heres
non protinus alendae sufficit paternae familiae. Interim illi esuriunt
strenue nisi strenue latrocinentur. Nam quid faciant? Siquidem ubi
errando paululum vestes ac valetudinem attrivere, morbo iam
squalidos atque obsitos pannis, neque generosi dignantur accipere 10
neque audent rustici: non ignari eum qui, molliter educatus in otio
ac deliciis, solitus sit accinctus acinace ac caetra totam viciniam
vultu nebulonico despicere et contemnere omnes prae se, haudquaquam idoneum fore qui cum ligone ac marra maligna mercede ac
victu parco, fideliter inserviat pauperi. 15

Ad haec ille, Atqui nobis, inquit, hoc hominum genus in primis
fovendum est. In his enim, utpote hominibus animi magis excelsi
ac generosioris quam sunt opifices aut agricolae, consistunt vires ac
robur exercitus si quando sit confligendum bello.

Profecto, inquam ego, eadem opera dicas licet belli gratia fov- 20
endos esse fures, quibus haud dubie numquam carebitis dum habeb-
itis hos. Quin neque latrones sunt instrenui milites neque milites
ignavissimi latronum, adeo inter has artes belle convenit. At hoc
vitium, tamen frequens est vobis, non proprium; est enim omnium
fere gentium commune. Nam Gallias infestat alia praeterea pestis 25

they bleed white by constantly raising their rents. (This is the only instance of their tightfistedness, because they are prodigal in everything else, ready to spend their way to the poorhouse.) What's more, they drag around with them a great train of idle servants, who have never learned any trade by which they could make a living.[22] As soon as their master dies, or they themselves fall ill, they are promptly turned out of doors, for lords would rather support idlers than invalids, and the heir is often unable to maintain as big a household as his father had, at least at first. Those who are turned out soon set about starving, unless they set about stealing.[23] What else can they do? Then when a wandering life has taken the edge off their health and the gloss off their clothes, when their faces look worn and their garments are tattered, men of rank will not care to engage them. And country folk dare not do so, for they don't have to be told that one who has been raised softly to idle pleasures, who has been used to swaggering about like a bully with sword and buckler, is likely to look down on the whole neighbourhood and despise everybody else as beneath him. Such a man can't be put to work with spade and mattock; he will not serve a poor man faithfully for scant wages and sparse diet."

'"But we ought to encourage these men in particular", said the lawyer. "In case of war the strength and power of our army depend on them, because they have a bolder and nobler spirit than workmen and farmers have."

'"You may as well say that thieves should be encouraged for the sake of wars", I answered, "since you will never lack for thieves as long as you have men like these. Just as thieves are not bad soldiers, soldiers turn out to be enterprising robbers, so nearly are these two ways of life related.[24] But this problem, though frequent here, is not yours alone; it is common to almost all nations. France suffers from an even more pestiferous plague. Even in peacetime, if you

---

[22] Some of these retainers were household servants; others constituted the remnants of the private armies which, in a feudal society, followed every lord. In the reign of Henry VII the latter kind of retaining was sharply curtailed.

[23] Cf. *Republic* VIII.552C: 'all winged drones have been created without stings, but . . . our two-footed ones vary, and some have stings and some not; and . . . the stingless type end their days as beggars, the stinging type as what we call criminals'. For Plato as for Hythloday beggary and theft are always found together, because they are consequences of the same social defects: 'in any state where there are beggars there are also, hidden away somewhere, thieves and pick-pockets and temple robbers and all such practitioners of crime' (552D).

[24] The close kinship between the professions of soldier and robber is a frequent theme of Erasmus and other humanists. See, for example, Erasmus' *Complaint of Peace* (CWE, XXVII, 316–17).

pestilentior: tota patria stipendiariis, in pace quoque (si illa pax est), oppleta atque obsessa militibus, eadem persuasione inductis qua vos otiosos hic ministros alendos esse censuistis. Nempe quod moro-sophis visum est in eo sitam esse publicam salutem si in promptu semper adsit validum firmumque praesidium maxime veteranorum, 5

Quam perniciem adferant perpetua militum praesidia

neque enim confidunt inexercitatis quicquam: ut vel ideo quaeren-dum eis bellum sit, ne imperitos habeant milites, et homines iugul-andi gratis, ne (ut habet facete Sallustius) manus aut animus incipiat per otium torpescere. At quam sit perniciosum huiusmodi beluas alere et Gallia suo malo didicit et Romanorum, Carthaginiensium, 10 ac Syrorum, tum multarum gentium exempla declarant, quorum omnium non imperium modo sed agros quoque atque adeo urbes ipsas parati ipsorum exercitus aliis atque aliis occasionibus evert-erunt. Quam vero non magnopere necessarium vel hinc elucescit, quod ne Galli quidem milites armis ab unguiculis exercitatissimi 15 cum evocatis comparati vestris admodum saepe gloriantur superi-ores sese discessisse, ut ne quid dicam amplius ne praesentibus videar adblandiri[7] vobis. Sed nec vestri illi vel opifices urbici vel rudes atque agrestes agricolae otiosos generosorum stipatores cre-duntur valde pertimescere, nisi aut hi quibus ad vires atque audac- 20 iam corpus contigit ineptius, aut quorum animi vis inopia rei famil-iaris infringitur. Adeo periculum nullum est ne quorum valida et robusta corpora (neque enim nisi selectos dignantur generosi corrumpere) nunc vel elanguescunt otio vel negotiis prope mulieb-ribus emolliuntur, iidem bonis artibus instructi ad vitam et virilibus 25 exercitati laboribus, effeminentur. Certe utcumque sese haec habet res, illud mihi nequaquam videtur publicae rei conducere, in eventum belli, quod numquam habetis nisi quum vultis, infinitam eius generis turbam alere quod infestat pacem, cuius tanto maior

---

[7] This non-classical verb is given by Latham, *Dictionary of Medieval Latin from British Sources*, under *abblandior*, with the meaning 'to flatter, to be pleasing'.

can call it peace, the whole country is crowded and overrun with foreign mercenaries, imported on the same principle that you've given for your noblemen keeping idle servants.[25] Wise fools[26] think that the public safety depends on having ready a strong army, preferably of veteran soldiers. They think inexperienced men are not reliable, and they sometimes hunt out pretexts for war, just so they may have trained soldiers; hence men's throats are cut for no reason – lest, as Sallust neatly puts it, 'hand and spirit grow dull through lack of practice.'[27] But France has learned to her cost how pernicious it is to feed such beasts. The examples of the Romans, the Carthaginians, the Syrians and many other peoples show the same thing; for not only their governments but their fields and even their cities were ruined more than once by their own standing armies.[28] Besides, this preparedness is unnecessary: not even the French soldiers, practised in arms from their cradles, can boast of having often got the best of your raw recruits.[29] I shall say no more on this point, lest I seem to flatter present company. At any rate, neither your town workmen nor your rough farm labourers – except for those whose physique isn't suited for strength or boldness, or whose spirit has been broken by the lack of means to support their families – seem to be much afraid of those flocks of idle retainers. So you need not fear that retainers, once strong and vigorous (for that's the only sort the gentry deign to corrupt), but now soft and flabby because of their idle, effeminate life, would be weakened if they were taught practical crafts to earn their living and trained to manly labour. However that may be, though, I certainly cannot think it's in the public interest to maintain for the emergency of war such a vast multitude of people who trouble and disturb the peace: you never have war unless you choose it, and

The mischief of standing armies

[25] In the early sixteenth century, French infantry forces were mainly Swiss and German mercenaries.

[26] *Morosophi* (transliterated from Greek). The term is used in Lucian's 'Alexander', and in *The Praise of Folly*. The modern word 'sophomore' is the same combination reversed.

[27] Paraphrased from *Bellum Catilinae* XVI.3.

[28] Roman history is full of such episodes, dating from the emergence of standing armies in the first century BC. At the end of the First Punic War (241 BC), the Carthaginians' mercenaries turned on their masters. The victimisers of the Syrians that Hythloday has in mind are probably the Mamelukes, a military caste of foreign extraction that ruled, from the thirteenth century to the early sixteenth, a state that included much of the Middle East.

[29] Past English victories over the French included Crécy (1346), Poitiers (1356) and Henry V's triumph at Agincourt (1415). The preferability of citizen to mercenary armies was a frequent topic of Italian political writing of More's time. It is, for example, an article of faith for Machiavelli (*The Prince*, chapters 12 and 13).

haberi ratio quam belli debeat. Neque haec tamen sola est furandi necessitas. Est alia magis, quantum credo, peculiaris vobis.

Quaenam est ea? inquit Cardinalis.

Oves, inquam, vestrae, quae tam mites esse tamque exiguo solent ali, nunc (uti fertur) tam edaces atque indomitae esse coeperunt ut ₅ homines devorent ipsos: agros, domos, oppida vastent ac depopulentur. Nempe quibuscumque regni partibus nascitur lana tenuior atque ideo pretiosior, ibi nobiles et generosi atque adeo abbates aliquot, sancti viri, non his contenti reditibus fructibusque annuis qui maioribus suis solebant ex praediis crescere, nec habentes satis ₁₀ quod otiose ac laute viventes nihil in publicum prosint, nisi etiam obsint: arvo nihil relinquunt, omnia claudunt pascuis, demoliuntur domos, diruunt oppida, templo dumtaxat stabulandis ovibus relicto, et tamquam parum soli perderent apud vos ferarum saltus ac vivaria, illi boni viri habitationes omnes et quicquid usquam est culti vertunt ₁₅ in solitudinem. Ergo ut unus helluo, inexplebilis ac dira pestis patriae, continuatis agris aliquot millia iugerum uno circumdet saepto, eiciuntur coloni; quidam suis etiam aut circumscripti fraude aut vi oppressi exuuntur, aut fatigati iniuriis adiguntur ad venditionem. Itaque quoquo pacto emigrant miseri, viri, mulieres, mariti, ₂₀ uxores, orbi, viduae, parentes cum parvis liberis et numerosa magis quam divite familia, ut multis opus habet manibus res rustica, emigrant, inquam, e notis atque assuetis laribus, nec inveniunt quo se recipiant. Supellectilem omnem haud magno vendibilem etiamsi manere possit emptorem, quum extrudi necesse est minimo ven- ₂₅ umdant. Id quum brevi errando insumpserint, quid restat aliud denique quam ut furentur et pendeant – iuste, scilicet – aut vagentur atque mendicent? Quamquam tum quoque velut errones coniciuntur in carcerem quod otiosi obambulent, quorum operam nemo est qui conducat, quum illi cupidissime offerant. Nam rusticae rei cui ₃₀

peace is always more to be considered than war. Yet this is not the only force driving men to thievery. There is another that, as I see it, applies more specially to you Englishmen."

' "What is that?" said the Cardinal.

' "Your sheep", I said, "that commonly are so meek and eat so little; now, as I hear, they have become so greedy and fierce that they devour human beings themselves.[30] They devastate and depopulate fields, houses and towns. For in whatever parts of the land sheep yield the finest and thus the most expensive wool, there the nobility and gentry, yes, and even a good many abbots – holy men – are not content with the old rents that the land yielded to their predecessors. Living in idleness and luxury without doing society any good no longer satisfies them; they have to do positive harm. For they leave no land free for the plough: they enclose every acre for pasture; they destroy houses and abolish towns, keeping the churches – but only for sheep-barns. And as if enough of your land were not already wasted on game-preserves and forests for hunting wild animals, these worthy men turn all human habitations and cultivated fields back to wilderness. Thus, so that one greedy, insatiable glutton, a frightful plague to his native country, may enclose thousands of acres within a single fence, the tenants are ejected; and some are stripped of their belongings by trickery or brute force, or, wearied by constant harassment, are driven to sell them. One way or another, these wretched people – men, women, husbands, wives, orphans, widows, parents with little children and entire families (poor but numerous, since farming requires many hands) – are forced to move out. They leave the only homes familiar to them, and can find no place to go. Since they must leave at once without waiting for a proper buyer, they sell for a pittance all their household goods, which would not bring much in any case. When that little money is gone (and it's soon spent in wandering from place to place), what finally remains for them but to steal, and so be hanged – justly, no doubt – or to wander and beg? And yet if they go tramping, they are jailed as idle vagrants. They would be glad to work, but they can find no one who will hire them. There

---

[30] This vivid image introduces Hythloday's treatment of the social dislocation brought about by 'enclosure' – the gradual amalgamation and fencing, over a period extending from the twelfth to the nineteenth century, of the open fields of the feudal system: one incentive to enclosure was the increasing profitability of the wool trade. There were (and are) apologists for enclosure, but Hythloday's view was widely shared, and there is no doubt that the increase in sheep farming, which required large grazing lands and little manpower, greatly worsened the lot of many labourers and resulted in the destruction of many villages.

assueverunt nihil est quod agatur ubi nihil seritur. Siquidem unus opilio atque bubulcus sufficit ei terrae depascendae pecoribus in cuius cultum ut sementi faciendae sufficeret multae poscebantur manus.

Atque hac ratione fit ut multis in locis annona multo sit carior. Quin lanarum quoque adeo increvit pretium ut a tenuioribus qui pannos inde solent apud vos conficere prorsus emi non possint, atque ea ratione plures ab opere ablegantur in otium. Nam post aucta pascua infinitam ovium vim absumpsit tabes, velut eorum cupiditatem ulciscente deo immissa in oves lue, quam in ipsorum capita contortam esse fuerat iustius. Quod si maxime increscat ovium numerus, pretio nihil decrescit tamen: quod earum, si monopolium appellari non potest quod non unus vendit, certe oligopolium est. Reciderunt enim fere in manus paucorum eorundemque divitum quos nulla necessitas urget ante vendendi quam libet, nec ante libet quam liceat quanti libet.

Iam cetera quoque pecorum genera ut aeque cara sint eadem ratio est, atque hoc etiam amplius, quod dirutis villis atque imminuta re rustica, non sint qui feturam curent. Neque enim divites illi ut ovium sic etiam armentorum fetus educant: sed aliunde macra empta vili posteaquam suis pascuis pinguerint magno revendunt. Ideoque, sicuti reor, nondum sentitur totum huius rei incommodum. Nempe adhuc his modo locis reddunt cara ubi vendunt. Ceterum ubi aliquandiu celerius extulerint illinc quam nasci possint, tum demum ibi quoque paulatim decrescente copia ubi coemuntur, necesse est hic insigni laboretur inopia. Ita qua re vel maxime felix haec vestra videbatur insula, iam ipsam paucorum improba cupiditas vertit in perniciem. Nam haec annonae caritas in causa est cur quisque quam possint plurimos e familia dimittat: quo, quaeso, nisi mendicatum, aut quod generosis animis persuadeas facilius, latrocinatum?

Quid quod ad miseram hanc egestatem atque inopiam adiungitur importuna luxuries. Nam et ministris nobilium et opificibus et ipsis propemodum rusticis et omnibus denique ordinibus, multum est insolentis apparatus in vestibus, nimius in victu luxus. Iam ganea,

is no need for farm labour, in which they have been trained, when there is no land left to be planted. One herdsman or shepherd can look after a flock of beasts large enough to stock an area that used to require many hands to make it grow crops.

'"This enclosing has led to sharply rising food prices in many districts. Also, the price of raw wool has risen so much that poor people among you who used to make cloth can no longer afford it, and so great numbers are forced from work to idleness. One reason is that after so much new pasture-land was enclosed, rot killed a countless number of the sheep – as though God were punishing greed by sending on the beasts a murrain that rightly should have fallen on the owners! But even if the number of sheep should increase greatly, the price will not fall a penny, because the wool trade, though it can't be called a monopoly because it isn't in the hands of a single person, is concentrated in so few hands (an oligopoly, you might say), and these so rich, that the owners are never pressed to sell until they have a mind to, and that is only when they can get their price.

'"For the same reason other kinds of livestock are also priced exorbitantly, the more so because, with farmhouses being torn down and farming in decay, nobody is left to breed the cattle. These rich men will not breed calves as they do lambs, but buy them lean and cheap, fatten them in their pastures, and then sell them dear. I don't think the full impact of this bad system has yet been felt. We know these dealers hurt consumers where the fattened cattle are sold. But when, over a period of time, they keep buying beasts from other localities faster than they can be bred, a gradually diminishing supply where they are bought will inevitably lead to severe shortages. So your island, which seemed specially fortunate in this matter, will be ruined by the crass avarice of a few. For the high cost of living causes everyone to dismiss as many retainers as he can from his household; and what, I ask, can these men do but rob or beg? And a man of courage is more easily persuaded to steal than to beg.

'"To make this miserable poverty and scarcity worse, they exist side by side with wanton luxury.[31] The servants of noblemen, tradespeople, even some farmers – people of every social rank – are given to ostentatious dress and gourmandising. Look at the

---

[31] Extravagant display was not in fact characteristic of the reign of the parsimonious Henry VII (the period in which Hythloday is supposed to be addressing Cardinal Morton). More seems to be projecting onto the earlier period the taste for display associated with the reign of Henry VIII.

lustra, lupanar et aliud lupanar tabernae vinariae, cervisiariae, postremo tot improbi ludi, alea, charta, fritillus, pila, sphaera, discus,
an non haec celeriter exhausta pecunia recta suos mystas mittunt
aliquo latrocinatum? Has perniciosas pestes eicite, statuite ut villas
atque oppida rustica aut hi restituant qui diruere, aut ea cedant 5
reposituris atque aedificare volentibus. Refrenate coemptiones istas
divitum ac velut monopolii exercendi licentiam. Pauciores alantur
otio, reddatur agricolatio, lanificium instauretur ut sit honestum
negotium quo se utiliter exerceat otiosa ista turba, vel quos hactenus
inopia fures fecit vel qui nunc errones aut otiosi sunt ministri, fures 10
nimirum utrique futuri.

Certe nisi his malis medemini, frustra iactetis exercitam in vind-
icanda furta iustitiam, nempe speciosam magis quam aut iustam aut
utilem. Siquidem quum pessime sinitis educari et mores paulatim
ab teneris annis corrumpi, puniendos videlicet tum demum quum 15
ea flagitia viri designent quorum spem de se perpetuam a pueritia
usque praebuerant, quid aliud, quaeso, quam facitis fures et iidem
plectitis?

Iam me haec loquente iuris ille consultus interim se ad dicendum
composuerat ac statuerat secum modo illo sollemni disputantium 20
uti qui diligentius repetunt quam respondent: adeo bonam partem
laudis ponunt in memoria. Belle, inquit, dixisti profecto quum sis
videlicet hospes qui magis audire his de rebus aliquid potueris quam
exacte quicquam cognoscere, id quod ego paucis efficiam perspicuum. Nam primum ordine recensebo quae tu dixisti, deinde osten- 25
dam quibus in rebus imposuit tibi nostrarum rerum ignoratio, postremo rationes tuas omnes diluam atque dissolvam. Igitur ut a primo
quod sum pollicitus exordiar, quattuor mihi visus es –

Expressit morem
ei Cardinali
familiarem
interpellandi si
quis loquacius
ageret

Tace, inquit Cardinalis: nam haud responsurus paucis videris qui
sic incipias. Quamobrem levabimus in praesenti te hac respondendi 30
molestia, servaturi tamen integrum id munus tibi in proximum con-
gressum vestrum, quem (nisi quid impediat aut te aut Raphaelem
hunc) crastinus dies velim referat. Sed interim abs te, mi Raphael,
perquam libenter audierim quare tu furtum putes ultimo supplicio
non puniendum, quamve aliam poenam ipse statuas quae magis 35

cook-shops, the brothels, the bawdy houses and those other places just as bad, the wine-bars and ale-houses. Look at all the crooked games of chance like dice, cards, backgammon, tennis, bowling and quoits, in which money slips away so fast. Don't all these pastimes lead their devotees straight to robbery? Banish these blights, make those who have ruined farmhouses and villages restore them or hand them over to someone who will restore and rebuild. Restrict the right of the rich to buy up anything and everything, and then to exercise a kind of monopoly.[32] Let fewer people be brought up in idleness. Let agriculture be restored, and the wool-manufacture revived as an honest trade, so there will be useful work for the idle throng, whether those whom poverty has already made thieves or those who are only vagabonds or idle servants now, but are bound to become thieves in the future.

' "Certainly, unless you cure these evils it is futile to boast of your justice in punishing theft. Your policy may look superficially like justice, but in reality it is neither just nor expedient. If you allow young folk to be abominably brought up and their characters corrupted, little by little, from childhood; and if then you punish them as grown-ups for committing the crimes to which their training has consistently inclined them, what else is this, I ask, but first making them thieves and then punishing them for it?"

'As I was speaking thus, the lawyer had prepared his answer, choosing the solemn style of disputants who are better at summing up than at replying, and who like to show off their memory. So he said to me, "You have talked very well for a stranger, but you have heard more than you've been able to understand correctly, as I will make clear to you in a few words. First, I will summarise what you said; then I will show how you have been misled by ignorance of our ways; finally, I will refute all your arguments and demolish them. And so to begin with the first thing I promised, on four points you seemed to me —"

' "Hold your tongue", said the Cardinal, "for you won't be fin- *Illustrates the* ished in a few words if this is the way you start. We will spare you *Cardinal's* *informal way of* the trouble of answering now and put off the whole task until your *interrupting a* *babbler* next meeting, which will be tomorrow if your affairs and Raphael's permit it. Meanwhile, my dear Raphael, I'd be glad to hear why you think theft should not be punished with the extreme penalty, or what other punishment you think would be more conducive to

[32] A number of laws to control gambling and ale-houses, restrict monopolies and provide for the rebuilding of towns and the restoration of pastures to tillage were in fact passed, with small result, in the reigns of both Henry VII and Henry VIII.

conducat in publicum. Nam tolerandum ne tu quidem sentis. At si
nunc per mortem quoque tamen in furtum ruitur, proposita semel
vitae securitate, quae vis, quis metus posset absterrere maleficos?
qui mitigatione supplicii velut praemio quodam ad maleficium se
invitatos interpretarentur.   5

Omnino mihi videtur, inquam, pater benignissime, homini vitam
eripi propter ereptam pecuniam prorsus iniquum esse. Siquidem
cum humana vita ne omnibus quidem fortunae possessionibus paria
fieri posse arbitror. Quod si laesam iustitiam, si leges violatas hac
rependi poena dicant, haud pecuniam: quidni merito summum illud   10
ius summa vocetur iniuria? Nam neque legum probanda sunt tam

Manliana imperia Manliana imperia ut sicubi in levissimis parum obtemperetur ilico
ex Livio stringant gladium, neque tam Stoica scita ut omnia peccata adeo
exsistiment paria, uti nihil iudicent interesse occidatne aliquis hominem an nummum ei surripiat, inter quae (si quicquam aequitas   15
valet) nihil omnino simile aut affine. Deus vetuit occidi quemquam,
et nos tam facile occidimus ob ademptam pecuniolam? Quod si
quis interpretetur illo dei iussu interdictam necis potestatem nisi
quatenus humana lex declaret occidendum, quid obstat quominus
homines eodem modo constituant inter se quatenus stuprum   20
admittendum sit, adulterandum, peierandum? Siquidem quum deus
non alienae modo, verumetiam suae cuique mortis ius ademerit, si
hominum inter se consensus de mutua caede certis placitis consen-
tientium adeo debet valere ut illius praecepti vinculis eximat suos
satellites, qui sine ullo exemplo dei eos interemerint quos humana 25
sanctio iussit occidi: an non hoc pacto praeceptum illud dei tantum
iuris est habiturum quantum humana iura permiserint? Ac fiet nimirum ut ad eundem modum omnibus in rebus statuant homines quatenus divina mandata conveniat observari. Denique lex Mosaica,
quamquam inclemens et aspera nempe in servos et quidem obstin- 30
atos lata, tamen pecunia furtum haud morte multavit. Ne putemus

68

the common good. For surely even you don't think it should go entirely unpunished. Even as it is, fear of death does not restrain the malefactors; once they were sure of their lives, as you propose, what force or fear could withhold them? They would look on a mitigation of the punishment as an invitation to commit crimes, almost a reward."

' "It seems to me, most kind and reverend father", I said, "that it's altogether unjust to take someone's life for taking money. In fact, I think that nothing in the world that fortune can bestow can be put on a par with a human life. If they say the thief suffers, not for the money, but for violation of justice and transgression of laws, then this extreme justice should properly be called extreme injury.[33] We ought not to approve of edicts so Manlian that they unsheathe the sword for the smallest violations.[34] Nor should we accept the Stoic decree that all crimes are equal,[35] as if there were no difference between killing a man and taking a coin from him. If equity means anything, there is no proportion or relation at all between these two crimes. God has forbidden us to kill anyone; shall we kill so readily for the theft of a bit of small change? Perhaps it will be argued that God's commandment against killing does not apply where human law allows it. But what then prevents men from making other laws in the same way, determining to what extent rape, adultery and perjury ought to be permitted? God has forbidden each of us not only to take the life of another but also to take his own life. If mutual consent to certain laws about killing one another has such force that it entitles men to exempt their agents from this command and allows them to kill those condemned by human decrees where God has given us no precedent, what is this but giving that command of God only as much force as human laws allow? The result will be that in every situation men will decide for themselves how far it suits them to observe the laws of God. Finally, the law of Moses was harsh and severe, as for an enslaved and stubborn people, but it punished theft with a fine, not death.[36]

Manlian edicts from Livy

[33] The phrase echoes the adage *summum ius, summa iniuria* (quoted by Cicero, *De officiis* I.x.33), which has a long history in discussions of equity.

[34] According to Livy, the Roman general Manlius (fourth century BC) executed his own son for violating one of his ordinances (VIII.vii.1–22). 'Manlian edicts' was therefore proverbial for inexorable decrees.

[35] Cicero ridicules this Stoic paradox (*De finibus* IV.ix.21–3, xxvii.75–xxviii.77); it is also criticised by Horace (*Satires* I.iii.96–124).

[36] The Mosaic law on theft is spelled out in the first verses of Exodus 22. It provides various penalties for theft, but nowhere death. This law is contrasted with the 'new law' of Christ, under which England is supposed to be operating. Note, though, that the Mosaic law prescribes death as the penalty for certain other

deum in nova lege clementiae, qua pater imperat filiis, maiorem indulsisse nobis invicem saeviendi licentiam.

Haec sunt cur non licere putem. Quam vero sit absurdum atque etiam perniciosum reipublicae furem atque homicidam ex aequo puniri nemo est, opinor, qui nesciat. Nempe quum latro conspiciat 5 non minus imminere discriminis dumtaxat furti damnato quam si praeterea convincatur homicidii, hac una cogitatione impellitur in caedem eius quem alioqui fuerat tantum spoliaturus. Quippe praeterquam quod deprehenso nihil sit plus periculi, est etiam in caede securitas maior, et maior celandi spes, sublato facinoris indice. 10 Itaque dum fures nimis atrociter studemus perterrefacere, in bonorum incitamus perniciem.

Iam quod quaeri solet quae punitio possit esse commodior, hoc meo iudicio haud paulo facilius est repertu quam quae possit esse deterior. Cur enim dubitemus eam viam utilem esse castigandis sce- 15 leribus quam scimus olim tam diu placuisse Romanis administrandae reipublicae peritissimis? Nempe hi magnorum facinorum convictos in lapidicinas atque fodienda metalla damnabant, perpetuis asservandos vinculis. Quamquam ego quod ad hanc rem attinet *Respublica* nullius institutum gentis magis probo quam id quod interea dum 20 *Polyleritarum* peregrinabar in Perside observatum apud vulgo dictos Polyleritas *apud Persas* adnotavi. Populum neque exiguum neque imprudenter institutum, et nisi quod tributum quotannis Persarum pendit regi, cetera liberum ac suis permissum legibus. Ceterum quoniam longe ab mari, montibus fere circumdati, et suae terrae nulla in re malignae[8] 25 contenti fructibus, neque adeunt alios saepe neque adeuntur. Tamen ex vetusto more gentis neque fines prorogare student et quos habent ab omni facile iniuria et montes tuentur et pensio quam rerum potenti persolvunt. Immunes prorsus ab militia, haud perinde splendide atque commode, felicesque magis quam nobiles aut clari 30 degunt. Quippe ne nomine quidem opinor praeterquam conterminis admodum satis noti.

Ergo apud hos furti qui peraguntur quod sustulere domino

---

[8] All texts until 1548 print *maligne*, but syntax requires *malignae*, modifying *terrae*.

Let us not think that in his new law of mercy, where he rules us as a father rules his children, God has given us greater licence to be cruel to one another.

' "These are the reasons why I think this punishment is wrong. And surely there is no one who doesn't know how absurd and even dangerous for society it is to punish theft and murder alike. If the thief realises that theft by itself carries the same peril as murder, that thought alone will encourage him to kill the victim whom otherwise he would only have robbed. Apart from the fact that he is in no greater danger if he is caught, murder is safer, since he conceals both crimes by killing the witness. Thus while we strive to terrify thieves with extreme cruelty, we really urge them to kill the innocent.

' "As for the usual question of what more suitable punishment can be found, in my judgement it would be far easier to find a better one than a worse. Why should we question the value of the punishments which we know were long used by the ancient Romans, who were most expert in the arts of government? They condemned those convicted of heinous crimes to work in shackles for the rest of their lives in stone quarries and mines. But on this point, of all the alternatives I prefer the method which I observed in my Persian travels practised among the people commonly called the Polylerites.[37] They are a nation of no small size, not badly governed, free and subject only to their own laws, except that they pay annual tribute to the Persian king. Living far from the sea, they are nearly surrounded by mountains; and since they are content with the products of their own land (it is by no means unfruitful), they do not visit other nations and are not much visited. By ancient tradition, they make no effort to enlarge their boundaries, and they are easily protected by their mountains and by the tribute paid to their overlord. Thus they fight no wars, and live in a comfortable rather than a glorious manner, more contented than renowned or glorious. Indeed, I think they are hardly known by name to anyone but their immediate neighbours.

The Polylerite society near the Persians

' "In their land, whoever is found guilty of theft must make resti-

crimes, and that Hythloday does not always condemn capital punishment. Surtz observes that Hythloday 'never asserts that capital punishment is not a just punishment for murder' (CW, IV, 342); nor, as Colin Starnes points out, does he deny that it should be 'the remedy of last resort' – as it is with the Polylerites (p. 73 below) and the Utopians (p. 193). See *The New Republic* (Waterloo, Ontario, 1990), p. 82n.

[37] More's coinage from *polus* ('much') plus *leros* ('nonsense'): 'the People of Much Nonsense'.

Adnotandum
nobis, qui secus
facimus
reddunt, non, quod alibi fieri solet, principi: utpote cui tantum iuris esse censent in rem furtivam quantum ipsi furi. Sin res perierit, pretio ex bonis furum confecto ac persoluto tum reliquo uxoribus eorum atque liberis integro, ipsi damnantur in opera.

Ac nisi atrociter commissum furtum est neque clauduntur ergas- 5
tulo neque gestant compedes, sed liberi ac soluti in publicis occupantur operibus. Detrectantes ac languidius gerentes sese, non tam vinculis coercent quam excitant verberibus. Strenuam navantes operam, absunt a contumeliis, noctu tantum nominatim censiti cubiculis includuntur. Praeter assiduum laborem nihil incommodi 10
est in vita. Aluntur enim haud duriter qui publicae rei serviunt e publico: alibi aliter. Siquidem alicubi quod impenditur in eos ex eleemosyna colligitur: atque ea via, quamquam incerta, tamen ut est ille populus misericors, nulla reperitur uberior. Alibi reditus quidam publici ad id destinantur. Est ubi certum in eos usus tribu- 15
tum viritim conferunt. Quin aliquot in locis nullum publicum opus faciunt, sed ut privatus quisque eget mercenariis, ita illorum cuiuspiam in eum diem operam stata mercede conducit apud forum, paulo minoris quam quanti liberam fuerat conducturus. Praeterea fas est servilem ignaviam flagris corripere. Sic fit uti numquam 20
opere careant, et praeter victum aliquid quoque die ab singulis publico inferatur aerario.

At idem hodie
famuli nobilium
pulchrum sibi
ducunt
Uno quodam colore vestiuntur et omnes et soli, capillo non abraso verum paulo supra auriculas attonso, e quarum altera paululum praescinditur. Cibum cuique[9] ab amicis dari, potumque, ac 25
sui coloris vestem licet: pecuniam datam esse danti pariter atque accipienti capitale, neque minus periculosum etiam homini libero quacumque de causa nummum a damnato recepisse, et servos item (sic enim damnatos vocant) arma contingere. Suos quaeque regio propria distinguit nota, quam abiecisse capitale est, ut vel extra 30
suos conspici fines, vel cum alterius regionis servo quicquam esse collocutum. At neque tutior fugae meditatio quam ipsa est fuga. Quin conscium talis fuisse consilii in servo nex est, in libero serv-

---

[9] *cuique* ('each') from 1518M, N; 1516 and 1517 print *cuiquam* ('anyone').

72

tution to the owner, not (as elsewhere) to the prince;[38] they think the prince has precisely as much right to the stolen goods as the thief himself. If the stolen property has disappeared, its value is made up from the thief's belongings and is paid back. All the rest is handed over to his wife and children, while the thief himself is sentenced to hard labour.

To be noted by us, who do otherwise

'"Unless their crimes were compounded with atrocities, thieves are neither imprisoned nor shackled, but go free and unconstrained about their work on public projects. If they shirk and do their jobs slackly, they are not chained, but they are whipped. If they work hard, they undergo no humiliation, except that at night after roll call they are locked in their cells. Apart from constant labour, their life is not uncomfortable. As workers for the public good, they are decently fed out of the public stores, though in different ways in different places. In some districts they are supported by alms. Unreliable as this support may seem, the Polylerites are so compassionate that no way is found more rewarding. In other places, public revenues are set aside for their support or a special tax is levied on every individual for their use; and in some localities they do not do public work, but anyone in need of workmen can go to the market and hire a convict by the day at a set rate, a little less than that for free men. If they are lazy, it is lawful to whip them. Thus the convicts never lack work, and each brings a little profit every day into the public treasury beyond the cost of his keep.

'"All of them, and only they, are dressed in clothes of the same distinctive colour. Their hair is not shaved off, but trimmed a little above the ears, and the tip of one ear is cut off. Their friends are allowed to give them food, drink or clothing, as long as it is of the proper colour; but to give them money is death, to both the giver and the taker. It is just as dangerous a crime for any free man to take money from them, for whatever reason; and it is also a capital crime for any of these slaves (as the condemned are called) to touch weapons. In each district of the country they wear a special badge. It is a capital crime to discard the badge, to be seen beyond the bounds of one's own district, or to talk with a slave of another district. Plotting escape is no more secure than escape itself: indeed, for any slave to be privy to an escape-plot is death, and for a free

Yet nowadays the servants of noblemen think such a haircut quite handsome

---

[38] Erasmus also condemns this common European practice, in *The Education of a Christian Prince* (CWE, XXVII, 270). In general, the principles underlying Polylerite criminal justice are similar to those expounded in Plato's *Laws*, where the legitimate aims of punishment are said to be to deter crime, reform the criminal, and redress the injury to the victim (IX.862C–D).

itus. Contra indici praemia decreta sunt: libero pecunia, servo libertas, utrique vero venia atque impunitas conscientiae, ne quando persequi malum consilium quam paenitere sit tutius.

Huius rei haec lex atque hic ordo est quem dixi. Qui quantum habeat humanitatis et commodi facile patet, quando sic irascitur ut 5 vitia perimat, servatis hominibus atque ita tractatis ut bonos esse necesse sit, et quantum ante damni dederunt tantum reliqua vita resartiant. Porro ne ad pristinos relabantur mores adeo nullus est metus, ut viatores quoque quibus iter aliquo institutum est non aliis viae ducibus sese tutiores arbitrentur quam servis illis ad quamque 10 regionem subinde commutatis. Nempe ad perpetrandum latrocinium nihil habent usquam non importunum: manus inermes, pecunia tantum sceleris index, deprehenso parata vindicta, neque spes ulla prorsus fugiendi quoquam. Quo enim pacto falleret ac tegeret fugam homo nulla vestium parte populo similis, nisi abeat nudus? 15 quin sic quoque fugientem proderet auricula. At ne inito saltem consilio coniurent in rempublicam, id demum scilicet periculum est. Quasi in tantam venire spem ulla possit vicinia non tentatis ac sollicitatis ante multarum regionum servitiis. Quae tantum absunt a facultate conspirandi, ut ne convenire quidem et colloqui aut salu- 20 tare se mutuo liceat. Ut credantur interim id consilium intrepide credituri suis, quod reticentibus periculosum, prodentibus maximo esse bono sciant? Quum contra nemo sit prorsus exspes, obediendo ac perferendo, bonamque de se praebendo spem emendatioris in posterum vitae, posse his modis fieri ut libertatem aliquando recup- 25 eret, quippe nullo non anno restitutis aliquot commendatione patientiae.

Haec quum dixissem atque adiecissem nihil mihi videri causae quare non hic modus haberi vel in Anglia possit, multo maiore cum fructu quam illa iustitia quam iuris ille peritus tantopere laudaverat, 30 sub haec ille, nempe iureconsultus: Numquam, inquit, istud sic stabiliri queat in Anglia, ut non in summum discrimen adducat rempublicam: et simul haec dicens commovit caput ac distorsit labrum, atque ita conticuit. Et omnes qui aderant pedibus in eius ibant sententiam. 35

Tum Cardinalis, Non est, inquit, proclive divinare commodene an secus res cessura sit, nullo prorsus facto periculo. Verum si, pronuntiata mortis sententia, differri executionem iubeat princeps

man, slavery. On the other hand, there are rewards for informers – money for a free man, freedom for a slave, and for both of them pardon and amnesty for knowing about the plot. Thus it can never be safer to persist in an illicit scheme than to repent of it.

'"These then are their laws and policy in this matter. It is clear how mild and practical they are, for the aim of the punishment is to destroy vices and save men. The men are treated so that they necessarily become good, and they have the rest of their lives to make up for the damage they have done. There is so little danger of recidivism that even travellers going from one part of the country to another think slaves the most reliable guides, changing them at the boundary of each district. Nowhere do the slaves have any chance of committing robbery, since they are unarmed, and any money in their possession is evidence of a crime. If caught, they would be punished, and there is utterly no hope of escaping any-where. Since every bit of a slave's clothing is unlike the usual cloth-ing of the country, how could one escape, unless he fled naked? And even then his cropped ear would give him away. But isn't there at least the danger of the slaves forming a conspiracy against the government? As if slaves of a single district could hope to suc-ceed unless they involved in their plot slave-gangs from many other districts! And they are so far from being able to form a conspiracy that they are not even allowed to meet or talk together, or to greet one another. How can we believe that anyone would dare to trust his comrades with such a plot when they know it is so dangerous to remain silent and so advantageous to reveal it? Besides, no one is quite without hope of gaining his freedom eventually if he accepts his punishment in a spirit of patient obedience and gives promise of future good conduct. Indeed, never a year goes by in which some are not pardoned as a reward for submissive behaviour."

'When I had finished this account, I added that I saw no reason why this policy could not be adopted even in England, and with much greater advantage than the "justice" which my legal antagon-ist had praised so highly. But the lawyer said, "Such a system could never be established in England without putting the commonwealth in serious peril." And so saying, he shook his head, made a wry face, and fell silent. And all who were present tripped over them-selves to get on his side.

'Then the Cardinal said, "It is not easy to guess whether this scheme would work well or not, since it has never been tried. But perhaps when the death sentence has been passed on a thief, the

atque hunc experiatur morem, cohibitis asylorum privilegiis, tum
vero si res comprobetur eventu esse utilis, rectum fuerit eam stabiliri. Alioqui tunc quoque adficere supplicio eos qui sunt ante dam-
nati neque minus e republica fuerit neque magis iniustum quam si
nunc idem fieret, nec ullum interea nasci ex ea re potest periculum. 5
Quin mihi certe videntur errones quoque ad eundem posse modum
non pessime tractari, in quos hactenus tam multis editis legibus
nihil promovimus tamen.

Haec ubi dixit Cardinalis, quae me narrante contempserant
omnes, eadem nemo non certatim laudibus est prosecutus, maxime 10
tamen illud de erronibus, quoniam hoc ab ipso adiectum est.

Nescio an quae sunt secuta silere praestiterit, erant enim ridicula:
sed narrabo tamen, nam non erant mala et aliquid ad hanc rem

Festivus dialogus
fratris et morionis

pertinebant. Astabat forte parasitus quidam, qui videri volebat imitari morionem, sed ita simulabat ut propior vero esset, tam frigidis 15
dictis captans risum ut ipse saepius quam dicta sua rideretur. Excid-
ebant homini tamen interdum quaedam adeo non absurda, ut fidem
adagio facerent, Crebro iactu iaci aliquando Venerem. Is ergo,
dicente quodam e conviviis iam meo sermone bene provisum esse
furibus, atque a Cardinale etiam cautum de erronibus, restare nunc 20
uti his praeterea consuleretur publicitus quos ad egestatem morbus
aut senectus impulisset, atque ad labores unde vivi possit reddidisset
impotes.

Sine, inquit, me: nam ego et hoc recte ut fiat videro. Etenim hoc
genus hominum misere cupio aliquo e conspectu amoliri meo, ita 25
me male vexarunt saepe, cum querulis illis opplorationibus flagitar-
ent pecuniam, quas numquam tamen tam commode potuerunt occi-
nere ut nummum a me extorquerent. Quippe semper alterum
evenit, ut aut non libeat dare aut ne liceat quidem quando nihil est
quod detur. Itaque nunc coeperunt sapere. Nam ne perdant operam 30

Proverbium vulgo
iactatum apud
mendicos

ubi me praeterire vident praetermittunt taciti: ita nihil a me sperant
amplius, non hercule magis quam si essem sacerdos. Sed illos ego

king might reprieve him for a time without right of sanctuary,[39] and thus see how the plan worked. If it turned out well, the practice might be made law; if not, he could then carry out the punishment of the man already condemned. This would be no more perilous to the public or unjust to the criminal than if the condemned person had been put to death at once, and in the meantime the experiment would involve no risk. In fact, I think it would not be a bad idea to treat vagabonds this way too, for though we have passed many laws against them, they have had no real effect as yet."

'When the Cardinal had said this, they all vied with one another in praising enthusiastically ideas which they had received with contempt when I suggested them; and they particularly liked the idea about vagabonds because it was the Cardinal's addition.

'I don't know whether it might not be better to keep quiet about what followed, because it was silly, but I'll tell it anyhow, for there's no harm in it, and it has some bearing on our subject. There was a parasite standing around, who liked to play the fool, and did it in such a way that you could hardly tell him from the real thing. *The friar and the fool: a merry dialogue* He was constantly making jokes, but so awkwardly that we laughed more at him than at them; yet sometimes a rather clever thing came out, confirming the old proverb that one who throws the dice often will sooner or later make a lucky cast. One of the company happened to say that in my speech I had taken care of the thieves, and the Cardinal of the vagabonds, so now all that was left to do was to take care of the poor, whom sickness or old age had reduced to poverty and kept from earning a living.

'"Leave that to me", said the fool, "and I'll see to it that it's taken care of properly. These are people I'm desperately eager to get out of my sight, having been so often vexed with them when they wail and whine and demand money – though they never cry out finely enough to extract a single penny from me. For they can't win with me: either I don't want to give them anything, or I haven't anything to give them. Now they're getting wise; they don't waste their breath, but let me pass without a word or a hope – no more, *An old saying bandied about among beggars*[40] by heaven, than if I were a priest. But I would make a law dividing

---

[39] In earlier days almost any criminal could take sanctuary in any church and be safe from the law. Beginning in the reign of Henry VII, the privilege was gradually abridged. The issue was much disputed in More's time, and is debated in his *Richard* III (CW, II, 27–33).

[40] The gloss is puzzling: there is no proverb in More's text at this point, nor does the text even seem to allude to any saying found in dictionaries of proverbs. Surtz (CW, IV, 346) suggests that the allusion is to the parable of the good Samaritan, in which a priest callously passes by the wounded man on the roadside (Luke 10: 31).

mendicos omnes lata lege distribui ac dispartiri iubeo in Benedicti-
norum coenobia et fieri laicos ut vocant monachos: mulieres
moniales esse impero.

Subrisit Cardinalis et approbat ioco, ceteri etiam serio.[10] Ceterum
theologus quidam frater hoc dicto in sacerdotes ac monachos adeo 5
est exhilaratus ut iam ipse quoque coeperit ludere, homo alioqui
prope ad torvitatem gravis. At ne sic quidem, inquit, extricaberis a
mendicis nisi nobis quoque prospexeris fratribus.

Atqui, inquit parasitus, hoc iam curatum est. Nam Cardinalis
egregie prospexit vobis quum statueret de coercendis atque opere 10
exercendis erronibus, nam vos estis errones maximi.

Hoc quoque dictum, quum coniectis in Cardinalem oculis eum
viderent non abnuere, coeperunt omnes non illibenter arripere,

Allusit ad illud Horatianum,[11] italo perfusus aceto
excepto fratre. Nam is (neque equidem miror), tali perfusus aceto,
sic indignatus est atque incanduit, ut nec a conviciis quidem potuerit 15
temperare: hominem vocavit nebulonem, detractorem, susurronem
et filium perditionis, minas interim terribiles citans e scriptura sacra.
Iam scurra serio scurrari coepit, et erat plane in sua palaestra.

Noli, inquit, irasci, bone frater: scriptum est, *In patientia vestra
possidebitis animas vestras.* 20

Ut servat decorum in narratione
Rursum frater (referam enim ipsius verba), Non irascor, inquit,
furcifer, vel saltem non pecco. Nam Psalmista dicit, *Irascimini et
nolite peccare.*

Admonitus deinde frater a Cardinale suaviter ut suos affectus
compesceret, Non, domine, inquit, ego loquor nisi ex bono zelo 25
sicut debeo, nam viri sancti habuerunt bonum zelum, unde dicitur,

Apparet fratrem ob imperitiam zelus abusum neutro genere sicut hoc scelus
Zelus domus tuae comedit me, et canitur in ecclesiis, *Irrisores Helizei, dum conscendit domum dei, zelus calvi sentiunt,* sicut fortasse
sentiet iste derisor, scurra, ribaldus.[12]

---

[10] The entire passage from *Ceterum theologus* through to *nosque dimisit* (80:13) was
omitted from certain late-sixteenth- and seventeenth-century editions.

[11] *Horatianum* (1518M, N) corrects *persianum* (1516, 1517) – an error probably
stemming from the fact that one Persius (not the poet) is the target of the Italian
vinegar in Horace's satire.

[12] *ribaldus* is very late Latin. As the gloss points out, the friar's Latinity is not of
the finest.

up and parcelling out all these beggars among the Benedictine monasteries, where the men could become lay brothers, as they're
called,[41] and the women I would make nuns."

'The Cardinal smiled and passed it off as a joke; the rest took it
seriously. But a certain friar, a theologian, found such pleasure in
this jest at the expense of priests and monks that he too began to
make merry, though generally he was grave to the point of sour-
ness. "Even so you will not get rid of the beggars", he began,
"unless you provide for us friars too."

' "But you have been taken care of already", said the parasite.
"The Cardinal provided for you splendidly when he said vagabonds
should be arrested and put to work, for you friars are the greatest
vagabonds of all."

'When the company, watching the Cardinal closely, saw that he
did not disdain this joke any more than the other, they all took it
up with a will – except for the friar. Not surprisingly, he was stung
by the vinegar and flew into such a violent rage that he could not
keep from abusing the fool. He called him a knave, a slanderer, a
sneak and a "son of perdition",[43] quoting the meanwhile terrible
denunciations from Holy Scripture. Now the jester began to jest
in earnest, for he was clearly on his own ground.

An Horatian allusion: 'Doused with Italian vinegar'[42]

' "Don't get angry, good friar", he said, "for it is written, *In your
patience you will possess your souls*".[44]

'In reply, the friar said, and I quote his very words: "I am not
angry, you gallows-bird, or at least I do not sin, for the Psalmist
says, *Be angry, and sin not*."[45]

How his people speak in character!

'At this point the Cardinal gently cautioned the friar to calm
down, but he answered, "No, my lord, I speak only from righteous
zeal, as I ought to. For holy men have had righteous zeal. That is
why it is said, *The zeal of your house has eaten me up*,[46] and we
sing in church, *Those who mocked Elisha as he went up to the house
of God felt the zeal of the baldhead*.[47] Just so this mocker, this
joker, this guttersnipe may well feel it."

Out of ignorance, the friar uses 'zelus' as if it were a neuter noun, like 'scelus'[48]

[41] 'Lay brothers' lived and worked in monasteries (performing mostly menial tasks)
but were not admitted to clerical orders.
[42] *Satires* I.vii.32.
[43] John 17:12, II Thessalonians 2:3.
[44] Luke 21:19.
[45] Psalms 4:4 (The Vulgate translates as *Irascimini* ('Be angry') the Hebrew word
that is rendered 'Stand in awe' in the Authorised Version.)
[46] Psalms 69:9.
[47] Some children mocked the prophet Elisha for his baldness. But his curse brought
two bears out of the woods, who tore to pieces forty-two of the mockers: II
Kings 2:23–4. The friar quotes a medieval hymn, ascribed to Adam of St Victor,
that is based on this cautionary tale.
[48] In the Latin, the friar incorrectly says *zelus* instead of *zelum*.

Facis, inquit Cardinalis, bono fortassis affectu, sed mihi videris facturus, nescio an sanctius, certe sapientius, si te ita compares ne cum homine stulto et ridiculo ridiculum tibi certamen instituas.

Non, domine, inquit, non facerem sapientius. Nam Solomon ipse sapientissimus dicit: *Responde stulto secundum stultitiam eius*, sicut 5 ego nunc facio, et demonstro ei foveam in quam cadet nisi bene praecaveat. Nam si multi irrisores Helizei qui erat tantum unus calvus senserunt zelus calvi, quanto magis sentiet unus derisor multorum fratrum in quibus sunt multi calvi? et etiam habemus bullam papalem per quam omnes qui derident nos sunt excommunicati. 10

Cardinalis, ubi vidit nullum fieri finem, nutu ablegato parasito ac aliam in rem commodum verso sermone, paulo post surgit e mensa atque audiendis clientum negotiis dedit se, nosque dimisit.

En, mi More, quam longo te sermone oneravi, quod tam diu facere plane puduisset me, nisi tu et cupide flagitasses et sic videreris 15 audire tamquam nolles quicquam eius confabulationis omitti, quae quamquam aliquanto perstrictius, narranda tamen mihi fuit omnino propter eorum iudicium, qui quae me dicente spreverant, eadem rursus evestigio non improbante Cardinale etiam ipsi comprobarunt: usqueadeo assentantes ei ut parasiti quoque eius inventis quae 20 dominus per iocum non aspernabatur adblandirentur et serio propemodum admitterent, ut hinc possis aestimare quanti me ac mea consilia aulici forent aestimaturi.[13]

Profecto, mi Raphael, inquam, magna me adfecisti voluptate, ita sunt abs te dicta prudenter simul et lepide omnia. Praeterea visus 25 mihi interim sum non solum in patria versari verumetiam repuerascere quodammodo iucunda recordatione Cardinalis illius in cuius aula puer sum educatus. Cuius viri memoriae quod tu tam impense faves, non credas, mi Raphael, quanto mihi sis effectus hoc nomine charior, cum esses alioqui charissimus. Ceterum non possum adhuc 30 ullo pacto meam demutare sententiam. Quin te plane putem, si animum inducas tuum uti ne ab aulis principum abhorreas, in publicum posse te tuis consiliis plurimum boni conferre. Qua re[14] nihil magis incumbit tuo, hoc est boni viri, officio. Siquidem cum tuus

---

[13] 1516 and 1517 print for *aestimaturi* the near-synonym *existimaturi*, which may imply a scruple more of 'value highly', a scruple less of 'judge exactly'.
[14] *Qua re* ('than which') instead of *Quare* ('why') as in all four early texts.

'"Perhaps you mean well", said the Cardinal, "but I think you would act if not in a holier at least in a wiser way, if you didn't set your wit against a fool's wit and try to spar with a buffoon."

'"No, my lord", he said, "I would not act more wisely. For Solomon himself, wisest of men, said, *Answer a fool according to his folly*,[49] and that's what I'm doing now. I am showing him the pit into which he will fall[50] if he does not take care. For if the many mockers of Elisha, who was only one bald man, felt the zeal of a baldhead, how much more of an effect shall be felt by a single mocker of many friars, among whom are a great many baldheads! And besides, we have a papal bull, by which all who mock at us are excommunicated."

'When the Cardinal saw there was no end to the matter, he nodded to the fool to leave and tactfully turned the conversation to another subject. Soon after, he rose from table and, going to hear petitioners, dismissed us.

'Look, my dear More, what a long story I have inflicted on you. I would be quite ashamed if you had not yourself eagerly insisted on it, and seemed to listen as if you did not want any part to be left out. Though I ought to have related this conversation more concisely, I did feel bound to recount it, so you might see how those who had rejected what I said approved of it immediately afterwards, when they saw the Cardinal did not disapprove. In fact they went so far in their flattery that they indulged and almost took seriously ideas that their master tolerated only as the clowning of a parasite. From this episode you can see how little courtiers would value me or my advice.'

'Certainly, my dear Raphael', I said, 'you have given me great pleasure, for everything you've said has been both wise and witty. Furthermore, as you spoke, I seemed somehow to be a child and in my own native land once more, through the pleasant recollection of that Cardinal in whose court I was brought up as a lad. Dear as you are to me on other accounts, you cannot imagine, my friend Raphael, how much dearer you are because you honour his memory so highly. Still, I by no means give up my former opinion: indeed, I am fully persuaded that if you could overcome your aversion to court life, your advice to a prince would be of the greatest advantage to the public welfare. No part of a good man's duty – and that means yours – is more important than this. Your friend Plato thinks

---

[49] Proverbs 26:5. The preceding verse, however, says 'Answer not a fool according to his folly, lest thou also be like unto him.'
[50] Alluding to Psalms 7:15.

censeat Plato respublicas ita demum futuras esse felices si aut
regnent philosophi aut reges philosophentur, quam procul aberit
felicitas si philosophi regibus nec dignentur saltem suum impertiri
consilium?

Non sunt, inquit ille, tam ingrati quin id libenter facerent, immo 5
multi libris editis iam fecerunt, si hi qui rerum potiuntur essent
parati bene consultis parere. Sed bene haud dubie praevidit Plato,
nisi reges philosophentur ipsi, numquam futurum ut, perversis
opinionibus a pueris imbuti atque infecti penitus, philosophantium
comprobent consilia: quod ipse quoque experiebatur apud Dionys- 10
ium. An non me putas, si apud aliquem regem[15] decreta sana proponerem et perniciosa malorum semina conarer illi evellere, protinus aut eiciendum aut habendum ludibrio?

Age, finge me apud regem esse Gallorum atque in eius considere
consilio, dum in secretissimo secessu praesidente rege ipso in 15
corona prudentissimorum hominum, magnis agitur studiis quibus
artibus ac machinamentis Mediolanum retineat ac fugitivam illam
Tecte Gallos Neapolim ad se retrahat: postea vero evertat Venetos ac totam Ital-
dehortatur ab iam subiciat sibi. Deinde Flandros, Brabantos, totam postremo Bur-
Italia paranda gundiam suae faciat ditionis, atque alias praeterea gentes quarum 20
regnum iam olim animo invasit.[16] Hic dum alius suadet feriendum
cum Venetis foedus, tantisper duraturum dum ipsis fuerit commodum, cum illis communicandum consilium, quin deponendam
quoque apud eosdem aliquam praedae partem quam, rebus ex sententia peractis, repetat: dum alius consulit conducendos Germanos, 25

---

[15] *regem* instead of *regum* (as in all texts), for correctness.
[16] The rest of Hythloday's account – from *Hic dum* through *putas excipiendam?*
(86:28) – is syntactically one very long (464 words) sentence. But the early editions
break it up by numerous periods, as we also have done, to make it manageable;
more boldly, we've paragraphed it.

that commonwealths will be happy only when philosophers become kings or kings become philosophers.[51] No wonder we are so far from happiness when philosophers do not condescend even to assist kings with their counsels.'

'They are not so ungracious', said Raphael, 'but that they would gladly do it; in fact, many have already done it in published books, if the rulers were only willing to take their good advice. But doubtless Plato was right in foreseeing that unless kings became philosophical themselves the advice of philosophers would never influence them, deeply immersed as they are and infected with false values from boyhood on. Plato himself had this experience with Dionysius.[52] If I proposed wise laws to some king, and tried to root out of his soul the seeds of evil and corruption, don't you suppose I would be either kicked out forthwith, or made into a laughing stock?

'Imagine, if you will, that I am at the court of the King of France.[53] Suppose me to be sitting in his royal council, meeting in secret session with the King himself presiding and surrounded by all his most judicious councillors hard at work devising a set of crafty machinations by which the King might keep hold of Milan and recover Naples, which has proved so slippery;[54] then overthrow the Venetians and subdue all Italy; next add to his realm Flanders, Brabant and the whole of Burgundy, besides some other nations he has long had in mind to invade. One man urges him to make an alliance with the Venetians for just as long as it suits their own convenience – to develop a common strategy with them, and even allow them a share of the loot, which can be recovered later when things work out according to plan. While one recommends hiring

Indirectly he discourages the French from seizing Italy

---

[51] *Republic* V.473C–D; cf. *Epistles* VII.326A–B.

[52] Plato is reported to have made three visits to Syracuse, where he conspicuously failed to reform either the tyrant Dionysius the Elder or his son Dionysius the Younger. See Plato, Epistle VII; Plutarch, 'Dion' IV.i–v.3, IX.i–xx.2.

[53] At the time of writing, Francis I was King of France. At the time of Hythloday's supposed visit to England, the French King was either Charles VIII (d. 1498) or Louis XII (d. 1515). All three were would-be imperialists with hereditary claims to Milan and Naples, and all three bogged down in the intricacies of Italian political intrigue. In general, the advice of the councillors in this passage closely conforms to actual French policies in the period. Scathing denunciation of such policies is characteristic of Erasmian humanism. (See R.P. Adams, *The Better Part of Valor*.) Rabelais probably had More's passage in mind in *Gargantua and Pantagruel* I.xxxiii, where he sketched King Picrochole's insanely tottery schemes of world conquest.

[54] France gained Milan in 1499, lost it in 1512, and regained it at the Battle of Marignano in September 1515. Naples was won in 1495, lost in 1496, won again in 1501, and lost again in 1504.

Elvetii conducticii alius pecunia demulcendos Elvetios, alius adversum[17] numen imper-
atoriae maiestatis auro, velut anathemate, propitiandum. Dum alii
videtur cum Arragonum rege componendas esse res, et alieno Nava-
riae regno velut pacis auctoramento cedendum, alius interim censet
Castelliae principem aliqua spe affinitatis irretiendum atque aulicos   5
nobiles aliquot in suam factionem certa pensione esse pertrahendos.

    Dum maximus omnium nodus occurrit quid statuendum interim
de Anglia sit. Ceterum de pace tractandum tamen, et constringenda
firmissimis vinculis semper infirma societas; amici vocentur, suspic-
iantur ut inimici. Habendos igitur paratos velut in statione Scotos,   10
ad omnem intentos occasionem, si quid se commoveant Angli, protinus immittendos. Ad haec fovendum exsulem nobilem aliquem
occulte, namque id aperte ne fiat prohibent foedera, qui id regnum
sibi deberi contendat, ut ea velut ansa contineat suspectum sibi
principem.   15

    Hic, inquam, in tanto rerum molimine, tot egregiis viris ad
bellum sua certatim consilia conferentibus, si ego homuncio surgam
ac verti iubeam vela, omittendam Italiam censeam et domi dicam
esse manendum, unum Galliae regnum fere maius esse quam ut
commode possit ab uno administrari, ne sibi putet rex de aliis adici-   20
endis esse cogitandum. Tum si illis proponerem decreta Acho-

---

[17] *adversus* modifying *alius* is the reading of 1518M, N; we follow 1516 and 1517
in printing *adversum* modifying *numen*.

German mercenaries,[55] his neighbour proposes paying the Swiss to *Swiss mercenaries* stay neutral. A fourth suggests soothing the offended divinity of his imperial majesty with a votive offering, as it were, of gold.[56] Still another thinks a settlement should be made with the King of Aragon, and that, as a reward for peace, he should be given Navarre, which belongs to somebody else.[57] Meanwhile, someone suggests snaring the Prince of Castile by the prospect of a marriage alliance, and by drawing some nobles of his court onto their side by granting them pensions.[58]

'The knottiest problem of all is what to do, in the meantime, about England. They agree that peace should be made, and that the alliance, which is weak at best, should be strengthened as much as possible. Let the English be proclaimed as friends, yet suspected as enemies. And let the Scots be kept like sentinels in constant readiness, poised to attack the English on the spot in case they stir ever so little.[59] Also a banished nobleman with pretensions to the English throne must be secretly encouraged (treaties forbid doing it openly), and in this way they will have a bridle to restrain a king whom they do not trust.[60]

'Now in a meeting like this one, where so much is at stake, where so many distinguished men are competing to think up schemes of warfare, what if an insignificant fellow like me were to get up and advise going on another tack entirely?[61] Suppose I said the King should leave Italy alone and stay at home, because the kingdom of France by itself is almost too much for one man to govern well, and the King should not dream of adding others to it?[62] Then imagine

---

[55] Among the mercenaries of Europe, the German foot soldiers were surpassed only by the Swiss.

[56] Maximilian of Habsburg, the Holy Roman Emperor, was notoriously impecunious.

[57] Ferdinand II of Aragon took the southern part of Navarre in 1512, and annexed it to Castile (of which he was regent) in 1515.

[58] Charles, Prince of Castile, was the future Holy Roman Emperor. The question of a French marriage for him, which would unite the two great European powers, was continually in the air. (He was engaged ten different times – always for financial or dynastic reasons – before he was twenty.) On the use of international bribery as an everyday tactic of European statecraft, see James W. Thompson and Saul K. Padover, *Secret Diplomacy*, 2nd edn (New York, 1963), pp. 56–60.

[59] The Scots, as traditional enemies of England, were traditional allies of France.

[60] The French had in fact supported various pretenders to the English throne – most recently, Richard de la Pole, the inheritor of the Yorkist claim.

[61] The advice that Hythloday imagines himself as giving is precisely the kind that Erasmian humanists offered in numerous political writings. Surtz documents many parallels (*CW*, IV, 358–61).

[62] Cf. More's epigram 'De cupiditate regnandi': 'Among many kings there will be scarcely one, if there is really one, who is satisfied to have one kingdom. And yet among many kings there will be scarcely one, if there is really one, who rules a single kingdom well' (*CW*, III, Part II, 257).

Exemplum
adnotandum riorum populi, Utopiensium insulae ad Euronoton oppositi, qui
quum olim bellum gessissent ut regi suo aliud obtinerent regnum
quod affinitatis antiquae causa sibi contendebat hereditate deberi,
consecuti tandem id, ubi viderunt nihilo sibi minus esse molestiae in
retinendo quam in quaerendo pertulerunt, verum assidua pullulare ₅
semina vel internae rebellionis vel externae incursionis in deditos,
ita semper aut pro illis aut contra pugnandum, numquam dari facultatem dimittendi exercitus, compilari interim se, efferri foras pecuniam, alienae gloriolae suum impendi sanguinem, pacem nihilo
tutiorem, domi corruptos bello mores, imbibitam latrocinandi libid- ₁₀
inem, confirmatam caedibus audaciam, leges esse contemptui quod
rex in duorum curam regnorum distractus minus in utrumvis
animum posset intendere.

Cum viderent alioqui tantis malis nullum finem fore, inito
tandem consilio, regi suo humanissime fecerunt optionem retinendi ₁₅
utrius regni vellet, nam utriusque non fore potestatem, se plures
esse quam qui a dimidiato possint rege gubernari, quum nemo sit
libenter admissurus mulionem sibi cum alio communem. Ita coactus
est ille bonus princeps, novo regno cuipiam ex amicis relicto (qui
brevi etiam post eiectus est), antiquo esse contentus. ₂₀

Praeterea si ostenderem omnes hos conatus bellorum quibus tot
nationes eius causa tumultuarentur, quum thesauros eius exhausiss-
ent ac destruxissent populum, aliqua tandem fortuna frustra ces-
suros tamen: proinde avitum regnum coleret, ornaret quantum
posset, et faceret quam florentissimum. Amet suos et ametur a suis, ₂₅
cum his una vivat imperetque suaviter, atque alia regna valere sinat,
quando id quod nunc ei contigisset satis amplum superque esset.
Hanc orationem quibus auribus, mi More, putas excipiendam?

Profecto non valde pronis, inquam.

I told about the decrees of the Achorians,[63] who live off to the   *A notable*
south-southeast of the island of Utopia. Long ago these people   *example*
went to war to gain another realm for their king, who claimed that
he had rightfully inherited it by virtue of an ancient marriage tie.
When they had conquered it, they saw that keeping it was going
to be no less trouble than getting it had been. The seeds of fighting
were always springing up: their new subjects were continually
rebelling or being attacked by foreign invaders; the Achorians had
to be constantly at war for them or against them, and they saw no
hope of ever being able to disband their army. In the meantime,
they were being heavily taxed, money flowed out of their kingdom,
their blood was being shed for someone else's petty pride, and
peace was no closer than it had ever been. At home the war corrupted their citizens by encouraging lust for robbery and murder;
and the laws fell into contempt because their king, distracted with
the cares of two kingdoms, could give neither his proper attention.

'When they saw that the list of these evils was endless, they took
counsel together, and very courteously offered their king his choice
of keeping whichever of the two kingdoms he preferred, because
he couldn't rule them both. They were too numerous a people,
they said, to be ruled by half a king; adding that a man would not
willingly share even a muledriver with someone else. The worthy
prince was thus obliged to be content with his own realm and give
his new one to a friend, who before long was driven out.

'Moreover, suppose I showed that all this war-mongering, by
which so many different nations were kept in turmoil for his sake,
would exhaust his treasury and demoralise his people, yet in the end
come to nothing through one mishap or another.[64] And therefore he
should look after his ancestral kingdom, improve it as much as
possible, and make it as flourishing as it could conceivably be
made.[65] He should love his people and be loved by them; he should
live among them, govern them kindly, and let other kingdoms
alone, since the one that had fallen to his lot was big enough, if not
too big, for him. How do you think, my dear More, this speech of
mine would be received?'

'Not very enthusiastically, I'm sure', said I.

[63] From *a-* ('without') plus *choros* ('place', 'country'): 'the People without a
Country'.
[64] Francis lost Milan in 1520 and, in a catastrophic effort to regain it in 1525, was
defeated and taken prisoner by Charles V.
[65] Hythloday is thinking of the adage 'Spartam nactus es, hanc orna', which Erasmus
discusses at length in *Adages* II.v.1 (*CWE*, XXXIII, 237–43).

Pergamus[18] ergo, inquit, si consiliariis cum rege quopiam tract-
antibus, et comminiscentibus quibus technis ei queant coacervare
thesauros, dum unus intendendam consulit aestimationem monetae
quum ipsi sit eroganda pecunia, deiciendam rursus infra iustum
quum fuerit corroganda, uti et multum aeris parvo dissolvat et pro 5
parvo multum recipiat: dum alius suadet ut bellum simulet atque,
eo praetextu coacta pecunia, cum visum erit faciat pacem sanctis
caerimoniis, quo plebeculae oculis fiat praestigium, miseratus videlicet humanum sanguinem princeps pius: dum alius ei suggerit in
mentem antiquas quasdam et tineis adesas leges longa desuetudine 10
antiquatas, quas quod nemo latas meminisset, omnes sint trans-
gressi: earum ergo mulctas iubeat exigi, nullum uberiorem
proventum esse, nullum magis honorificum, utpote qui iustitiae
prae se personam ferat: dum ab alio admonetur uti sub magnis
mulctis multa prohibeat, maxime talia quae ne fiant in rem sit 15
populi. Post pecunia cum illis dispenset quorum commodis obstat
interdictum: sic et a populo gratiam iniri, et duplex adferri compen-
dium, vel dum hi mulctantur quod quaestus cupiditas pellexit in
casses, vel dum aliis vendit privilegia tanto pluris quanto scilicet
fuerit melior princeps, utpote qui gravatim quicquam contra populi 20
commodum privato cuiquam indulgeat, et ob id non nisi magno
pretio.

Dum alius ei persuadet obstringendos sibi iudices qui quavis in
re pro regio iure disceptent, accersendos praeterea in palatium atque
invitandos uti coram se de suis rebus disserant: ita nullam causam 25
eius tam aperte iniquam fore, in qua non aliquis eorum vel contra-
dicendi studio vel pudore dicendi eadem vel quo gratiam ineant,
apud eum aliquam reperiant rimam qua possit intendi calumnia. Sic
dum iudicibus diversa sentientibus, res per se clarissima disputatur
et veritas in quaestionem venit, ansam commodum regi dari pro 30
suo commodo ius interpretandi. Ceteros aut pudore accessuros aut

---

[18] Like the account of the French privy council, Hythloday's second *exemplum*
consists, syntactically, of a single gargantuan sentence – comprising 926 words
and running through to *narraturus fabulam?* at 94:18–19. Again the early editions
ignore this fact, dividing up the sentence with periods, and again we follow their
lead (though not always their particular divisions).

'Well, let's go on', he said. 'Suppose that a king and his councillors are deliberating about various schemes for filling his treasury. One man recommends increasing the value of money when the king pays his debts and devaluing it when he collects his revenues. Thus he can discharge a huge debt with a small payment, and collect a large sum when only a small one is due him.[66] Another suggests a make-believe war, so that money can be raised under that pretext; then when the money is in, he can make peace with holy ceremonies – which the deluded common people will attribute to the prince's piety and compassion for the lives of his subjects.[67] Another councillor calls to mind some old moth-eaten laws, antiquated by long disuse, which no one remembers being made and therefore everyone has transgressed, and suggests that the king levy fines for breaking them. There's no richer source of income, nor any that looks more creditable, since it can be made to wear the mask of justice.[68] Another recommendation is that he forbid under particularly heavy fines many practices, especially such as are contrary to the public interest; afterwards, for money he can grant the special interests dispensations from his own rules. Thus he gains the favour of the people and makes a double profit, from fines imposed on those who've fallen into his trap and from selling dispensations. The higher the price, the better the prince, since he is very reluctant to grant a private person the right to obstruct the public welfare, and therefore does it only for a great price.

'Another councillor proposes that he work on the judges so they will decide every case in the royal interest. Moreover, they should be frequently summoned to the palace and asked to debate his affairs in the royal presence. However unjust his claims, one or another of the judges, whether from love of contradiction, or desire to seem original, or simply to serve his own interest, will be able to find some loophole to introduce chicanery. If the judges give differing opinions, the clearest matter in the world can be made cloudy and truth itself brought into question. The king is given a convenient handle to interpret the law in his favour, and everyone

---

[66] Dodges of this kind were practised by Edward IV, Henry VII and (after *Utopia* was written) Henry VIII. In general, the policies satirised in this continuation find more parallels in recent English practice than elsewhere, though European parallels also abound.

[67] Something like this happened in 1492, when Henry VII not only pretended war with France on behalf of Brittany and levied taxes for the war (which was hardly fought) but collected a bribe from Charles VIII for not fighting it.

[68] Henry VII's ministers Empson and Dudley were notorious masters in this practice – and Cardinal Morton was also involved in it.

metu, sic intrepide fertur postea pro tribunali sententia. Neque enim deesse praetextus potest pronuntianti pro principe. Nempe cui satis est aut aequitatem a sua parte esse aut verba legis aut contortum scripti sensum aut, quae legibus denique omnibus praeponderat apud religiosos iudices, principis indisputabilem praerogativam.   5

Dum omnes in Crassiano illo consentiunt atque conspirant, *Crassi divitis* nullam auri vim satis esse principi cui sit alendus exercitus, prae-*dictum* terea, nihil iniuste regem facere, ut maxime etiam velit, posse. Quippe omnia omnium eius esse, ut homines etiam ipsos, tantum vero cuique esse proprium quantum regis benignitas ei non adem- 10 erit, quod ipsum ut quam minimum sit principis multum referre, ut cuius tutamentum in eo situm sit ne populus divitiis ac libertate lasciviat, quod hae res minus patienter ferant dura atque iniusta imperia: quum contra egestas atque inopia retundat animos ac patientes reddat, adimatque pressis generosos rebellandi spiritus.   15

Hic si ego rursus assurgens contendam haec consilia omnia regi et inhonesta esse et perniciosa, cuius non honor modo sed securitas quoque in populi magis opibus sita sit quam suis: quos si ostendam regem sibi deligere sua causa, non regis, videlicet uti eius labore ac studio ipsi commode vivant tutique ab iniuriis: eoque magis ad 20 principem eam pertinere curam ut populo bene sit suo quam ut

else will acquiesce from shame or fear. Thus the judgement can be boldly handed down in court; nor can there be any lack of pretexts for someone ruling in the prince's favour. Either equity is on the king's side, or the letter of the law makes for him, or a twisted interpretation of a document, or the factor which in the end out-weighs all laws for scrupulous judges, the indisputable prerogative of the prince.[69]

'Then all the councillors agree with the famous maxim of Crassus: a king can never have enough gold, because he must main-tain an army.[70] Further, that a king, even if he wants to, can do no wrong, for all property belongs to the king, and so do his subjects themselves; a man owns nothing but what the king, in his goodness, sees fit not to take from him. It is important for the king to leave his subjects as little as possible, because his own safety depends on keeping them from getting too frisky with wealth and freedom. For riches and liberty make people less patient to endure harsh and unjust commands, whereas poverty and want blunt their spirits, make them docile, and grind out of the oppressed the lofty spirit of rebellion.[71]

Saying of Crassus the Rich

'Now at this point, suppose I were to get up again and declare that all these counsels are both dishonourable and ruinous to the king? Suppose I said his honour and his safety alike rest on the people's resources rather than his own? Suppose I said that people choose a king for their own sake, not his, so that by his efforts and troubles they may live in comfort and safety? This is why, I would say, it is the king's duty to take more care of his people's welfare

[69] The limits of royal prerogative, and the duties of judges (who served by royal appointment) in respect to it, was in the course of becoming an issue of the utmost importance. For an overview, see John W. Allen, *A History of Political Thought in the Sixteenth Century* (1928; rpt 1957), pp. 121–68.

[70] Hythloday adapts his source, which is Cicero's *De officiis*: 'Crassus ... not long since declared that no amount of wealth was enough for the man who aspired to be the foremost citizen of the state, unless with the income from it he could maintain an army' (I.viii.25).

[71] The underlying schema of the fiscal policy developed in the foregoing paragraphs was provided by Aristotle's discussion in the *Politics* of the two ways in which tyrannies can be preserved. The first embraces the traditional acts of the tyrant: he will prohibit 'everything likely to produce ... mutual confidence and a high spirit' in the citizens (V.xi.5); his 'first end and aim is to break the spirit of ... [his] subjects', because 'a poor-spirited man will never plot against anybody' (xi.15). Impoverishing the citizens is a principal means to this end. Alternatively, 'the tyrant should act, or at any rate appear to act, in the role of a good player of the part of King' (xi.19). He should, for example, 'levy taxes, and require other contributions, in such a way that they can be seen to be intended for the proper management of public services, or to be meant for use ... on military emergen-cies' (xi.21).

sibi, non aliter ac pastoris officium est oves potius quam semet pascere, quatenus opilio est.

Nam quod populi egestatem censeant pacis praesidium esse, longissime aberrare eos ipsa res docet: nempe ubi plus rixarum comperias quam inter mendicos? Quis intentius mutationi rerum studet quam cui minime placet praesens vitae status? Aut cui denique audacior impetus ad conturbanda omnia, spe alicunde lucrandi, quam cui iam nihil est quod possit perdere? Quod si rex aliquis adeo aut contemptus esset aut invisus suis ut aliter eos continere in officio non possit nisi contumeliis, compilatione et sectione grassetur eosque redigat ad mendicitatem, praestiterit illi profecto regno abdicare[19] quam his retinere artibus, quibus quamquam imperii nomen retineat, certe amittit maiestatem: neque enim regiae dignitatis est imperium in mendicos exercere, sed in opulentos potius atque felices. Quod ipsum sensit certe vir erecti ac sublimis animi Fabricius, cum responderet malle se imperare divitibus quam divitem esse. Et profecto unum aliquem voluptate ac deliciis fluere, gementibus undique ac lamentantibus aliis, hoc non est regni sed carceris esse custodem. Denique ut imperitissimus medicus est qui morbum nescit nisi morbo curare, ita qui vitam civium non novit alia via corrigere quam ademptis vitae commodis, is se nescire fateatur imperare liberis.

Quin aut inertiam potius mutet suam aut superbiam, nam his fere vitiis accidit ut populus eum vel contemnat vel habeat odio. Vivat innocuus de suo, sumptus ad reditus accommodet, refrenet maleficia et recta institutione suorum praeveniat potius quam sinat increscere quae deinde puniat. Leges abrogatas consuetudine haud temere revocet, praesertim quae diu desitae numquam desideratae sunt. Neque umquam commissi nomine eiusmodi quicquam capiat quale privatum quempiam iudex velut iniquum ac vafrum non pateretur accipere.

[19] *se abdicare* in 1516, 1517 and some later editions.

than of his own, just as it is the duty of a shepherd who cares about his job to feed the sheep rather than himself.[72]

'They are absolutely wrong in thinking that the people's poverty guarantees public peace: experience shows the contrary. Where will you find more squabbling than among beggars? Who is more eager to change things than the man who is most discontented with his present position? Who is more reckless about creating disorder than the man who knows he has nothing to lose and thinks he may have something to gain? If a king is so hated or despised by his subjects that he can keep them in hand only by maltreatment, plundering, confiscation and reducing them to beggary, he'd do much better to abdicate his throne than to retain it by such methods, through which he keeps the name of authority but loses all the majesty of a king. A king has no dignity when he exercises authority over beggars, only when he rules over prosperous and happy subjects. This was certainly what that noble and lofty spirit Fabricius meant, when he replied that he would rather be a ruler of rich men than be rich himself.[73] Indeed a lone individual who enjoys a life of pleasure and self-indulgence while all about him are grieving and groaning is acting like a jailer, not a king. Finally, just as an incompetent doctor can cure his patient of one disease only by throwing him into another, so it's an incompetent monarch who knows no other way to reform his people than by depriving them of all life's benefits. Such a king openly confesses his incapacity to rule free men.

'He should correct his own sloth or arrogance, because these are the vices that cause people to despise or hate him. Let him live on his own income without wronging others, and limit his spending to his income. Let him curb crime, and by training his subjects wisely keep them from misbehaviour, instead of letting trouble breed and then punishing it. Let him not rashly revive antiquated laws, especially if they have been long forgotten and never missed. And let him never take money as a fine for some crime when a judge would regard an ordinary subject as wicked and deceitful for claiming it.

---

[72] Again Hythloday's advice is the same as that offered by More speaking in his own person (e.g., *Epigrams, CW,* III, Part II, 163–5, 169), as well as by other humanists and their classical sources. See *CW,* IV, 366–71.

[73] Gaius Fabricius Luscinus took part in the wars against Pyrrhus, King of Epirus (280–275 BC). The saying that is attributed to him here was actually coined by his colleague Manius Curius Dentatus (Plutarch, *Moralia* 194F), but it is quite in his spirit.

Hic si proponerem illis Macarensium legem qui et ipsi non longe
admodum absunt ab Utopia, quorum rex quo primum die auspica-
tur imperium magnis adhibitis sacrificiis iuriiurando astringitur
numquam se uno tempore supra mille auri pondo in thesauris
habiturum, aut argenti quantum eius auri pretium aequet. Hanc 5
legem ferunt ab optimo quodam rege institutam, cui maiori curae
fuit patriae commodum quam divitiae suae, velut obicem acervan-
dae pecuniae tantae quanta faceret inopiam eius in populo. Nempe
eum thesaurum videbat suffecturum sive regi adversus rebelles sive
regno adversus hostium incursiones esset confligendum, ceterum 10
minorem esse quam ut animos faciat invadendi aliena, quae potissima condendae legis causa fuit. Proxima, quod sic prospectum
putavit ne desit pecunia quae in cottidiana civium commutatione
versetur, et quum regi necesse est erogare quicquid thesauro supra
legitimum accrevit modum, non quaesiturum censuit occasiones 15
iniuriae. Talis rex et malis erit formidini et a bonis amabitur. Haec
ergo atque huiusmodi si ingererem apud homines in contrariam
partem vehementer inclinatos, quam surdis essem narraturus
fabulam?

Surdissimis, inquam, haud dubie: neque hercule miror, neque 20
mihi videntur (ut vere dicam) huiusmodi sermones ingerendi aut
talia danda consilia, quae certus sis numquam admissum iri. Quid
enim prodesse possit aut quomodo in illorum pectus influere sermo
tam insolens, quorum praeoccupavit animos atque insedit penitus
diversa persuasio? Apud amiculos in familiari colloquio non 25
insuavis est haec philosophia scholastica. Ceterum in consiliis principum, ubi res magnae magna auctoritate aguntur, non est his rebus
locus.

Hoc est, inquit ille, quod dicebam, non esse apud principes locum
philosophiae. 30

Immo, inquam, est verum,[21] non huic scholasticae quae quidvis
putet ubivis convenire: sed est alia philosophia civilior quae suam

Mira lex Macarensium (gloss)

Proverbium[20] (gloss)

Philosophia scholastica (gloss)

---

[20] This gloss first appeared in 1518N.
[21] An emendation proposed by Otto Foss (recorded in *CW*, V, Part II, 1033) would
place the punctuation before, not after, *verum*, changing its sense from 'true' to
'but'.

'Suppose I should then describe for them the law of the Macarians,[74] a people who also live not far from the Utopians. On the day
that their king first assumes office, he must take an oath confirmed
by solemn ceremonies never to have in his treasury at any one time
more than a thousand pounds of gold, or its equivalent in silver.[75]
They say this law was made by an excellent king, who cared more
for his country's welfare than for his own wealth, and wanted to
prevent any king from heaping up so much money as to impoverish
his people. He thought this sum would enable a king to put down
rebellions or repel hostile invasions, but would not be large enough
to tempt him into aggressive adventures. Though this was the primary reason for the law, he also wanted to ensure an ample supply
of money for the daily business of the citizens. Finally, he thought
that a king who has to distribute all the excess money in the treasury
to the people will not look for ways to gain it wrongfully. Such a
king will be feared by evil-doers, and just as much beloved by the
good. – Now, don't you suppose if I set these ideas and others like
them before men strongly inclined to the contrary, they would turn
deaf ears to me?'

Wonderful law of the Macarians

Proverb

'Stone deaf, indeed, there's no doubt about it', I said, 'and by
heaven it's no wonder! To tell you the truth, I don't think you
should thrust forward ideas of this sort, or offer advice that you
know for certain will not be listened to. What good can it do?
When your listeners are already prepossessed against you and
firmly convinced of opposite opinions, how can you win over their
minds with such out-of-the-way speeches? This academic philosophy is pleasant enough in the private conversation of close
friends, but in the councils of kings, where great matters are debated
with great authority, there is no room for it.'[76]

'That is just what I was saying', Raphael replied. 'There is no
place for philosophy in the councils of kings.'

'Yes, it is true', I said, 'that there is no place for this school philosophy which supposes every topic suitable for every occasion.[77]

Philosophy of the schools

---

[74] From *makarios*: 'blessed', 'happy'.
[75] Again More seems to glance at Henry VII, who died with a huge sum in his
treasury.
[76] This position is informed by the rhetorical and ethical doctrine of *decorum*, propriety of words or actions. (On *decorum*, see Cicero, *Orator* XXII.74, *De officiis*
I.xxvii-xlii.) The ensuing argument reflects the ancient conflict between rhetoric
and philosophy, which centres in the tension between persuasion and truth.
[77] Complaints that philosophers fail to consider context – whether in the interpretation of literary works or in their mistaken notions about style and rhetorical
strategy – constitute a main theme of humanist attacks on scholasticism. See, for
example, More's 'Letter to Dorp', CW, XV, 49–55.

novit scaenam, eique sese accommodans, in ea fabula quae in manibus est suas partes concinne et cum decoro tutatur. Hac utendum
est tibi. Alioquin dum agitur quaepiam Plauti comoedia, nugantibus
inter se vernulis, si tu in proscaenium prodeas habitu philosophico
et recenseas ex *Octavia* locum in quo Seneca disputat cum Nerone, 5
nonne praestiterit egisse mutam personam quam aliena recitando
talem fecisse tragicomoediam? Corruperis enim perverterisque
praesentem fabulam dum diversa permisces, etiamsi ea quae tu
adfers meliora fuerint. Quaecumque fabula in manu est, eam age
quam potes optime, neque ideo totam perturbes quod tibi in 10
mentem venit alterius quae sit lepidior.

Sic est in republica, sic in consultationibus principum. Si radicitus
evelli non possint opiniones pravae nec receptis usu vitiis mederi
queas ex animi tui sententia, non ideo tamen deserenda respublica
est, et in tempestate navis destituenda est,[22] quoniam ventos inhibere 15
non possis. At neque insuetus et insolens sermo inculcandus quem
scias apud diversa persuasos pondus non habiturum, sed obliquo
ductu conandum est atque adnitendum tibi uti pro tua virili omnia
tractes commode, et quod in bonum nequis vertere efficias saltem
ut sit quam minime malum. Nam ut omnia bene sint fieri non 20
potest, nisi omnes boni sint, quod ad aliquot abhinc annos adhuc
non exspecto.

Hac, inquit, arte nihil fieret aliud quam ne dum aliorum furori
mederi studeo, ipse cum illis insaniam. Nam si vera loqui volo talia
loquar necesse est. Ceterum falsa loqui sitne philosophi nescio: 25

ὁμοίωσις mira

κωφὸν πρόσωπον

---

[22] *est* is not present in 1516 or 1517. The Latin seems better without it.

But there is another philosophy, better suited for the role of a citizen, that takes its cue, adapts itself to the drama in hand and acts its part neatly and appropriately. This is the philosophy for you to use.[78] Otherwise, when a comedy of Plautus is being played, and the household slaves are cracking trivial jokes together, you come onstage in the garb of a philosopher and repeat Seneca's speech to Nero from the *Octavia*.[79] Wouldn't it be better to take a silent role than to say something inappropriate and thus turn the play into a tragicomedy? You pervert a play and ruin it when you add irrelevant speeches, even if they are better than the play itself. So go through with the drama in hand as best you can, and don't spoil it all just because you happen to think of a play by someone else that might be more elegant.

A striking comparison

A mute part

'That's how things go in the commonwealth, and in the councils of princes. If you cannot pluck up bad ideas by the root, or cure long-standing evils to your heart's content, you must not therefore abandon the commonwealth. Don't give up the ship in a storm because you cannot hold back the winds. You must not deliver strange and out-of-the-way speeches to people with whom they will carry no weight because they are firmly persuaded the other way. Instead, by an indirect approach, you must strive and struggle as best you can to handle everything tactfully – and thus what you cannot turn to good, you may at least make as little bad as possible.[80] For it is impossible to make everything good unless all men are good, and that I don't expect to see for quite a few years yet.'

'The only result of this', he said, 'will be that while I try to cure the madness of others, I'll be raving along with them myself. For if I wish to speak the truth, I will have to talk in the way I've described. Whether it's the business of a philosopher to tell lies, I

---

[78] Cf. Cicero, *Orator* XXXV.123: 'This ... is the form of wisdom that the orator must especially employ – to adapt himself to occasions and persons ... one must not speak in the same style at all times, nor before all people'; *De officiis* I.xxxi.114: 'if at some time stress of circumstances shall thrust us aside into some uncongenial part, we must devote to it all possible thought, practice, and pains, that we may be able to perform it, if not with propriety [*si non decore*], at least with as little impropriety as possible'.

[79] Most of the plays of the Roman comic dramatist Plautus involve low intrigue: needy young men, expensive prostitutes, senile moneybags and clever slaves, in predictable combinations. The tragedy *Octavia*, involving Seneca as a character, but not by him (though long supposed to be so), is full of high seriousness. In the passage to which More alludes (ll. 440–592), Seneca lectures Nero on the abuses of power.

[80] This is consistent with the advice of rhetoricians (e.g., Quintilian II.xvii.26–9, III.viii.38–9) and some humanists (e.g., Erasmus, *Correspondence*, CWE, II, 79, 81–2).

certe non est meum. Quamquam ille meus sermo ut fuerit fortasse
ingratus illis atque molestus, ita non video cur videri debeat usque
ad ineptias insolens. Quod si aut ea dicerem quae fingit Plato in
Utopiensium
instituta sua republica aut ea quae faciunt Utopienses in sua, haec quamquam
essent (ut certe sunt) meliora, tamen aliena videri possint, quod hic 5
singulorum privatae sunt possessiones, illic omnia sunt communia.

Mea vero oratio[23] (nisi quod ad eos qui statuissent secum ruere
diversa via praecipites, iucundus esse non potest qui revocet ac prae-
monstret pericula) alioquin quid habuit quod non ubivis dici vel
conveniat vel oporteat? Equidem si omittenda sunt omnia tamquam 10
insolentia atque absurda quaecumque perversi mores hominum
fecerunt ut videri possint aliena, dissimulemus oportet apud Christianos pleraque omnia quae CHRISTUS docuit ac dissimulari
usqueadeo vetuit ut ea quoque quae ipse in aures insusurrasset suis,
palam in tectis iusserit praedicari. Quorum maxima pars ab istis 15
moribus longe est alienior quam mea fuit oratio, nisi quod contio-
natores, homines callidi, tuum illud consilium secuti puto, quando
mores suos homines ad CHRISTI normam gravatim paterentur
aptari, doctrinam eius velut regulam plumbeam accommodaverunt
ad mores, ut aliquo saltem pacto coniungerentur scilicet. Qua re 20
nihil video quid profecerint nisi ut securius liceat esse malos.

Atque ipse profecto tantundem proficiam in consiliis principum.
Nam aut diversa sentiam, quod perinde fuerit ac si nihil sentiam,
aut eadem, et ipsorum adiutor sim, ut inquit Mitio Terentianus,
insaniae. Nam obliquus ille ductus tuus non video quid sibi velit, 25
quo censes adnitendum si non possint omnia reddi bona tamen ut
tractentur commode, fiantque quoad licet quam minime mala.
Quippe non est ibi dissimulandi locus, nec licet conivere:

---

[23] *Mea vero oratio* is the reading of 1516, 1517 and 1518M. 1518N reads *Meus vero
sermo*, apparently influenced by *ille meus sermo* two sentences above. On Prévost's insupportable claim that the 1518N variant shows More's involvement in
that edition, see Appendix, pp. 273–4 below.

don't know, but it certainly isn't mine. Perhaps my advice may be repugnant and irksome to them, but I don't see why it should be considered outlandish to the point of folly. What if I told them the kind of thing that Plato imagines in his republic, or that the Utopians actually practise in theirs? However superior those institutions might be (and they certainly are), yet here they would seem alien, because private property is the rule here, and there all things are held in common.

Utopian
institutions

'People who have made up their minds to rush headlong down the opposite road are never pleased with the man who calls them back and points out the dangers of their course. But, apart from that, what did I say that could not and should not be said everywhere? Indeed, if we dismiss as outlandish and absurd everything that the perverse customs of men have made to seem alien to us, we shall have to set aside, even in a community of Christians, most of the teachings of Christ. Yet he forbade us to dissemble them, and even ordered that what he had whispered in the ears of his disciples should be preached openly from the housetops.[81] Most of his teachings are far more alien from the common customs of mankind than my discourse was. But preachers, like the crafty fellows they are, have found that people would rather not change their lives to fit Christ's rule, and so, following your advice, I suppose, they have adjusted his teaching to the way people live, as if it were a leaden yardstick.[82] At least in that way they can get the two things to correspond in some way or other. The only real thing they accomplish that I can see is to make people feel more secure about doing evil.

'And indeed this is all that I myself would accomplish in the councils of princes. For either I would have different ideas from the others, and that would be like having no ideas at all, or I would agree with them, and that, as Mitio says in Terence, would merely confirm them in their madness.[83] As for that "indirect approach" of yours, I simply don't know what you mean. You think I should try hard to urge my case tactfully, so that what cannot be made good can at least be made as little bad as possible. In a council, there is no way to dissemble or look the other way. You must

---

[81] Matthew 10:27; Luke 12:3.

[82] A flexible measuring rod of lead was particularly useful in the sort of ancient building known as the 'Lesbian' style, because of the great number of curved mouldings. Aristotle uses the leaden rule as a metaphor for adaptable moral standards (*Nicomachean Ethics* V.x.7).

[83] *Adelphoe* I.145–7.

approbanda sunt aperte pessima consilia, et decretis pestilentissimis
subscribendum est. Speculatoris vice fierit ac paene proditoris etiam
qui improbe consulta maligne laudaverit. Porro nihil occurrit in
quo prodesse quicquam possis, in eos delatus collegas qui vel
optimum virum facilius corruperint quam ipsi corrigantur, quorum   5
perversa consuetudine vel depravaberis vel ipse integer atque inno-
cens alienae malitiae stultitiaeque praetexeris, tantum abest ut
aliquid possit in melius obliquo illo ductu convertere.

Quamobrem pulcherrima similitudine declarat Plato cur merito
sapientes abstineant a capessenda republica. Quippe quum populum   10
videant in plateas effusum assiduis imbribus perfundi, nec persuad-
ere queant illis ut se subducant pluviae tectaque subeant: gnari nihil
profuturos sese si exeant quam ut una compluantur, semet intra
tecta continent, habentes satis quando alienae stultitiae non possunt
mederi si ipsi saltem sint in tuto.   15

Quamquam profecto, mi More (ut ea vere dicam quae meus
animus fert), mihi videtur ubicumque privatae sunt possessiones,
ubi omnes omnia pecuniis metiuntur, ibi vix umquam posse fieri
ut cum republica aut iuste agatur aut prospere, nisi vel ibi sentias
agi iuste ubi optima quaeque perveniunt ad pessimos, vel ibi feliciter 20
ubi omnia dividuntur in paucissimos, nec illos habitos undecumque
commode, ceteris vero plane miseris.

Quamobrem quum apud animum meum reputo prudentissima
atque sanctissima instituta Utopiensium, apud quos tam paucis legibus tam commode res administrantur ut et virtuti pretium sit, et   25
tamen aequatis rebus omnia abundent omnibus, tum ubi his eorum
moribus ex adverso comparo tot nationes alias, semper ordinantes
nec ullam satis ordinatam umquam earum omnium, in quibus quod
quisque nactus fuerit suum vocat privatum, quorum tam multae
indies conditae leges non sufficiunt vel ut consequatur quisquam   30
vel ut tueatur vel ut satis internoscat ab alieno illud quod suum
invicem quisque privatum nominat (id quod facile indicant infinita
illa tam assidue nascentia quam numquam finienda litigia), haec,
inquam, dum apud me considero, aequior Platoni fio, minusque
demiror dedignatum illis leges ferre ullas qui recusabant eas quibus 35
ex aequo omnes omnia partirentur commoda. Siquidem facile prae-

openly approve the worst proposals and endorse the most vicious policies. A man who praised wicked counsels only half-heartedly would be suspected as a spy, perhaps a traitor. And there is no way for you to do any good when you are thrown among colleagues who would more readily corrupt the best of men than be reformed themselves. Either they will seduce you by their evil ways, or, if you remain honest and innocent, you will be made a screen for the knavery and folly of others. You wouldn't stand a chance of changing anything for the better by that "indirect approach".

'This is why Plato in a very fine comparison[84] declares that wise men are right in keeping away from public business. They see the people swarming through the streets and getting soaked with rain; they cannot persuade them to go indoors and get out of the wet. If they go out themselves, they know they will do no good, but only get drenched with the others. So they stay indoors and are content to keep at least themselves dry, since they cannot remedy the folly of others.

'But as a matter of fact, my dear More, to tell you what I really think, wherever you have private property, and money is the measure of all things, it is hardly ever possible for a commonwealth to be just or prosperous – unless you think justice can exist where all the best things are held by the worst citizens, or suppose happiness can be found where the good things of life are divided among very few, where even those few are always uneasy, and where the rest are utterly wretched.

'So I reflect on the wonderfully wise and sacred institutions of the Utopians, who are so well governed with so few laws.[85] Among them virtue has its reward, yet everything is shared equally, and everyone lives in plenty. I contrast with them the many other nations, none of which, though all are constantly passing new ordinances, can ever order its affairs satisfactorily. In such nations, whatever a man can get he calls his own private property; but all the mass of laws enacted day after day don't enable him to secure his own or to defend it, or even to distinguish it from someone else's property – as is shown by innumerable and interminable lawsuits, fresh ones every day. When I consider all these things, I become more sympathetic to Plato, and wonder the less that he refused to make any laws for people who rejected laws requiring all goods to be shared equally by all. Wisest of men, he saw easily

---

[84] *Republic* VI.496D–E.
[85] On the small number of Utopian laws (though they are supplemented by an oppressive number of codes, customs and conventions), see p. 195.

vidit homo prudentissimus unam atque unicam illam esse viam ad
salutem publicam si rerum indicatur aequalitas: quae nescio an
umquam possit observari ubi sua sunt singulorum propria. Nam
quum certis titulis quisque quantum potest ad se converrit,[24]
quantacumque fuerit rerum copia, eam omnem pauci inter se partiti, 5
reliquis relinquunt inopiam: fereque accidit ut alteri sint alterorum
sorte dignissimi, quum illi sint rapaces, improbi, atque inutiles,
contra hi modesti viri ac simplices, et cottidiana industria in publicum quam in semet benigniores.

Adeo mihi certe persuadeo res aequabili ac iusta aliqua ratione 10
distribui aut feliciter agi cum rebus mortalium, nisi sublata prorsus
proprietate, non posse. Sed manente illa, mansuram semper apud
multo maximam multoque optimam hominum partem egestatis et
aerumnarum anxiam atque inevitabilem sarcinam. Quam ut fateor
levari aliquantulum posse, sic tolli plane contendo non posse. 15
Nempe si statuatur ne quis supra certum agri modum possideat et
uti sit legitimus cuique census pecuniae: si fuerit legibus quibusdam
cautum ut neque sit princeps nimium potens neque populus nimis
insolens: tum magistratus ne ambiantur, neu dentur venum aut
sumptus in illis fieri sit necesse – alioquin et occasio datur per 20
fraudem ac rapinas sarciendae pecuniae, et fit necessitas eis muner-
ibus praeficiendi divites quae potius fuerant administranda pru-
dentibus – talibus, inquam, legibus, quemadmodum aegra assiduis
solent fomentis fulciri corpora deploratae valetudinis, ita haec
quoque mala leniri queant ac mitigari. Ut sanentur vero atque in 25
bonum redeant habitum nulla omnino spes est dum sua cuique
sunt propria. Quin dum unius partis curae studes, aliarum vulnus

---

[24] This reading of 1518M is more vivid (and more difficult) than the *convertit* ('turns
to his own use') of 1516, 1517 and 1518N.

that the one and only path to the public welfare lies through equal allocation of goods.[86] I doubt whether such equality can ever be achieved where property belongs to individuals. However abundant goods may be, when everyone, by whatever pretexts, tries to scrape together for himself as much as he can, a handful of men end up sharing the whole pile, and the rest are left in poverty. The result generally is two sorts of people whose fortunes ought to be interchanged: the rich are rapacious, wicked and useless, while the poor are unassuming, modest men, whose daily labour benefits the public more than themselves.

'Thus I am wholly convinced that unless private property is entirely abolished, there can be no fair or just distribution of goods, nor can the business of mortals be conducted happily. As long as private property remains, by far the largest and best part of the human race will be oppressed by a distressing and inescapable burden of poverty and anxieties. This load, I admit, may be lightened to some extent, but I maintain it cannot be entirely removed. Laws might be made that no one should own more than a certain amount of land or receive more than a certain income. Or laws might be passed to prevent the prince from becoming too powerful and the populace too insolent. It might be made illegal for public offices to be solicited or put up for sale or made burdensome for the office-holder by great expense. Otherwise, officials are tempted to get their money back by fraud or extortion, and only rich men can accept appointment to positions which ought to go to the wise. Laws of this sort, I agree, may have as much effect as poultices continually applied to sick bodies that are past cure. The social evils I mentioned may be alleviated and their effects mitigated for a while, but so long as private property remains, there is no hope at all of effecting a cure and restoring society to good health. While you try to cure one part, you aggravate the wound

[86] Diogenes Laertius reports that 'the Arcadians and Thebans, when they were founding Megalopolis, invited Plato to be their legislator; but . . . when he discovered that they were opposed to equality of possessions, he refused to go' (III.23). In the *Republic* Plato recommends communism only for the ruling class (the Guardians), but in the *Laws* (V.739B–C) he says that the best commonwealth would be one in which communism was applied across the board. Given its approval by Plato, Plutarch and, traditionally, Pythagoras, as well as the stress in the New Testament on the communal life of the earliest Christians, communism had long been respectable as a theoretical position. The first proverb discussed in Erasmus' *Adages* is *Amicorum communia omnia* ('Between friends all is common'), and Erasmus remarks that 'it is extraordinary how Christians dislike this common ownership of Plato's . . . although nothing was ever said by a pagan philosopher which comes closer to the mind of Christ' (*CWE*, XXXI, 30).

exasperaveris, ita mutuo nascitur ex alterius medela alterius morbus, quando nihil sic adici cuiquam potest ut non idem adimatur alii.

At mihi, inquam, contra videtur, ibi numquam commode vivi posse ubi omnia sint communia. Nam quo pacto suppetat copia rerum, unoquoque[25] ab labore subducente se, utpote quem neque 5 sui quaestus urget ratio, et alienae industriae fiducia reddit segnem? At quum et stimulentur inopia neque quod quisquam fuerit nactus id pro suo tueri ulla possit lege, an non necesse est perpetua caede ac seditione laboretur? Sublata praesertim auctoritate ac reverentia magistratuum, cui quis esse locus possit apud homines tales quos 10 inter nullum discrimen est, ne comminisci quidem queo.

Non miror, inquit, sic videri tibi, quippe cui eius imago rei aut nulla succurrit aut falsa. Verum si in Utopia fuisses mecum, moresque eorum atque instituta vidisses praesens ut ego feci, qui plus annis quinque ibi vixi, neque umquam voluissem inde discedere 15 nisi ut novum illum orbem proderem, tum plane faterere populum recte institutum nusquam alibi te vidisse quam illic.

Atqui profecto, inquit Petrus Aegidius, aegre persuadeas mihi, melius institutum populum in novo illo quam in hoc noto nobis orbe reperiri, ut in quo neque deteriora ingenia et vetustiores opinor 20 esse quam in illo respublicas et in quibus plurima ad vitam commoda longus invenit usus, ut ne adiciam apud nos casu reperta quaedam quibus excogitandis nullum potuisset ingenium sufficere.

Quod ad vetustatem, inquit ille, rerum attinet publicarum, tum pronuntiare posses rectius, si historias illius orbis perlegisses, 25 quibus si fides haberi debet, prius apud eos erant urbes quam homines apud nos. Iam vero quicquid hactenus vel ingenium invenit vel casus repperit, hoc utrobique potuit exstitisse. Ceterum ego certe puto ut illis praestemus ingenio, studio tamen atque industria longe a tergo relinquimur. 30

---

[25] 1516 and 1517 print *quolibet* in place of *unoquoque*.

in other parts. Suppressing the disease in one place causes it to break out in another, since you cannot give something to one person without taking it away from someone else.'[87]

'But I don't see it that way', I said. 'It seems to me that people cannot possibly live well where all things are in common. How can there be plenty of commodities where every man stops working? The hope of gain does not spur him on, and by relying on others he will become lazy. If men are impelled by need, and yet no man can legally protect what he has obtained, what can follow but continual bloodshed and turmoil, especially when respect for magistrates and their authority has been lost? I for one cannot even conceive of authority existing among men who are not distinguished from one another in any respect.'[88]

'I'm not surprised that you think of it this way', he said, 'since you have no image, or only a false one, of such a commonwealth. But you should have been with me in Utopia and seen with your own eyes their manners and customs, as I did – for I lived there more than five years, and would never have left, if it had not been to make that new world known to others. If you had seen them, you would frankly confess that you had never seen a well-governed people anywhere but there.'

'Come now', said Peter Giles, 'you will have a hard time persuading me that one can find in that new world a better-governed people than in the world we know. Our minds are not inferior to theirs, and our governments, I believe, are older. Long experience has helped us develop many conveniences of life, to say nothing of chance discoveries that human ingenuity could never have hit upon.'

'As for the relative ages of the governments', Raphael said, 'you might judge more accurately if you had read the histories of that part of the world. If we are to believe these records, they had cities there before there were even people here. What ingenuity has discovered or chance hit upon could have turned up just as well there as here. For the rest, I really think that even if we surpass them in natural intelligence, they leave us far behind in their diligence and zeal to learn.

---

[87] Plato repeatedly uses the metaphor of disease, and of the statesman as physician, in much the same way. Cf. *Republic* IV.425E–426A; *Statesman* 297E–298E; Epistle VII 330C–331A – and Plutarch, 'Lycurgus' V.2.

[88] These objections to communism derive from the critique of the *Republic* in Aristotle's *Politics* (II.i–v). Aristotle's arguments had been assimilated to the scholastic tradition by Aquinas' commentary on the *Politics*.

Nam (ut ipsorum habent annales) ante appulsum illuc nostrum de rebus nostris (quos illi vocant Ultra-aequinoctiales) nihil umquam quicquam audierant, nisi quod olim annis abhinc ducentis supra mille, navis quaedam apud insulam Utopiam naufragio periit, quam tempestas eo detulerat. Eiecti sunt in litus Romani quidam atque 5 Aegyptii, qui postea numquam inde discessere.

Hanc unam occasionem vide quam commodam illis sua fecit industria. Nihil artis erat intra Romanum imperium unde possit aliquis esse usus quod non illi aut ab expositis hospitibus didicerint aut acceptis quaerendi seminibus adinvenerint. Tanto bono fuit illis 10 aliquos hinc semel illuc esse delatos. At si qua similis fortuna quempiam antehac illinc huc perpulerit, tam penitus hoc obliteratum est quam istud quoque forsan excidet posteris me aliquando illic fuisse. Et ut illi uno statim congressu quicquid a nobis commode inventum est fecerunt suum: sic diu futurum puto priusquam nos accipiamus 15 quicquam quod apud illos melius quam nobis est institutum. Quod unum maxime esse reor in causa cur quum neque ingenio neque opibus inferiores simus eis, ipsorum tamen res quam nostra prudentius administretur et felicius efflorescat.

Ergo, mi Raphael, inquam, quaeso te atque obsecro, describe 20 nobis insulam: nec velis esse brevis, sed explices ordine agros, fluvios, urbes, homines, mores, instituta, leges ac denique omnia quae nos putes velle cognoscere. Putabis autem velle quicquid adhuc nescimus.

Nihil, inquit, faciam libentius, nam haec in promptu habeo. Sed 25 res otium poscit.

Eamus ergo, inquam, intro pransum: mox tempus nostro arbitratu sumemus.

Fiat, inquit. Ita ingressi prandemus. Pransi in eundem reversi locum, in eodem sedili consedimus, ac iussis ministris ne quis inter- 30 pellaret, ego ac Petrus Aegidius hortamur Raphaelem ut praestet quod erat pollicitus. Is ergo ubi nos vidit intentos atque avidos audiendi, quum paulisper tacitus et cogitabundus assedisset, hunc in modum exorsus est.

PRIMI LIBRI FINIS. 35
SEQUITUR SECUNDUS.[26]

---

[26] 1518M and N omit this line.

'According to their chronicles, they had heard nothing of Ultra-equatorials (that's their name for us) until we arrived, except that once, some twelve hundred years ago, a ship which a storm had blown towards Utopia was wrecked on their island. Some Romans and Egyptians were cast ashore, and never departed.

'Now note how the Utopians profited, through their diligence, from this one chance event. They learned every single useful art of the Roman empire either directly from their guests or by using the seeds of ideas to discover these arts for themselves. What benefits from the mere fact that on a single occasion some people from this part of the world landed there! If in the past a similar accident has brought anyone here from their land, the incident has been completely forgotten, as our future generations will perhaps forget that I was ever there. From one such accident they made themselves masters of all our useful inventions, but I suspect it will be a long time before we adopt any institutions of theirs which are better than ours. This readiness to learn is, I think, the really important reason for their being better governed and living more happily than we do, though we are not inferior to them in brains or resources.'

'Then let me implore you, my dear Raphael', said I, 'describe that island to us. Don't try to be brief, but explain in order their fields, rivers, towns, people, manners, institutions, laws – everything, in short, that you think we would like to know. And you can assume we want to know everything we don't know yet.'

'There's nothing I'd rather do', he said, 'for these things are fresh in my mind. But it will take quite some time.'

'In that case', I said, 'let's first go to luncheon. Afterwards, we shall have all the time we want.'

'Agreed', he said. So we went in and had lunch. Then we came back to the same spot, and sat down on the same bench. I ordered my servants to make sure that no one interrupted us. Peter Giles and I urged Raphael to fulfil his promise. When he saw that we were attentive and eager to hear him, he sat silent and thoughtful a moment, and then began as follows.

THE END OF BOOK I.
BOOK II FOLLOWS.

———

SERMONIS QUEM
RAPHAEL HYTHLODAEUS
DE OPTIMO REIPUBLICAE STATU HABUIT
LIBER SECUNDUS
PER THOMAM MORUM
CIVEM ET VICECOMITEM LONDINENSEM

Situs et forma
Utopiae novae
insulae

Utopiensium insula in media sui parte (nam hac latissima est) millia
passuum ducenta porrigitur, magnumque per insulae spatium non
multo angustior, fines versus paulatim utrimque tenuatur. Hi velut
circumducti circino quingentorum ambitu millium, insulam totam 10
in lunae speciem renascentis effigiant. Cuius cornua fretum
interfluens millibus passuum plus minus undecim dirimit, ac per
ingens inane diffusum, circumiectu undique terrae prohibitis ventis,
vasti in morem lacus, stagnans magis quam saeviens, omnem prope
eius terrae alvum pro portu facit, magnoque hominum usu naves 15
quaqua versus transmittit. Fauces hinc vadis inde saxis formidolo-

Locus natura
tutus unico
praesidio
defenditur

sae. In medio ferme interstitio una rupes eminet, eoque innoxia, cui
inaedificatam turrim praesidio tenent; ceterae latentes et insidiosae.
Canales solis ipsis noti, atque ideo non temere accidit uti exterus
quisquam hunc in sinum, nisi Utopiano duce, penetret, ut in quem 20
vix ipsis tutus ingressus est, nisi signis quibusdam e litore viam

THE DISCOURSE OF
RAPHAEL HYTHLODAY
ON THE BEST STATE OF A COMMONWEALTH,
BOOK II:
AS RECOUNTED BY THOMAS MORE,
CITIZEN AND UNDERSHERIFF OF LONDON

The island of the Utopians is two hundred miles across in the *Site and shape of* middle part, where it is widest, and nowhere much narrower than *Utopia the new* this except towards the two ends, where it gradually tapers. These *island* ends, curved round as if completing a circle five hundred miles in circumference, make the island crescent-shaped, like a new moon.[1] Between the horns of the crescent, which are about eleven miles apart, the sea enters and spreads into a broad bay. Being sheltered from the wind by the surrounding land, the bay is not rough, but placid and smooth instead, like a big lake. Thus nearly the whole inner coast is one great harbour, across which ships pass in every direction, to the great advantage of the people. What with shallows on one side and rocks on the other, the mouth of the bay is peril- ous.[2] Near mid-channel, there is one reef that rises above the water, *Being naturally* and so presents no danger in itself; a tower has been built on top *safe, the entry is* of it, and a garrison is kept there. Since the other rocks lie under *single fort* the water, they are very dangerous. The channels are known only to the Utopians, so hardly any strangers enter the bay without one of their pilots; and even they themselves could not enter safely if they did not direct their course by some landmarks on the coast.

---

[1] Utopia is similar to England in size, though not at all in shape. For a detailed account of its geography, and the inconsistencies thereof, see Brian R. Goodey, 'Mapping "Utopia": A comment on the geography of Sir Thomas More', *The Geographical Review*, 60 (1970), 15–30.
   The main topics and the order of Hythloday's account may owe something to Aristotle's treatment of the ideal commonwealth in *Politics* VII–VIII. Aristotle's discussion of the optimal 'human material' and territory for a polis is followed by a checklist of the six 'services' that must be provided for: food; arts and crafts; arms; 'a certain supply of property, alike for domestic use and for military purposes'; public worship; and a deliberative and judicial system (VII.iv–viii).

[2] A number of the geographical features of Utopia recall the dicta of ideal- commonwealth literature. Aristotle, for example, says that the best territory for a polis is one that is 'difficult of access to enemies, and easy of egress for its inhabitants' (*Politics* VII.v.3). There are, though, some features in which the Uto- pians' territory is *not* ideal: on the shortage of iron, see p. 147; on the poor climate and soil, p. 179.

Stratagema ex mutatis signis regentibus. His in diversa translatis loca, hostium quamlibet numerosam classem facile in perniciem traherent.

Ab altera parte non infrequentes portus. At ubique descensus in terram ita natura munitus aut arte ut ingentes copiae[1] paucis inde queant propugnatoribus arceri. Ceterum uti fertur, utique ipsa loci 5 facies prae se fert, ea tellus olim non ambiebatur mari. Sed Utopus, *Utopia insula ab Utopo duce* cuius utpote victoris nomen refert insula (nam ante id temporis Abraxa dicebatur), quique rudem atque agrestem turbam ad id quo nunc ceteros prope mortales antecellit cultus humanitatisque *Hoc plus erat quam Isthmum perfodere* perduxit, primo protinus appulsu victoria potitus, passuum millia 10 quindecim qua parte tellus continenti adhaesit exscindendum curavit, ac mare circum terram duxit; quumque ad id operis non incolas modo coegisset (ne contumeliae loco laborem ducerent) sed suos *Facile fertur quod omnibus commune est* praeterea milites omnes adiungeret, in tantam hominum multitudinem opere distributo incredibili celeritate res perfecta ut[2] finitimos 15 (qui initio vanitatem incepti riserant) admiratione successus ac terrore perculerit.

---

[1] In 1516 and 1517, the sentence beginning *At ubique* reads *At nusquam descensus in terram non ita natura munitus aut arte: quin ingentes copiae*, etc. The reading (1518M, N) is less strained, but it is certainly possible that the change was not More's.

[2] *ut* inserted as in 1563, to govern *perculerit*.

Should these landmarks be shifted about, the Utopians could easily lure to destruction an enemy fleet, however big it was. *The trick of shifting landmarks*

On the outer side of the island, harbours are found not infrequently; but everywhere the coast is rugged by nature, and so well fortified that a few defenders could beat off the attack of a strong force. They say (and the appearance of the place confirms this) that their land was not always surrounded by the sea. But Utopus, who conquered the country and gave it his name (for it had previously been called Abraxa),[3] and who brought its rude, uncouth inhabitants to such a high level of culture and humanity that they now surpass almost every other people, also changed its geography. *Utopia named after Utopus the commander* After winning the victory at his first assault, he had a channel cut fifteen miles wide where the land joined the continent, and thus caused the sea to flow around the country. He put not only the natives to work at this task, but all his own soldiers too, so that the vanquished would not think the labour a disgrace.[5] With the work divided among so many hands, the project was finished quickly, and the neighbouring peoples, who at first had laughed at the folly of the undertaking, were struck with wonder and terror at its success. *This was a bigger job than digging across the Isthmus*[4] *Many hands make light work*

[3] The Greek Gnostic Basilides (second century) postulated 365 heavens, and gave the name 'Abraxas' to the highest of them. The Greek letters that constitute the term have numerical equivalents summing to 365, but what 'Abraxas' actually means nobody knows. Erasmus refers to it several times; for him, as Baker-Smith says, it 'obviously means a far-fetched fantasy' (*More's 'Utopia'*, p. 55n).

The prototypes of Utopus are the legendary lawgivers of Greek tradition – Solon, Lycurgus, Pythagoras and others – who founded or regenerated polities. See Frank E. and Fritzie P. Manuel, *Utopian Thought in the Western World* (Cambridge, Mass., 1979), pp. 93–5.

[4] The Isthmus of Corinth joins the Peloponnesian peninsula to the rest of Greece. The failure of various attempts to excavate a canal across it made this difficult task proverbial. Alan F. Nagel calls attention to a tradition (recorded in Holinshed, Camden and *The Faerie Queene* II.x.5) that England was originally attached to the European continent. See 'Lies and the limitable inane: Contradiction in More's *Utopia*', *Renaissance Quarterly*, 26 (1973), 174n.

[5] This is the first of several passages in *Utopia* stressing the dignity of labour. Frank and Fritzie Manuel observe that 'More's rehabilitation of the idea of physical labor was a milestone in the history of utopian thought, and was incorporated into all socialist systems' (*Utopian Thought in the Western World*, p. 127). The principal sources of this attitude are Christian; in particular, the monastic orders constituted a paradigm of a society in which all are workers. (Monasticism is the one European institution that the Utopians are said to admire (p. 221), and such Utopian institutions as their uniform dress (pp. 125, 133) and common meals (p. 141) – generally, their communal way of life – recall the monastic rules.) By contrast, in classical political theory and practice manual labour was normally assigned to members of the lower orders (including especially slaves) and to women.

Insula civitates habet quattuor et quinquaginta spatiosas omnes ac magnificas, lingua, moribus, institutis, legibus prorsus eisdem. Idem situs omnium, eadem ubique, quatenus per locum licet, rerum facies. Harum quae proximae inter se[3] sunt millia quattuor ac viginti separant. Nulla rursus est tam deserta, e qua non ad aliam urbem 5 pedibus queat unius itinere diei perveniri.

Cives quaqua ex urbe terni senes ac rerum periti tractatum de rebus insulae communibus quotannis conveniunt Amaurotum. Nam ea urbs (quod tamquam in umbilico terrae sita maxime iacet omnium partium legatis opportuna) prima princepsque habetur. 10 Agri ita commode civitatibus assignati sunt ut ab nulla parte minus soli quam XII[4] passuum millia una quaevis habeat: ab aliqua multo etiam amplius, videlicet qua parte longius urbes inter se disiunguntur. Nulli urbi cupido promovendorum finium. Quippe quos habent, agricolas magis eorum se quam dominos putant. Habent 15 ruri per omnes agros commode dispositas domos rusticis instrumentis instructas. Hae habitantur civibus per vices eo commigrantibus. Nulla familia rustica in viris mulieribusque pauciores habet quam quadraginta, praeter duos ascripticios servos, quibus pater materque familias graves ac maturi praeficiuntur, et singulis 20 tricenis familiis phylarchus[5] unus. E quaqua familia viginti quotannis in urbem remigrant, hi qui biennium ruri complevere. In horum locum totidem recentes ex urbe surrogantur, ut ab his qui annum ibi fuere atque ideo rusticarum peritiores rerum instituantur, alios anno sequente docturi ne, si pariter omnes ibi novi agricola- 25 tionisque rudes essent, aliquid in annona per imperitiam peccaretur. Is innovandorum agricolarum mos, etsi sollemnis sit ne quisquam invitus asperiorem vitam cogatur continuare diutius, multi tamen

Oppida Utopiae insulae

Similitudo concordiam facit

Urbium inter se mediocre intervallum

Distributio agrorum

At hinc hodie pestis rerumpublicarum omnium

Prima cura agricolationis

---

[3] *se* added from 1516, 1517. 1518M has *inter sunt* (and 1518N *intersunt*), which makes little sense.
[4] Twelve (miles) as in 1516 and 1517, rather than twenty as in 1518M, N. The arithmetic of the latter figure is impossible.
[5] *phylarchus* as in 1516, 1517, not *philarchus* as in 1518M, N. In the Greek, γύλαρχος = ruler of a φυλή ('tribe'), γύλαρχος = fond of rule.

BOOK II

There are fifty-four cities[6] on the island, all spacious and magnificent, entirely identical in language, customs, institutions and laws. So far as the location permits, all of them are built on the same plan and have the same appearance. The nearest are twenty-four miles apart, and the farthest are not so remote that a person cannot travel on foot from one to another in a day.

The towns of Utopia

Likeness breeds concord

A middling distance between cities

Once a year each city sends three of its old and experienced citizens to Amaurot[7] to consider affairs of common interest to the island. Amaurot lies at the navel of the land, so to speak, and convenient to every other district, so it acts as a capital. Every city has enough ground assigned to it so that at least twelve miles of farmland are available in every direction, though where the cities are farther apart, their territories are much more extensive. No city wants to enlarge its boundaries, for the inhabitants consider themselves cultivators rather than landlords. At proper intervals all over the countryside they have houses furnished with farm equipment. These houses are inhabited by citizens who come to the country by turns. No rural household has fewer than forty men and women in it, besides two slaves bound to the land. A master and mistress, serious and mature persons, are in charge of each household, and over every thirty households is placed a single phylarch.[9] Each year twenty persons from each household move back to the city after completing a two-year stint in the country. In their place, twenty substitutes are sent out from town, to learn farm work from those who have already been in the country for a year and are therefore better skilled in farming. They, in turn, will teach those who come the following year. If all were equally untrained in farm work and new to it, they might harm the crops out of ignorance. This custom of alternating farm workers is the usual procedure, so that no one has to perform such heavy labour unwillingly for too long; but

Distribution of land

But today this is the curse of all countries[8]

Farming is the prime occupation

---

[6] Although the primary reference here is to the cities themselves, the word More uses – *civitas* – is the Latin equivalent of the Greek *polis*, 'city-state'. In fact each of the fifty-four Utopian *civitates* is, like the Greek *polis*, constituted of a central city and its surrounding countryside. Though federated, they also resemble the Greek city-states in functioning as largely independent political units. Throughout Book II, the concentration on the *civitas* is the most striking indication of More's debt to Greek political theory. In number, the Utopian cities match the number of counties in England and Wales – given as fifty-three in William Harrison's 1587 *Description of England* (ed. Georges Edelen (Ithaca, 1968), p. 86) – plus London.

[7] From *amauroton*, 'made dark or dim'.

[8] Although Utopia exists in the present, the glosses repeatedly refer to it as if it belonged to the distant past, like classical Greece and Rome.

[9] Greek *phylarchos*, 'ruler of a tribe'. Cf. textual note 5 opposite.

quos rusticae rei studium natura delectat plures sibi annos
impetrant.

Agricolarum officia Agricolae terram colunt, nutriunt animalia, ligna comparant
atque in urbem qua[6] commodum est terra marive convehunt. Pullo-
Mira ratio fovendi ova rum infinitam educant multitudinem mirabili artificio. Neque enim 5
incubant ova gallinae, sed magnum eorum numerum calore quodam
aequabili foventes animant educantque. Hi simulatque e testa prodi-
ere homines vice matrum comitantur et agnoscunt.

Usus equorum Equos alunt perquam paucos nec nisi ferocientes neque alium in
usum quam exercendae rebus equestribus iuventuti. Nam omnem 10
Usus bovum seu colendi seu vehendi laborem boves obeunt, quos ut fatentur
equis impetu cedere, sic patientia vincere, nec tot obnoxios morbis
putant; ad haec minore impendio et operae et sumptus ali, ac
denique laboribus emeritos in cibum tandem usui esse.

Cibus ac potus Semente in solum panem utuntur. Nam aut uvarum vinum bibunt 15
aut pomorum pirorumve aut denique aquam nonnumquam meram:
saepe etiam qua mel aut glycyrrhizam incoxerint, cuius haud exig-
uam habent copiam. Quum exploratum habeant (habent enim
certissimum) quantum annonae consumat urbs et circumiectus urbi
Modus sementis conventus, tamen multo amplius et sementis faciunt et pecudum 20
educant quam quod in suos usus sufficiat, reliquum impertituri fin-
itimis. Quibuscumque rebus opus est quae res ruri non habentur,
eam supellectilem omnem ab urbe petunt, et sine ulla rerum commutatione a magistratibus urbanis nullo negotio consequuntur.
Nam illo singulo quoque mense plerique ad festum diem conven- 25
iunt. Quum frumentandi dies instat, magistratibus urbanis agricolarum phylarchi denuntiant quantum civium numerum ad se mitti
Mutua opera quantum valeat conveniat: quae multitudo frumentatorum, quum ad ipsum diem
opportune adsit, uno prope sereno die tota frumentatione
defunguntur. 30

DE URBIBUS, AC NOMINATIM DE AMAUROTO

Urbium qui unam norit omnes noverit, ita sunt inter se (quatenus
loci natura non obstat) omnino similes. Depingam igitur unam

[6] The *qua* is Ciceronian shorthand (*Pro Caecina* 8) for *qua via*, by whatever path.

many of them who take a natural pleasure in farm life are allowed
to stay extra years.

The farm workers till the soil, feed the animals, procure wood *Farmers' jobs*
and take their produce to the city by land or water, whichever is
convenient. They breed an enormous number of chickens by a most *A notable way of*
marvellous method. The farmers, not hens, keep the eggs alive and *hatching eggs*
hatch them, maintaining them at an even, warm temperature.[10] As
soon as they come out of the shell, the chicks recognise the humans
and follow them around instead of their mothers.

They raise very few horses, and those full of mettle, which they *Uses of the horse*
keep only to exercise the young people in the art of horsemanship.
For all the work of ploughing and hauling they use oxen, which *Uses of oxen*
they agree are inferior to horses over the short haul, but which can
hold out longer under heavy burdens, are less subject to disease (as
they suppose), and besides can be kept with less cost and trouble.
Moreover, when oxen are too old for work, they can be used for
meat.

Grain they use only to make bread.[11] For they drink wine made *Food and drink*
of grapes, apple or pear cider, or simple water, which they sometimes boil with honey or liquorice, of which they have plenty.
Although they know very well, down to the last detail, how much
food each city and its surrounding district will consume, they pro- *Method of*
duce much more grain and cattle than they need for themselves, *planting*
and share the surplus with their neighbours. Whatever goods the
folk in the country need which cannot be had there, they request
of the town magistrates, and, giving nothing in exchange, they get
what they want without any trouble. They generally go to town
once a month in any case, to observe the feast day. When harvest
time approaches, the phylarchs in the country notify the town
magistrates how many hands will be needed. The crowd of harves-
ters comes at just the right time, and in about one day of good *The advantage of*
weather they can get in the whole crop. *collective labour*

THEIR CITIES, ESPECIALLY AMAUROT

If you know one of their cities you know them all, for they're
exactly alike, except where geography itself makes a difference. So

---

[10] It's not entirely clear what is meant here. Though artificial incubation is mentioned in Pliny's *Naturalis Historia* (X.lxxvi.154), it was not practised in More's
time.
[11] I.e., they don't, like the English, use it to make beer and ale.

quampiam (neque enim admodum refert quam). Sed quam potius quam Amaurotum? qua nec ulla dignior est quippe cui senatus gratia reliquae deferunt, nec ulla mihi notior ut in qua annos quinque perpetuo vixerim.

Amauroti primariae Utopiensium urbis descriptio

Situm est igitur Amaurotum in leni deiectu montis, figura fere quadrata. Nam latitudo eius paulo infra collis incepta verticem, millibus passuum duobus ad flumen Anydrum pertinet, secundum ripam aliquanto longior. Oritur Anydrus millibus octoginta supra Amaurotum, modico fonte, sed aliorum occursu fluminum atque in his duorum etiam mediocrium auctus, ante urbem ipsam quingentos in latum passus extenditur. Mox adhuc amplior, sexaginta millia prolapsus, excipitur oceano. Hoc toto spatio quod urbem ac mare interiacet, ac supra urbem quoque aliquot millia, sex horas perpetuas influens aestus ac refluus alternat celeri flumine. Quum sese pelagus infert triginta in longum millia, totum Anydri alveum suis occupat undis, profligato retrorsum fluvio. Tum aliquanto ultra liquorem eius salsugine corrumpit, dehinc paulatim dulcescens amnis, sincerus urbem perlabitur, ac refugientem vicissim purus et incorruptus ad ipsas prope fauces insequitur.

Anydri fluminis descriptio

Idem fit apud Anglos in flumine Thamysi

Urbs adversae fluminis ripae non pilis ac sublicibus ligneis sed ex opere lapideo egregie arcuato ponte commissa est, ab ea parte quae longissime distat a mari, quo naves totum id latus urbis possint inoffensae praetervehi. Habent alium praeterea fluvium,[7] haud magnum quidem illum sed perquam placidum ac iucundum. Nam ex eodem scaturiens monte in quo civitas collocatur mediam illam per devexa perfluens Anydro miscetur. Eius fluvii caput fontemque, quod paulo extra urbem nascitur, munimentis amplexi Amaurotani iunxerunt oppido, ne si qua vis hostium ingruat, intercipi atque averti aqua neve corrumpi queat. Inde canalibus coctilibus diversim

Et in hoc Londinum cum Amauroto convenit

Usus aquae potabilis

---

[7] For *fluvium*, 1516 prints *gurgitem*, meaning 'abyss' or 'whirlpool', hardly compatible with the stream as *perquam placidum ac iucundum* (next line).

I will describe one of them, and no matter which. But what one rather than Amaurot, the most worthy of all? – since its eminence is acknowledged by the other cities that send representatives to the senate there; besides which, I know it best because I lived there for five full years.

Description of Amaurot, principal city of Utopia

Well, then, Amaurot lies up against a gently sloping hill; the town is almost square in shape. From a little below the crest of the hill, its shorter side runs down two miles to the river Anyder;[12] its length along the river bank is somewhat greater. The Anyder rises from a small spring eighty miles above Amaurot, but other streams flow into it, two of them being pretty big, so that as it runs by Amaurot the river has grown to a width of about five hundred yards. It continues to grow even larger until at last, sixty miles farther along, it is lost in the ocean. In all this stretch between the sea and the city, and also for some miles above the city, the river is tidal, ebbing and flowing every six hours with a swift current. When the tide comes in, it fills the whole Anyder with salt water for about thirty miles, driving the fresh water back. Even above that, for several miles farther, the water is brackish; but higher up it gradually becomes free of salt, and the river is fresh as it runs through the city. When the tide ebbs, the river runs fresh and clean nearly all the way to the sea.

Description of the river Anyder

Just like the Thames in England

The two banks of the river at Amaurot are linked by a bridge, built not on wooden pillars and piles but on remarkable stone arches. It is placed at the upper end of the city farthest removed from the sea, so that ships can sail along the entire length of the city quays without obstruction.[13] There is also another stream, not particularly large but very gentle and pleasant, that gushes out of the hill on which the city is situated and, following the slope of the terrain, flows down through the centre of town and into the Anyder.[14] The inhabitants of Amaurot have walled around the head and source of this stream, which is somewhat outside the city, and joined it to the town proper, so that if they should be attacked the enemy would not be able to cut off and divert the stream, or poison it. Water from the stream is carried by tile pipes into various sec-

Here too London is just like Amaurot

A source of drinking water

---

[12] From *anydros*, 'waterless'. The description of the Anyder and the situation of Amaurot correspond in detail to the Thames and London, except that the Thames rises about twice as far above London as the Anyder above Amaurot. The situation of Amaurot – a well-watered site on sloping ground – also chimes with Aristotle's recommendations for the territory of an ideal polis (*Politics* VII.x.1–2)

[13] This is an improvement on the situation of London Bridge, which was in the lower part of town.

[14] Except in its pleasantness, this second stream resembles London's Fleet Ditch.

ad inferiores urbis partes aqua derivatur. Id sicubi locus fieri vetat, cisternis capacibus collecta pluvia tantundem usus adfert.

Moenium munimenta Murus altus ac latus oppidum cingit, turribus ac propugnaculis frequens. Arida fossa sed alta lataque ac veprium saepibus impedita tribus ab lateribus circumdat moenia, quarto flumen ipsum pro 5
Plateae cuiusmodi fossa est. Plateae cum ad vecturam tum adversus ventos descriptae
Aedificia commode. Aedificia neutiquam sordida, quorum longa et totum per vicum perpetua series adversa domorum fronte conspicitur. Has vicorum frontes via distinguit pedes viginti lata. Posterioribus
Horti aedibus adhaerentes aedium partibus, quanta est vici longitudo, hortus adiacet latus et 10 vicorum tergis undique circumseptus.

Nulla domus est quae non ut ostium in plateam ita posticum in hortum habeat. Quin bifores quoque facili tractu manus apertiles
Haec sapiunt communitatem Platonis ac dein sua sponte coeuntes quemvis intromittunt; ita nihil usquam privati est. Nam domos ipsas uno quoque decennio sorte commut- 15 ant. Hos hortos magnifaciunt: in his vineas, fructus, herbas, flores habent tanto nitore cultuque ut nihil fructuosius usquam viderim, nihil elegantius. Qua in re studium eorum non ipsa voluptas modo sed vicorum quoque invicem de suo cuiusque horti cultu certamen
Utilitas hortorum etiam Maroni praedicata accendit. Et certe non aliud quicquam temere urbe tota reperias sive 20 ad usum civium sive ad voluptatem commodius. Eoque nullius rei quam huiusmodi hortorum maiorem habuisse curam videtur is qui condidit.

Nam totam hanc urbis figuram iam inde ab initio descriptam ab ipso Utopo ferunt. Sed ornatum ceterumque cultum, quibus unius 25 aetatem hominis haud suffecturam vidit, posteris adiciendum

tions of the lower town. Where the terrain makes this impractical, they collect rain water in cisterns, which serve just as well.

The town is surrounded by a thick, high wall, with many towers and battlements. On three sides it is also surrounded by a dry ditch, broad and deep and filled with thorn hedges; on its fourth side the river itself serves as a moat. The streets are conveniently laid out both for use by vehicles and for protection from the wind. Their buildings are by no means shabby. Long unbroken rows of houses face each other down the whole block. The housefronts along each block are separated by a street twenty feet wide.[15] Behind the houses, a large garden – as long on each side as the block itself – is hemmed in on all sides by the backs of the houses.

Every house has a front door to the street and a back door to the garden. The double doors, which open easily with a push of the hand and close again automatically, let anyone come in – so there is nothing private anywhere. Every ten years they exchange the houses themselves by lot.[16] The Utopians are very fond of these gardens of theirs. They raise vines, fruits, herbs and flowers, so well cared for and flourishing that I have never seen any gardens more productive or elegant than theirs. They keep interested in gardening, partly because they delight in it, and also because of the competition among the blocks, which challenge one another to produce the best gardens. Certainly you will not easily find anything else in the whole city more useful or more pleasant to the citizens. And from that fact it appears that the city's founder must have made such gardens a primary object of his consideration.

They say that from the beginning the whole city was planned by Utopus himself, but that he left to posterity matters of adornment and improvement such as he saw could not be perfected in one

Fortified city walls

Streets, of what sort

Buildings

Gardens next to the houses

This smacks of Plato's community

Virgil also wrote in praise of gardens[17]

---

[15] Lavish, by sixteenth-century standards. Goodey observes that the layout of Amaurot is reminiscent of Roman urban planning: 'Twenty feet was the average width of Roman city streets, which, again like Amaurotum, were bordered by fairly high-density housing blocks that surrounded large courtyards used for recreation. As in Amaurotum, the rectangular block pattern was the most evident feature of the Roman urban plan. In the Roman city this pattern was broken only by the insertion of major public buildings, again a feature of the Utopian city' ('Mapping "Utopia"', p. 29). The notable *difference* from Roman arrangements lies in the fact that the Utopian courtyards are merged in the communal gardens.

[16] Cf. Plato, *Republic* V.416D: the Guardians 'shall have no private property beyond the barest essentials ... none of them shall possess a dwelling-house or other property to which all have not the right of entry'. The Carthusian monks, among whom More sojourned for a few years, regularly exchange dwellings.

[17] In the *Georgics* (IV.116–48).

reliquit. Itaque scriptum in annalibus habent, quos ab capta usque insula mille septingentorum ac sexaginta annorum complectentes historiam diligenter et religiose perscriptos asservant, aedes initio humiles ac veluti casas et tuguria fuisse, e quolibet ligno temere factas, parietes luto obductos. Culmina in aciem fastigiata[8] stra- ₅ mentis operuerant. At nunc omnis domus visenda forma tabulatorum trium, parietum facies aut silice aut caementis aut latere coctili constructae, in alvum introrsus congesto rudere.[9] Tecta in planum subducta quae intritis quibusdam insternunt nullius impendii, sed ea temperatura quae nec igni obnoxia sit et tolerandis ₁₀

Vitreae aut linteatae fenestrae

tempestatum iniuriis plumbum superet. Ventos a fenestris vitro (nam eius ibi creberrimus usus est) expellunt, interim etiam lino tenui quod perlucido oleo aut sucino[10] perlinunt, gemino nimirum commodo. Siquidem ad eum modum fit ut et plus lucis transmittat et ventorum minus admittat. ₁₅

DE MAGISTRATIBUS

Triginta quaeque familiae magistratum sibi quotannis eligunt, quem sua prisca lingua syphograntum vocant, recentiore phylarchum.

---

[8] From *fastigio*, a variant form of *fastigo*.
[9] 1516 describes the walls (*parietum facies*) as *silice, aut lapide duro, aut denique coctili constructae*; roofs are covered with *sementis* (i.e., *caementis*), not *intritis*.
[10] *sucinum* means 'amber'. But since amber is fossil resin, it is not a long step to the meaning required by the passage: 'resin' or 'gum'.

man's lifetime. Their records began 1,760 years ago[18] with the conquest of the island, were diligently compiled, and are carefully preserved in writing. From these records it appears that the first houses were low, like cabins or peasant huts, built slapdash out of any sort of lumber, with mud-plastered walls. The roofs, rising up to a central point, were thatched with straw. But now their houses are all three storeys high and handsomely constructed; the outer sections of the walls are made of fieldstone, quarried rock or brick, and the space between is filled up with gravel and cement.[19] The roofs are flat and are covered with a kind of plaster that is cheap but formulated so as to be fireproof, and more weather-resistant even than lead.[20] Glass (of which they have a good supply) is used in windows to keep out the weather; and they also use thin linen cloth treated with clear oil or gum so that it has the double advantage of letting in more light and keeping out more wind.

Windows of glass or linen

THEIR OFFICIALS

Once a year, every group of thirty households elects an official, called the syphogrant in their ancient language,[21] but now known

---

[18] Counting from 1516, this takes us back to 244 BC, when Agis IV became King of Sparta: he was put to death for proposing egalitarian reforms. See Plutarch's 'Agis'; and R.J. Schoeck, 'More, Plutarch, and King Agis: Spartan history and the meaning of *Utopia*', *Philological Quarterly*, 35 (1956), 366–75; rpt *Essential Articles for the Study of Thomas More*, ed. R.S. Sylvester and G.P. Marc'hadour (Hamden, Conn., 1977), pp. 275–80.

[19] The housing of modern Amaurot is considerably more impressive than that of early sixteenth-century London, where dwellings were normally of timber and of at most two storeys.

[20] The Utopians' roof-covering may be the plaster of Paris spoken of in Harrison's *Description of England*, which was made of 'fine alabaster burned, . . . whereof in some places we have great plenty and that very profitable against the rage of fire' (p. 196). Glass windows were uncommon in England. Oiled linen, sheets of horn and lattices of wicker or wood were used instead.

[21] 'Syphogrant' appears to be constructed from Greek *sophos* ('wise') – or perhaps *sypheos* ('of the sty') – plus *gerontes* ('old men'). For 'tranibor' (below), the etymology seems to be *traneis* or *tranos* ('clear', 'plain', 'distinct') plus *boros* ('devouring', 'gluttonous'). Although Hythloday says that these terms have been displaced by the more unambiguously respectful 'phylarch' and 'protophylarch' (translated as 'head phylarch'), in the remainder of his account he invariably uses the 'older' terms. 'Phylarch' occurs twice before this passage, but never again; 'protophylarch' occurs only this once.

The Utopian form of government is republican: syphogrants are elected by the households, and the syphogrants of each city elect – and can remove – the governor (below), as well as the class of scholars, from which all high officials

Traniborus
Utopiensium
lingua sonat
praefectum
primarium
Syphograntis decem cum suis familiis traniborus olim, nunc proto-
phylarchus dictus, praeficitur. Demum syphogranti omnes, qui sunt
ducenti, iurati lecturos sese quem maxime censent utilem suffragiis
occultis renuntiant principem, unum videlicet ex his quattuor quos
Mira ratio creandi
magistratus
eis populus nominavit. Nam a quaque urbis quarta parte selectus ₅
unus commendatur senatui. Principis magistratus perpetuus est in
Tyrannis invisa
bene institutae
reipublicae
omnem illius vitam, nisi tyrannidis adfectatae suspicio impediat.
Traniboros quotannis eligunt, ceterum haud temere commutant:
reliqui magistratus omnes annui.

    Tranibori tertio quoque die, interdum si res postulat saepius, in ₁₀
Cito dirimendae
controversiae,
quas nunc data
opera in
immensum
prorogant
consilium cum principe veniunt. De republica consultant, con-
troversias privatorum (si quae sunt, quae perquam paucae sunt)
mature dirimunt. Syphograntos semper in senatum duos asciscunt,
atque omni die diversos, cautumque ut ne quid ratum sit quod ad
Nihil subito
statuendum
rempublicam pertineat, de quo non tribus in senatu diebus ante ₁₅
agitatum quam decretum sit. Extra senatum aut comitia publica de
rebus communibus inire consilia capitale habetur. Haec eo ferunt
instituta ne proclive esset coniuratione principis ac tranibororum,
oppresso per tyrannidem populo, statum reipublicae mutare. Atque
ideo quicquid magni momenti iudicatur ad syphograntorum comitia ₂₀
defertur, qui cum suis familiis communicata re post inter se consultant ac suum consilium renuntiant senatui. Interdum ad totius insulae consilium res defertur.

Utinam idem
hodie fiat in
nostris consiliis
    Quin id quoque moris habet senatus, ut nihil quo die primum
proponitur eodem disputetur, sed in sequentem senatum differatur, ₂₅
ne quis ubi quod in buccam primum venerit temere effutierit, ea
Hoc sibi volebat
vetus proverbium,
ἐν νυκτὶ βουλή
potius excogitet postea quibus decreta tueatur sua quam quae ex
reipublicae usu sint, malitque salutis publicae quam opinionis de se

as the phylarch. Over every group of ten syphogrants with their households there is another official, once called the tranibor but now known as the head phylarch. All the syphogrants, two hundred in number,[22] elect the governor. They take an oath to choose the man they think best qualified; and then by secret ballot they elect the governor from among four men commended to the senate by the people of the four sections of the city.[23] The governor holds office for life, unless he is suspected of aiming at a tyranny. Though the tranibors are elected annually, they are not changed for light or casual reasons. All their other officials hold office for a single year only.

In the Utopian tongue 'tranibor' means 'chief official'

A notable way of electing officials

Tyranny hateful to the well-ordered commonwealth

The tranibors meet to consult with the governor every other day, more often if necessary: they discuss affairs of state and settle disputes between private parties (if there are any, and there are very few), acting as quickly as possible. The tranibors always invite two syphogrants to the senate chamber, different ones every day. There is a rule that no decision can be made on a matter of public business unless it has been discussed in the senate on three separate days. It is a capital offence to make plans about public business outside the senate or the popular assembly. The purpose of these rules, they say, is to prevent governor and tranibors from conspiring together to alter the government and enslave the people. Therefore all matters which are considered important are first laid before the assembly of syphogrants. They talk the matter over with the households they represent, consult among themselves, and then report their recommendation to the senate. Sometimes a question is brought before the general council of the whole island.

A quick ending to disputes, which now are endlessly and deliberately prolonged

No abrupt decisions

The senate also has a standing rule never to debate a matter on the same day that it is first introduced but to put it off till the next meeting. This they do so that a man will not blurt out the first thought that occurs to him, and then devote all his energies to defending his own proposals, instead of considering the common

Would that the same rules prevailed in our modern councils

This is the old saying, 'to sleep on a decision'

are chosen (p. 131). The particular republic that the Utopian arrangements would be most likely to call to mind was Venice, whose 'mixed' constitution combined the institutions of Doge (the elected head of government), Senate and Grand Council. The famous stability of this constitution was thought to be owed to its embodiment of Plato's view (*Laws* III.691D–693E, IV.712B–E) that the soundest form of government was an amalgam of monarchy, aristocracy and democracy. See Skinner, *The Foundations of Modern Political Thought*, I, 139–42.

22 Because there are 6,000 families in each city (p. 135), with thirty families per syphogrant.

23 While each city has a governor, there is no governor over the whole island, so that when the national council meets at Amaurot (p. 113) there's nobody for it to advise – no executive.

iacturam facere, perverso quodam ac praepostero pudore ne initio parum prospexisse videatur. Cui prospiciendum initio fuit ut consulto potius quam cito loqueretur.

DE ARTIFICIIS

Agricolatio
communis
omnium, quam
nunc in paucos
contemptos
reicimus

Ars una est omnibus viris mulieribusque promiscua agricultura, cuius nemo est expers. Hac a pueritia erudiuntur omnes, partim in schola traditis praeceptis, partim in agros viciniores urbi quasi per ludum educti, non intuentes modo sed per exercitandi corporis occasionem tractantes etiam.

Praeter agriculturam (quae est omnibus, ut dixi, communis) quilibet unam quampiam tamquam suam docetur. Ea est fere aut lanificium, aut operandi lini studium, aut caementariorum, aut fabri seu

Artes ad
necessitatem non
ad luxum
discendae

Cultus similitudo

ferrarii seu materiarii artificium. Neque enim aliud est opificium ullum quod numerum aliquem dictu dignum occupet illic. Nam vestes – quarum, nisi quod habitu sexus discernitur et caelibatus a coniugio, una per totam insulam forma est, eademque per omne aevum perpetua, nec ad oculum indecora et ad corporis motum habilis, tum ad frigoris aestusque rationem apposita – eas, inquam, quaeque sibi familia conficit.

Nemo civium
expers artificii

Sed ex aliis illis artibus unusquisque aliquam discit, nec viri modo sed mulieres etiam. Ceterum hae velut imbecilliores leviora tractant: lanam fere linumque operantur. Viris artes reliquae magis laboriosae mandantur. Maxima ex parte quisque in patriis artibus educatur

Ad quam quisque
natura sit
appositus, eam
discat artem

nam eo plerique natura feruntur. Quod si quem animus alio trahat, in eius opificii cuius capitur studio familiam quampiam adoptione traducitur, cura non a patre modo eius sed magistratibus etiam praestita ut gravi atque honesto patrifamilias mancipetur. Quin si quis unam perdoctus artem, aliam praeterea cupiverit, eodem modo per-

interest. They know that some men have such a perverse and pre-
posterous sense of shame that they would rather jeopardise the
general welfare than their own reputation by admitting they were
short-sighted in the first place. They should have had enough fore-
sight at the beginning to speak with consideration rather than haste.

THEIR OCCUPATIONS

Farming is the one job at which everyone works, men and women
alike, with no exception. They are trained in it from childhood,
partly in the schools, where they learn theory, partly through field
trips to nearby farms, which make something like a game of practical instruction.[24] On these trips they don't just observe, but frequently pitch in and get a workout by doing the jobs themselves.

Agriculture is everyone's business, though now we put it off on a despised few

Besides farm work (which, as I said, everybody performs), each
person is taught a particular trade of his own, such as wool-
working, linen-making, masonry, metal-work or carpentry. No
other craft is practised by any considerable number of them.[25] Their
clothing – which is, except for the distinction between the sexes
and between married and unmarried persons, the same throughout
the whole island and throughout one's lifetime, and which is by no
means unattractive, does not hinder bodily movement and serves
for warm as well as cold weather – this clothing, I say, each family
makes for itself.

Trades taught to satisfy need, not greed

A uniform dress code

Every person (and this includes women as well as men) learns
one of the trades I mentioned. As the weaker sex, women practise
the lighter crafts, such as working in wool or linen; the other,
heavier jobs are assigned to the men. Ordinarily, the son is trained
to his father's craft, for which most feel a natural inclination. But
if anyone is attracted to another occupation, he is transferred by
adoption into a family practising that trade. Both his father and the
authorities take care that he is assigned to a grave and responsible
householder. After someone has mastered one trade, if he wants to
learn another he gets the same permission. When he has learned

No citizen without a trade

Everyone to learn the trade for which his nature fits him

[24] Both Plato (*Laws* I.643B–C, VII.797A–B) and Aristotle (*Politics* VII.xvii.5) stress
the educational potential of games. In particular, Plato says that a 'man who
intends to be a good farmer must play [in childhood] at farming' (*Laws* I.643C).

[25] One would have thought that considerable numbers would also have been
employed making such things as pottery, harness, bread and books, or in mining
or the merchant marine. Presumably all professionals – doctors, for example –
are drawn from the class of scholars (p. 131).

mittitur. Utramque nactus, utram velit exercet, nisi alterutra civitas magis egeat.

Syphograntorum praecipuum ac prope unicum negotium est *Otiosi pellendi e* curare ac prospicere ne quisquam desideat otiosus, sed uti suae *republica* quisque arti sedulo incumbat, nec ab summo mane tamen ad 5 multam usque noctem perpetuo labore velut iumenta fatigatus. Nam ea plus quam servilis aerumna est, quae tamen ubique fere opificum vita est, exceptis Utopiensibus. Qui cum in horas vigin- *Moderandus* tiquattuor aequales diem connumerata nocte dividant, sex dumtaxat *opificum labor* operi deputant, tres ante meridiem a quibus prandium ineunt, atque 10 a prandio duas pomeridianas horas quum interquieverint, tres deinde rursus labori datas cena claudunt. Quum primam horam ab meridie numerent, sub octavam cubitum eunt. Horas octo somnus vindicat.

Quicquid inter operis horas ac somni cibique medium esset, id 15 suo cuiusque arbitrio permittitur, non quo per luxum aut segnitiem abutatur, sed quod, ab opificio suo liberum, ex animi sententia in aliud quippiam studii bene collocet. Has intercapedines plerique *Studia literarum* impendunt literis. Sollemne est enim publicas cottidie lectiones haberi antelucanis horis, quibus ut intersint ei dumtaxat adiguntur 20 qui ad literas nominatim selecti sunt. Ceterum ex omni ordine mares simul ac feminae, multitudo maxima ad audiendas lectiones, alii alias, prout cuiusque fert natura, confluit. Hoc ipsum tempus tamen, si quis arti suae malit insumere, quod multis usu venit (quorum animus in nullius contemplatione disciplinae consurgit), 25 haud prohibetur, quin laudatur quoque ut utilis reipublicae.

Lusus in cenis Super cenam tum unam horam ludendo producunt, aestate in hortis, hieme in aulis illis communibus in quibus comedunt. Ibi aut

both, he pursues the one he likes better, unless the city needs one more than the other.[26]

The chief and almost the only business of the syphogrants is to take care and see to it that no one sits around in idleness, and to make sure that everyone works hard at his trade. But no one has to be exhausted with endless toil from early morning to late at night like a beast of burden. Such wretchedness, really worse than slavery, is the common lot of workmen almost everywhere except in Utopia.[27] Of the twenty-four equal hours into which they divide the day and the night, the Utopians devote only six to work. They work three hours before noon, when they go to lunch. After lunch, they rest for two hours, then go to work for another three hours. Then they have supper, and about eight o'clock (counting the first hour after noon as one) they go to bed, and sleep eight hours.

The other hours of the day, when they are not working, eating or sleeping, are left to each person's individual discretion, provided that free time is not wasted in roistering or sloth but used properly in some chosen occupation. Generally these intervals are devoted to intellectual activity. For they have an established custom of giving daily public lectures before dawn;[28] attendance at these lectures is required only of those who have been specifically chosen to devote themselves to learning, but a great many other people of all kinds, both men and women,[29] gather to hear them. Depending on their interests, some go to one lecture, some to another. But if anyone would rather devote his spare time to his trade, as many do who are not suited to the intellectual life, this is not prohibited; in fact, such persons are commended as specially useful to the commonwealth.

After supper, they devote an hour to recreation, in their gardens during the summer, or during winter in the common halls where they have their meals. There they either play music or amuse them-

The idle are expelled from the commonwealth

Workmen not to be overtasked

The pursuit of learning

Entertainment at supper

---

[26] The fact that all Utopians have at least two occupations (agriculture and one of the crafts), and in some cases three, brings them into implicit conflict with Plato, who strongly insists that in a well-ordered commonwealth each individual would have one and only one profession (*Republic* II.370A–C; *Laws* VIII.846D–E).

[27] In England, for example, an 'Act concerning Artificers & Labourers', 1514–15, made exorbitant demands upon the time of workmen: daybreak to nightfall from mid-September to mid-March; before 5 a.m. to between 7 and 8 p.m. from mid-March to mid-September (*The Statutes of the Realm*, III (1822), 124–6).

[28] In the universities of More's time, lectures normally began between 5 and 7 a.m.

[29] Humanists were pioneers in forwarding the education of women. Celibate Erasmus was greatly impressed by the erudite daughters of his married fellow humanists, including Margaret More. See 'The Abbot and the learned lady' in Erasmus' *Colloquies*, trans. Craig R. Thompson (Chicago, 1965), pp. 217–23.

musicen exercent aut se sermone recreant. Aleam atque id genus
ineptos ac perniciosos ludos ne cognoscunt quidem, ceterum duos
habent in usu ludos latrunculorum ludo non dissimiles. Alterum
numerorum pugnam in qua numerus numerum praedatur, alterum
in quo collata acie cum virtutibus vitia confligunt. Quo in ludo 5
perquam scite ostenditur et vitiorum inter se discidium et adversus
virtutes concordia: item quae vitia quibus se virtutibus opponant,
quibus viribus aperte oppugnent, quibus machinamentis ab obliquo
adoriantur, quo praesidio virtutes vitiorum vires infringant, quibus
artibus eorum conatus eludant, quibus denique modis alterutra pars 10
victoriae compos fiat.

Sed hoc loco ne quid erretis quiddam pressius intuendum est.
Etenim quod sex dumtaxat horas in opere sunt, fieri fortasse potest
ut inopiam aliquam putes necessariarum rerum sequi. Quod tam
longe abest ut accidat ut id temporis ad omnium rerum copiam 15
quae quidem ad vitae vel necessitatem requirantur vel commodita-
tem, non sufficiat modo sed supersit etiam, id quod vos quoque
intelligetis si vobiscum reputetis apud alias gentes quam magna
populi pars iners degit. Primum mulieres fere omnes, totius summae
dimidium: aut sicubi mulieres negotiosae sunt, ibi ut plurimum 20
earum vice viri stertunt. Ad haec sacerdotum ac religiosorum, quos
vocant, quanta quamque otiosa turba! Adice divites omnes, maxime
praediorum dominos quos vulgo generosos appellant ac nobiles.
His adnumera ipsorum famulitium,[11] totam videlicet illam caetrato-
rum nebulonum colluviem. Robustos denique ac valentes mendicos 25
adiunge, morbum quempiam praetexentes inertiae. Multo certe pauciores esse quam putaras invenies eos quorum labore constant haec
omnia quibus mortales utuntur.

Expende nunc tecum ex his ipsis quam pauci in necessariis opificiis versantur, siquidem ubi omnia pecuniis metimur, multas artes 30
necesse est exerceri inanes prorsus ac superfluas, luxus tantum ac
libidinis ministras. Nam haec ipsa multitudo quae nunc operatur,
si partiretur in tam paucas artes quam paucas commodus naturae

At nunc alea
principum lusus
est

Lusus utiles
quoque

Otiosorum
hominum genera

δορυφόρημα
nobilium

Prudentissime
dictum

---

[11] *famulitium*, frequent in classical Latin in the sense of a family of domestic slaves,
is extended here by More to mean a private army of retainers.

selves with conversation. They know nothing about gambling with *But now dicing is the sport of princes* dice or other such foolish and ruinous games, but they do play two games not unlike chess. One is a battle of numbers, in which one number captures another. The other is a game in which the vices fight a battle against the virtues. The game is ingeniously set up to *Their games are useful too* show how the vices oppose one another, yet combine against the virtues; then, what vices oppose what virtues, how they try to assault them with open force or undermine them indirectly through trickery, how the defences of the virtues can break the strength of the vices or skilfully elude their plots; and finally, by what means one side or the other gains the victory.

But at this point you may get a wrong impression if we don't go back and consider one matter more carefully. Because they allot only six hours to work, perhaps you might think the necessities of life would be in scant supply. This is far from the case. Their working hours are ample to provide not only enough but more than enough of the necessities and even the conveniences of life. You will easily appreciate this if you consider how large a part of the population in other countries lives without doing any work at all. In the first place, hardly any of the women, who are a full half *Kinds of idlers* of the population, work;[30] or, if they do, then as a rule their husbands lie snoring in bed. Then there is a great lazy gang of priests and so-called religious.[31] Add to them all the rich, especially the landlords, who are commonly called gentlemen and nobles. Include with them their retainers, that cesspool of worthless swashbucklers. *Noblemen's bodyguards* Finally, reckon in with these the sturdy and lusty beggars who feign some disease as an excuse for their idleness. You will certainly find that all the things which satisfy the needs of mortals are pro- *A very shrewd observation* duced by far fewer hands than you had supposed.

And now consider how few of those who do work are doing really essential things. For where money is the measure of every-thing, many vain and completely superfluous trades are bound to be carried on simply to satisfy luxury and licentiousness. Suppose the multitude of those who now work were limited to a few trades and set to producing just those commodities that nature really

---

[30] A strange statement, in view of the fact that women had the same, or heavier, domestic duties in the sixteenth century as in the twentieth. In Utopia, they are responsible for some at least of these duties – cooking, childcare (p. 141) – in addition to practising a craft and taking their turn at farm work. Numerous problems, such as who does the laundry, who cleans the house, who tends the garden, are solved by the simple expedient of not mentioning them.

[31] I.e., members of the various religious orders.

usus postulat, in tanta rerum abundantia quantam nunc esse necesse sit, pretia nimirum viliora forent quam ut artifices inde vitam tueri suam possent. At si isti omnes quos nunc inertes artes distringunt, ac tota insuper otio ac desidia languescens turba (quorum unus quivis earum rerum quae aliorum laboribus suppeditantur quantum 5 duo earundem operatores consumit), in opera universi atque eadem utilia collocarentur, facile animadvertis quantulum temporis ad suppeditanda omnia quae vel necessitatis ratio vel commoditatis efflagitet (adde voluptatis etiam quae quidem vera sit ac naturalis) abunde satis superque foret. 10

Atque id ipsum in Utopia res ipsa perspicuum facit. Nam illic in tota urbe cum adiacente vicinia vix hominibus quingentis[12] ex omni virorum ac mulierum numero quorum aetas ac robur operi sufficit, *Ne magistratus quidem ab opere cessant* vacatio permittitur. In his syphogranti (quamquam leges eos labore solverunt) ipsi tamen sese non eximunt, quo facilius exemplo suo 15 reliquos ad labores invitent. Eadem immunitate gaudent hi quibus[13] commendatione sacerdotum persuasus populus occultis syphograntorum suffragiis ad perdiscendas disciplinas perpetuam vacationem indulget. Quorum si quis conceptam de se spem fefellerit ad opifices retruditur: contraque non rarenter usu venit ut mechanicus quis- 20 piam subsicivas illas horas tam naviter impendat literis, tantum diligentia proficiat, ut opificio suo exemptus in literatorum classem *Soli literati ad magistratus vocantur* provehatur. Ex hoc literatorum ordine legati, sacerdotes, tranibori ac ipse denique deligitur princeps, quem illi prisca ipsorum lingua Barzanem, recentiore Ademum appellant. Reliqua fere multitudo 25 omnis, quum neque otiosa sit nec inutilibus opificiis occupata, proclivis aestimatio est quam paucae horae quantum boni operis pariant.

Ad ea quae commemoravi, hoc praeterea facilitatis accedit quod in necessariis plerisque artibus minore opera quam aliae gentes opus 30

---

[12] *hominibus quingentis*, following 1517 against *homines quingenti* of the other texts; as indirect object of *permittitur*, no other form is possible.

[13] *quibus*, following 1518N, construed as indirect object of *indulget* with direct object *vacationem*; the other texts have *quos*.

requires.[32] They would be bound to produce so much that prices would drop and the workmen would be unable to make a living. But suppose again that all the workers in useless trades were put to useful ones, and that the whole crowd of languid idlers (each of whom consumes as much as any two of the workmen who provide what he consumes) were assigned to productive tasks – well, you can easily see how little time would be enough and more than enough to produce all the goods that human needs and conveniences call for – yes, and human pleasure too, as long as it is true and natural pleasure.

The experience of Utopia makes this perfectly apparent. For there, in the whole city and its surrounding countryside barely five hundred of those men and women whose age and strength make them fit for work are exempted from it.[33] Among these are the syphogrants, who by law are free not to work; yet they don't take advantage of the privilege, preferring to set a good example to their fellow citizens. Some others are also permanently exempted from work so that they may devote themselves to study, but only on the recommendation of the priests[34] and through a secret vote of the syphogrants. If any of these scholars disappoints the hopes they had for him, he is sent packing, to become a workman again. On the other hand, it happens not infrequently that a craftsman devotes his leisure so earnestly to study, and makes such progress by his diligence, that he is released from his craft and promoted to the order of learned men. From this scholarly class are chosen ambassadors, priests, tranibors and the governor himself, who used to be called Barzanes, but in their modern tongue is known as Ademus.[35] Since almost all the rest of the populace is neither idle nor engaged in useless trades, it is easy to see why they produce so much in such a short working day.

Apart from all this, they have it easier because in most of the necessary crafts they need less labour than people elsewhere do.

Not even officials dodge work

Only the learned hold public office

[32] The notion that a well-ordered commonwealth would not countenance trades other than those that supply legitimate human needs is traceable to Plato (*Republic* II.372D–373D). Plutarch says that Lycurgus, the lawgiver of Sparta, 'banished the unnecessary and superfluous arts' ('Lycurgus' IX.3).

[33] Two hundred of these are syphogrants; presumably the governor, the twenty tranibors and the thirteen priests (p. 231) are also exempt. The rest must be scholars, and the ambassadors drawn from their ranks.

[34] The priests are in charge of the education of children (p. 231).

[35] 'Barzanes': probably Hebrew *bar*, 'son of', plus *Zanos*, Doric poetic form of the genitive of Zeus. A potent Chaldean magician named Mithrobarzanes figures in Lucian's 'Menippus', which More had translated. 'Ademus': Greek α-privative plus *demos*, 'people': hence 'Peopleless'.

habent. Nam primum aedificiorum aut structura aut refectio ideo
tam multorum assiduam ubique requirit operam, quod quae pater
aedificavit heres parum frugi paulatim dilabi sinit; ita quod minimo
tueri potuit, successor eius de integro, impendio magno, cogitur
instaurare. Quin frequenter etiam quae domus alii ingenti sumptu 5
stetit, hanc alius delicato animo contemnit, eaque neglecta atque
ideo brevi collapsa, aliam alibi impensis non minoribus extruit. At
apud Utopienses compositis rebus omnibus et constituta republica,
rarissime accidit uti nova collocandis aedibus area deligatur, et non
modo remedium celeriter praesentibus vitiis adhibetur sed etiam 10
imminentibus occurritur. Ita fit ut minimo labore diutissime
perdurent aedificia et id genus opifices vix habeant interdum quod
agant, nisi quod materiam dolare domi et lapides interim quadrare
atque aptare iubentur, quo (si quod opus incidat) maturius possit
exsurgere. 15

Iam in vestibus vide quam paucis operis egeant. Primum dum in
opere sunt corio neglectim aut pellibus amiciuntur quae in septen-
nium durent. Quum procedunt in publicum, superinduunt chlamy-
dem vestem quae rudiores illas vestes contegat; eius per totam insulam unus color est atque is nativus. Itaque lanei panni non modo 20
multo minus quam[14] usquam alibi sufficit, verum is ipse quoque
multo minoris impendii est. At lini minor est labor eoque usus
crebrior, sed in lineo solus candor, in laneo sola mundities conspicitur, nullum tenuioris fili pretium est. Itaque fit ut quum alibi nusquam uni homini quattuor aut quinque togae laneae diversis color- 25
ibus ac totidem sericiae tunicae sufficiant, delicatioribus paulo ne
decem quidem, ibi una quisque contentus est plerumque in biennium. Quippe nec causa est ulla cur plures adfectet, quas consecutus
neque adversus frigus esset munitior neque vestitu videretur vel pilo
cultior. 30

Quamobrem quum et omnes utilibus sese artibus exerceant et
ipsarum etiam opera pauciora sufficiant, fit nimirum ut abundante
rerum omnium copia, interdum in reficiendas (si quae detritae sunt)
vias publicas immensam multitudinem educant. Persaepe etiam

---

[14] *quam*, 1516, 1517; *quae*, 1518M, N.

First of all, building and repairing houses everywhere demands the *Avoiding expense* constant labour of many men, because what a father has built, his *in building* thriftless heir lets fall into ruin; and then his successor has to reconstruct, at great expense, what could have been kept up at a very small charge. Even more, when a man has built a splendid house at vast cost, someone else may think he has better taste, let the first house fall to ruin, and then build another one somewhere else for just as much money. But among the Utopians, where everything has been well-ordered and the commonwealth properly established, building a new house on a new site is a rare event. They are not only quick to repair deterioration but foresighted in preventing it. The result is that their buildings last for a very long time with minimum repairs; and workmen of that sort sometimes have so little to do that they are set to shaping timber and squaring stone for prompt use in case of future need.

Consider, too, how little labour their clothing requires. Their work clothes are unpretentious garments made of leather or pelts, *How to do so in* which last seven years. When they go out in public, they cover *clothing* these rough work clothes with a cloak. Throughout the entire island, these cloaks are of the same colour, which is that of natural wool.[36] As a result, they not only need less woollen cloth than people anywhere else, but what they do need is also less expensive. Even so, they use linen cloth most, because it requires least labour. They like linen cloth to be white and wool cloth to be clean; but they do not value fineness of texture. Everywhere else a man may not be satisfied with four or five woollen cloaks of different colours and as many silk shirts – or if he's a bit of a fop, even ten are not enough. But there everyone is content with a single cloak, and generally wears it for two years. There is no reason why he should want any more garments, for if he had them, he would not be better protected against the cold, nor would he appear the least bit more fashionable.

Since there is an abundance of everything – as a result of everyone working at useful trades and the trades requiring less work – they sometimes assemble great numbers of people to work on the roads,

[36] More's letter to Erasmus of *c.* 4 December 1516 – in which he reports a daydream of being King of Utopia – identifies this garment as a Franciscan habit (*Selected Letters*, p. 85). The Carthusians, with whom More lived for some years (Introduction, p. xix), wore garments of undyed wool. The biographical sketch of More that Erasmus included in a letter to Ulrich von Hutten says that 'Simple clothes please . . . [More] best, and he never wears silk or scarlet or a gold chain, except when it is not open to him to lay it aside' (*CWE*, VII, 18).

quum nec talis cuiuspiam operis usus occurrat, pauciores horas operandi publice denuntient. Neque enim supervacaneo labore cives invitos exercent magistratus, quandoquidem eius reipublicae institutio hunc unum scopum in primis respicit: ut quoad per publicas necessitates licet, quam plurimum temporis ab servitio corporis ad 5 animi libertatem cultumque civibus universis asseratur. In eo enim sitam vitae felicitatem putant.

DE COMMERCIIS MUTUIS

———

Sed iam quo pacto sese mutuo cives utantur, quae populi inter se commercia, quaeque sit distribuendarum rerum forma, videtur 10 explicandum.

Quum igitur ex familiis constet civitas, familias ut plurimum cognationes efficiunt. Nam feminae (ubi maturuerint) collocatae maritis in ipsorum domicilia concedunt. At masculi filii ac deinceps nepotes in familia permanent, et parentum antiquissimo parent, nisi 15 prae senecta mente parum valuerit; tunc enim aetate proximus ei sufficitur. Verum ne civitas aut fieri infrequentior aut ultra modum *Numerus civium* possit increscere, cavetur ne ulla familia (quarum millia sex quaeque civitas, excepto conventu, complectitur) pauciores quam decem pluresve quam sexdecim puberes habeat. Impuberum enim nullus prae- 20 finiri numerus potest. Hic modus facile servatur, transcriptis his in rariores familias qui in plenioribus excrescunt. At si quando in totum plus iusto abundaverit, aliarum urbium suarum infrequentiam sarciunt.[15] Quod si forte per totam insulam plus aequo moles intumuerit, tum ex qualibet urbe descriptis civibus in conti- 25 nente proximo, ubicumque indigenis agri multum superest et cultu vacat, coloniam suis ipsorum legibus propagant, ascitis una terrae

---

[15] In place of *sarciunt*, 1517 has the rare near-synonym *resartiunt*.

134

if any need repairs. And when there is no need even for this sort of work, then they very often proclaim a shorter work day, since the magistrates never force their citizens to perform useless labour. The chief aim of their constitution is that, as far as public needs permit, all citizens should be free to withdraw as much time as possible from the service of the body and devote themselves to the freedom and culture of the mind. For in that, they think, lies the happiness of life.

SOCIAL RELATIONS

Now it would be well to explain how the citizens behave towards one another, the nature of their social relations and their system of distributing goods.

Each city, then, consists of households, the households consisting generally of blood-relations. When the women grow up and are married, they move into their husbands' households. On the other hand, male children and grandchildren remain in the family, and are subject to the oldest member, unless his mind has started to fail from old age, in which case the next oldest takes his place. To keep the cities from becoming too sparse or too crowded, they take care that each household (there are six thousand of them in each city, *The number of citizens* exclusive of the surrounding countryside) should have no fewer than ten nor more than sixteen adults. They cannot, of course, regulate the number of minor children in a family.[37] The limit on adults is easily observed by transferring individuals from a household with too many into a household with too few. But if a city has too many people, the extra persons serve to make up the shortage of population in other cities. And if the population throughout the entire island exceeds the quota, they enrol citizens out of every city and plant a colony under their own laws on the mainland near them, wherever the natives have plenty of unoccupied and uncultiv-

---

[37] If an average household includes thirteen adults, then there are approximately 78,000 adults per city. Those on two-year tours of agricultural duty may or may not be included. Allowing for children and slaves, the population of each Utopian city must be in excess of 100,000, making them larger than all but the greatest European cities of the time.

The closest parallel to the Utopian arrangements is found in Plato's *Laws* (V. 740A–741A), where the ideal figure of 5,040 households for the polis is maintained by relocating children, manipulating the birthrate and establishing colonies.

indigenis si convivere secum velint. Cum volentibus coniuncti in idem vitae institutum eosdemque mores, facile coalescunt, idque utriusque populi bono. Efficiunt enim suis institutis ut ea terra utrisque abunda sit, quae alteris ante[16] parca ac maligna videbatur. Renuentes ipsorum legibus vivere, propellunt his finibus quos sibi ipsi describunt; adversus repugnantes, bello confligunt. Nam eam iustissimam belli causam ducunt quum populus quispiam eius soli quo ipse non utitur sed velut inane ac vacuum possidet, aliis tamen qui ex naturae praescripto inde nutriri debeant usum ac possessionem interdicat.

Si quando ullas ex suis urbibus aliquis casus eousque imminuerit ut ex aliis insulae partibus servato suo cuiusque urbis modo resarciri non possint (quod bis dumtaxat ab omni aevo pestis grassante saevitia fertur contigisse) remigrantibus e colonia civibus replentur. Perire enim colonias potius patiuntur quam ullam ex insulanis urbibus imminui.

Sic excludi potest otiosa turba ministrorum   Sed ad convictum civium revertor. Antiquissimus (ut dixi) praeest familiae. Ministri sunt uxores maritis et liberi parentibus atque in summa minores natu maioribus. Civitas omnis in quattuor aequales partes dividitur. In medio cuiusque partis forum est omnium rerum. Eo in certas domos opera cuiusque familiae convehuntur atque in horrea singulae seorsum species distributae sunt. Ab his quilibet paterfamilias quibus ipse suique opus habent petit ac sine pecunia, sine omni prorsus hostimento, quicquid petierit aufert. Quare enim negetur quicquam? quum et omnium rerum abunde satis sit nec timor ullus subsit ne quisquam plus quam sit opus flagitare velit? Nam cur supervacua petiturus putetur is qui certum habeat nihil *Rapacitas unde* sibi umquam defuturum? Nempe avidum ac rapacem aut timor carendi facit in omni animantum genere, aut in homine sola reddit

---

[16] *ante*, following 1516 and 1517 in preference to the *aut* of 1518M, N.

ated land. Those natives who want to live with the Utopians are
adopted by them. When such a merger occurs, the two peoples
gradually and easily blend together, sharing the same way of life
and customs, much to the advantage of both. For by their policies
the Utopians make the land yield an abundance for all, though
previously it had seemed too poor and barren even to support the
natives. But those who refuse to live under their laws they drive
out of the land they claim for themselves; and against those who
resist them, they wage war. They think it is perfectly justifiable to
make war on people who leave their land idle and waste yet forbid
the use and possession of it to others who, by the law of nature,
ought to be supported from it.[38]

If for any reason the population of one city shrinks so sharply
that it cannot be made up without reducing others below their
quota, the numbers are restored by bringing people back from the
colonies. This has happened only twice, they say, in their whole
history, both times in consequence of a frightful plague. They
would rather let their colonies disappear than allow any of the cities
on their island to get too small.

But to return to the communal life of the citizens. The oldest of
every household, as I said, is the ruler. Wives act as servants to
their husbands, children to their parents, and generally the younger
to their elders.[39] Every city is divided into four equal districts, and
in the middle of each district is a market for all kinds of commodities. Whatever each household produces is brought here and stored
in warehouses, each kind of goods in its own place. Here the head
of every household looks for what he or his family needs, and
carries off what he wants without any sort of payment or compensation. Why should anything be refused him? There is plenty
of everything, and no reason to fear that anyone will claim more
than he needs. For why would anyone be suspected of asking for
more than is needed, when he knows there will never be any shortage? Fear of want, no doubt, makes every living creature greedy

*Thus they
eliminate crowds
of idle servants*

*The sources of
greed*

---

[38] On the law of nature, see p. 11n. A fundamental principle of this law is that all
things are common; from this it follows that, as Surtz says, 'a nation may take
possession of wasteland necessary for its survival' (*CW*, IV, 416). Similar arguments were applied to colonisation of the New World – to which, as Baker-Smith
observes, the Utopians' proceedings bear 'a painful similarity' (*More's 'Utopia'*,
p. 186).

[39] It is scarcely necessary to say that this patriarchy finds strong support in innumerable classical, Biblical and later texts. See, for example, Aristotle, *Politics*
I.xii.1–2, and Ephesians 5:22–6:4. The Utopians are perhaps especially interested
in reinforcing it as a way of countering the disruptive effects supposed to be
entailed in communism (cf. p. 105).

superbia quae gloriae sibi ducit superflua rerum ostentatione ceteros antecellere, quod vitii genus in Utopiensium institutis nullum omnino locum habet.

Adiuncta sunt foris (quae commemoravi) fora cibaria, in quae non holera modo arborumque fructus[17] et panes comportantur, sed pisces praeterea, quadrupedumque et avium quicquid esculentum est, extra urbem locis appositis ubi fluento tabum ac sordes eluantur. Hinc deportant pecudes occisas depuratasque manibus famulorum. Nam neque suos cives patiuntur assuescere laniatu animalium, cuius usu clementiam, humanissimum naturae nostrae affectum, paulatim deperire putant: neque sordidum quicquam atque immundum, cuius putredine corruptus aer morbum posset invehere, perferri in urbem sinunt.

Tabes ac sordes pestem invehit civitatibus

Ex pecudum laniena didicimus et homines iugulare

Habet praeterea quilibet vicus aulas quasdam capaces, aequali ab sese invicem intervallo distantes, nomine quamque suo cognitas. Has colunt syphogranti, quarum unicuique triginta familiae, videlicet ab utroque latere quindecim, sunt ascriptae cibum ibi sumpturae. Obsonatores cuiusque aulae certa hora conveniunt in forum ac relato suorum numero cibum petunt.

Cura aegrotorum

Sed prima ratio aegrotorum habetur, qui in publicis hospitiis curantur. Nam quattuor habent in ambitu civitatis hospitia, paulo extra muros, tam capacia ut totidem oppidulis aequari possint, tum ut neque aegrotorum numerus quamlibet magnus anguste collocaretur et per hoc incommode, tum quo hi qui tali morbo tenerentur cuius contagio solet ab alio ad alium serpere longius ab aliorum coetu semoveri possint. Haec hospitia ita sunt instructa atque omnibus rebus quae ad salutem conferant referta, tum tam tenera ac sedula cura adhibetur, tam assidua medicorum peritissimorum praesentia, ut quum illuc nemo mittatur invitus, nemo tamen fere in tota urbe

---

[17] *arborumque fructus] fructusque* 1516, 1517; *quadrupedumque . . . est] carnesque* 1516, *carnesque &* 1517; *Hinc deportant]* omitted 1516, 1517; *occisas depuratasque]* 1516; *occisae depurataeque]* 1517. The erroneous omission of *Hinc deportant* in 1516 was corrected in 1517 by changing *pecudes . . . depuratasque* to the nominative case so that it could be taken with *comportantur*. In 1518M and 1518N the omitted phrase was restored. On the significance of such passages – where 1517 and 1518M, N correct 1516 differently – see Appendix, p. 273.

and rapacious, and man, besides, develops these qualities out of sheer pride, which glories in getting ahead of others by a superfluous display of possessions. But this sort of vice has no place whatever in the Utopian scheme of things.

Next to the marketplaces of which I just spoke are the food markets, where people bring all sorts of vegetables, fruit and bread. Fish, meat and poultry are also brought there from designated places not far outside the city, where running water can carry away all the blood and refuse. Bondsmen do the slaughtering and cleaning in these places: citizens are not allowed to do such work.[40] The Utopians feel that slaughtering our fellow creatures gradually destroys the sense of compassion, the finest sentiment of which our human nature is capable. Besides, they don't allow anything dirty or filthy to be brought into the city, lest the air become tainted by putrefaction and thus infectious.

Filth and refuse spread disease in cities

By butchering beasts we learn to slaughter men

Every square block has its own spacious halls, equally distant from one another, and each known by a special name. In these halls live the syphogrants. Thirty families are assigned to each hall – fifteen from each side of it – to take their meals in common.[41] The stewards of all the halls meet at a fixed time in the market and requisition food according to the number of persons for whom each is responsible.

But first consideration goes to the sick, who are cared for in public hospitals. Every city has four of these, built at the city limits slightly outside the walls, and spacious enough to appear like little towns. The hospitals are large for two reasons: so that the sick, however numerous they may be, will not be packed closely and uncomfortably together, and also so that those with contagious diseases, such as might pass from one to the other, can be isolated. These hospitals are well ordered and supplied with everything needed to cure the patients, who are nursed with tender and watchful care. Highly skilled physicians are in constant attendance. Consequently, though nobody is sent there against his will, still there

Caring for the sick

---

[40] The bondsmen (Latin *famuli*), who are mentioned only here, should possibly be distinguished from the slaves (Latin *servi*) who are referred to several times. But on p. 171 Hythloday notes that the Utopians have assigned hunting 'to their butchers, who, as I said before, are all slaves' (*servi*).

[41] Each side of each square block, then, has thirty houses – fifteen on each side of the syphogrant's hall. (Cf. p. 119.)

According to Plutarch, Lycurgus instituted the common messes of Sparta as part of his plan 'to attack luxury . . . and remove the thirst for wealth' ('Lycurgus' X). For similar reasons the institution was incorporated into the ideal commonwealths of Plato and Aristotle (*Republic* III.416E; *Politics* VII.x.10).

sit qui adversa valetudine laborans non ibi decumbere quam domi suae praeferat.

Quum aegrotorum obsonator cibos ex medicorum praescripto receperit, deinceps optima quaeque inter aulas aequabiliter pro suo cuiusque numero distribuuntur, nisi quod principis, pontificis et tranibororum respectus habetur, ac legatorum etiam et exterorum omnium (si qui sunt, qui pauci ac raro sunt): sed his quoque cum adsunt domicilia certa atque instructa parantur. Ad has aulas prandii *Convivia communia promiscuaque* cenaeque statis horis tota syphograntia convenit, aeneae tubae clangore commonefacta, nisi qui aut in hospitiis aut domi decumbunt. *Ut ubique libertatis habetur ratio, ne quid fiat a coactis* Quamquam nemo prohibetur postquam aulis est satisfactum e foro domum cibum petere, sciunt enim neminem id temere facere, nam etsi domi prandere nulli vetitum sit nemo tamen hoc libenter facit cum neque honestum habeatur et stultum sit deterioris parandi prandii sumere laborem cum lauto atque opiparum praesto apud aulam tam propinquam sit.

In hac aula ministeria omnia in quibus paulo plus sordis aut laboris est obeunt servi. *Feminae ministrae in conviviis* Ceterum coquendi parandique cibi officium et totius denique instruendi convivii solae mulieres exercent, cuiusque videlicet familiae per vices. Tribus pluribusve mensis pro numero convivarum discumbitur. Viri ad parietem, feminae exterius collocantur ut si quid his subiti oboriatur mali, quod uterum gerentibus interdum solet accidere, imperturbatis ordinibus exsurgant atque inde ad nutrices abeant.

Sedent illae quidem seorsum cum lactentibus in cenaculo quodam ad id destinato, numquam sine foco atque aqua munda nec absque cunis interim, ut et reclinare liceat infantulos et ad ignem cum velint exemptos fasciis liberare ac ludo reficere. Suae quaeque soboli nutrix est nisi aut mors aut morbus impediat. Id cum accidit, uxores syphograntorum propere nutricem quaerunt, nec id difficile est. *Laude et officio cives optime invitantur ad recte agendum* Nam quae id praestare possunt nulli officio sese offerunt libentius, quoniam et omnes eam misericordiam laude prosequuntur, et qui educatur nutricem parentis agnoscit loco.

In antro[18] *Educatio sobolis* nutricum considunt pueri omnes qui primum lustrum non explevere. Ceteri impuberes, quo in numero ducunt quicumque sexus alteriusutrius intra nubiles annos sunt, aut ministrant discumbentibus aut qui per aetatem nondum valent astant tamen atque id summo cum silentio. Utrique quod a sedentibus porrigitur eo vescuntur, nec aliud discretum prandendi tempus habent.

---

[18] *antro* ('cave') is an odd word here; a suggestion has been made (*CW*, V, Part II, 1034) to emend to *atrio*.

is hardly anyone in the whole city who would not rather be treated for an illness at the hospital than at home.

When the hospital steward has received the food prescribed for the sick by their doctors, the best of the remainder is fairly divided among the halls according to the number in each, except that special regard is paid to the governor, the high priest and the tranibors, as well as to ambassadors and foreigners, if there are any. In fact, there are very few; but when they do come, they have certain furnished houses assigned to them. At the hours of lunch and supper, a brazen trumpet summons the entire syphogranty to assemble in their hall, except for those who are bedridden in the hospitals or at home. After the halls have been served with their quotas of food, nothing prevents an individual from taking home food from the marketplace. They realise that no one would do this without good reason. For while it is not forbidden to eat at home, no one does it willingly, because it is not thought proper; and besides, it would be stupid to work at preparing a worse meal at home when there is an elegant and sumptuous one near at hand in the hall. *Meals in common, mixing all groups* *Note how freedom is granted everywhere, lest people act under compulsion*

In this hall, slaves do all the particularly dirty and heavy chores. But planning the meal, as well as preparing and cooking the food, is carried out by the women alone, with each family taking its turn. Depending on the number, they sit down at three or more tables. The men sit with their backs to the wall, the women on the outside, so that if a woman has a sudden qualm or pain, such as occasionally happens during pregnancy, she may get up without disturbing the others and go off to the nurses. *Women prepare the meals*

A separate dining room is assigned to the nurses and infants, with a plentiful supply of cradles, clean water and a warm fire. Thus the nurses may lay the infants down, or remove their swaddling clothes before the fire and let them renew their strength by playing. Each child is nursed by its own mother, unless death or illness prevents. When that happens, the wives of the syphogrants quickly find a nurse. The problem is not difficult: any woman who can volunteers more willingly than for any other service, since everyone applauds her kindheartedness, and the child itself regards its nurse as its natural mother. *Honour and praise incite people to act properly*

Children under the age of five sit together in the nurses' den. All other minors, among whom they include boys and girls up to the age of marriage, either wait on table, or, if not old and strong enough for that, stand by in absolute silence. Both groups eat whatever is handed to them by those sitting at the table, and have no other set time for their meals. *Raising the young*

In medio primae mensae, qui summus locus est et cui (nam ea mensa suprema in parte cenaculi transversa est) totus conventus conspicitur, syphograntus cum uxore considet. His adiunguntur duo ex natu maximis. Sedent enim per omnes mensas quaterni. At si templum in ea syphograntia situm est, sacerdos eiusque uxor cum syphogranto sedent ut praesideant. Ab utraque parte collocantur iuniores, post senes rursus, atque hoc pacto per totam domum; et aequales inter se iunguntur et dissimilibus tamen immiscentur, quod ideo ferunt institutum ut senum gravitas ac reverentia (quum nihil ita in mensa fieri dicive potest ut eos ab omni parte vicinos effugiat) iuniores ab improba verborum gestuumque licentia cohibeat.

Ciborum fercula non a primo loco deinceps apponuntur, sed senioribus primum omnibus (quorum insignes loci sunt) optimus quisque cibus infertur, deinde reliquis aequaliter ministratur. At senes lautitias suas (quarum non tanta erat copia ut posset totam per domum affatim distribui) pro suo arbitratu circumsedentibus impertiuntur. Sic et maioribus natu suus servatur honos et commodi tantundem tamen ad omnes pervenit.

Omne prandium cenamque ab aliqua lectione auspicantur quae ad mores faciat, sed brevi tamen, ne fastidio sit. Ab hac seniores honestos sermones sed neque tristes ac infacetos ingerunt. At nec longis logis totum occupant prandium, quin audiunt libenter iuvenes quoque, atque adeo de industria provocant quo et indolis cuiusque et ingenii per convivii libertatem prodentis sese capiant experimentum.

Prandia breviuscula sunt, cenae largiores, quod labor illa, has somnus et nocturna quies excipit, quam illi ad salubrem concoctionem magis efficacem putant. Nulla cena sine musica transigitur, nec ullis caret secunda mensa bellariis. Odores incendunt et unguenta spargunt nihilque non faciunt quod exhilarare convivas possit. Sunt enim hanc in partem aliquanto procliviores ut nullum voluptatis genus (ex quo nihil sequatur incommodi) censeant interdictum.

Hoc pacto igitur in urbe convivunt: at ruri, qui longius ab sese dissiti sunt, omnes domi quisque suae comedunt. Nulli enim famil-

Sacerdos supra principem. At nunc etiam et episcopi eis mancipiorum vice sunt

Iuniores maioribus admixti

Senum habita ratio

Id hodie vix monachi observant

Sermones in conviviis

Id hodie medici damnant

Musica in convivio

Voluptas innoxia non aspernanda

At the middle of the first table sits the syphogrant with his wife. This is the place of greatest honour, and from this table, which is placed at the highest level of the hall and crosswise to the other tables, the whole gathering can be seen. Two of the eldest sit next to them – for the seating is always by groups of four. But if there is a church in the district, the priest and his wife sit with the syphogrant so as to preside. On both sides of them sit younger people, next to them older people again, and so through the hall: thus those of about the same age sit together, yet are mingled with others of a different age. The reason for this, as they explain it, is that the dignity of the aged, and the respect due to them, may restrain the younger people from improper freedom of words or gestures, since nothing said or done at table can pass unnoticed by the old, who are present on every side.

Priest before prince. But now even bishops act as servants to royalty

Young mixed with old

Dishes of food are not served down the tables in order from top to bottom, but all the old persons, who are seated in conspicuous places, are served first with the best food, and then equal shares are given to the rest. The old people, as they feel inclined, give their neighbours a share of those delicacies which were not plentiful enough to go around. Thus due respect is paid to seniority, yet everyone enjoys some of the benefits.

Respect for the elderly

They begin every lunch and supper with some reading on a moral topic,[42] but keep it brief lest it become a bore. Taking their cue from this, the elders introduce proper topics of conversation, but not gloomy or dull ones. They never monopolise the conversation with long monologues, but are eager to hear what the young people say. In fact, they deliberately draw them out, in order to discover the natural temper and quality of each one's mind, as revealed in the freedom of mealtime talk.

Nowadays even monks scarcely do this

Table talk

Their lunches are light, their suppers more generous, because lunch is followed by work, supper by rest and a night's sleep, which they think particularly helpful to good digestion. No evening meal passes without music, and the dessert course is never scanted; they burn incense and scatter perfume, omitting nothing which will cheer up the diners. For they are somewhat inclined to think that no kind of pleasure is forbidden, provided harm does not come of it.

Modern physicians condemn this practice

Music at mealtimes

Innocent pleasures are not to be rejected

This is the pattern of life in the city; but in the country, where they are farther removed from neighbours, they all eat in their

---

[42] Humanists were fond of this ancient social custom – which, as the gloss implies, lingered longest in the monasteries. Stapleton says it was the practice at More's table (*The Life and Illustrious Martyrdom of Sir Thomas More*, p. 89).

iae quicquam ad victum deest, quippe a quibus id totum venit quo
vescantur urbici.

DE PEREGRINATIONE UTOPIENSIUM

At si quos aut amicorum alia in urbe commorantium aut ipsius
etiam videndi loci desiderium ceperit, a syphograntis ac traniboris 5
suis veniam facile impetrant, nisi si quis usus impediat. Mittitur
ergo simul numerus aliquis cum epistula principis quae et datam
peregrinandi copiam testatur et reditus diem praescribit. Vehiculum
datur cum servo publico qui agat boves et curet. Ceterum nisi mulieres in coetu habeant, vehiculum velut onus et impedimentum 10
remittitur. Toto itinere cum nihil secum efferant, nihil defit tamen,
ubique enim domi sunt. Si quo in loco diutius uno die commoren-
tur, suam ibi quisque artem exercet atque ab artis eiusdem opificibus humanissime tractantur.

Si semet auctore quisquam extra suos fines vagetur, deprehensus 15
sine principis diplomate contumeliose habitus pro fugitivo reducitur
castigatus acriter. Idem ausus denuo servitute plectitur. Quod si
quem libido incessat per suae civitatis agros palandi venia patris
et consentiente coniuge non prohibetur. Sed in quodcumque rus
pervenerit, nullus ante cibus datur quam antemeridianum operis 20
pensum aut quantum ante cenam ibi laborari solet absolverit. Hac
lege quovis intra suae urbis fines ire licet. Erit enim non minus
utilis urbi quam si in urbe esset.

Iam videtis quam nulla sit usquam otiandi licentia, nullus inertiae
praetextus, nulla taberna vinaria, nulla cervisiaria, nusquam lupanar, 25
nulla corruptelae occasio, nullae latebrae, conciliabulum nullum,
sed omnium praesentes oculi necessitatem aut consueti laboris aut
otii non inhonesti faciunt. Quem populi morem necesse est omnium
rerum copiam sequi. Atque ea quum aequabiliter ad omnes perven-
iat fit nimirum ut inops esse nemo aut mendicus possit. 30

In senatu Amaurotico[19] (quem, uti dixi, terni quotannis omni ex
urbe frequentant), ubi primum constiterit quae res quoque loco

*O sanctam
rempublicam, et
vel Christianis
imitandam*

*Aequabilitas facit
ut omnibus
sufficiat*

---

[19] 1516 prints *Mentirano* instead of *Amaurotico* as in the other three texts. On the
significance of this variant, see Appendix, p. 271.

own homes. No family lacks for food since, after all, whatever city-dwellers eat comes originally from those in the country.

THE TRAVELS OF THE UTOPIANS

Any individuals who want to visit friends living in another city, or simply to see the place itself, can easily obtain permission from their syphogrants and tranibors, unless there is some need for them at home. They travel together in groups, taking a letter from the governor granting leave to travel and fixing a day of return. They are given a wagon and a public slave to drive the oxen and look after them, but unless women are in the company they dispense with the wagon as a burden and a hindrance. Wherever they go, though they take nothing with them, they never lack for anything, because they are at home everywhere. If they stay more than a day in one place, each one practises his trade there, and is kindly received by his fellow artisans.

Anyone who takes upon himself to leave his district without permission, and is caught without the governor's letter, is treated with contempt, brought back as a runaway, and severely punished. If he is bold enough to try it a second time, he is made a slave. Anyone who is eager to stroll about his own district is not prevented, provided he first obtains his father's permission and his spouse's consent. But wherever he goes in the countryside, he gets no food until he has completed either a morning's or an afternoon's stint of work.[43] On these terms he may go where he pleases within his own district, yet be just as useful to the city as if he were in it.

So you see that nowhere is there any chance to loaf or any pretext for evading work; there are no wine-bars, or ale-houses, or brothels; no chances for corruption; no hiding places; no spots for secret meetings. Because they live in the full view of all, they are bound to be either working at their usual trades or enjoying their leisure in a respectable way. Such customs must necessarily result in plenty of life's good things, and since they share everything equally, it follows that no one can ever be reduced to poverty or forced to beg.

In the senate at Amaurot (to which, as I said before, three representatives come every year from each city), they first determine

O sacred society, worthy of imitation, even by Christians!

Equality for all results in enough for each

---

[43] The Utopians in this rule agree with St Paul: II Thessalonians 3:10.

abundet, rursum cuius alicubi malignior proventus fuerit, alterius inopiam alterius protinus ubertas explet, atque id gratuito faciunt, nihil vicissim ab his recipientes quibus donant. Sed quae de suis rebus unicuipiam urbi dederint nihil ab ea repetentes, ab alia cui nihil impenderunt quibus egent accipiunt. Ita tota insula velut una 5 familia est.

Respublica nihil aliud quam magna quaedam familia est

At postquam satis provisum ipsis est (quod non antea factum censent quam in biennium propter anni sequentis eventum prospexerint), tum ex his quae supersunt magnam vim frumenti, mellis, lanae, lini, ligni, cocci et conchyliorum, vellerum, cerae, sebi, 10 corii, ad haec animalium quoque in alias regiones exportant. Quarum rerum omnium septimam partem inopibus eius regionis dono dant, reliquam pretio mediocri venditant. Quo ex commercio non eas modo merces quibus domi egent (nam id fere nihil est praeter ferrum) sed argenti atque auri praeterea magnam vim in 15 patriam reportant. Cuius rei diutina consuetudine supra quam credi possit ubique iam earum rerum copia abundant. Itaque nunc parum pensi habent praesente ne pecunia an in diem vendant, multoque maximam partem habeant in nominibus, in quibus tamen faciendis non privatorum umquam, sed confectis ex more instrumentis pub- 20 licam urbis fidem sequuntur. Civitas ubi solutionis dies advenerit a privatis debitoribus exigit creditum atque in aerarium redigit: eiusque pecuniae quoad ab Utopiensibus repetatur usura fruitur. Illi maximam partem numquam repetunt. Nam quae res apud se nullum habet usum, eam ab his auferre quibus usui est haud aequum 25 censent. Ceterum si res ita poscat ut eius aliquam partem alii populo mutuam daturi sint, tum demum poscunt, aut quum bellum geren- dum est, quam in rem unam totum illum thesaurum quem habent domi servant, uti aut extremis in periculis aut in subitis praesidio sit, potissimum quo milites externos (quos libentius quam suos cives 30 obiciunt discrimini) immodico stipendio conducant, gnari multitud- ine pecuniae hostes ipsos plerumque mercabiles, et vel proditione vel infestis etiam signis inter se committi.

Negotiatio Utopiensium

Ut nusquam non meminerunt suae communitatis

Qua ratione possit esse utilis[20] pecunia

Satius est bellum pecunia aut arte declinare quam multa sanguinis humani iactura gerere

Hanc ob causam inaestimabilem thesaurum servant; at non ut thesaurum tamen sed ita habent quomodo me narrare profecto 35

---

[20] The texts print *vilis*; but we accept Lupton's emendation (correcting his misprint of *utiles* to *utilis*), as truer to the immediate context.

where there are shortages and surpluses, and promptly satisfy one district's shortage with another's surplus. These are outright gifts; those who give get nothing in return from those who receive. Though they give freely to one city asking for nothing in return, they get what they need from another to which they gave nothing. Thus the whole island is like a single family.[44]

The commonwealth is nothing but a kind of extended family

After they have accumulated enough for themselves – and this they consider to be a full two-years' store, because next year's crop is always uncertain – then they export their surpluses to other countries: great quantities of grain, honey, wool, flax, timber, scarlet and purple dyestuffs, hides, wax, tallow and leather, as well as livestock. One seventh of all these things they give freely to the poor of the importing country, and the rest they sell at moderate prices. In exchange they receive not only such goods as they lack at home (in fact, about the only important thing they lack is iron) but immense quantities of silver and gold. They have been carrying on trade for a long time now, and have accumulated a greater supply of the precious metals than you would believe possible. As a result, they now care very little whether they sell for cash or on credit, and most payments to them actually take the form of promissory notes. However, in all such transactions, they never trust individuals but insist that the foreign city become officially responsible. When the day of payment comes, the city collects the money from private debtors, puts it into the treasury, and enjoys the use of it till the Utopians claim payment. Most of it, in fact, is never claimed. The Utopians think it is hardly right to take what they don't need away from people who do need it. But if there is a need to lend some part of the money to another nation, then they call it in – as they do also when they must wage war. This is the only reason that they keep such an immense treasure at home, as a protection against extreme peril or sudden emergency. They use it above all to hire, at extravagant rates of pay, foreign mercenaries, whom they would much rather risk in battle than their own citizens. They know very well that for large enough sums of money many of the enemy's soldiers themselves can be bought off or set at odds with one another, either openly or secretly.

Utopian business dealings

Nowhere do they fail to be mindful of their community

How money can be useful

Better to avoid war by bribery or guile than to wage it with great loss of human blood

For this reason, therefore, they have a vast treasure in reserve, but they do not keep it like a treasure. I'm really quite ashamed to

---

[44] According to Plutarch, Lycurgus, returning from a journey just after harvest, and seeing 'the heaps of grain standing parallel and equal to one another . . . said to them that were by: "All Laconia looks like a family estate newly divided among many brothers"' ('Lycurgus' VIII.4).

O artificem

deterret pudor, metuentem ne fidem oratio non sit habitura, quod eo iustius vereor quo magis mihi sum conscius, nisi vidissem praesens, quam aegre potuissem perduci ipse ut alteri idem recensenti crederem. Necesse est enim fere quam quicque est ab eorum qui audiunt moribus alienum, tam idem procul illis abesse a fide. 5 Quamquam prudens rerum aestimator minus fortasse mirabitur, quum reliqua eorum instituta tam longe ab nostris differant, si argenti quoque atque auri usus ad ipsorum potius quam ad nostri moris rationem accommodetur. Nempe quum pecunia non utantur ipsi sed in eum servent eventum qui ut potest usu venire ita fieri 10 potest ut numquam incidat, interim aurum argentumque (unde ea fit) sic apud se habent ut ab nullo pluris aestimetur quam rerum

Aurum ferro vilius, quantum ad usum attinet

ipsarum natura meretur, qua quis non videt quam longe infra ferrum sunt? ut sine quo non hercule magis quam absque igni atque aqua vivere mortales queant, quum interim auro argentoque nullum 15 usum quo non facile careamus natura tribuerit, nisi hominum stultitia pretium raritati fecisset,[21] quin contra, velut parens indulgentissima, optima quaeque in propatulo posuerit, ut aerem, aquam ac tellurem ipsam, longissime vero vana ac nihil profutura semoverit.

Ergo haec metalla si apud eos in turrim aliquam abstruderentur, 20 princeps ac senatus in suspicionem venire posset (ut est vulgi stulta sollertia) ne, deluso per technam populo, ipsi aliquo inde commodo fruerentur. Porro si phialas inde aliaque id genus opera fabre excusa conficerent, siquando incidisset occasio ut conflanda sint rursus atque in militum eroganda stipendium, vident nimirum fore ut aegre 25 patiantur avelli quae semel in delitiis habere coepissent. His rebus uti occurrant, excogitavere quandam rationem, ut reliquis ipsorum institutis consentaneam, ita ab nostris (apud quos aurum tanti fit ac tam diligenter conditur) longissime abhorrentem, eoque nisi peritis non credibilem. Nam quum in fictilibus e terra vitroque eleg- 30

O magnificam auri contumeliam

antissimis quidem illis sed vilibus tamen edant bibantque, ex auro atque argento non in communibus aulis modo sed in privatis etiam domibus matellas passim ac sordidissima quaeque vasa conficiunt. Ad haec catenas et crassas compedes quibus coercent servos eisdem

---

[21] *quum . . . fecisset* was omitted from 1516.

tell you how they do keep it, because you probably won't believe me; I would not have believed it myself if someone else had simply *O crafty fellow!* told me about it, but I was there and saw it with my own eyes. As a general rule, the more different anything is from what the listeners are used to, the harder it is to believe. But considering that all their other customs are so unlike ours, a sensible judge will perhaps not be surprised that they treat gold and silver quite differently from the way we do. After all, they never do use money among themselves, but keep it only for a contingency that may or may not actually arise. So in the meanwhile they keep gold and silver (of which money is made) in such a way that no one will value them beyond what the metals themselves deserve. Anyone can see, for *As far as utility* example, that iron in itself is far superior to either;[45] men could not *goes, gold is* *inferior to iron* live without iron, by heaven, any more than without fire or water. But Nature granted to gold and silver no function with which we cannot easily dispense. Human folly has made them precious because they are rare. In contrast, Nature, like a most indulgent mother, has placed her best gifts out in the open, like air, water and the earth itself; vain and unprofitable things she has hidden away in remote places.

And so, if in Utopia gold and silver were kept locked up in some tower, smart fools among the common people might concoct a story that the governor and senate were out to cheat ordinary folk and get some advantage for themselves. Of course, the gold and silver might be put into plate-ware and such handiwork, but then they see that in case of necessity the people would not want to give up articles on which they had begun to fix their hearts – only to melt them down for soldiers' pay. To avoid these problems they thought of a plan which conforms with the rest of their institutions as sharply as it contrasts with our own. Unless one has actually seen it working, their plan may seem incredible, because we prize gold so highly and are so careful about guarding it. While they eat from earthenware dishes and drink from glass cups, finely made but inexpensive, their chamber pots and all their humblest vessels, *O magnificent* for use in the common halls and even in private homes, are made *scorn for gold!* of gold and silver.[46] Moreover, the chains and heavy shackles of

---

[45] More expresses the same view *in propria persona* in two works of 1534: *A Dialogue of Comfort against Tribulation* (CW, XII, 207); *A Treatise upon the Passion* (CW, XIII, 8).

[46] Tacitus reports of the ancient Germans that 'One may see among them silver vessels . . . treated as of no more value than earthenware' (*Germania* 5). Vespucci notes the Indians' indifference to gold and gems (*Four Voyages*, p. 98), as does the explorer Pietro Martire d'Anghiera (1457–1526), who tells of a tribe that

Aurum gestamen   ex metallis operantur. Postremo quoscumque aliquod crimen
infamium   infames facit ab horum auribus anuli dependent aurei, digitos aurum
cingit, aurea torques ambit collum, et caput denique auro vincitur.
Ita omnibus curant modis uti apud se aurum argentumque in igno-
minia sint, atque hoc pacto fit ut haec metalla, quae ceterae gentes   5
non minus fere dolenter ac viscera sua distrahi patiuntur, apud Utopienses si semel omnia res postularet efferri nemo sibi iacturam
unius fecisse assis videretur.

Margaritas praeterea legunt in litoribus quin in rupibus quibusdam adamantes ac pyropos quoque: neque tamen quaerunt, sed   10
Gemmae   oblatos casu perpoliunt. His ornant infantulos qui, ut primis pueri-
puerorum deliciae   iae annis talibus ornamentis gloriantur ac superbiunt, sic ubi plusculum accrevit aetatis, cum animadvertunt eiusmodi nugis non nisi
pueros uti, nullo parentum monitu sed suomet ipsorum pudore
deponunt, non aliter ac nostri pueri quum grandescunt nuces, bullas   15
et pupas abiciunt.

Itaque haec tam diversa ab reliquis gentibus instituta quam
diversas itidem animorum affectiones pariant[22] numquam aeque
Elegantissima   mihi atque in Anemoliorum legatis inclaruit. Venerunt hi Amauro-
fabula   tum (dum ego aderam) et quoniam magnis de rebus tractatum veni-   20
ebant, adventum eorum terni illi cives ex qualibet urbe praevener-
ant. Sed omnes finitimarum gentium legati, qui eo ante appulerant,
quibus Utopiensium perspecti mores erant, apud quos sumptuoso
vestitui nihil honoris haberi intelligebant, sericum contemptui esse,
aurum etiam infame sciebant, cultu quam poterant modestissimo   25
venire consueverant. At Anemolii, quod longius aberant ac minus
cum illis commercii habuerant, quum accepissent eodem omnes
eoque rudi corporis cultu esse, persuasi non habere eos quo non
utebantur, ipsi etiam superbi magis quam sapientes decreverunt
apparatus elegantia deos quosdam repraesentare et miserorum   30
oculos Utopiensium ornatus sui splendore praestringere.

Itaque ingressi sunt legati tres cum comitibus centum, omnes
vestitu versicolori, plerique serico, legati ipsi (nam domi nobiles

---

[22] *pariant*] 1517; *pariāt*] 1516; *pariat*] 1518M, N.

slaves are also made of these metals. Finally, criminals who are to *Gold the mark of infamy* bear the mark of some disgraceful act are forced to wear golden rings in their ears and on their fingers, golden chains around their necks, and even golden headbands. Thus they hold up gold and silver to scorn in every conceivable way. As a result, if they had to part with their entire supply of these metals, which other people give up with as much agony as if they were being disembowelled, no one would feel it any more than the loss of a penny.

They pick up pearls by the seashore, and also diamonds and garnets from certain cliffs, but never go out of set purpose to look for them.[47] If they happen to find some, they polish them and give *Gems the playthings of children* them as decorations to the children, who feel proud and pleased with such ornaments during the early years of childhood. But when they have grown a bit older and notice that only small children like this kind of toy, they lay them aside. Their parents don't have to say anything; they simply put these trifles away out of shame, just as our children, when they grow up, put away their marbles, baubles and dolls.

These customs so different from those of other people also produce a quite different cast of mind: this never became clearer to me than it did in the case of the Anemolian[48] ambassadors, who came to *A neat tale* Amaurot while I was there. Because they came to discuss important business, the national council had assembled ahead of time, three citizens from each city. The ambassadors from nearby nations, who had visited Utopia before and knew the local customs, understood that fine clothing was not respected in that land, silk was despised, and gold a badge of contempt; therefore they always came in the very plainest of their clothes. But the Anemolians, who lived farther off and had had fewer dealings with them, had heard only that they all dressed alike and very simply; so they took for granted that their hosts had nothing to wear that they didn't put on. Being themselves rather more proud than wise, they decided to dress as elegantly as the very gods, and dazzle the eyes of the poor Utopians with the splendour of their garb.

And so the three ambassadors made a grand entry with a suite of a hundred attendants, all in clothing of many colours, and most

'used kitchen and other common utensils made of gold' (*De Orbe Novo: The Eight Decades of Peter Martyr D'Anghera*, trans. Francis A. MacNutt, 2 vols. (New York and London, 1912; rpt New York, 1970), I, 221).

[47] Similarly, Tacitus reports of the ancient Britons that though their sea produces pearls, 'they are gathered only when thrown up on shore' (*Agricola* 12).

[48] From *anemolios*, 'windy'.

erant) amictu aureo, magnis torquibus et inauribus aureis, ad haec
anulis aureis in manibus, monilibus insuper appensis in pileo quae
margaritis ac gemmis adfulgebant, omnibus postremo rebus ornati
quae apud Utopienses aut servorum supplicia aut infamium dede-
cora aut puerorum nugamenta fuere. Itaque operae pretium erat ₅
videre quo pacto cristas erexerint ubi suum ornatum cum Utopiensium vestitu (nam in plateis sese populus effuderat) contulere. Contraque non minus erat voluptatis considerare quam longe sua eos
spes exspectatioque fefellerat, quamque²³ longe ab ea existimatione
aberant, quam se consecuturos putaverant. Nempe Utopiensium ₁₀
oculis omnium, exceptis perquam paucis qui alias gentes aliqua
idonea de causa inviserant, totus ille splendor apparatus pudendus
videbatur, et infimum quemque pro dominis reverenter salutantes,
legatos ipsos ex aurearum usu catenarum pro servis habitos, sine
ullo prorsus honore praetermiserunt. Quin pueros quoque vidisses ₁₅
qui gemmas ac margaritas abiecerant ubi in legatorum pileis adfixas
conspexerunt, compellare matrem ac latus fodere: En mater, quam
ὦ τεχνίτην magnus nebulo margaritis adhuc et gemmulis utitur, ac si esset
puerulus?²⁴ At parens serio etiam illa: Tace, inquit, fili: est, opinor,
quispiam e morionibus legatorum. ₂₀

Alii catenas illas aureas reprehendere utpote nullius usus quippe
tam graciles ut eas facile servus infringere, tam laxas rursus uti quum
fuerit libitum possit excutere et solutus ac liber quovis aufugere.

Verum legati postquam ibi unum atque alterum diem versati
tantam auri vim in tanta vilitate conspexerunt, nec in minore contu- ₂₅
melia quam apud se honore habitam vidissent, ad haec in unius
fugitivi servi catenas compedesque plus auri atque argenti con-
gestum quam totus ipsorum trium apparatus constiterat, sub-
sidentibus pennis, omnem illum cultum quo sese tam arroganter
extulerant pudefacti seposuerunt, maxime vero postquam famil- ₃₀
iarius cum Utopiensibus collocuti mores eorum atque opiniones
didicere.

---

²³ The *quamquam* of 1518M should be *quamque*, as in the other texts.
²⁴ For *puerulus* ('little boy'), 1518N substitutes *parvulus* ('child').

in silk. Being noblemen at home, the ambassadors were arrayed in cloth of gold, with heavy gold chains round their necks, gold earrings, gold rings on their fingers and sparkling strings of pearls and gems hanging on their caps. In fact, they were decked out in all the articles which in Utopia are used to punish slaves, shame wrongdoers or entertain infants. It was a sight to see how they strutted when they compared their finery with the dress of the Utopians, who had poured out into the streets. But it was just as funny to see how wide they fell of the mark, and how far they were from getting the consideration they thought they would get. Except for a very few Utopians who for some good reason had visited foreign countries, all the onlookers considered this splendid pomp a mark of disgrace. They therefore bowed to all the humblest of the party as lords, and took the ambassadors, because of their golden chains, to be slaves, passing them by without any reverence at all. You might have seen children, who had themselves thrown away their pearls and gems, nudge their mothers when they saw the ambassadors' jewelled caps and say, 'Look at that big lout, mother, who's still wearing pearls and jewels as if he were a little boy!' But the *O what a craftsman!* mother, in all seriousness, would say, 'Quiet, son, I think he is one of the ambassadors' fools.'

Others found fault with the golden chains as useless because they were so flimsy any slave could break them, and so loose that he could easily shake them off and run away anywhere he wanted, foot-loose and fancy-free.

But after the ambassadors had spent a couple of days among the Utopians, they saw the immense amounts of gold which were as thoroughly despised there as they were prized at home. They saw too that more gold and silver went into making chains and shackles for a single runaway slave than into costuming all three of them. Somewhat ashamed and crestfallen, they put away all the finery in which they had strutted so arrogantly – especially after they had talked with the Utopians enough to learn their customs and opinions.[49]

[49] The story of the Anemolian ambassadors owes something to Lucian's 'The Wisdom of Nigrinus', in which a visiting millionaire makes a fool of himself by stalking around Athens in a purple robe: 'with his crowd of attendants and his gay clothes and jewelry, ... [he] expected to be looked up to as a happy man. But they thought the creature unfortunate, and undertook to educate him ... His gay clothes and his purple gown they stripped from him very neatly by making fun of his flowery colours, saying "Spring already?" "How did that peacock get here?" "Perhaps it's his mother's" and the like' (sect. 13). Herodotus tells how an Ethiopian king scorned the gift of a golden necklace and armlets brought by emissaries of Cambyses: 'the king smiled, and, thinking them to be

Dubius dixit ob
gemmas
facticias aut certe
dubium dixit
exiguum ac
malignum

Mirantur illi siquidem quemquam esse mortalium quem exiguae gemmulae aut lapilli dubius oblectet fulgor, cui quidem stellam aliquam atque ipsum denique solem liceat intueri, aut quemquam tam insanum esse ut nobilior ipse sibi ob tenuioris lanae filum videatur, siquidem hanc ipsam (quantumvis tenui filo sit) ovis olim gestavit nec aliud tamen interim quam ovis fuit. Mirantur item aurum suapte natura tam inutile nunc ubique gentium aestimari tanti ut homo ipse per quem atque adeo in cuius usum id pretii obtinuit minoris multo quam aurum ipsum aestimetur, usqueadeo ut plumbeus quispiam et cui non plus ingenii sit quam stipiti nec minus

Quam vere et
quam apte

etiam improbus quam stultus, multos tamen et sapientes et bonos viros in servitute habeat, ob id dumtaxat quod ei magnus contigit aureorum numismatum cumulus; quem si qua fortuna aut aliqua legum stropha (quae nihil minus ac fortuna ipsa summis ima permiscet), ab ero illo ad abiectissimum totius familiae suae nebulonem transtulerit, fit nimirum paulo post ut in famuli sui famulitium concedat velut appendix additamentumque numismatum.

Quanto plus
sapiunt Utopiani
quam
Christianorum
vulgus

Ceterum multo magis eorum mirantur ac detestantur insaniam qui divitibus illis quibus neque debent quicquam neque sunt obnoxii, nullo alio respectu quam quod divites sunt, honores tantum non divinos impendunt, idque cum eos tam sordidos atque avaros cognoscunt ut habeant certo certius ex tanto nummorum cumulo viventibus illis ne unum quidem nummulum umquam ad se venturum.

Has atque huiusmodi opiniones partim ex educatione conceperunt, in ea educti republica cuius instituta longissime ab his stultitiae generibus absunt, partim ex doctrina et literis. Nam etsi haud multi cuiusque urbis sunt qui ceteris exonerati laboribus soli disciplinae deputantur (hi videlicet in quibus a pueritia egregiam indolem, eximium ingenium, atque animum ad bonas artes propensum deprehendere), tamen omnes pueri literis imbuuntur, et populi bona pars viri feminaeque per totam vitam horas illas quas ab operibus liberas diximus in literis collocant.

Studia et
disciplinae
Utopiensium

Disciplinas ipsorum lingua perdiscunt. Est enim neque verborum inops nec insuavis auditu nec ulla fidelior animi interpres est. Eadem fere (nisi quod ubique corruptior alibi aliter) magnam eius

They marvel that any mortal can take pleasure in the dubious sparkle of a tiny little jewel or gemstone, when he has a star, or the sun itself, to look at. They are amazed at the madness of any man who considers himself a nobler fellow because he wears clothing of specially fine wool. No matter how fine the thread, they say, a sheep wore it once, and still was nothing but a sheep.[50] They are surprised that gold, a useless commodity in itself, is everywhere valued so highly that man himself, who for his own purposes conferred this value on it, is considered far less valuable than the gold – so much so that a dunderhead who has no more brains than a post, and who is as vicious as he is foolish, should command a great many wise and good men, simply because he happens to have a big pile of gold coins. Yet if this master should lose his money to the lowest rascal in his household (as can happen by chance or through some legal trick – for the law can produce reversals as violent as Fortune herself), he would soon become the servant of his servant, as if he were personally attached to the coins, and a mere appendage to them. Even more than this, they are appalled at those people who practically worship a rich man, though they neither owe him anything nor are under his thumb in any way. What impresses them is simply the fact that the man is rich. Yet all the while they know he is so mean and grasping that as long as he lives not a single little penny out of that great mound of money will ever come their way.

'Dubious' because the gems are fake, or their glitter is feeble and scanty

How true and how apt!

How much wiser are the Utopians than the ruck of Christians

These and the like attitudes the Utopians have picked up partly from their upbringing, since the institutions of their commonwealth are completely opposed to such folly, partly from instruction and good books. For though not many people in each city are excused from labour and assigned to scholarship full-time (these are persons who from childhood have given evidence of excellent character, unusual intelligence and devotion to learning), every child gets an introduction to good literature, and throughout their lives many people, men and women alike, devote the free time I've mentioned to reading.

They study all the branches of learning in their native tongue, which is not deficient in terminology or unpleasant in sound and adapts itself as well as any to the expression of thought. This same language, or something close to it, is diffused through much of that

Training and studies of the Utopians

fetters, said: "We have stronger chains than these"' – a claim that he demonstrated by taking the emissaries to a prison where they were bound with golden fetters (III.22–3).

[50] The source is Lucian's 'Demonax' (sect. 41). More repeated the idea years later in *A Treatise upon the Passion* (*CW*, XIII, 8).

orbis plagam pervagatur.

Ex omnibus his philosophis quorum nomina sunt in hoc noto nobis orbe celebria ante nostrum adventum ne fama quidem cuius-
Musica, quam eo pervenerat, et tamen in musica, dialecticaque ac numerandi
Dialectica,
Arithmetica et metiendi scientia eadem fere quae nostri illi veteres invenere. ₅
Ceterum ut antiquos omnibus prope rebus exaequant, ita nupero-
Apparet hoc loco rum inventis dialecticorum longe sunt impares. Nam ne ullam
subesse nasum quidem regulam invenerunt earum quas de restrictionibus, ampli-
ficationibus ac suppositionibus acutissime excogitatis in parvis
logicalibus passim hic ediscunt pueri. Porro secundas intentiones ₁₀
tam longe abest ut investigare suffecerint ut nec hominem ipsum in
communi, quem vocant, quamquam (ut scitis) plane colosseum et
quovis gigante maiorem, tum a nobis praeterea digito demon-
Astrologia stratum, nemo tamen eorum videre potuerit. At sunt in astrorum
cursu et caelestium orbium motu peritissimi. Quin instrumenta ₁₅
quoque diversis figuris sollerter excogitarunt, quibus solis ac lunae
et ceterorum item astrorum quae in ipsorum horizonte visuntur
At hi regnant motiones ac situs exactissime comprehensos habent. Ceterum amic-
inter Christianos
hodie itias atque errantium discidia siderum ac totam denique illam ex

part of the world, except that everywhere else it is corrupted to various degrees.

Before we came there the Utopians had never so much as heard about a single one of those philosophers[51] whose names are so celebrated in our part of the world. Yet in music, dialectic, arithmetic and geometry[52] they have found out just about the same things as our great men of the past. But while they equal the ancients in almost all subjects, they are far from matching the inventions of our modern logicians. In fact they have not discovered even one of those elaborate rules about restrictions, amplifications and suppositions which young men here study in the *Parva logicalia*.[53] They are so far from being able to speculate on 'second intentions'[54] that not one of them was able to see 'man-in-general', though we pointed straight at him with our fingers, and he is, as you well know, colossal and bigger than any giant.[55] On the other hand, they have learned to plot expertly the courses of the stars and the movements of the heavenly bodies. To this end they have devised a number of different instruments by which they compute with the greatest exactness the course and position of the sun, the moon and the other stars that are visible in their area of the sky. As for the conjunctions and oppositions of the planets and that whole deceitful

Music, dialectic and mathematics

The passage seems a bit satiric

The study of the stars

Yet these astrologers are revered by Christians to this day

51 As the following sentences indicate, 'philosophers' is used here in the old, broad sense that includes those learned in the natural and mathematical sciences as well as students of metaphysics and moral philosophy.

52 Music, arithmetic and geometry, together with astronomy (below), constitute the advanced division – the *quadrivium* – of the traditional Seven Liberal Arts. Dialectic joins with grammar and rhetoric to constitute the elementary division – the *trivium*. Grammar and rhetoric would be encompassed in the Utopians' study of 'good literature'.

53 Of several late-medieval treatises called *Parva logicalia*, the best-known consists of the second half of the *Summulae logicales* of Peter of Spain (d. 1277). More mounts a sustained attack on the 'modern logicians' (i.e., scholastic dialecticians) in his long open letter to the Dutch theologian and philologist Maarten van Dorp, composed in the same year (1515) in which he wrote Book II of *Utopia*. In the letter, More suggests that the *Parva logicalia* is 'so called probably because it contains little logic': 'it is worth having a look at its chapters on so-called suppositions, on ampliations, restrictions, and appellations, and everywhere else, to see all of the pointless and even false little precepts it does contain' (*CW*, XV, 29). On the technical terms, see the discussion in Daniel Kinney's introduction to the letter (XV, liv–lv).

54 'First intentions' are the direct apprehensions of things; 'second intentions' are purely abstract conceptions, derived from considering the relations of first intentions.

55 The Utopians' blindness to 'man-in-general' (i.e., man as a 'universal') makes them just opposite to the scholastic philosophers mocked by Erasmus' Folly, who, 'though ignorant even of themselves and sometimes not able to see the ditch or stone lying in their path, either because most of them are half-blind or because their minds are far away . . . still boast that they can see ideas, universals, separate forms, prime matters, quiddities, ecceities' (*CWE*, XXVII, 126).

astris divinandi imposturam ne somniant quidem. Imbres, ventos ac ceteras tempestatum vicissitudines signis quibusdam longo per-

Physica omnium
incertissima

spectis usu praesentiunt. Sed de causis earum rerum omnium et de fluxu maris eiusque salsitate et in summa de caeli mundique origine ac natura, partim eadem quae veteres philosophi nostri disserunt, 5 partim ut illi inter se dissident, ita hi quoque dum novas rerum rationes adferunt ab omnibus illis dissentiunt, nec inter se tamen usquequaque conveniunt.

Ethica

In ea philosophiae parte qua de moribus agitur eadem illis disput-

Ordo bonorum

antur quae nobis. De bonis animi quaerunt et corporis et externis, 10 tum utrum boni nomen omnibus his an solis animi dotibus conven-

Fines bonorum

iat. De virtute disserunt ac voluptate, sed omnium prima est ac princeps controversia quanam in re, una pluribusve, sitam hominis

Utopiani
felicitatem
honesta voluptate
metiuntur

felicitatem putent. At hac in re propensiores aequo videntur in factionem voluptatis assertricem[25] ut qua vel totam vel potissimam 15 felicitatis humanae partem definiant. Et quo magis mireris, ab reli-

---

[25] Hythloday coins the adjective *assertrix* by analogy with such classical forms as *dispensatrix* (as in Budé's letter, 10:16). One example of the same form as a feminine noun (with the meaning 'supporter') is given in the principal dictionary of classical Latin, *Thesaurus linguae Latinae*, 10 vols. to date (Leipzig, 1900–).

business of divination by the stars, they have never so much as dreamed of it.[56] From long experience in observation, they are able to forecast rains, winds and other changes in the weather. But as to the causes of the weather, of the tides in the sea and its saltiness, and, finally, the origins and nature of the heavens and the earth, they have various opinions. To some extent they treat of these matters as our ancient philosophers did, but they are also like them in disagreeing with one another. So too, when they propose a new theory they differ from our ancient philosophers and yet reach no consensus at all among themselves.

Physics the most uncertain study of all

In matters of moral philosophy, they carry on the same arguments as we do. They inquire into the goods of the mind and goods of the body and external goods.[57] They ask whether the name of 'good' can be applied to all three, or whether it refers only to goods of the mind.[58] They discuss virtue and pleasure, but their chief concern is what to think of human happiness, and whether it consists of one thing or of more.[59] On this point, they seem rather too much inclined to the view which favours pleasure, in which they conclude that all or the most important part of human happiness consists.[60] And what is more surprising, they seek support for this

Ethics

Higher and lower goods

Supreme goods

The Utopians consider honest pleasure the measure of happiness

---

[56] More wrote a number of Latin poems ridiculing judicial astrology (see CW, III, Part II, 133–7, 159, 167, 215–7).

[57] This threefold classification of goods appears in Plato (*Laws* III.697B, V.743E), but is especially associated with Aristotle (*Nicomachean Ethics* I.viii.2, *Politics* VII.i.3–4) and Aristotelian tradition. Of course the Utopians have never heard of Plato, Aristotle or any other European philosopher, and one point of the account of Utopian philosophy is that natural reason will lead earnest, ingenious thinkers to the same set of problems and positions at any time and place. The other, main point is to argue that the moral norms derivable from reason are consistent with those of Christianity.

[58] The first position is especially that of the Aristotelians, the second that of the Stoics.

[59] The topics of virtue and pleasure are linked especially in discussions – like Cicero's *De finibus* – of the relative merits of Stoic and Epicurean ethics. The idea that happiness is the end of life is axiomatic in all the major philosophical schools; whether it depends on one thing or more than one depends on how many *goods* there are.

[60] I.e., the Utopians are inclined to the Epicurean position. The remark launches a long passage that constitutes, as Surtz points out (*The Praise of Pleasure*, pp. 9–11), a praise of pleasure reminiscent of Erasmus' praise of folly. The praise of pleasure, and of Epicurus, had an important precedent in Lorenzo Valla's *De vero falsoque bono* (1444–9), which in its original version (1431) was called *De voluptate*. Valla's work furthered the gradual, qualified humanist rehabilitation of Epicurus that began with Petrarch and Boccaccio and in which (after Valla) Ficino, Pico and Erasmus played a part: these writers pointed out that, contrary to popular opinion, Epicurus did not mean by 'pleasure' mere sensuality. See, in addition to Surtz, D.C. Allen, 'The rehabilitation of Epicurus and his theory of pleasure in the early Renaissance' (*Studies in Philology*, 41 (1944), 1–15); Edgar

gione quoque (quae gravis et severa est fereque tristis et rigida)
petunt tamen sententiae tam delicatae patrocinium. Neque enim de

Principia
philosophiae e
religione petenda

felicitate disceptant umquam quin principia quaedam ex religione
deprompta cum[26] philosophia quae rationibus utitur coniungant,
sine quibus ad verae felicitatis investigationem mancam atque imbe- 5
cillam per se rationem putant.

Theologia
Utopiensium

Animorum
immortalitas, de
qua hodie non
pauci etiam
Christiani
dubitant

Ea principia sunt huiusmodi: animam esse immortalem ac dei
beneficentia ad felicitatem natam; virtutibus ac benefactis nostris
praemia post hanc vitam, flagitiis destinata supplicia. Haec tametsi
religionis sint, ratione tamen censent ad ea credenda et concedenda 10
perduci; quibus e medio sublatis sine ulla cunctatione pronuntiant
neminem esse tam stupidum qui non sentiat petendam sibi per fas
ac nefas voluptatem. Hoc tantum caveret ne minor voluptas obstet
maiori, aut eam persequatur quam invicem retaliet dolor. Nam

---

[26] Early editions print *tum*; like several previous editors, we correct to *cum*, governed by *coniungant*.

comfortable opinion from their religion, which is serious and strict, indeed almost stern and forbidding. For they never discuss happiness without joining to the rational arguments of philosophy certain principles drawn from religion. Without these religious principles, they think that reason by itself is weak and defective in its efforts to investigate true happiness. *First principles of philosophy to be sought in religion*

The religious principles they invoke are of this nature: that the soul is immortal, and by God's beneficence born for happiness; and that after this life, rewards are appointed for our virtues and good deeds, punishments for our sins. Though these are indeed religious principles, they think that reason leads us to believe and accept them.[62] And they add unhesitatingly that if these beliefs were rejected, no one would be so stupid as not to feel that he should seek pleasure, regardless of right and wrong. His only care would be to keep a lesser pleasure from standing in the way of a greater one, and to avoid pleasures that are inevitably followed by pain.[63] *Utopian theology*

The immortality of the soul, about which nowadays no small number even of Christians have their doubts[61]

Wind, *Pagan Mysteries in the Renaissance*, pp. 48–71; Logan, *The Meaning of More's 'Utopia'*, pp. 144–7, 154–63; and *The Cambridge History of Renaissance Philosophy*, ed. Charles B. Schmitt *et al.* (Cambridge, 1988), pp. 374–86. Vespucci's observation about the Indians may also be relevant: 'Since their life is so entirely given over to pleasure, I should style it Epicurean' (*Quattuor navigationes*, p. 97; see also *Mundus novus*, p. 6).

[61] The immortality of the soul, formulated as a dogma of the Church by the Lateran Council of 1513, was the subject of much philosophical discussion in the fifteenth and sixteenth centuries. (For an overview, see Paul Oskar Kristeller, *Renaissance Thought and Its Sources* (New York, 1979), pp. 181–96.) The individual most prominently associated with doubts about immortality was Pietro Pompanazzi, a Paduan Aristotelian who in 1516 published a treatise *On the Immortality of the Soul*, which argues 'that immortality cannot be demonstrated on purely natural or Aristotelian grounds, but must be accepted as an article of faith' (Kristeller, p. 192).

[62] Thomistic theology supports this view. As Surtz observes, Aquinas maintains that 'man, without supernatural grace, can come to the knowledge . . . of moral and religious truths, such as the existence and perfections of God, the immortality and spirituality of the soul, the duties of man toward his Creator, and the punishments and rewards of the future life' ('Interpretations of *Utopia*', *Catholic Historical Review*, 38 (1952), 163). In *A Dialogue Concerning Heresies* (1529), More says that 'all the whole number of the old philosophers . . . found out by nature and reason that there was a god either maker or governor or both of all this whole engine of the world' (*CW*, VI, 73).

Since Epicurus maintained the indifference of the gods and the mortality of the soul, these principles sharply distinguish Utopian philosophy from classical Epicureanism and lead the Utopians to a view of the good life similar to the Christian view.

[63] This is the first of three citations of Epicurus' rules for choosing between competing pleasures (see Introduction, p. xxxii). The rules find perhaps their most influential statement in Cicero's dialogue *De finibus*, where the Epicurean Torquatus explains that 'The wise man always holds . . . to this principle of selection: he rejects pleasures to secure other greater pleasures, or else he endures pains to avoid worse pains' (I.x.33; cf. I.x.36). Another formulation occurs in a letter of

Ut non quaevis
expetenda
voluptas, ita nec
dolor adfectandus
nisi virtutis causa

virtutem asperam ac difficilem sequi ac non abigere modo suavita- tem vitae sed dolorem etiam sponte perpeti cuius nullum exspectes fructum (quis enim potest esse fructus si post mortem nihil assequeris quum hanc vitam totam insuaviter, hoc est misere, traduxeris?), id vero dementissimum ferunt.

Nunc vero non in omni voluptate felicitatem sed in bona atque honesta sitam putant; ad eam enim velut ad summum bonum natu- ram nostram ab ipsa virtute pertrahi, cui soli²⁷ adversa factio felicit- atem tribuit.

Hoc iuxta Stoicos

Nempe virtutem definiunt secundum naturam vivere, ad id siqui- dem a deo institutos esse nos. Eum vero naturae ductum sequi quisquis in appetendis fugiendisque rebus obtemperat rationi. Rationem porro mortales primum omnium in amorem ac venera- tionem divinae maiestatis incendere, cui debemus et quod sumus et quod compotes esse felicitatis possumus. Secundum id commonet atque excitat nos ut vitam quam licet minime anxiam ac maxime laetam ducamus ipsi, ceterisque omnibus ad idem obtinendum adiu- tores nos pro naturae societate praebeamus. Neque enim quisquam umquam fuit tam tristis ac rigidus assecla virtutis et osor voluptatis qui ita labores, vigilias et squalores indicat tibi, ut non idem aliorum inopiam atque incommoda levare te pro tua virili iubeat, et id laud- andum humanitatis nomine censeat hominem homini saluti ac sola- cio esse, si humanum est maxime (qua virtute nulla est homini magis propria) aliorum mitigare molestiam et, sublata tristitia, vitae iucun-

---

²⁷ Early texts print *sola* modifying *factio*; like some previous editors, we print *soli* modifying *cui*, referring to *virtute*. The other faction attributes felicity to virtue alone.

They think you would have to be actually crazy to pursue harsh and painful virtue, give up the pleasures of life, and suffer pain from which you can expect no advantage. For if there is no reward after death, you have no compensation for having passed your entire existence without pleasure, that is, miserably.[64] *Not every pleasure is desirable, neither is pain to be sought, except for the sake of virtue*

To be sure, they think happiness is found, not in every kind of pleasure, but only in good and honest pleasure. Virtue itself, they say, draws our nature to pleasure of this sort, as to the supreme good. There is an opposed school which declares that virtue is itself happiness.[65]

They define virtue as living according to nature; and God, they say, created us to that end. When an individual obeys the dictates of reason in choosing one thing and avoiding another, he is following nature.[66] Now above all reason urges us to love and venerate the Divine Majesty to whom we owe our existence and our capacity for happiness. Secondly, nature prescribes that we should lead a life as free of anxiety and as full of joy as possible, and that we should help all others – because of our natural fellowship – toward that end. The most hard-faced eulogist of virtue and the grimmest enemy of pleasure, while he invites you to toil and sleepless nights and mortification, still admonishes you to relieve the poverty and distress of others as best you can. It is especially praiseworthy, they think, when we provide for the comfort and welfare of our fellow creatures. Nothing is more humane (and humanity is the virtue most proper to human beings) than to relieve the misery of others, remove all sadness from their lives, and restore them to enjoyment, *This is like Stoic doctrine*

Epicurus quoted by Diogenes Laertius: 'since pleasure is our first and native good, for that reason we do not choose every pleasure whatsoever, but ofttimes pass over many pleasures when a greater annoyance ensues from them' (X.129). The Utopians accept these rules of selection, but recognise that their application leads to quite different conclusions about the good life depending on whether religious principles are factored into the individual's calculations.

[64] The Utopians, that is, reject the claim that purely rational and mundane considerations provide sufficient sanction for moral behaviour. In this respect, too, they differ from Epicurus, who thought that the mental pleasure of moral actions and the fear of detection in wrongdoing provided adequate incentives to virtue (cf. Diogenes Laertius X.131–2).

[65] This second position is that of the Stoics, who declared that virtue constitutes happiness, whether it leads to pleasure or not – indeed, that a man who is enduring great misery may derive happiness from his knowledge of his own virtuous behaviour. As the following marginal gloss points out, the Utopians' *definition* of virtue is also Stoic. See, for example, Cicero, *De finibus* III.ix.31.

[66] Throughout the ensuing discussion, 'reason' has the sense of 'right reason' – the faculty that, according to a conception passed on by the Stoics to the Middle Ages and the Renaissance, enables human beings to distinguish right and wrong with instinctive clarity; that is, to apprehend the natural law.

ditati, hoc est voluptati, reddere.[28] Quidni natura quemque instiget
ut sibimet idem praestet? Nam aut mala est vita iucunda, id est

*At nunc quidam
accerunt dolores
velut in his sita sit
religio, cum
ferendi potius sint
si incidant ad
pietatis officium
tendenti, aut
naturae necessitate
accidant*

voluptuaria, quod si est non solum neminem ad eam debes adiutare
sed omnibus utpote noxiam ac mortiferam quantum potes adimere;
aut si conciliare aliis eam ut bonam non licet modo sed etiam debes, 5
cur non tibi in primis ipsi? cui non minus propitium esse te quam
aliis decet. Neque enim quum te natura moneat uti in alios bonus
sis, eadem te rursus iubet in temet saevum atque inclementem esse.
Vitam ergo iucundam, inquiunt, id est voluptatem, tamquam opera-
tionum omnium finem, ipsa nobis natura praescribit, ex cuius prae- 10
scripto vivere virtutem definiunt. At quum natura mortales invitet
ad hilarioris vitae mutuum subsidium (quod certe merito facit,
neque enim tam supra generis humani sortem quisquam est ut solus
naturae curae sit, quae universos ex aequo fovet quos eiusdem
formae communione complectitur), eadem te nimirum iubet etiam 15
atque etiam observare, ne sic tuis commodis obsecundes ut aliorum
procures incommoda.

Pacta et leges   Servanda igitur censent non inita solum inter privatos pacta sed
publicas etiam leges quas aut bonus princeps iuste promulgavit aut
populus nec oppressus tyrannide nec dolo circumscriptus, de parti- 20
endis vitae commodis, hoc est materia voluptatis, communi consensu sanxit. His inoffensis legibus, tuum curare commodum prudentiae[29] est: publicum praeterea, pietatis. Sed alienam voluptatem
praereptum ire dum consequare tuam, ea vero iniuria est: contra

*Officia vitae
mutua*   tibi aliquid ipsi demere quod addas aliis, id demum est humanitatis 25
ac benignitatis officium, quod ipsum numquam tantum aufert commodi quantum refert. Nam et beneficiorum vicissitudine pensatur
et ipsa benefacti conscientia ac recordatio charitatis eorum et bene-

---

[28] We assume an unwritten *eos*, referring back to *aliorum*, as the direct object of
reddere.
[29] Following Lupton, we print *prudentiae* instead of *prudentia* (early texts) to parallel *pietatis.*

that is, pleasure. Well, then, why doesn't nature equally invite all of us to do the same thing for ourselves? Either a joyful life (that is, one of pleasure) is a good thing, or it isn't. If it isn't, then you should not help anyone to it – indeed, you ought to take it away from everyone you can, as being harmful and deadly to them. But if you are allowed, indeed obliged, to help others to such a life, why not first of all yourself, to whom you owe no less favour than to anyone else? For when nature prompts you to be kind to your neighbours, she does not mean that you should be cruel and merciless to yourself. Thus, they say, nature herself prescribes for us a joyous life, in other words, pleasure, as the goal of all our actions; and living according to her rules is to be defined as virtue.[67] But as nature bids mortals to make one another's lives cheerful, as far as they can – and she does so rightly, for no one is placed so far above the rest that he is nature's sole concern, and she cherishes equally all those to whom she has granted the same form – so she repeatedly warns you not to seek your own advantage in ways that cause misfortune to others.

But now some people cultivate pain as if it were the essence of religion, rather than incidental to performance of a pious duty or the result of natural necessity – and thus to be borne, not pursued

Consequently, they think that one should abide not only by private agreements but by those public laws which control the distribution of vital goods, such as are the very substance of pleasure. Any such laws, when properly promulgated by a good king, or ratified by the common consent of a people free of tyranny and deception, should be observed. So long as they are observed, to pursue your own interests is prudent; to pursue the public interest as well is pious; but to pursue your own pleasure by depriving others of theirs is unjust. On the other hand, to decrease your own pleasure in order to augment that of others is a work of humanity and benevolence, which never fails to reward the doer over and above his sacrifice. You may be repaid for your kindness, and in any case your consciousness of having done a good deed, and recalling the affection and good will of those whom you have bene-

Contracts and laws

Mutual assistance

---

[67] The argument is not inconsistent with the Stoic position as expounded by Seneca: 'Our motto, as you know, is "Live according to Nature"; but it is quite contrary to nature to torture the body, to hate unlaboured elegance, to be dirty on purpose, to eat food that is not only plain, but disgusting and forbidding . . . Philosophy calls for plain living, but not for penance; and we may perfectly well be plain and neat at the same time' (*Epistulae morales* V.4–5). Seneca, who is highly sympathetic to Epicurus, also points out the rapprochement between Stoicism and Epicureanism that the Utopians' views imply: 'the teachings of Epicurus are upright and holy and, if you consider them closely, austere; for his famous doctrine of pleasure is reduced to small and narrow proportions, and the rule that we Stoics lay down for virtue, this same rule he lays down for pleasure – he bids that it obey Nature' (VII.xiii.1).

volentiae quibus benefeceris plus voluptatis adfert animo quam fuisset illa corporis qua abstinuisti. Postremo (quod facile persuadet
animo libenter assentienti religio) brevis et exiguae voluptatis vicem
ingenti ac numquam interituro gaudio rependit deus. Itaque hoc
pacto censent, et excussa sedulo et perpensa re, omnes actiones 5
nostras, atque in his virtutes etiam ipsas, voluptatem tandem velut
finem felicitatemque respicere.

Voluptas quid   Voluptatem appellant omnem corporis animive motum stat-
umque in quo versari natura duce delectet. Appetitionem naturae
non temere addunt. Nam ut quicquid natura iucundum est, ad quod 10
neque per iniuriam tenditur nec iucundius aliud amittitur nec labor
succedit, non sensus modo sed recta quoque ratio persequitur, ita
Falsae voluptates quae praeter naturam dulcia sibi mortales vanissima conspiratione
confingunt (tamquam in ipsis esset perinde res ac vocabula
commutare), ea omnia statuunt adeo nihil ad felicitatem facere ut 15
plurimum officiant etiam, vel eo quod quibus semel insederunt, ne
veris ac genuinis oblectamentis usquam vacet locus, totum prorsus
animum falsa voluptatis opinione praeoccupant. Sunt enim perquam
multa quae quum suapte natura nihil contineant suavitatis immo
bona pars amaritudinis etiam plurimum, perversa tamen[30] improba- 20
rum cupiditatum illecebra non pro summis tantum voluptatibus
habeantur, verumetiam inter praecipuas vitae causas numerentur.

In hoc adulterinae voluptatis genere eos collocant quos ante
Error eorum qui memoravi qui quo meliorem togam habent eo sibi meliores ipsi
sibi ob cultum
placent videntur; qua una in re bis errant. Neque enim minus falsi sunt 25
quod meliorem putant togam suam quam quod se. Cur enim si
vestis usum spectes, tenuioris fili lana praestet crassiori? At illi
tamen, tamquam natura non errore praecellerent, attollunt cristas
et sibimet quoque pretii credunt inde non nihil accedere; eoque
honorem quem vilius vestiti sperare non essent ausi, elegantiori 30

---

[30] Instead of the *tum* (abbreviated *tũ*) of the early editions, the context clearly
requires the emendation proposed by three seventeenth-century editions and by
Lupton: *tamen* (abbreviated *tñ*).

fited, gives your mind more pleasure than your body would have drawn from the things you forfeited. Finally, as religion easily persuades a well-disposed mind to believe, God will requite the loss of a brief and transitory pleasure here with immense and never-ending joy in heaven. And so they conclude, after carefully considering and weighing the matter, that all our actions, including even the virtues exercised within them, look toward pleasure as their happiness and final goal.[68]

By pleasure they understand every state or movement of body or mind in which we find delight according to the behests of nature.[69] They have good reason for adding that the desire is according to nature. By following our senses and right reason we may discover what is pleasant by nature: it is a delight that does not injure others, does not preclude a greater pleasure, and is not followed by pain. But all pleasures which are against nature, and which men agree to call 'delightful' only by the emptiest of fictions (as if one could change the real nature of things just by changing their names), do not, they have decided, really make for happiness; in fact, they say such pleasures often preclude happiness. And the reason is that once they have taken over someone's mind, they leave no room for true and genuine delights, and they completely fill the mind with a false notion of pleasure. For there are a great many things which have no genuine sweetness in them but are for the most part actually bitter – yet which, through the perverse enticement of evil desires, are not only considered very great pleasures but are even included among the primary reasons for living.

Among the pursuers of this false pleasure, they include those whom I mentioned before, the people who think themselves finer folk because they wear finer clothes. On this one point, these people are twice mistaken: first in supposing their clothes better than anyone else's, and then in thinking themselves better. As far as a garment's usefulness goes, why is fine woollen thread better than coarse? Yet they strut about and think their clothes make them more substantial, as if they were exalted by nature herself, rather than their own fantasies. Therefore, honours they would never have dared to expect if they were plainly dressed they demand as right-

What pleasure is

False pleasures

Mistaken pride in fancy dress

---

[68] This is Epicurus' view, as reported by Diogenes Laertius: 'we choose the virtues too on account of pleasure and not for their own sake' (X.138).

[69] Both Plato (*Philebus* 36C–52B) and Aristotle (*Nicomachean Ethics* I.viii.11, VII.v.1) acknowledge the importance to the good life of physical as well as mental pleasures and distinguish between true pleasures – which are 'pleasant by nature' – and false ones. The ensuing discussion relies heavily on their arguments.

togae velut suo iure exigunt, et praetermissi negligentius indignantur.

Stulti honores   At hoc ipsum quoque, vanis et nihil profuturis honoribus adfici, an non eiusdem inscitiae est? Nam quid naturalis et verae voluptatis adfert nudatus alterius vertex, aut curvati poplites? Hocine tuorum ⁵ poplitum dolori medebitur? aut tui capitis phrenesim levabit? In hac fucatae voluptatis imagine mirum quam suaviter insaniunt ei *Vana nobilitas*   qui nobilitatis opinione sibi blandiuntur ac plaudunt quod eiusmodi maioribus nasci contigerit quorum longa series dives (neque enim nunc aliud est nobilitas) habita sit, praesertim in praediis, nec pilo ¹⁰ quidem minus sibi nobiles videntur etiamsi maiores nihil inde reliquerint aut relictum ipsi obligurierint.

Stultissima voluptas ex gemmis   His adnumerant eos qui gemmis ac lapillis (ut dixi) capiuntur ac dei quodammodo sibi videntur facti si quando eximium aliquem consequantur, eius praesertim generis quod sua tempestate maximo ¹⁵ *Opinio hominum pretium addit aut adimit gemmis*   apud suos aestimetur: neque enim apud omnes neque omni tempore eadem genera sunt in pretio. Sed nec nisi exemptum auro ac nudum comparant, immo ne sic quidem nisi adiurato venditore et praestanti cautionem veram gemmam ac lapidem verum esse: tam solliciti sunt ne oculis eorum veri loco adulterinus imponat. At spectaturo tibi ²⁰ cur minus praebeat oblectamenti facticius quem tuus oculus non discernit a vero? Uterque ex aequo valere debet tibi, non minus hercule quam caeco.

Quid hi qui superfluas opes asservant ut nullo acervi usu sed sola contemplatione delectentur? Num veram percipiunt an falsa potius ²⁵ voluptate luduntur? Aut hi qui diverso vitio aurum quo numquam sint usuri, fortasse nec visuri amplius, abscondunt et, solliciti ne perdant, perdunt. Quid enim aliud est usibus demptum tuis et

fully due to their fancy suit, and they grow indignant if someone passes them by without showing special respect.

Isn't it the same kind of stupidity to be pleased by empty, merely *Foolish honours* ceremonial honours? What true or natural pleasure can you get from someone's bent knee or bared head? Will the creaks in your own knees be eased thereby, or the madness in your head? The phantom of false pleasure is illustrated by others who are pleasantly mad with delight over their own blue blood, flatter themselves on their nobility, and gloat over all the long line of rich ancestors they *Empty nobility* happen to have (and wealth is the only sort of nobility these days), and especially over their ancient family estates. Even if these ancestors have left them no estates to inherit, or if they've squandered all of their inheritance, they don't consider themselves a bit less noble.[70]

In the same class they put those people I described before, who *The silliest* are captivated by jewels and gemstones, and think themselves *pleasure of all: gemstones* divinely happy if they get a good specimen, especially of the sort that happens to be fashionable in their country at the time – for *Popular opinion* not every country nor every era values the same kinds. But col- *gives gems their value or takes it* lectors will not make an offer for a stone till it's taken out of its *away* gold setting, and even then they will not buy unless the dealer guarantees and gives security that it is a true and genuine stone. What they fear is that their eyes will be deceived by a counterfeit. But why should a counterfeit give any less pleasure, if, when you look at it, your eyes cannot distinguish it from a genuine gem? Both should be of equal value to you – no less so, by heaven, than they would be to a blind man.[71]

What about those who pile up money, not for any real purpose, but just to look at it? Do they feel a true pleasure, or aren't they simply deluded by a show of pleasure? Or what about those with the opposite vice, who hide away gold they will never use and perhaps never even see again? In their anxiety not to lose it, they actually do lose it. For what else happens when you deprive your-

---

[70] This passage – like the catalogue of false pleasures as a whole – is close in substance and tone to *The Praise of Folly*. Folly comments on 'those who are no better than the humblest worker but take extraordinary pride in an empty title of nobility' (*CWE*, XXVII, 116).

[71] There are similar sentiments in More's *Treatise upon the Passion* (*CW*, XIII, 8) and *The Four Last Things* (after 1520) (*English Works*, 1, 461). Erasmus' Folly tells how someone with a name like hers (i.e., *Morus*) 'made his new bride a present of some jewels which were copies, and . . . persuaded her that they were not only real and genuine but also of unique and incalculable value' (*CWE*, XXVII, 118).

omnium fortasse mortalium telluri reddere? Et tu tamen abstruso
Mira fictio et
aptissima
thesauro velut animi iam securus laetitia gestis. Quem si quis furto
sustulerit cuius tu ignarus furti decem post annis obieris, toto illo
decennio quo subtractae pecuniae superfuisti, quid tua retulit sur-
reptum an salvum fuisse? Utroque certe modo tantundem usus ad 5
te pervenit.

Ad has tam ineptas laetitias, aleatores (quorum insaniam auditu,
non usu, cognovere), venatores praeterea atque aucupes adiungunt.
Alea
Nam quid habet, inquiunt, voluptatis talos in alveum proicere, quod
toties fecisti ut si quid voluptatis inesset, oriri tamen potuisset ex 10
frequenti usu satietas? Aut quae suavitas esse potest ac non fastid-
Venatio
ium potius in audiendo latratu atque ululatu canum? Aut qui maior
voluptatis sensus est cum leporem canis insequitur quam quum
canis canem? Nempe idem utrobique agitur, accuritur enim, si te
cursus oblectet. At si te caedis spes, laniatus exspectatio sub oculis 15
peragendi retinet, misericordiam potius movere debet, spectare
lepusculum a cane, imbecillum a validiore, fugacem ac timidum a
At haec hodie ars
est deorum
aulicorum
feroce, innoxium denique a crudeli discerptum. Itaque Utopienses
totum hoc venandi exercitium, ut rem liberis indignam, in lanios
(quam artem per servos obire eos supra diximus) reiecerunt. Infi- 20
mam enim eius partem esse venationem statuunt, reliquas eius
partes et utiliores et honestiores ut quae et multo magis conferant[31]
et animalia necessitatis dumtaxat gratia perimant, quum venator ab
miseri animalculi caede ac laniatu nihil nisi voluptatem petat. Quam
spectandae necis libidinem in ipsis etiam bestiis aut ab animi crud- 25
elis affectu censent exoriri, aut in crudelitatem denique assiduo tam
efferae voluptatis usu defluere.

[31] 1516 prints *conservant*, the other editions *conferant*.

self, and perhaps all other people too, of a chance to use your gold, by burying it in the ground? And yet, when you've hidden your treasure away, you are overjoyed, as if your mind were now at ease. Suppose someone stole it, and you died ten years later, know- *A strange fancy, and much to the point* ing nothing of the theft. During all those ten years, what did it matter to you whether the money was stolen or not? In either case, it was equally useless to you.[72]

To these foolish pleasures they add gambling, which they have heard about, though they've never tried it, as well as hunting and hawking. What pleasure can there be, they say, in throwing dice *Dicing* on a playing-table? If there were any pleasure in the action, wouldn't doing it over and over again make one tired of it? What pleasure can there be in listening to the barking and howling of *Hunting* dogs – isn't that rather a disgusting noise? Is any more pleasure felt when a dog chases a hare than when a dog chases a dog? If what you like is fast running, there's plenty of that in both cases; they're just about the same. But if what you really want is slaughter, if you want to see a creature torn apart under your eyes – you ought to feel nothing but pity when you see the little hare fleeing from the hound, the weak creature tormented by the stronger, the fearful and timid beast brutalised by the savage one, the harmless hare killed by the cruel hound. And so the Utopians, who regard this *Yet today this is the chosen art of our court-divinities* whole activity of hunting as unworthy of free men, have accordingly assigned it to their butchers, who, as I said before, are all slaves. In their eyes, hunting is the lowest thing even butchers can do. In the slaughterhouse, their work is more useful and honest, since there they kill animals only out of necessity; whereas the hunter seeks nothing but his own pleasure from killing and mutilating some poor little creature. Taking such relish in the sight of slaughter, even if only of beasts, springs, in their opinion, from a cruel disposition, or else finally produces cruelty, through the constant practice of such brutal pleasures.[73]

---

[72] There is a very similar passage in More's *Dialogue of Comfort* (CW, XII, 210).

[73] In one of More's Latin poems (CW, III, Part II, 123), a hunter 'looks on and smiles' as his hound tears a rabbit to pieces: 'Insensate breed, more savage than any beast, to find cruel amusement in bitter slaughter!' Similarly, Folly satirises those who 'declare they take unbelievable pleasure in the hideous blast of the hunting horn and baying of the hounds ... All they achieve by this incessant hunting and eating wild game is their own degeneration – they're practically wild beasts themselves' (CWE, XXVII, 112–13). By contrast, hunting is praised as good exercise and good practice for war by Plato (*Laws* VII.823B–824B) and other classical and later writers, including many of More's and Erasmus' fellow humanists.

Haec igitur et quicquid est eiusmodi (sunt enim innumera), quamquam pro voluptatibus mortalium vulgus habeat, illi tamen quum natura nihil insit suave, plane statuunt cum vera voluptate nihil habere commercii. Nam quod vulgo sensum iucunditate perfundunt (quod voluptatis opus videtur) nihil de sententia decedunt. 5 Non enim ipsius rei natura sed ipsorum perversa consuetudo in causa est, cuius vitio fit ut amara pro dulcibus amplectantur, non *Citta*[32] *in gravidis* aliter ac mulieres gravidae picem et sebum corrupto gustu melle mellitius arbitrantur. Nec cuiusquam tamen aut morbo aut consuetudine depravatum iudicium mutare naturam, ut non aliarum 10 rerum, ita nec voluptatis potest.

Verae voluptatis Voluptatum quas veras fatentur species diversas faciunt. Siquidem *species* alias animo, corpori alias tribuunt. Animo dant intellectum eamque dulcedinem quam veri contemplatio pepererit. Ad haec suavis additur bene actae vitae memoria et spes non dubia futuri boni. 15

Voluptate corporis Corporis voluptatem in duas partiuntur formas, quarum prima sit ea quae sensum perspicua suavitate perfundit, quod alias earum instauratione partium fit quas insitus nobis calor exhauserit (nam hae cibo potuque redduntur), alias dum egeruntur illa quorum copia corpus exuberat. Haec suggeritur dum excrementis intestina pur- 20 gamus aut opera liberis datur aut ullius prurigo partis frictu scalptuve lenitur. Interdum vero voluptas oritur nec reddita quicquam quod membra nostra desiderent, nec ademptura quo laborent, ceterum quae sensus nostros tamen vi quadam occulta sed illustri motu titillet adficiatque, et in se convertat, qualis ex musica nascitur. 25

Alteram corporeae voluptatis formam eam volunt esse quae in quieto atque aequabili corporis statu consistat, id est nimirum sua cuiusque nullo interpellata malo sanitas. Haec siquidem, si nihil eam doloris oppugnet, per se ipsa delectat etiamsi nulla extrinsecus adhibita voluptate moveatur. Quamquam enim sese minus effert 30 minusque offert sensui quam tumida illa edendi bibendique libido, nihilo tamen setius multi eam statuunt voluptatum maximam.

Valeat possessor Omnes fere Utopienses magnam et velut fundamentum omnium ac *oportet* basim fatentur ut quae vel sola placidam et optabilem vitae conditionem reddat, et qua sublata nullus usquam reliquus sit cuiquam 35

---

[32] Medieval Latin *citta*, from Greek κίττα (Attic form of κίσσα), 'magpie', is equivalent to classical Latin *pica* and, like that word, acquired the secondary, medical sense of 'unnatural appetites' (with reference to the pie's miscellaneous feeding).

Common opinion considers these activities, and countless others like them, to be pleasures; but the Utopians say flatly they have nothing at all to do with real pleasure, since there's nothing naturally pleasant about them. They often please the senses, and in this they are like pleasure, but that does not alter their view. The enjoyment doesn't arise from the nature of the experience itself but from the perverse habits of the mob, which cause them to mistake the bitter for the sweet, just as pregnant women whose taste has been distorted sometimes think pitch and tallow taste sweeter than honey. A person's taste may be depraved by disease or by custom, but that doesn't change the nature of pleasure or of anything else. *Morbid tastes of pregnant women*

They distinguish several classes of pleasures which they confess to be genuine, attributing some to the mind and others to the body. Those of the mind are knowledge and the delight that arises from contemplating the truth, the gratification of looking back on a well-spent life, and the unquestioning hope of happiness to come. *Classes of true pleasure*

Pleasures of the body they also divide into two classes. The first is that which fills the senses with immediate delight. Sometimes this happens when bodily organs that have been weakened by natural heat are restored with food and drink; sometimes it happens when we eliminate some excess in the body, as when we move our bowels, generate children, or relieve an itch somewhere by rubbing or scratching it. Now and then pleasure arises, not from restoring a deficiency or discharging an excess, but from something that affects and excites our senses with a hidden but unmistakable force, and attracts them to itself. Such is the power of music.[74] *Bodily pleasures*

The second kind of bodily pleasure they describe as nothing but the calm and harmonious state of the body, its state of health when undisturbed by any disorder. Health itself, when not oppressed by pain, gives pleasure, without any external excitement at all. Even though it appeals less directly to the senses than the gross gratifications of eating and drinking, many still consider this to be the greatest pleasure of all. Most of the Utopians regard it as the foundation and basis of all the pleasures, since by itself alone it can make life peaceful and desirable, whereas without it there is no *To enjoy anything, one needs good health*

[74] The source is Plato, who distinguishes between the bodily pleasures that occur 'when things are restored to their natural condition' (*Philebus* 42D) and 'those the want of which is unfelt and painless, whereas the satisfaction furnished by them is felt by the senses, pleasant, and unmixed with pain' (51B). The Utopians also agree with Plato in denying (below) that the 'mere absence of pain' constitutes a pleasure. But they differ from him in regarding health as a pleasure: for Plato, health is an example of the neutral state between pain and pleasure. See *Philebus* 42C–44B, 51A; *Republic* IX.583C–585A.

voluptati locus. Nam dolore prorsus vacare, nisi adsit sanitas, stu-
porem certe non voluptatem vocant.

Iamdudum explosum est apud eos decretum illorum qui stabilem
et tranquillam sanitatem (nam haec quoque quaestio naviter apud
eos agitata est) ideo non habendam pro voluptate censebant quod 5
praesentem non posse dicerent nisi motu quopiam extrario sentiri.
Verum contra nunc in hoc prope universi conspirant sanitatem vel
in primis voluptati esse. Etenim quum in morbo, inquiunt, dolor
sit, qui voluptati implacabilis hostis est, non aliter ac sanitati
morbus, quidni vicissim insit sanitatis tranquillitati voluptas? Nihil 10
enim ad hanc rem referre putant seu morbus dolor esse seu morbo
dolor inesse dicatur, tantundem enim utroque modo effici. Quippe
si sanitas aut voluptas ipsa sit aut necessario voluptatem pariat velut
calor igni gignitur, nimirum utrobique efficitur ut quibus immota
sanitas adest, his voluptas abesse non possit. 15

Praeterea dum vescimur, inquiunt, quid aliud quam sanitas quae
labefactari coeperat adversus esuriem (cibo commilitone) depugnat?
In qua dum paulatim invalescit, ille ipse profectus ad solitum vigo-
rem suggerit illam qua sic reficimur voluptatem. Sanitas ergo quae
in conflictu laetatur eadem non gaudebit adepta victoriam? Sed pris- 20
tinum robur quod solum toto conflictu petiverat tandem feliciter
assecuta, protinus obstupescet nec bona sua cognoscet atque ample-
xabitur? Nam quod non sentiri sanitas dicta est, id vero perquam
procul a vero putant. Quis enim vigilans, inquiunt, sanum esse se
non sentit, nisi qui non est? Quemne tantus aut stupor aut lethargus 25
astringit ut sanitatem non iucundam sibi fateatur ac delectabilem?
At delectatio quid aliud quam alio nomine voluptas est?

Amplectuntur ergo in primis animi voluptates (eas enim primas
omnium principesque ducunt), quarum potissimam partem censent
ab exercitio virtutum bonaeque vitae conscientia proficisci. Earum 30

possibility of any other pleasure. Mere absence of pain, without positive health, they regard as insensibility, not pleasure.

Some have maintained that a stable and tranquil state of health is not really a pleasure, on the ground that the presence of health cannot be felt except in contrast to its opposite. The Utopians (who have considered the matter thoroughly) long ago rejected this opinion. Quite the contrary, they nearly all agree that health is crucial to pleasure. Since pain is inherent in disease, they say, and pain is the bitter enemy of pleasure just as disease is the enemy of health, then pleasure must be inherent in quiet good health. Whether pain is the disease itself or just an accompanying effect makes, they think, no real difference, since the effect is the same either way. Indeed, whether health is itself a pleasure or simply the cause of pleasure (as fire is the cause of heat), the fact remains that those who have stable health must also have pleasure.

When we eat, they say, what happens is that health, which was starting to fade, takes food as its ally in the fight against hunger. While our health gains strength, the simple process of returning vigour gives us pleasure and refreshment. If our health feels delight in the struggle, will it not rejoice when the victory has been won? When at last it is happily restored to its original strength, which was its aim all through the conflict, will it at once become insensible and fail to recognise and embrace its own good? The idea that health cannot be felt they consider very far from the truth. What man, when he's awake, can fail to feel that he's in good health – except one who isn't? Is anyone so torpid and dull that he won't admit health is agreeable and delightful to him? And what is delight except pleasure under another name?

Among the various pleasures, then, they seek primarily those of the mind, and prize them most highly. The foremost mental pleasure, they believe, arises from practice of the virtues and consciousness of a good life.[75] Among pleasures of the body, they give

---

[75] The formulation is from Cicero, who in *De senectute* maintains that 'the most suitable defences of old age are the principles and practice of the virtues, which, if cultivated in every period of life, bring forth wonderful fruits at the close of a long and busy career, not only because they never fail you even at the very end of life . . . but also because it is most delightful to have the consciousness of a life well spent and the memory of many deeds worthily performed' (III. 9).

The idea that pleasures can be ranked is found in both Plato (*Philebus* 57A–59D, 61D–E) and Aristotle (*Nicomachean Ethics* X.v.6–7). Both assert the superiority of mental pleasures to bodily ones (as does Epicurus: Diogenes Laertius X.137), but differ from the Utopians in regarding philosophic contemplation as the highest mental pleasure (*Republic* IX.583A; cf. 585D–586C; *Nicomachean Ethics* X.vii.1–viii.8).

voluptatum quas corpus suggerit, palmam sanitati deferunt. Nam
edendi bibendique suavitatem et quicquid eandem oblectamenti
rationem habet, appetenda quidem sed non nisi sanitatis gratia statuunt, neque enim per se iucunda esse talia, sed quatenus adversae
valetudini clanculum surrepenti resistunt. Ideoque sapienti sicuti   5
magis deprecandos morbos quam optandam medicinam, et dolores
profligandos potius quam asciscenda solacia, ita hoc quoque voluptatis genere non egere quam deliniri praestiterit.

    Quo voluptatis genere si quisquam se beatum putet, is necesse
est fateatur se tum demum fore felicissimum si ea vita contigerit   10
quae in perpetua fame, siti, pruritu, esu, potatione, scalptu, fric-
tuque traducatur – quae quam non foeda solum sed misera etiam
sit, quis non videt? Infimae profecto omnium hae voluptates sunt,
ut minime sincerae, neque enim umquam subeunt nisi contrariis
coniunctae doloribus. Nempe cum edendi voluptate copulatur esur-   15
ies, idque non satis aequa lege, nam ut vehementior ita longior
quoque dolor est. Quippe et ante voluptatem nascitur et nisi voluptate una commoriente non exstinguitur. Huiusmodi ergo voluptates,
nisi quatenus expetit necessitas, haud magni habendas putant.
Gaudent tamen etiam his, gratique agnoscunt naturae parentis   20
indulgentiam, quae fetus suos ad id quod necessitatis causa tam
assidue faciundum erat etiam blandissima suavitate pelliceat.
Quanto enim in taedio vivendum erat si ut ceterae aegritudines quae
nos infestant rarius ita hi quoque cottidiani famis ac sitis morbi
venenis ac pharmacis amaris essent abigendi?   25

    At formam, vires, agilitatem, haec ut propria iucundaque naturae
dona libenter fovent. Quin eas quoque voluptates quae per aures,
oculos ac nares admittuntur, quas natura proprias ac peculiares esse
homini voluit (neque enim aliud animantium genus aut mundi
formam pulchritudinemque suspicit, aut odorum nisi ad cibi discri-   30
men ulla commovetur gratia, neque consonas inter se discordesque
sonorum distantias internoscit), et has, inquam, ut iucunda quaedam vitae condimenta persequuntur. In omnibus autem hunc
habent modum ne maiorem minor impediat, neu dolorem aliquando
voluptas pariat – quod necessario sequi censent si inhonesta sit.   35

first place to health. As for eating, drinking and other delights of that sort, they consider them desirable, but only for the sake of health. They are not pleasant in themselves, but only as ways to withstand the insidious encroachments of sickness. A wise man would rather escape sickness altogether than have a medicine against it; he would rather prevent pain than find a palliative. And so it would be better not to need this kind of pleasure at all than to be assuaged by it.

Anyone who thinks happiness consists of this sort of pleasure must confess that his ideal life would be one spent in an endless round of hunger, thirst and itching, followed by eating, drinking, scratching and rubbing. Who can fail to see that such an existence is not only disgusting but miserable? These pleasures are certainly the lowest of all, as they are the most adulterated – for they never occur except in connection with the pains that are their contraries.[76] Hunger, for example, is linked to the pleasure of eating, and by no equal law, since the pain is sharper and lasts longer; it precedes the pleasure, and ends only when the pleasure ends with it. So they think pleasures of this sort should not be highly rated, except insofar as they are necessary to life. Yet they enjoy these pleasures too, and acknowledge gratefully the kindness of Mother Nature, who coaxes her children with enticing delight to do what in any case they must do from necessity. How wretched life would be if the daily diseases of hunger and thirst had to be overcome by bitter potions and drugs, like some other diseases that afflict us less often!

Beauty, strength and agility, as special and pleasant gifts of Nature, they joyfully cherish. The pleasures of sound, sight and smell they also pursue as the agreeable seasonings of life, recognising that Nature intended them to be the particular province of man. No other kind of animal contemplates with delight the shape and loveliness of the universe, or enjoys odours (except in the way of searching for food), or distinguishes harmonious from dissonant sounds. But in all their pleasures, they observe this rule, that the lesser shall not interfere with the greater, and that no pleasure shall carry pain with it as a consequence. If a pleasure is dishonourable, they think it will inevitably lead to pain.

---

[76] There is a similar passage in More's 1533 treatise, *The Answer to a Poisoned Book* (CW, XI, 32). The idea that the restorative pleasures are contaminated by being mixed with the opposite pains comes directly from the *Philebus* (46C-D), as does the notion of a life given over to itching and scratching (46D, 47B; cf. *Gorgias* 494B-D).

At certe formae decus contemnere, vires deterere, agilitatem in pigritiam vertere, corpus exhaurire ieiuniis, sanitati iniuriam facere et cetera naturae blandimenta respuere, nisi quis haec sua commoda negligat dum aliorum publicave[33] ardentius procurat, cuius laboris vice maiorem a deo voluptatem exspectet: alioquin ob inanem virtutis umbram nullius bono semet adfligere vel quo adversa ferre minus moleste possit, numquam fortasse ventura – hoc vero putant esse dementissimum, animique et in se crudelis et erga naturam ingratissimi, cui tamquam debere quicquam dedignetur, omnibus eius beneficiis renuntiat.

Adnotandum et hoc diligenter   Haec est eorum de virtute ac voluptate sententia, qua nisi sanctius aliquid inspiret homini caelitus immissa religio, nullam investigari credunt humana ratione veriorem. Qua in re rectene an secus sentiant excutere nos neque tempus patitur neque necesse est, quippe qui narranda eorum instituta non etiam tuenda suscepimus. Ceterum hoc mihi certe persuadeo, utut sese habeant haec decreta, *Felicitas Utopiensium ac descriptio* nusquam neque praestantiorem populum neque feliciorem esse rempublicam.

Corpore sunt agili vegetoque, virum amplius quam statura promittat, nec ea tamen improcera. Et quum neque solo sint usquequaque fertili, nec admodum salubri caelo, adversus aerem ita sese temperantia victus muniunt, terrae sic medentur industria, ut nusquam gentium sit frugis pecorisque proventus uberior, aut hominum vivaciora corpora paucioribusque morbis obnoxia. Itaque non ea modo quae vulgo faciunt agricolae diligenter ibi administrata conspicias, ut terram natura maligniorem arte atque opera iuvent, sed populi manibus alibi radicitus evulsam silvam, alibi consitam videas. Qua in re habita est non ubertatis sed vecturae ratio, ut essent ligna aut mari aut fluviis aut urbibus ipsis viciniora: minore enim cum labore terrestri itinere fruges quam ligna longius adferuntur.

Gens facilis ac faceta, sollers, otio gaudens, corporis laborum (quum est usus) satis patiens (ceterum alias haudquaquam sane

---

[33] *publicamve* (all texts) might be justified on the strength of an implicit *rem*, but *publicave* (Michels and Ziegler; Delcourt) relies on the tangible *commoda*. Lupton's emendation *publicumve* (to wit, *commodum*) would also be acceptable.

Moreover, they think it is crazy for a man to despise beauty of form, to impair his strength, to grind his agility down to torpor, to exhaust his body with fasts, to ruin his health and to scorn all other natural delights, unless by so doing he can more zealously serve the welfare of others or the common good. Then indeed he may expect a greater reward from God. But otherwise to inflict pain on oneself without doing anyone any good – simply to gain the empty and shadowy appearance of virtue, or to be able to bear with less distress adversities that may never come – this they consider to be absolutely crazy, the token of a mind cruel to itself as well as most ungrateful to Nature – as if, to avoid being in her debt, it is rejecting all her gifts.[77]

This is the way they think about virtue and pleasure. Human reason, they think, can attain to no truer conclusions than these, unless a revelation from heaven should inspire men with holier notions. In all this, I have no time now to consider whether they are right or wrong, and don't feel obliged to do so. I have undertaken only to describe their principles, not to defend them. But of this I am sure, that whatever their principles are, there is not a more excellent people or a happier commonwealth anywhere in the whole world. *Note this and note it well*

The happiness of the Utopians, and a description of them

In body they are nimble and vigorous, and stronger than you would expect from their stature, though they're by no means tiny. Their soil is not very fertile, nor their climate of the best, but they protect themselves against the weather by temperate living, and improve their soil by industry, so that nowhere do grain and cattle flourish more plentifully, nowhere are people's bodies more vigorous or less susceptible to disease. There you can not only observe that they do all the things farmers usually do to improve poor soil by hard work and technical knowledge, but you can see a forest which they tore up by the roots with their own hands and moved to another site. They did this not so much for the sake of better growth but to make transport easier, by having wood closer to the sea, the rivers, or the cities themselves. For grain is easier than wood to carry by land over a long distance.

The people are easy-going, cheerful, clever, and like their leisure. They can stand heavy labour when it is useful, but otherwise they

---

[77] Note that the Utopians utterly reject the idea of practising ascetic denial in order to strengthen oneself against possible future adversity. In later, theological works, though, More takes for granted the efficacy of fasting in 'taming of the flesh against the sin imminent and to come' (*The Confutation of Tyndale's Answer*, *CW*, VIII, Part I, 67; cf. 71).

appetens), animi studiis infatigata. Qui quum a nobis accepissent
de literis et disciplina Graecorum (nam in Latinis praeter historias
ac poetas nihil erat quod videbantur magnopere probaturi) mirum
quanto studio contenderunt ut eas liceret ipsis nostra interpretatione perdiscere. Coepimus ergo legere, magis adeo primum ne ₅
recusare laborem videremur quam quod fructum eius aliquem sper-
aremus. At ubi paulum processimus, ipsorum diligentia fecit ut nostram haud frustra impendendam animo statim praeciperemus.
Siquidem literarum formas tam facile imitari, verba tam expedite
pronuntiare, tam celeriter mandare memoriae, et tanta cum fide ₁₀
reddere coeperunt, ut nobis miraculi esset loco, nisi quod pleraque
pars eorum qui non sua solum sponte accensi verum senatus quoque
decreto iussi, ista sibi discenda sumpserunt, e numero schol-
asticorum selectissimis ingeniis et matura aetate fuerunt. Itaque
minus quam triennio nihil erat in lingua quod requirerent; bonos ₁₅
auctores, nisi obstet libri menda, inoffense perlegerent. Eas literas,
ut equidem conicio, ob id quoque facilius arripuerunt quod nonnihil illis essent cognatae. Suspicor enim eam gentem a Graecis origi-
nem duxisse propterea quod sermo illorum, cetera fere Persicus,
nonnulla Graeci sermonis vestigia servet in urbium ac magistratuum ₂₀
vocabulis.

Habent ex me (nam librorum sarcinam mediocrem loco mercium
quarto navigaturus in navem conieci, quod mecum plane decrev-
eram numquam potius redire quam cito) Platonis opera pleraque,
Aristotelis plura, Theophrastum item de plantis, sed pluribus, quod ₂₅
doleo, in locis mutilum. In librum enim dum navigabamus negligentius habitum cercopithecus inciderat, qui lasciviens ac ludi-
bundus paginas aliquot hinc atque inde evulsas laceravit. Ex his qui
scripsere grammaticam, Lascarem habent tantum, Theodorum enim
non advexi mecum, nec dictionarium aliquem praeter Hesychium ₃₀
ac Dioscoridem. Plutarchi libellos habent charissimos, et Luciani

Utilitas linguae graecae

Docilitas Utopiensium mira

At nunc stipites et caudices dicantur literis: felicissima ingenia voluptatibus corrumpuntur

are not very fond of it. In intellectual pursuits they are tireless. When they heard from us about the literature and learning of the Greeks (for we thought that, except for the historians and poets, there was nothing in Latin that they would value), it was wonderful to behold how eagerly they sought to learn Greek through our instruction. We therefore began to read with them, at first more to avoid seeming lazy than out of any expectation they would profit by it. But after a short trial, their diligence immediately convinced us that ours would not be wasted. They picked up the forms of letters so easily, pronounced the language so aptly, memorised it so quickly, and began to recite so accurately, that it seemed like a miracle. Most of our pupils were established scholars, of course, picked for their unusual ability and mature minds; and they studied with us, not just of their own free will, but at the command of the senate. Thus in less than three years they had perfect control of the language, and could read the best authors fluently, unless the text was corrupt. I have a feeling they picked up Greek more easily because it was somewhat related to their own tongue. Though their language resembles Persian in most respects, I suspect their race descends from the Greeks because, in the names of cities and in official titles, they retain some vestiges of the Greek tongue.

Before leaving on the fourth voyage[78] I placed on board, instead of merchandise, a good-sized packet of books; for I had resolved not to return at all rather than come home soon. Thus they received from me most of Plato's works and more of Aristotle's, as well as Theophrastus' book *On Plants*,[79] though the latter, I'm sorry to say, was somewhat mutilated. During the voyage I carelessly left it lying around, a monkey got hold of it, and from sheer mischief ripped out a few pages here and there and tore them up. Of the grammarians they have only Lascaris, for I did not take Theodorus with me, nor any dictionary except that of Hesychius; and they have Dioscorides.[80] They are very fond of Plutarch's writings, and delighted with the witty persiflage of Lucian.[81] Among the poets

The usefulness of the Greek tongue

The Utopians' wonderful aptitude for learning

But now clods and blockheads are assigned to learning, while the best minds are corrupted by pleasures

[78] The Latin says 'for the fourth time' (*quarto*): but either we are to understand the word as in the translation or else it is a slip, since we know (from p. 45) that Hythloday accompanied Vespucci only on the last three of his four voyages.

[79] Theophrastus was a pupil of Aristotle. His views were still current in the Renaissance.

[80] Constantinus Lascaris and Theodorus Gaza wrote Renaissance grammars of Greek. The Greek dictionary of Hesychius (fifth century AD?) was first printed in 1514. Dioscorides (first century AD) wrote a treatise on drugs and herbs (not properly a dictionary), which was printed in 1499.

[81] 'Plutarch's writings' presumably includes the *Moralia* as well as the *Parallel Lives* of eminent Greeks and Romans. For Lucian, see Introduction, p. xxv.

quoque facetiis ac lepore capiuntur. Ex poetis habent Aristophanem, Homerum atque Euripidem, tum Sophoclem minusculis. Aldi formulis. Ex historicis Thucydidem atque Herodotum, necnon Herodianum.

Quin in re medica quoque sodalis meus Tricius Apinatus advexerat secum parva quaedam Hippocratis opuscula ac Microtechnen Galeni, quos libros magno in pretio habent. Siquidem etsi omnium *Medicina* fere gentium re medica minime egent, nusquam tamen in maiore *utilissima* honore est vel eo ipso quod eius cognitionem numerant inter pulcherrimas atque utilissimas partes philosophiae. Cuius ope philosophiae dum naturae secreta scrutantur, videntur sibi non solum *Contemplatio* admirabilem inde voluptatem percipere, sed apud auctorem quoque *naturae* eius atque opificem summam inire gratiam. Quem,[34] ceterorum more artificum, arbitrantur mundi huius visendam machinam homini (quem solum tantae rei capacem fecit) exposuisse spectandam, eoque chariorem habere curiosum ac sollicitum inspectorem, operisque sui admiratorem, quam eum qui velut animal expers mentis tantum ac tam mirabile spectaculum stupidus immotusque neglexerit.

Utopiensium itaque exercitata literis ingenia mire valent ad inventiones artium quae faciant aliquid ad commodae vitae compendia. Sed duas tamen debent nobis, chalcographorum et faciendae chartae, nec solis tamen nobis sed sibi quoque bonam eius partem. Nam quum ostenderemus eis libris chartaceis impressas ab Aldo literas, et de chartae faciendae materia ac literas imprimendi facultate loqueremur aliquid, magis quam explicaremus (neque enim quisquam erat nostrum qui alterutram calleret), ipsi statim acutissime coniecerunt rem. Et quum ante pellibus, corticibus ac papyro

----

[34] *Quem* (referring to *auctorem . . . atque opificem*) is the reading of 1517; *quae* of the other early texts. *ceterorum more artificum* makes sense only with *quem*.

they have Aristophanes, Homer and Euripides, together with Sophocles in the small typeface of the Aldine edition.[82] Of the historians they possess Thucydides and Herodotus, as well as Herodian.[83]

As for medical books, a comrade of mine named Tricius Apinatus[84] brought with him some small treatises by Hippocrates, and the *Microtechne* of Galen.[85] They were delighted to have these books because, even though there is hardly a country in the world that needs medicine less, still it is nowhere held in greater honour, *Medicine the most* since they consider a knowledge of it one of the finest and most *useful of studies* useful parts of philosophy.[86] They think that when, with the help of philosophy, they explore the secrets of nature, they are gratifying not only themselves but the author and maker of nature. They *Contemplation of* suppose that like other artists he created this beautiful mechanism *nature* of the world to be admired – and by whom, if not by man, who is alone in being able to appreciate so great a thing? Therefore he is bound to prefer a careful observer and sensitive admirer of his work before one who, like a brute beast, looks on such a grand and wonderful spectacle with a stupid and inert mind.

Once stimulated by learning, the minds of the Utopians are wonderfully quick to seek out those various skills which make life more agreeable. Two inventions, to be sure, they owe to us: the art of printing and the manufacture of paper. At least they owe these arts partly to us, though also in good measure to themselves. While we were showing them the books printed on paper in Aldine letters, we talked about what paper is made of and how letters are printed, though without going into details, for none of us had had any practical experience of either skill. But with great sharpness of mind they immediately conceived how to do it. While previously they had written only on vellum, bark and papyrus, they now undertook

---

[82] The first modern edition of Sophocles was that of Aldus Manutius in 1502. The house of Aldus, where Erasmus lived and worked for a while, was distinguished both for its list of Greek and Latin works and for its contributions to the art of book design.

[83] Thucydides and Herodotus are the great historians of classical Greece. Herodian (c. 175–250 AD) wrote a history of the Roman emperors of the second and third centuries.

[84] A learned joke (in keeping with Hythloday's own name) based on a passage in the *Epigrams* of Martial. Martial says of one set of his poems that *Sunt apinae tricaeque*: 'They're trifles and toys' (XIV.i).

[85] Hippocrates (fifth century BC) and Galen (second century AD) were the most influential Greek medical writers. The *Microtechne* is a medieval summary of Galen's ideas.

[86] As earlier (p. 157), 'philosophy' is employed in its old, inclusive sense.

tantum scriberent, iam chartam ilico facere et literas imprimere tentarunt. Quae quum primo non satis procederent, eadem saepius experiendo brevi sunt utrumque consecuti, tantumque effecerunt ut, si essent Graecorum exemplaria librorum, codices deesse non possent. At nunc nihil habent amplius quam a me commemoratum 5 est. Id vero quod habent impressis iam libris in multa exemplariorum millia propagavere.

Quisquis eo spectandi gratia venerit quem insignis aliqua dos ingenii aut longa peregrinatione usum multarum cognitio terrarum commendet (quo nomine gratus fuit noster appulsus) pronis animis 10 excipitur. Quippe libenter audiunt quid ubique terrarum geratur. Ceterum mercandi gratia non admodum frequenter appellitur. Quid enim ferrent nisi aut ferrum aut, quod quisque referre mallet, aurum argentumve? Tum quae ex ipsis exportanda sint, ea consultius putant ab se efferri quam ab aliis illinc peti, quo et exteras undique 15 gentes exploratiores habeant neque maritimarum rerum usum ac peritiam oblitum eant.

DE SERVIS

Mira huius gentis Pro servis neque bello captos habent nisi ab ipsis gesto neque
aequitas servorum filios neque denique quemquam quem apud alias gentes 20 servientem possent comparare, sed aut si cuius apud se flagitium in servitium vertitur, aut quos apud exteras urbes (quod genus multo frequentius est) admissum facinus destinavit supplicio, eorum enim multos, interdum aestimatos vili, saepius etiam gratis impetratos, auferunt. Haec servorum genera non in opere solum perpetuo, 25 verumetiam in vinculis habent, sed suos durius quos eo deploratiores ac deteriora meritos exempla censent quod tam praeclara educatione ad virtutem egregie instructi contineri tamen ab scelere non

to make paper and print with type. Their first attempts were not altogether successful, but with practice they soon mastered both arts. They became so proficient that, if they had the texts of the Greek authors, they would have no lack of volumes. But now they have no more than those I mentioned – which, however, they have reprinted in thousands of copies.

Any sightseer coming to their land who has some special intellectual gift, or who has travelled widely and knows about many countries, is sure of a warm welcome. That is why we were received so kindly. Indeed they love to hear what is happening throughout the world. Few merchants, however, go there to trade. What could they import, except iron – or else gold and silver, which everyone would rather take home than send abroad? As for the export trade, they prefer to do their own transportation, instead of letting strangers come there to fetch the goods. By carrying their own cargoes, they are able to learn more about foreign countries on all sides and keep their own navigational skills from getting rusty.

SLAVES

The only prisoners of war the Utopians keep as slaves are those captured in wars they fight themselves.[87] The children of slaves are not born into slavery,[88] nor are any slaves obtained from foreign countries. They are either their own citizens, enslaved for some heinous offence, or else foreigners who had been condemned to death in their own cities; the latter sort predominate. Sometimes the Utopians buy them at a low price; more often they ask for them, get them for nothing, and bring them home in considerable numbers. These kinds of slaves are not only kept constantly at work, but are always fettered. The Utopians, however, deal more harshly with their own people than with the others, feeling that they are worse and deserve stricter punishment because they had an excellent education and the best of moral training, yet still

The wonderful fairness of these people

[87] In classical times prisoners of war – civilians as well as soldiers – constituted a major source of slaves. By More's day there was general agreement that it was wrong for Christians to enslave Christian captives; but non-Christians – especially Africans and American Indians – were often regarded as a different matter. A later passage (p. 217) suggests that the Utopians enslave only the defenders of cities they have had to besiege.

[88] The non-hereditary character of Utopian slavery distinguishes it sharply from that of the classical world and from medieval serfdom.

potuerint. Aliud servorem genus est quum alterius populi mediastinus quispiam laboriosus ac pauper elegerit apud eos sua sponte servire. Hos honeste tractant ac nisi quod laboris utpote consuetis imponitur plusculum, non multo minus clementer ac cives habent. Volentem discedere (quod non saepe fit) neque retinent invitum neque inanem dimittunt.

De aegrotis   Aegrotantes, ut dixi, magno cum affectu curant, nihilque prorsus omittunt quo sanitati eos vel medicinae vel victus observatione restituant. Quin insanabili morbo laborantes assidendo, colloquendo, adhibendo demum quae possunt levamenta, solantur. Ceterum si non immedicabilis modo morbus sit, verumetiam perpetuo vexet atque discruciet, tum sacerdotes ac magistratus hortantur hominem, *Mors spontanea* quandoquidem omnibus vitae muniis impar, aliis molestus ac sibi gravis, morti iam suae supervivat, ne secum statuat pestem diutius ac luem alere, neve quum tormentum ei vita sit, mori dubitet: quin bona spe fretus, acerba illa vita velut carcere atque aculeo vel ipse semet eximat vel ab aliis eripi se sua voluntate patiatur. Hoc illum quum non commoda sed supplicium abrupturus morte sit, prudenter facturum; quoniam vero sacerdotum in ea re consiliis, id est interpretum dei, sit obsecuturus, etiam pie sancteque facturum.

Haec quibus persuaserint aut inedia sponte vitam finiunt aut sopiti sine mortis sensu solvuntur. Invitum vero neminem tollunt, nec officii erga eum quicquam imminuunt. Persuasos hoc pacto defungi honorificum, alioqui qui mortem sibi consciverit causa non

couldn't be restrained from wrongdoing.[89] A third class of slaves consists of hard-working penniless drudges from other nations who voluntarily choose slavery in Utopia. Such people are treated with respect, almost as kindly as citizens, except that they are assigned a little extra work, on the score that they're used to it. If one of them wants to leave, which seldom happens, no obstacles are put in his way, nor is he sent off empty-handed.

As I said before, they care for the sick with great affection, neg- *The sick* lecting nothing whatever in the way of medicine or diet which might restore them to health. Everything possible is done to mitigate the pain of those suffering from incurable diseases; and visitors do their best to console them by sitting and talking with them. But if the disease is not only incurable, but excruciatingly and unremittingly painful, then the priests and public officials come and remind the sufferer that he is now unequal to any of life's duties, a burden *Deliberate death* to himself and others; he has really outlived his own death. They tell him he should not let the pestilence prey on him any longer, but now that life is simply torture he should not hesitate to die but should rely on hope for something better; and since his life is a prison where he is bitterly tormented, he should escape from it on his own or allow others to rescue him from it.[90] This would be a wise act, they say, since for him death would put an end not to pleasure but to agony. In addition, he would be obeying the counsel of the priests, who are the interpreters of God's will; thus it would be a pious and holy act.[91]

Those who have been persuaded by these arguments either starve themselves to death of their own accord or, having been put to sleep, are freed from life without any sensation of dying. But they never force this step on a man against his will; nor, if he decides against it, do they lessen their care of him. The man who yields to their arguments, they think, dies an honourable death; but the suicide, who takes his own life without approval of priests and senate,

---

[89] For the same reason, Plato would punish lawbreakers among the citizens of his ideal commonwealth more severely than non-citizens who commit the same crime (*Laws* IX.854E).

[90] More was fond of the figure of the world as a prison. See his Latin poem no. 119 (*CW*, III, Part II, 167–9), *A Dialogue Concerning Heresies* (*CW*, VI, 259–77) and *The Four Last Things* (*English Works*, I, 479–80).

[91] Though in the ancient world suicide was regarded as an honourable way out of deep personal and political difficulties, neither suicide nor euthanasia was (or is) acceptable in Catholic Christianity. More discusses the 'wicked temptation' of suicide at length in *A Dialogue of Comfort against Tribulation* (1534) (*CW*, XII, 122–57); and cf. Hythloday's earlier reference to God's prohibition of self-slaughter (p. 69).

probata sacerdotibus et senatui, hunc neque terra neque igne dignantur, sed in paludem aliquam turpiter insepultus abicitur.

De coniugiis   Femina non ante annum duodevicesimum nubit, mas non nisi expletis quattuor etiam amplius. Ante coniugium mas aut femina si convincatur furtivae libidinis graviter in eum eamve animadvertitur, 5 coniugioque illis in totum interdicitur nisi venia principis noxam remiserit. Sed et pater et mater[35] familias cuius in domo admissum flagitium est, tamquam suas partes parum diligenter tutati, magnae obiacent infamiae. Id facinus ideo tam severe vindicant quod futurum prospiciunt ut rari in coniugalem amorem coalescerent, in quo 10 aetatem omnem cum uno videant exigendam, et perferendas insuper quas ea res adfert molestias, nisi a vago concubitu diligenter arceantur.

Porro in deligendis coniugibus ineptissimum ritum (ut nobis visum est) adprimeque ridiculum illi serio ac severe observant. Mul- 15
Et si parum   ierem enim, seu virgo seu vidua sit, gravis et honesta matrona proco
verecunde haud   nudam exhibet, ac probus aliquis vir vicissim nudam puellae
tamen incaute   procum sistit. Hunc morem quum velut ineptum ridentes improbaremus, illi contra ceterarum omnium gentium insignem demirari stultitiam, qui quum in equuleo comparando ubi de paucis agitur 20 nummis tam cauti sint ut, quamvis fere nudum, nisi detracta sella tamen omnibusque revulsis ephippiis, recusent emere, ne sub illis operculis ulcus aliquod delitesceret; in deligenda coniuge, qua ex re aut voluptas aut nausea sit totam per vitam comitatura, tam negligenter agant ut, reliquo corpore vestibus obvoluto, totam mulierem 25 vix ab unius palmae spatio (nihil enim praeter vultum visitur) aestiment adiungantque sibi, non absque magno (si quid offendat postea)

---

[35] We have adopted *et mater* from 1517, instead of the pleonastic *et materque* of the other three texts.

him they consider unworthy of either earth or fire, and they throw his body, unburied and disgraced, into a bog.

Women do not marry till they are eighteen, nor men till they are twenty-two.[92] Clandestine premarital intercourse, if discovered and proved, brings severe punishment on both man and woman; and the guilty parties are forbidden to marry for their whole lives, unless the governor by his pardon remits the sentence. Also both the father and mother of the household where the offence was committed suffer public disgrace for having been remiss in their duty. The reason they punish this offence so severely is that they suppose few people would join in married love – with confinement to a single partner and all the petty annoyances that married life involves – unless they were strictly restrained from promiscuous intercourse.

Marriages

In choosing marriage partners they solemnly and seriously follow a custom which seemed to us foolish and absurd in the extreme. Whether she be widow or virgin, the woman is shown naked to the suitor by a responsible and respectable matron; and similarly, some honourable man presents the suitor naked to the woman. We laughed at this custom, and called it absurd; but they were just as amazed at the folly of all other peoples. When men go to buy a colt, where they are risking only a little money, they are so cautious that, though the animal is almost bare, they won't close the deal until saddle and blanket have been taken off, lest there be a hidden sore underneath.[93] Yet in the choice of a mate, which may cause either delight or disgust for the rest of their lives, men are so careless that they leave all the rest of the woman's body covered up with clothes and estimate her attractiveness from a mere handsbreadth of her person, the face, which is all they can see. And so they marry, running great risk of bitter discord, if something in either's

Not very modest, but not so impractical either

---

[92] Canon law required that girls be at least twelve and boys at least fourteen at the time of marriage. In fact, even younger children were sometimes forced into marriage in Christian Europe.

[93] Plato's *Laws* commends with perfect seriousness a practice similar to the Utopians': 'when people are going to live together as partners in marriage, it is vital that the fullest possible information should be available . . . Boys and girls must dance together at an age when plausible occasions can be found for their doing so, in order that they may have a reasonable look at each other; and they should dance naked, provided sufficient modesty and restraint are displayed by all concerned' (VI.771E–772A). J.S. Cummins suggests that the Utopian custom may have had the purpose – hinted at in 'hidden sore' – of curbing the spread of syphilis, which had become a scourge in Europe (if not Utopia) by the time More wrote. See 'Pox and paranoia in Renaissance Europe', *History Today*, 38 (August 1988), 29.

male cohaerendi periculo. Nam neque omnes tam sapientes sunt ut solos mores respiciant, et in ipsorum quoque sapientum coniugiis, ad animi virtutes nonnihil additamenti corporis etiam dotes adiciunt. Certe tam foeda deformitas latere sub illis potest involucris ut alienare prorsus animum ab uxore queat, quum corpore iam seiungi 5 non liceat. Qualis deformitas si quo casu contingat post contractas nuptias suam quisque sortem necesse est[36] ferat: ante vero, ne quis capiatur insidiis, legibus caveri debet.

Idque tanto maiore studio fuit curandum quod et soli illarum orbis plagarum singulis sunt contenti coniugibus, et matrimonium 10 *Divortium* ibi haud saepe aliter quam morte solvitur, nisi adulterium in causa fuerit aut morum non ferenda molestia. Nempe alterutri sic offenso facta ab senatu coniugis mutandi venia; alter infamem simul ac caelibem perpetuo vitam ducit. Alioquin invitam coniugem cuius nulla sit noxa repudiare quod corporis obtigerit calamitas, id vero nullo 15 pacto ferunt. Nam et crudele iudicant tum quemquam deseri cum maxime eget solacio, et senectuti, quum et morbos adferat et morbus ipsa sit, incertam atque infirmam fidem fore.

Ceterum accidit interdum ut quum non satis inter se coniugum conveniant mores, repertis utrique aliis quibuscum sperent se suav- 20 ius esse victuros, amborum sponte separati, nova matrimonia contrahant, haud absque senatus auctoritate tamen, qui, nisi causa per se atque uxores suas diligenter cognita, divortia non admittit. Immo ne sic quidem facile, quod rem minime utilem sciunt firmandae coniugum charitati facilem novarum nuptiarum spem esse pro- 25 positam.

Temeratores coniugii gravissima servitute plectuntur, et si neuter erat caelebs iniuriam passi (velint modo) repudiatis adulteris coniu-

---

[36] *est*, following 1516, 1517 against 1518M, N, which omit.

person should offend the other. Not all people are so wise as to concern themselves solely with character; and even the wise appreciate the gifts of the body as a supplement to the virtues of the mind. There's no doubt that a deformity may lurk under clothing, serious enough to alienate a man's mind from his wife when his body can no longer lawfully be separated from her. If some disfiguring accident takes place after marriage, each person must bear his own fate; but beforehand everyone should be legally protected from deception.

There is extra reason for them to be careful, because in that part of the world they are the only people who practise monogamy,[94] and because their marriages are seldom terminated except by death – though they do allow divorce for adultery or for intolerably *Divorce* offensive behaviour. A husband or wife who is the aggrieved party in such a divorce is granted leave by the senate to take a new mate; the guilty party suffers disgrace and is permanently forbidden to remarry.[95] But they absolutely forbid a husband to put away his wife against her will and without any fault on her part, just because of some bodily misfortune; they think it cruel that a person should be abandoned when most in need of comfort; and they add that old age, since it not only entails disease but is a disease itself,[96] needs more than a precarious fidelity.

It happens occasionally that a married couple have incompatible characters, and have both found other persons with whom they hope to live more harmoniously. After getting approval of the senate, they may then separate by mutual consent and contract new marriages. But such divorces are allowed only after the senators and their wives have carefully investigated the case. Divorce is deliberately made difficult because they know that conjugal love will hardly be strengthened if each partner has in mind that a new marriage is easily available.

Violators of the marriage bond are punished with the strictest form of slavery. If both parties were married, both are divorced,

---

[94] In this respect the Utopians resemble the ancient Germans as portrayed by Tacitus: 'the marriage tie with them is strict: you will find nothing in their character to praise more highly. They are almost the only barbarians who are content with a wife apiece' (*Germania* 17).

[95] Although the Church in More's day permitted separation in the case of adultery, it did not allow the injured party to remarry. Erasmus, however, thought the Church was wrong on this point, and argued not only for the right of remarriage in cases of adultery but in general for a relaxation of canon law on the indissolubility of marriage. See the discussion in *CW*, IV, 482.

[96] The phrase comes from Terence's comedy *Phormio* (IV.i; l. 575).

gio inter se ipsi iunguntur, alioquin quibus videbitur. At si laesorum alteruter erga tam male merentem coniugem in amore persistat, tamen uti coniugii lege non prohibetur si velit in opera damnatum sequi: acciditque interdum ut alterius paenitentia, alterius officiosa sedulitas, miserationem commovens principi, libertatem rursus 5 impetret. Ceterum ad scelus iam relapso nex infligitur.

Aestimatio supplicii penes magistratum Ceteris facinoribus nullam certam poenam lex ulla praestituit, sed ut quodque atrox aut contra visum est, ita supplicium senatus decernit. Uxores mariti castigant et parentes liberos: nisi quid tam ingens admiserint ut id publice puniri morum intersit. Sed fere grav- 10 issima quaeque scelera servitutis incommodo puniuntur, id siquidem et sceleratis non minus triste, et reipublicae magis commodum arbitrantur quam si mactare noxios et protinus amoliri festinent. Nam et labore quam nece magis prosunt et exemplo diutius alios ab simili flagitio deterrent. Quod si sic habiti rebellent atque recal- 15 citrent, tum demum, velut indomitae beluae, quos coercere carcer et catena non potest, trucidantur. At patientibus non adimitur omnis omnino spes. Quippe longis domiti malis si eam paenitentiam prae se ferant quae peccatum testetur magis eis displicere quam poenam, principis interdum praerogativa, interdum suffragiis populi, aut 20 mitigatur servitus aut remittitur.

Stupri sollicitati poena Sollicitasse ad stuprum nihilo minus quam stuprasse periculi est. In omni siquidem flagitio certum destinatumque conatum aequant facto: neque enim id quod defuit ei putant prodesse debere per quem non stetit quominus nihil defuerit. 25

Voluptas e morionibus Moriones in deliciis habentur, quos ut adfecisse contumelia magno in probro est, ita voluptatem ab stultitia capere non vetant. Siquidem id morionibus ipsis maximo esse bono censent. Cuius[37] qui tam severus ac tristis est ut nullum neque factum neque dictum rideat, ei tutandum non credunt, veriti ne non satis indulgenter 30 curetur ab eo, cui non modo nulli usui sed ne oblectamento quidem (qua sola dote valet)[38] futurus esset.

---

[37] Lupton and Delcourt manage to make tortuous sense (Lupton calls the construction 'harsh') out of *cuius* (the reading of all four early editions) by making it refer to *morionis* understood from the preceding *morionibus* and taking it to modify *neque factum neque dictum*. To emend to the dative *cuivis* after *credunt*, modified by the *qui*-clause and reiterated by *ei*, might improve the grammar. Both Yale and Prévost, in fact, translate as if the text read *cuivis*. But since *cuius* is possible, we have let it stand.

[38] We have adopted *valet* from 1516 and 1517 instead of *valent* in 1518M and N in order to make the verb agree with *curetur* and *esset*.

and the injured parties may marry one another if they want, or someone else. But if one of the injured parties continues to love such an undeserving spouse, the marriage may go on, provided the innocent person chooses to share in the labour to which the slave is condemned. And sometimes it happens that the repentance of the guilty and the devotion of the innocent party so move the governor to pity that he restores both to freedom. But a relapse into the same crime is punished by death.

No other crimes carry fixed penalties; the senate decrees a specific punishment for each misdeed, as it is considered atrocious or venial. Husbands chastise their wives and parents their children, unless the offence is so serious that public punishment is called for. Generally, the gravest crimes are punished with slavery, for they think this deters offenders just as much as getting rid of them by immediate capital punishment, and convict labour is more beneficial to the commonwealth. Slaves, moreover, contribute more by their labour than by their death, and they are permanent and visible reminders that crime does not pay. If the slaves rebel against their condition, then, since neither bars nor chains can tame them, they are finally put to death like wild beasts. But if they are patient, they are not left altogether without hope. When subdued by long hardships, if they show by their behaviour that they regret the crime more than the punishment, their slavery is lightened or remitted altogether, sometimes by the governor's prerogative, sometimes by popular vote.

Assignment of punishments left to the magistracy

Attempted seduction is subject to the same penalty as seduction itself. They think that a crime clearly and deliberately attempted is as bad as one committed, and that failure should not confer advantages on a criminal who did all he could to succeed.

The penalty for soliciting to lewdness

They are very fond of fools, and think it contemptible to insult them.[97] There is no prohibition against enjoying their foolishness, and they even regard this as beneficial to the fools. If anyone is so solemn and severe that the foolish behaviour and comic patter of a clown do not amuse him, they don't entrust him with the care of such a person, for fear that one who gets not only no use from a fool but not even any amusement – a fool's only gift – will not treat him kindly.

Pleasure derived from fools

[97] Erasmus wrote of More that 'there is nothing in human life to which he cannot look for entertainment ... If he has to do with educated and intelligent people, he enjoys their gifts; if they are ignorant and stupid, he is amused by their absurdity' (*CWE*, VII, 19). More's household fool, Henry Patenson, appears in Holbein's sketch of the family.

Irridere deformem aut mutilum, turpe ac deforme non ei qui ridetur habetur sed irrisori, qui cuiquam quod in eius potestate non erat ut fugeret, id vitii loco stulte exprobret.

Fucata forma   Ut enim formam naturalem non tueri segnis atque inertis ducunt, sic adiumentum ab fucis quaerere infamis apud illos insolentia est.   5 Usu enim ipso sentiunt quam non ullum formae decus uxores aeque ac morum probitas et reverentia commendet maritis. Nam ut forma nonnulli sola capiuntur, ita nemo nisi virtute atque obsequio retinetur.

Et praemiis invitandi cives ad officium   Non poenis tantum deterrent a flagitiis, sed propositis quoque 10 honoribus ad virtutes invitant. Ideoque statuas viris insignibus et de republica praeclare meritis in foro collocant, in rerum bene gestarum memoriam simul ut ipsorum posteris maiorum suorum gloria calcar et incitamentum ad virtutem sit.

Damnatus ambitus   Qui magistratum ullum ambierit exspes omnium redditur. Con- 15 vivunt amabiliter, quippe nec magistratus ullus insolens aut terribilis

Honor magistratuum est; patres apellantur et exhibent. Eisdem defertur (ut debet) ab

Dignitas principis volentibus honor, non ab invitis exigitur. Ne principem quidem ipsum vestis aut diadema sed gestatus frumenti manipulus discernit, ut pontificis insigne est praelatus cereus. 20

Leges paucae   Leges habent perquam paucas, sufficiunt enim sic institutis paucissimae. Quin hoc in primis apud alios improbant populos, quod legum interpretumque volumina non infinita sufficiunt. Ipsi vero censent iniquissimum ullos homines his obligari legibus quae aut numerosiores sint quam ut perlegi queant, aut obscuriores quam ut 25

Advocatorum inutilis turba a quovis possint intellegi. Porro causidicos, qui causas tractent callide ac leges vafre disputent,[39] prorsus omnes excludunt. Censent enim ex usu esse ut suam quisque causam agat, eademque referat iudici quae narraturus patrono fuerat, sic et minus ambagum fore et facilius elici veritatem dum, eo dicente quem nullus patronus 30 fucum docuit, iudex sollerter expendit singula, et contra versutorum calumnias simplicioribus ingeniis opitulatur. Haec apud alias gentes

---

[39] *tractent . . . disputent*] 1518M, N; *tractant . . . disputent* 1516; *tractant . . . disputant* 1517. Here again 1517 and 1518 correct 1516 in different ways: 1517 makes both verbs indicative, and 1518 makes them both subjunctive. It would be possible to take the indicatives of 1517 restrictively: the Utopians exclude only the lawyers who are crafty, but not necessarily all lawyers (they do, after all, have some laws). But the characteristic subjunctives of 1518 have to be nonrestrictive: they exclude all lawyers, who are in fact crafty.

To deride a person for being deformed or crippled is considered ugly and disfiguring, not to the victim but to the mocker, who stupidly reproaches the cripple for something he cannot help.

Though they think it a sign of weak and sluggish character to neglect one's natural beauty, they consider cosmetics a disgraceful affectation. From experience they have learned that no physical attractions recommend a wife to her husband so effectually as an upright character and a respectful attitude. Though some men are captured by beauty alone, none are held except by virtue and compliance. *Artificial beauty*

They not only deter people from crime by penalties, but they incite them to virtue by public honours. Accordingly, they set up in the marketplace statues of distinguished men who have served their country well, thinking thereby to preserve the memory of their good deeds and to spur on citizens to emulate the glory of their ancestors. *Citizens to be encouraged by rewards to do their duty*

Any man who campaigns for a public office is disqualified for all of them. They live together in a friendly fashion, and their public officials are never arrogant or unapproachable. They are called 'fathers', and that indeed is the way they behave. Because officials never extort respect from the people against their will, the people respect them spontaneously, as they should. The governor himself is distinguished from his fellow citizens not by a robe or a crown but only by the sheaf of grain he bears, as the sign of the high priest is a wax candle carried before him.[98] *Running for office condemned* *Magistrates held in honour* *Dignity of the governor*

They have very few laws, for their training is such that very few suffice.[99] The chief fault they find with other nations is that even their infinite volumes of laws and interpretations are not adequate. They think it completely unjust to bind people by a set of laws that are too many to be read or too obscure for anyone to understand. As for lawyers, a class of men whose trade it is to manipulate cases and multiply quibbles, they exclude them entirely. They think it practical for each man to plead his own case, and say the same thing to the judge that he would tell his lawyer. This makes for less confusion and readier access to the truth. A man speaks his mind without tricky instructions from a lawyer, and the judge examines each point carefully, taking pains to protect simple folk against the *Few laws* *The useless crowd of lawyers*

[98] Grain (suggesting prosperity) and candle (suggesting vision) symbolise the special function of each.
[99] The idea that good education obviates the need for an elaborate system of law is common in the literature of the ideal commonwealth. See, for example, Plato, *Republic* IV.425C–D; Plutarch, 'Lycurgus' XIII.1–2.

in tanto perplexissimarum acervo legum difficile est observari. Ceterum apud eos unusquisque est legis peritus. Nam et sunt (ut dixi) paucissimae, et interpretationum praeterea ut quaeque est maxime crassa, ita maxime aequam censent. Nempe quum omnes leges (inquiunt) ea tantum causa promulgentur ut ab his quisque sui com- 5 monefiat officii, subtilior interpretatio paucissimos admonet (pauci enim sunt qui assequantur), quum interim simplicior ac magis obvius legum sensus omnibus in aperto sit. Alioquin, quod ad vulgus attinet, cuius et maximus est numerus et maxime eget admonitu, quid referat utrum legem omnino non condas an condi- 10 tam in talem interpreteris sententiam quam nisi magno ingenio et longa disputatione nemo possit eruere? ad quam investigandam neque crassum vulgi iudicium queat attingere neque vita in comparando victu occupata sufficere.

His eorum virtutibus incitati finitimi qui quidem liberi sunt et 15 suae spontis (multos enim ipsi iam olim tyrannide liberaverunt) magistratus sibi ab illis, alii quotannis, alii in lustrum, impetrant, quos defunctos imperio cum honore ac laude reducunt, novosque secum rursus in patriam revehunt. Atque hi quidem populi optime profecto ac saluberrime reipublicae suae consulunt, cuius et salus 20 et pernicies, quum ab moribus magistratuum pendeat, quosnam potuissent elegisse prudentius quam qui neque ullo pretio queant ab honesto deduci (utpote quod brevi sit remigraturis inutile) neque,[40] ignoti civibus, aut pravo cuiusquam studio aut simultate flecti? Quae duo mala, affectus atque avaritiae, sicubi incubuere iudiciis, 25 ilico iustitiam omnem, fortissimum reipublicae nervum, dissolvunt. Hos Utopiani populos quibus qui imperent ab ipsis petuntur appellant socios, ceteros quos beneficiis auxerunt amicos vocant.

De foederibus Foedera quae reliquae inter se gentes toties ineunt, frangunt, ac renovant, ipsi nulla cum gente feriunt. Quorsum enim foedus, 30 inquiunt, quasi non hominem homini satis natura conciliet, quam

---

[40] To complete a *neque* . . . *neque* construction we follow Lupton and Delcourt in adding, without textual authority, this second *neque*.

false accusations of the crafty. This sort of plain dealing is hard to find in other nations, where they have such a mass of incomprehensibly intricate laws. But in Utopia everyone is a legal expert. For the laws are very few, as I said, and they consider the most obvious interpretation of any law to be the fairest. As they see things, all laws are promulgated for the single purpose of advising every man of his duty. Subtle interpretations admonish very few, since hardly anybody can understand them, whereas the more simple and apparent sense of the law is open to everyone. If laws are not clear, they are useless; for simple-minded men (and most men are of this sort, and must be told where their duty lies), there might as well be no laws at all as laws which can be interpreted only by devious minds after endless disputes. The dull mind of the common man cannot understand such laws, and couldn't even if he studied them his whole life, since he has to earn a living in the meantime.

Some of their free and independent neighbours (the Utopians themselves previously liberated many of them from tyranny) have learned to admire the Utopian virtues, and now of their own accord ask the Utopians to supply magistrates for them. Of these magistrates, some serve for one year, others for five.[100] When their term of office is over, they bring them home with honour and praise, and take back new ones to their country. These peoples seem to have settled on an excellent scheme to safeguard the commonwealth. Since the welfare or ruin of a commonwealth depends on the character of the officials, where could they make a more prudent choice than among those who cannot be corrupted by money? For money is useless to them when they go home, as they soon must, and they can have no partisan or factional feelings, since they are strangers in the city over which they rule. Wherever they take root in men's minds, these two evils, greed and faction, soon destroy all justice, which is the strongest bond of any society. The Utopians call these people who have borrowed magistrates from them their allies; others whom they have benefited they call simply friends.

While other nations are constantly making, breaking and *Treaties* renewing treaties, the Utopians make none at all with any nation. If nature, they say, doesn't bind man adequately to his fellow man,

---

[100] Surtz notes the parallel with the Italian institution of the *podestà*, 'an official rather like the present-day city-manager, a professional administrator from outside the city, who stood above the factions within and who was employed for a limited and prescribed time' (*CW*, IV, 491).

qui contempserit, hunc verba scilicet putes curaturum? In hanc sententiam eo vel maxime trahuntur quod in illis terrarum plagis foedera pactaque principum solent parum bona fide servari.

Etenim in Europa, idque his potissimum partibus quas CHRISTI fides et religio possidet, sancta est et inviolabilis ubique maiestas 5 foedorum, partim ipsa iustitia et bonitate principum, partim summorum reverentia metuque pontificum, qui ut nihil in se recipiunt ipsi quod non religiosissime praestant, ita ceteros omnes principes iubent ut pollicitis omnibus modis immorentur, tergiversantes vero pastorali censura et severitate compellunt. Merito sane censent tur- 10 pissimam rem videri si illorum foederibus absit fides qui peculiari nomine fideles appellantur.

At in illo novo orbe terrarum quem circulus aequator vix tam longe ab hoc nostro orbe semovet quam vita moresque dissident, foederum nulla fiducia est: quorum ut quodque[41] plurimis ac 15 sanctissimis caerimoniis innodatum fuerit, ita citissime solvitur, inventa facile in verbis calumnia, quae sic interim de industria dictant callide ut numquam tam firmis astringi vinculis queant quin elabantur aliqua foedusque et fidem pariter eludant. Quam vafriciem, immo quam fraudem dolumque, si privatorum deprehenderent 20 intervenisse contractui, magno supercilio rem sacrilegam et furca dignam clamitarent, hi nimirum ipsi qui eius consilii principibus dati semet gloriantur auctores. Quo fit ut iustitia tota videatur aut non nisi plebea virtus et humilis quaeque longo intervallo subsidat infra regale fastigium, aut uti saltem duae sint, quarum altera vulgus 25 deceat, pedestris et humirepa,[42] neve usquam saepta transilire queat, multis undique restricta vinculis, altera principum virtus quae, sicuti

[41] *quodque*, following 1516 and 1517 in preference to *quoque* (1518M, N), which makes little sense.
[42] For the non-classical adjective *humirepa* (fem.), Latham (*Dictionary of Medieval Latin from British Sources*) gives only this place, with the meaning 'creeping on the ground'.

what good is a treaty? If a man scorns nature herself, is there any reason to think he will care about mere words? They are confirmed in this view by the fact that in that part of the world, treaties and alliances between princes are not generally observed with much good faith.

In Europe, of course, and especially in these regions where the Christian faith and religion prevail, the dignity of treaties is everywhere kept sacred and inviolable. This is partly because the princes are all so just and virtuous, partly also from the awe and reverence that everyone feels for the popes.[101] Just as the popes themselves never promise anything that they do not scrupulously perform, so they command all other princes to abide by their promises in every way. If someone declines to do so, by pastoral censure and sharp reproof they compel him to obey. They think, and rightly, that it would be shameful if people who are specifically called 'the faithful' acted in bad faith.

But in that new world, which is as distant from ours in customs and manners as by the distance the equator puts between us, nobody trusts treaties. The greater the formalities, the more numerous and solemn the oaths, the sooner the treaty will be broken. They easily find some defect in the wording, which often enough they deliberately inserted themselves. No treaty can be made so strong and explicit that a government will not be able to worm out of it, breaking in the process both the treaty and its own word. If such craft (not to call it deceit and fraud) were practised in private contracts, the politicians would raise a great outcry against both parties, calling them sacrilegious and worthy of the gallows. Yet the very same politicians think themselves clever fellows when they give this sort of advice to princes. Thus people are apt to think that justice is altogether a humble, plebeian virtue, far beneath the dignity of kings. Or else they conclude that there are two kinds of justice, one for the common herd, a lowly justice that creeps along the ground, hedged in everywhere and encumbered with chains; and the other, which is the justice of princes, much more majestic

---

[101] The European rulers of the time were in fact ruthless and casual violators of treaties. So also were two recent popes, Alexander VI and Julius II. Of the former, Machiavelli says admiringly that he 'never did anything else and never dreamed of anything else than deceiving men ... Never was there a man more effective in swearing and who with stronger oaths confirmed a promise, but yet honored it less' (*The Prince*, chapter 18; trans. Allan Gilbert, in Niccolò Machiavelli, *The Chief Works and Others*, 3 vols. (Durham, N.C., 1958), I, 65).

sit quam illa popularis augustior, sic est etiam longo intervallo
liberior, ut cui nihil non liceat nisi quod non libeat.

Hos mores, ut dixi, principum illic foedera tam male servantium
puto in causa esse ne ulla feriant Utopienses, mutaturi fortasse sententiam si hic viverent. Quamquam illis videtur ut optime serventur 5
male tamen inolevisse foederis omnino sanciendi consuetudinem:
qua fit ut (perinde ac si populum populo quos exiguo spatio collis
tantum aut rivus discriminat nulla naturae societas copularet) hostes
atque inimicos invicem sese natos putent, meritoque in mutuam
grassari perniciem, nisi foedera prohibeant, quin his ipsis quoque 10
initis non amicitiam coalescere, sed manere praedandi licentiam
quatenus per imprudentiam dictandi foederis nihil quod prohibeat
satis caute comprehensum in pactis est. At illi contra censent neminem pro inimico habendum a quo nihil iniuriae profectum est: naturae consortium foederis vice esse: et satius valentiusque homines 15
invicem benevolentia quam pactis, animo quam verbis, connecti.

DE RE MILITARI

Bellum utpote rem plane beluinam, nec ulli tamen beluarum formae
in tam assiduo atque homini est usu, summopere abominantur, contraque morem gentium ferme omnium nihil aeque ducunt inglorium 20
atque petitam e bello gloriam. Eoque, licet assidue militari sese
disciplina exerceant, neque id viri modo sed feminae quoque statis
diebus, ne ad bellum sint quum exigat usus inhabiles: non temere
capessunt tamen, nisi quo aut suos fines tueantur, aut amicorum
terris infusos hostes propulsent, aut populum quempiam tyrannide 25

and hence more free than common justice, so that it can do anything it wants and nothing it doesn't want.[102]

This royal practice of keeping treaties badly there is, I suppose, the reason the Utopians don't make any; perhaps if they lived here they would change their minds. However, they think it a bad idea to make treaties at all, even if they are faithfully kept. A treaty implies that people divided by some natural obstacle as slight as a hill or a brook are joined by no bond of nature; it assumes they are born rivals and enemies, and are right in trying to destroy one another except when a treaty restrains them. Besides, they see that treaties do not really promote friendship; for both parties still retain the right to prey on one another, insofar as careless drafting has left the treaty without sufficient provisions against it. The Utopians think, on the other hand, that no one should be considered an enemy who has done no harm, that the kinship of nature is as good as a treaty, and that men are united more firmly by good will than by pacts, by their hearts than by their words.

MILITARY PRACTICES

They utterly despise war as an activity fit only for beasts,[103] yet practised more by man than by any other animal. Unlike almost every other people in the world, they think nothing so inglorious as the glory won in battle. Yet on certain assigned days both men and women carry on vigorous military training, so they will be fit to fight should the need arise. But they go to war only for good reasons: to protect their own land, to drive invading armies from the territories of their friends, or to liberate an oppressed people,

---

[102] The idea that political morality differs from private, and the attendant notion that political necessity or *raison d'état* sometimes dictates policies that conflict with traditional morality, gained increasing acceptance in the late Middle Ages and the Renaissance. Aquinas notes Aristotle's demonstration (*Politics* III.iv.1–9) that the virtue of the good citizen is not always identical to that of the good man (*Sententia libri politicorum* III.3, in *Opera omnia* (Rome, 1882–), XLVIII, A 195–6). By the late fifteenth century, various Italian political writers were exploring the ways in which the virtues of a ruler might differ from those of ordinary people – explorations that culminated in Machiavelli.

[103] A false etymology derived Latin *bellum* ('war') from *belua* ('beast').

For the most part, the Utopians' attitudes towards war – basically pacifistic and thoroughly anti-chivalric – are similar to those of More and his humanist circle. For a full account, see R. P. Adams, *The Better Part of Valor*.

pressum miserati (quod humanitatis gratia faciunt) suis viribus tyranni iugo et servitute liberent. Quamquam auxilium gratificantur amicis, non semper quidem quo se defendant, sed interdum quoque illatas retalient atque ulciscantur iniurias. Verum id ita demum faciunt, si re adhuc integra consulantur ipsi, et probata causa, repetitis ac non redditis rebus, belli auctores inferendi sint: quod non tunc solum decernunt quoties hostili incursu abacta est praeda, verum tum quoque multo infestius quum eorum negotiatores usquam gentium, vel iniquarum praetextu legum vel sinistra derivatione bonarum, iniustam subeunt, iustitiae colore, calumniam.

Nec alia fuit eius origo belli quod pro Nephelogetis adversus Alaopolitas paulo ante nostram memoriam Utopienses gessere, quam apud Alaopolitas Nephelogetarum mercatoribus illata praetextu iuris (ut visum est ipsis) iniuria. Certe, sive illud ius sive ea iniuria fuit, bello tam atroci est vindicata, quum ad proprias utriusque partis vires odiaque, circumiectarum etiam gentium studia atque opes adiungerentur, ut florentissimis populorum aliis concussis, aliis vehementer adflictis, orientia ex malis mala Alaopolitarum servitus demum ac deditio finierit, qua in Nephelogetarum (neque enim sibi certabant Utopienses) potestatem concessere – gentis, florentibus Alaopolitarum rebus, haudquaquam cum illis conferendae.

Tam acriter Utopienses amicorum etiam in pecuniis iniuriam persequuntur, suas ipsorum non item: qui sicubi circumscripti bonis excidant, modo corporibus absit vis, hactenus irascuntur uti, quoad satisfactio fiat, eius commercio gentis abstineant, non quod minoris sibi curae cives quam socii sint, sed horum tamen pecuniam intercipi aegrius quam suam ferunt, propterea quod amicorum negotiatores, quoniam de suo perdunt privato, grave vulnus ex iactura sentiunt. At ipsorum civibus nihil nisi de publico[43] perit, prae-

---

[43] *publico*, following 1517 against the other texts' *publica*, to maintain parallel with *privato*. (*bono* or *thesauro* may be understood but is not needed.)

in the name of compassion and humanity, from tyranny and servitude.[104] They war not only to protect their friends from present danger, but sometimes to repay and avenge previous injuries. But they enter a conflict only if they themselves have been consulted in advance, have approved the cause, and have demanded restitution, but in vain, and only if they are the ones who begin the war. They take this final step not only when their friends have been plundered, but also, and even more fiercely, when their friends' merchants have been subjected to extortion anywhere in the world under the semblance of justice, either on the pretext of laws unjust in themselves or through the perversion of good laws.

This and no other was the cause of the war which the Utopians waged a little before our time on behalf of the Nephelogetes against the Alaopolitans.[105] Under pretext of right, a wrong (as they saw it) had been inflicted on some Nephelogete traders residing in Alaopolis. Whatever the rights and wrongs of the quarrel, it developed into a fierce war, to which, apart from the hostile forces of the two parties themselves, the neighbouring nations added their efforts and resources. Some prosperous nations were ravaged, others badly shaken. One trouble led to another, and in the end the Alaopolitans surrendered, and the Utopians (since they weren't involved on their own account) handed them over to be enslaved by the Nephelogetes – even though before the war the victors had not been remotely comparable in power to the Alaopolitans.

So sharply do the Utopians punish wrong done to their friends, even in matters of mere money; but they are not so strict in enforcing their own rights. When they are cheated out of their goods, so long as no bodily harm is done, their anger goes no further than cutting off trade relations with that nation till restitution is made. The reason is not that they care less for their own citizens than for their allies, but that the merchants of their friends, when they lose goods from their private stock, feel the loss more bitterly. The Utopian traders, by contrast, lose nothing but what belongs to the

---

[104] In the background is the ancient distinction between just and unjust wars. (A key locus is Cicero, *De officiis* I.xi.34–xiii.40.) It is not clear, though, that More would have approved of all the 'good reasons' for war listed here. Erasmus allows that purely defensive wars are just (*Complaint of Peace*, CWE, XXVII, 314), but he endorses Cicero's remark (*Epistulae ad familiares* VI.vi.5) that 'an unjust peace is far preferable to a just war'. More's friend and mentor John Colet stated unequivocally – in a sermon before the king – that for Christians *no* war is just (CWE, VIII, 243).

[105] More Greek compounds: 'People Born from the Clouds' and 'Citizens of a Country without People'.

terea quod abundabat domi ac veluti supererat, alioqui non emitten-
dum foras. Quo fit ut intertrimentum citra cuiusquam sensum
accidat. Quocirca nimis crudele censent id damnum multorum ulci-
sci mortibus cuius damni incommodum nemo ipsorum aut vita aut
victu persentiscat. Ceterum si quis suorum usquam per iniuriam ⁵
debilitetur aut occidatur,⁴⁴ sive id publico factum consilio sive privato sit, per legatos re comperta, nisi deditis noxiis placari non possunt quin ilico bellum denuntient. Noxae deditos aut morte aut
servitio puniunt.

*Magno empta
victoria*

Cruentae victoriae non piget modo eos sed pudet quoque, reput- ¹⁰
antes inscitiam esse quamlibet pretiosas merces nimio emisse. Arte
doloque victos, oppressos hostes impendio gloriantur, trium-
phumque ob eam rem publicitus agunt, et velut re strenue gesta
tropaeum erigunt. Tunc enim demum viriliter sese iactant et cum
virtute gessisse quoties ita vicerint quomodo nullum animal praeter ¹⁵
hominem potuit, id est, ingenii viribus. Nam corporis,⁴⁵ inquiunt,
ursi, leones, apri, lupi, canes, ceteraeque beluae dimicant: quarum
ut pleraeque nos robore ac ferocia vincunt, ita cunctae ingenio et
ratione superantur.

Hoc unum illi in bello spectant, uti id obtineant quod si fuissent ²⁰
ante consecuti, bellum non fuerant illaturi: aut si id res vetet, tam
severam ab his vindictam expetunt quibus factum imputant ut idem
ausuros in posterum terror absterreat. Hos propositi sui scopos
destinant quos mature petunt, at ita tamen uti prior vitandi periculi
cura quam laudis aut famae consequendae sit. ²⁵

Itaque protinus indicto bello schedulas ipsorum publico signo
roboratas locis maxime conspicuis hosticae terrae clam uno tempore
multas appendi procurant, quibus ingentia pollicentur praemia si
quis principem adversarium sustulerit: deinde minora, quamquam
illa quoque egregia, decernunt pro singulis eorum capitibus, ³⁰
quorum nomina in eisdem literis proscribunt. Hi sunt quos
secundum principem ipsum auctores initi adversus se consilii
ducunt. Quicquid percussori praefiniunt hoc geminant ei qui vivum
e proscriptis aliquem ad se perduxerit;⁴⁶ quin ipsos quoque pro-
scriptos praemiis eisdem, addita etiam impunitate, contra socios ³⁵

---

⁴⁴ The sense requires *occidatur* (1565–6 and Lupton) instead of *occidat* (all four early
texts).

⁴⁵ *viribus* should be understood with *corporis*, to maintain the contrast with *ingenii
viribus*.

⁴⁶ *perduxerit*, following 1517 against *perduxerint* in the other three editions: *qui*
refers to *ei*, which requires a singular form. *quin*: The reading of the texts, *quum*,
does not make good sense: its meanings ('when' or 'since') do not give an acceptable relationship between the two ideas (doubling the reward if the proscribed

commonwealth, more particularly goods that were already abundant at home, even superfluous, since otherwise they wouldn't have
been exported. Hence no one individual even notices the loss. So
small an injury, which affects neither the life nor the livelihood of
any of their own people, they consider it cruel to avenge by the
deaths of many people. On the other hand, if one of their own is
maimed or killed anywhere, whether by government decision or
by a private citizen, they first send envoys to look into the circumstances; then they demand that the guilty persons be surrendered;
and if that demand is refused, they are not to be put off, but at
once declare war. Those who devoted themselves to doing injury
are punished by death or slavery.

The Utopians are not only troubled but ashamed when their *Victory dearly*
forces gain a bloody victory, thinking it folly to pay too high a *bought*
price even for the best goods. But if they overcome the enemy by
skill and cunning, they exult mightily, celebrate a public triumph,
and raise a monument as for a glorious exploit. They boast that
they have really acted with manly and virile bravery when they have
won a victory such as no animal except man could have achieved – a
victory gained by strength of understanding. Bears, lions, boars,
wolves, dogs and other wild beasts fight with their bodies, they
say; and most of them are superior to us in strength and ferocity;
but we outdo them all in intelligence and rationality.

The only thing they aim at, in going to war, is to secure what
would have prevented the declaration of war, if the enemy had
conceded it beforehand. Or, if they cannot get that, they try to
take such bitter revenge on those who provoked them that they
will be afraid ever to do it again. These are their chief aims, which
they try to achieve quickly, yet in such a way as to avoid danger
rather than to win fame or glory.

As soon as war is declared, therefore, they have their secret agents
simultaneously post many placards, each marked with their official
seal, in the most conspicuous places throughout enemy territory.
In these proclamations they promise immense rewards to anyone
who will do away with the enemy prince. They offer smaller but
still substantial sums for killing any of a list of other individuals
whom they name. These are the persons whom they regard as most
responsible, after the prince, for plotting aggression against them.
The reward for an assassin is doubled for anyone who succeeds in
bringing in one of the proscribed men alive. In fact, they even offer
the same reward, plus a guarantee of personal safety, to any one of
the proscribed men who turns against his comrades. As a result,

invitant. Itaque fit celeriter ut et ceteros mortales suspectos habeant, et sibi invicem ipsi neque fidentes satis neque fidi sint, maximoque in metu et non minore periculo versentur. Nam saepenumero constat evenisse uti bona pars eorum et princeps in primis ipse ab his proderentur in quibus maximam spem reposuerunt. Tam facile ₅ quodvis in facinus impellunt munera, quibus illi nullum exhibent modum. Sed memores in quantum discrimen hortantur, operam dant uti periculi magnitudo beneficiorum mole compensetur: eoque non immensam modo auri vim sed praedia quoque magni reditus in locis apud amicos tutissimis propria ac perpetua pollicitantur et ₁₀ summa cum fide praestant.

Hunc licitandi mercandique hostis morem, apud alios improbatum velut animi degeneris crudele facinus, illi magnae sibi laudi ducunt tamquam prudentes qui maximis hoc pacto bellis sine ullo prorsus proelio defungantur, humanique ac misericordes etiam, qui ₁₅ paucorum nece noxiorum numerosas innocentium vitas redimant qui pugnando fuerint occubituri, partim e suis, partim ex hostibus, quorum turbam vulgusque non minus ferme quam suos miserantur, gnari non sua sponte eos bellum capessere sed principum ad id furiis agi. ₂₀

Si res hoc pacto non procedat, discidiorum semina iaciunt aluntque, fratre principis aut aliquo e nobilibus in spem potiundi regni perducto. Si factiones internae languerint, finitimas hostibus gentes excitant committuntque, eruto vetusto quopiam titulo quales numquam regibus desunt. ₂₅

Suas ad bellum opes polliciti pecuniam adfluenter suggerunt, cives parcissime, quos tam unice habent charos, tantique sese mutuo faciunt, ut neminem sint e suis cum adverso principe libenter commutaturi. At aurum argentumque, quoniam unum hunc in usum omne servant, haud gravatim erogant, utpote non minus commode ₃₀ victuri etiamsi universum impenderent. Quin praeter domesticas divitias est illis foris quoque infinitus thesaurus quo plurimae

persons are brought in alive; encouraging the proscribed to turn their comrades in). The meaning of *quin* ('going beyond what precedes') fits perfectly – and has in fact been followed (in the translation, not the text) by Robinson, Yale and Prévost.

the enemies of the Utopians quickly come to suspect all other mortals and even among themselves are neither trusting nor trustworthy, so that they live in the greatest fear and danger. They know very well that many of them, including especially their princes, have been betrayed by those in whom they placed complete trust – so effective are bribes as an incitement to crime. Hence the Utopians are lavish in their promises of bounty. Being well aware of the risks their agents must run, they make sure the payments are in proportion to the peril; thus they not only offer, but actually deliver, enormous sums of gold, as well as valuable landed estates in very secure locations on the territory of their friends.

Other nations condemn this custom of bidding for and buying the life of an enemy as the cruel villainy of a degenerate mind; but the Utopians consider it praiseworthy: wise, since it enables them to win tremendous wars without fighting any actual battles, and also merciful and humane, since it enables them, by the sacrifice of a few guilty men, to spare the lives of many innocent persons who would have died in the fighting, some on their side, some on the enemy's. They pity the mass of the enemy's soldiers almost as much as their own citizens, for they know common people do not go to war of their own accord, but are driven to it by the madness of princes.

If assassination does not work, they stir up dissensions by inciting the brother of the prince or some other member of the nobility to plot for the crown.[106] If internal discord dies down, they try to rouse up neighbouring peoples against the enemy by digging up ancient claims to dominion, of which kings always have an ample supply.

When they promise their resources to help in a war, they send money very freely, but commit their citizens very sparingly indeed. They hold their own people dear, and value one another so highly that they would not willingly exchange one of themselves for an enemy's prince. But gold and silver, all of which they keep for this purpose alone, they spend without hesitation; after all, they will continue to live just as well even if they expend the whole sum. Moreover, in addition to the wealth they have at home, they also have a vast treasure abroad since, as I said before, many nations owe

---

[106] The stratagems of this paragraph compare interestingly with the recommendations of the corrupt privy councillors in Hythloday's imaginary strategy session (p. 85).

gentes, uti ante dixi, in ipsorum aere sunt. Ita milites undique con-
ductos ad bellum mittunt, praesertim ex Zapoletis.

Gens haud ita
dissimilis
Helvetiis⁴⁷

Hic populus quingentis passuum millibus ab Utopia distat orien-
tem solem versus, horridus, agrestis, ferox: silvas montesque asp-
eros, quibus sunt innutriti, praeferunt. Dura gens, aestus, frigoris ₅
et laboris patiens, deliciarum expers omnium neque agriculturae
studens, et cum aedificiorum tum vestitus indiligens, pecorum dumtaxat curam habent. Magna ex parte venatu et raptu vivunt. Ad
solum bellum nati, cuius gerendi facultatem studiose quaerunt,
repertam cupide amplectuntur, et magno numero egressi, cuivis ₁₀
requirenti milites vili semet offerunt. Hanc unam vitae artem nov-
erunt, qua mors quaeritur.

Sub quibus merent acriter pro his et incorrupta fide dimicant.
Verum in nullum certum diem sese obstringunt, sed ea lege in partes
veniunt ut posteriore die,⁴⁸ vel ab hostibus oblato maiore stipendio ₁₅
sint staturi, eidem perendie rursus invitati plusculo remigrant.
Rarum oritur bellum in quo non bona pars illorum in utroque sint
exercitu. Itaque accidit cottidie ut sanguinis necessitudine coniuncti,
qui et eisdem in partibus conducti familiarissime semet invicem
utebantur, paulo post in contrarias distracti copias, hostiliter con- ₂₀
currant et infestis animis, obliti generis, immemores amicitiae,
mutuo sese confodiant, nulla alia causa in mutuam incitati perniciem
quam quod a diversis principibus exigua pecuniola conducti. Cuius
tam exactam habent rationem ut ad diurnum stipendium unius
accessione assis facile ad commutandas partes impellantur. Ita celer- ₂₅
iter imbiberunt avaritiam quae tamen nulli est eis usui, nam quae
sanguine quaerunt protinus per luxum, et eum tamen miserum,
consumunt.

Hic populus Utopiensibus adversus quosvis mortales militat
quod tanti ab his eorum conducatur opera quanti nusquam alibi. ₃₀
Utopienses siquidem ut bonos quaerunt quibus utantur, ita hos
quoque homines pessimos quibus abutantur. Quos quum usus

---

⁴⁷ Johann Froben, himself a Swiss, omitted this gloss from the two 1518 editions.
⁴⁸ In 1518M, N, *posteriore die* ('on the next day') replaced the less specific expression
of 1516, 1517, *postero die* ('at a later day' – not necessarily the very next one).

them money. So they hire mercenary soldiers from everywhere, especially the Zapoletes.[107]

These people live five hundred miles to the east of Utopia, and are rough, rude and fierce. The forests and mountains where they are bred are the kind of country they like: tough and rugged. They are a hard race, capable of standing heat, cold and drudgery, unacquainted with any luxuries, careless about their houses and their clothes; they don't till the fields but raise cattle instead. Most survive by hunting and stealing. These people are born for battle, which they seek out at every opportunity and eagerly embrace when they have found it. Leaving their own country in great numbers, they offer themselves for cheap hire to anyone in need of warriors. The only art they know for earning a living is the art which aims at death.

A people not so unlike the Swiss

For the people who pay them, they fight with great courage and complete loyalty, but they will not bind themselves to serve for any fixed period of time. They take sides on such terms that if someone, even the enemy, offers them more money tomorrow, they will take his part; and the day after tomorrow, if a trifle more is offered to bring them back, they'll return to their first employers. Hardly a war is fought in which a good number of them are not engaged on both sides. Thus it happens every day that men who are united by ties of blood and have served together in friendship, but who are soon after separated into opposing armies, meet in battle. Forgetful of kinship and comradeship alike, they furiously run each other through, driven to mutual destruction for no other reason than that they were hired for a paltry sum by opposing princes. They reckon up money so closely that they can easily be induced to change sides for an increase of only a penny a day. They have quickly picked up the habit of avarice, but none of the profit; for what they earn by blood-letting they immediately squander on debauchery of the most squalid sort.

Because the pay for their services is nowhere higher than what the Utopians offer, these people are ready to serve them against any mortals whatever. And the Utopians, as they seek out the best possible men for proper uses, hire these, the worst possible men, for improper uses. When the situation requires, they thrust the

---

[107] As the following gloss points out, the Zapoletes (from Greek: 'busy sellers') resemble the Swiss, who provided Europe's most feared and hated mercenaries. Many Italian princes, as well as the French, hired Swiss mercenaries; and popes have Swiss guards to this day.

postulat, magnis impulsos pollicitationibus, maximis obiciunt periculis, unde plerumque magna pars numquam ad exigenda promissa revertitur. Superstitibus quae sunt polliciti bona fide persolvunt, quo ad⁴⁹ similes ausus incendantur. Neque enim pensi quicquam habent quam multos ex eis perdant, rati de genere humano maxi- 5
mam merituros gratiam se si tota illa colluvie populi tam taetri ac nefarii orbem terrarum purgare possent.

Secundum hos, eorum copiis utuntur pro quibus arma capiunt, deinde auxiliaribus ceterorum amicorum turmis. Postremo suos cives adiungunt, e quibus aliquem virtutis probatae virum totius 10
exercitus summae praeficiunt. Huic duos ita substituunt uti, eo incolumi, ambo privati sint: capto aut interempto, alter e duobus velut hereditate succedat, eique ex eventu tertius, ne (ut sunt bellorum sortes variae) periclitante duce totus perturbetur exercitus.

E quaque civitate delectus exercetur ex his qui sponte nomen 15
profitentur. Neque enim invitus quisquam foras in militiam truditur, quod persuasum habeant si quis sit natura timidior, non ipsum modo nihil facturum strenue, sed metum etiam comitibus incussurum. Ceterum si quod bellum ingruat in patriam, ignavos huiusmodi, modo valeant corpore, in naves mixtos melioribus collocant, 20
aut in moenibus sparsim disponunt, unde non sit refugiendi locus. Ita suorum pudor, hostis in manibus, atque adempta fugae spes timorem obruunt, et saepe extrema necessitas in virtutem vertitur.

At sicuti ad externum bellum ex ipsis nemo protrahitur nolens, ita feminas volentes in militiam comitari maritos adeo non prohibent ut 25
exhortentur etiam et laudibus incitent. Profectas cum suo quamque viro pariter in acie constituunt. Tum sui quemque liberi, affines, cognati circumsistunt, ut hi de proximo sint mutuo sibi subsidio quos maxime ad ferendas invicem suppetias natura stimulat. In

---

⁴⁹ *quo ad*, following 1517 and 1518N against 1516 and 1518M, *quoad*. 'So far as' makes no sense in context.

Zapoletes into the positions of greatest danger by offering them immense rewards. Most of them never come back to collect their stipend, but the Utopians faithfully pay off those who do survive, to encourage them to try it again. As for how many Zapoletes get killed, the Utopians never worry about that, for they think they would deserve very well of mankind if they could sweep from the face of the earth all the dregs of that vicious and disgusting race.[108]

After the Zapoletes, they employ as auxiliaries the soldiers of the people for whom they have taken up arms, and then squadrons of their other friends. Last, they add their own citizens, including some man of known bravery to command the entire army. They also appoint two substitutes for him, who hold no rank as long as he is safe. But if the commander is captured or killed, one of these two substitutes becomes his successor, and in case of a mishap to him, the third.[109] Thus, despite the many accidents of war, they ensure that the whole army will not be disorganised through loss of the general.

In each city, soldiers are chosen from those who have volunteered. No one is forced to fight abroad against his will, because they think a man who is naturally fearful will act weakly at best, and may even spread panic among his comrades. But if their own country is invaded they call to arms even the fearful (as long as they are physically fit), placing them on shipboard among braver men, or here and there along fortifications, where there is no place to run away. Thus shame at failing their countrymen, the immediate presence of the enemy and the impossibility of flight often combine to overcome their fear, and they make a virtue out of sheer necessity.

Just as no man is forced into a foreign war against his will, so women are allowed to accompany their men on military service if they want to – not only not forbidden, but encouraged and praised for doing so. Each leaves with her husband, and they stand shoulder to shoulder in the line of battle; in addition, they place around a man his children and his blood- or marriage-relations, so that those who by nature have most reason to help one another may be closest

---

[108] Sixteenth-century accounts of horrors perpetrated by mercenaries – including an account by More of the sacking of Rome in 1527 (*Dialogue Concerning Heresies*, CW, VI, 370–2) – help to explain the Utopians' genocidal policy towards the Zapoletes. In *The Education of a Christian Prince*, Erasmus says of mercenaries that 'there is no class of men more abject and indeed more damnable' (CWE, XXVII, 283). How the Utopians reconcile their employment of the Zapoletes with their aim of minimising bloodshed and plunder in war is unclear.

[109] This is a Spartan practice. See Thucydides, *The Peloponnesian War* IV.xxxviii.

maximo probro est coniunx absque coniuge redux aut amisso parente reversus filius. Quo fit uti si ad ipsorum manus ventum sit, modo perstent hostes, longo et lugubri proelio ad internitionem usque decernatur.

Nempe ut omnibus curant modis ne ipsis dimicare necesse sit 5 modo bello possint vicaria conducticiorum manu defungi, ita quum vitari non potest quin ipsi ineant pugnam, tam intrepide capessunt quam quoad licuit prudenter detrectabant: nec tam primo ferociunt impetu quam mora sensim et duratione invalescunt tam offirmatis animis ut interimi citius quam averti queant. Quippe victus illa 10 securitas quae cuique domi est, ademptaque de posteris anxia cogitandi cura (nam haec solicitudo[50] generosos ubique spiritus frangit), sublimem illis animum et vinci dedignantem facit. Ad haec militaris disciplinae peritia fiduciam praebet. Postremo rectae opiniones (quibus et doctrina et bonis reipublicae institutis imbuti a pueris 15 sunt) virtutem addunt: qua neque tam vilem habent vitam ut temere prodigant neque tam improbe charam ut quum honestas ponendam suadeat avare turpiterque retineant.

Dux potissimum impetendus, quo citius finiatur bellum

Dum ubique pugna maxima fervet, lectissimi iuvenes coniurati devotique ducem sibi deposcunt adversum. Hunc aperte invadunt, 20 hunc ex insidiis adoriuntur. Idem eminus, idem comminus petitur, longoque ac perpetuo cuneo, summissis assidue in fatigatorum locum recentibus, oppugnatur. Raroque accidit (ni sibi fuga prospiciat) ut non intereat aut vivus in hostium potestatem veniat.

Si ab ipsis victoria sit, haudquaquam caede grassantur, fugatos 25 enim comprehendunt quam occidunt libentius. Neque umquam ita persequuntur fugientes ut non unam interim sub signis instructam aciem retineant: adeo ut si,[51] ceteris superati partibus, postrema acie sua victoriam adepti sint, elabi potius hostes universos sinant quam

---

[50] 1516–1518N have *solitudo*, first corrected to *solicitudo* in 1563. *illis animum* (below) is from 1517; the words are omitted from the other early editions.
[51] *ut si* adopted from 1517 in preference to *visi* (1518M) or *nisi* (1516, 1518N), to preserve the sense.

at hand for mutual support.[110] It is a matter of great reproach for either spouse to come home without the other, or for a son to return after losing a parent. The result is that if the enemy stands his ground, the hand-to-hand fighting is apt to be long and bitter, ending only when everyone is dead.

They take every precaution to avoid having to fight in person, so long as they can use mercenaries to wage war for them. But when they are forced to enter the battle, they are as bold in the struggle as they were prudent in putting it off as long as possible. In the first charge they are not fierce, but gradually as the fighting goes on they grow more determined, putting up a steady, stubborn resistance. Their spirit is so strong that they will die rather than yield ground. They are sure that everyone at home will be provided for, nor do they have any worry about the future of their families (for that sort of care often daunts the boldest courage); so their spirit is proud and unconquerable. Moreover, their skill in the arts of war gives them confidence; also they have been trained from infancy in sound principles of conduct (which their education and the good institutions of their society both reinforce), and that too adds to their courage. They don't hold life so cheap that they throw it away recklessly, nor so dear that they grasp it greedily at the price of shame when duty bids them give it up.

At the height of the battle, a band of the bravest young men, who have taken a special oath, devote themselves to seeking out the opposing general. They assail him directly, they lay secret traps for him, they hit at him from near and far. A long and continuous wedge of fresh men keep up the assault as the exhausted drop out. It rarely happens that they fail to kill or capture him, unless he takes flight.

The enemy general to be most fiercely attacked, so as to end the war sooner

When they win a battle, it never ends in a massacre, for they would much rather take prisoners than cut throats. They never pursue fugitives without keeping one line of their army drawn up under the colours. They are so careful of this that if they win the victory with this last reserve force (after the rest of their army has been beaten), they ordinarily let the enemy army escape instead of

---

[110] In the *Republic*, men and women 'will serve together, and take the children to war with them when they are old enough, to let them see, as they do in other trades, the job they will have to do when they grow up' (V.466E–467A). Tacitus says that among the Germans the 'strongest incentive to courage lies in this, that neither chance nor casual grouping makes the squadron or the wedge, but family and kinship: close at hand, too, are their dearest, whence is heard the wailing voice of woman and the child's cry' (*Germania* 7).

insequi fugientes perturbatis suorum ordinibus insuescant: memores sibimet haud semel usu venisse ut, mole totius exercitus victa profligataque, quum hostes victoria gestientes hac atque illac abeuntes persequerentur, pauci ipsorum in subsidiis collocati, ad occasiones intenti, dispersos ac palantes illos et praesumpta securitate negligentes derepente adorti, totius eventum proelii mutaverunt, extortaque e manibus tam certa et indubitata victoria, victi victores invicem vicerunt.[52]

Haud facile dictu est astutiores in struendis[53] insidiis an cautiores ad vitandas sient. Fugam parare credas quum nihil minus in animo habent: contra quum id consilii capiunt nihil minus cogitare putes. Nam si nimium sese sentiunt aut numero aut loco premi, tunc aut noctu agmine silente castra movent, aut aliquo stratagemate eludunt, aut interdiu ita sensim sese referunt, tali servato ordine ut non minus periculi sit cedentes quam instantes adoriri. Castra diligentissime communiunt fossa praealta lataque, terra quae egeritur introrsum reiecta, nec in eam rem opera mediastinorum utuntur. Ipsorum manibus militum res agitur, totusque exercitus in opere est, exceptis qui pro vallo in armis ad subitos casus excubant. Itaque tam multis adnitentibus, magna multumque amplexa loci munimenta omni fide citius perficiunt.

Formae armorum Armis utuntur ad excipiendos ictus firmis nec ad motum gestumve quemlibet ineptis adeo ut ne natando quidem molesta sentiant. Nam armati natare inter militaris disciplinae rudimenta consuescunt. Tela sunt eminus sagittae, quas acerrime simul et certissime iaculantur non pedites modo sed ex equis etiam. Comminus vero non gladii sed secures vel acie letales vel pondere seu caesim seu punctim feriant. Machinas excogitant sollertissime; factas accuratissime celant, ne ante proditae quam res postulet, ludibrio magis quam usui sint. In quibus fabricandis hoc in primis respiciunt, uti vectu faciles et habiles circumactu sint.

---

[52] *mutaverunt . . . vicerunt* is the reading of all four early editions. Given the *ut* near the beginning of the sentence, correctness would require the subjunctives *mutaverint . . . vicerint*.

[53] *in struendis* (Lupton) rather than *instruendis* (the texts).

pursuing fugitives with their own ranks in disorder. They recall what has happened more than once to themselves: that when the enemy seemed to have the best of the day, had routed the main Utopian force, and, exulting in their victory, had scattered to round up runaways, a few Utopians held in reserve and watching their opportunity have suddenly attacked the dispersed and straggling enemy just when he felt safe and had lowered his guard. Thereby they changed the fortune of the day, snatched certain victory out of the enemy's hands, and, though conquered themselves, conquered their conquerors.

It is not easy to say whether they are more crafty in laying ambushes or more clever in avoiding them. You would think they are about to run away when that is the last thing in their minds; when they are really ready to retreat, you would never guess it. If they are outnumbered, or if the terrain is unsuitable, they shift their ground silently by night or get away by some stratagem; or if they withdraw by day, they do so gradually, and in such good order that they are as dangerous to attack then as if they were advancing. They fortify their camps thoroughly, with a deep, broad ditch, the earth being thrown inward;[111] the work is done not by labourers but by the soldiers themselves with their own hands. The whole army pitches in, except for an armed guard posted outside the ditch to prevent surprise attack. With so many hands at work, they complete great fortifications, enclosing wide areas with unbelievable speed.

Their armour is strong enough to stand up under blows but does *Kinds of weapons* not prevent free movement of the body; indeed, it doesn't even interfere with swimming, and swimming in armour is a normal part of their training. For long-range fighting they use arrows, which they shoot with great force and accuracy, from horseback as well as on foot. At close quarters they use not swords but battle-axes, which because of their sharp edge and great weight are lethal weapons, whether used to slash or thrust. They are very skilful in inventing machines of war, but carefully conceal them, since if they were made known before they were needed, they might prove ridiculous rather than useful.[112] Their first consideration in designing them is to make them easy to move and aim.

---

[111] That is, to form a parapet – as explained in Vegetius, *Epitoma rei militaris* I.xxiv and III.viii.

[112] Perhaps because the enemy could prepare countermeasures or move out of range. The military devices of the Utopians are a patchwork of different notions from the common knowledge of the day. Their camps are fortified like Roman

De indutiis Initas cum hostibus indutias tam sancte observant ut ne lacessiti quidem violent. Hostilem terram non depopulantur neque segetes exurunt, immo ne hominum equorumve pedibus conterantur quantum fieri potest provident, rati in ipsorum usus crescere. Inermem neminem laedunt nisi idem speculator sit. Deditas urbes tuentur at nec expugnatas diripiunt, sed per quos deditio est impedita eos enecant, ceteris defensoribus in servitutem addictis; imbellem turbam omnem relinquunt intactam. Si quos deditionem suasisse compererint, his e damnatorum bonis aliquam partem impertiunt; reliqua sectione auxiliares donant, nam ipsorum nemo quicquam de praeda capit.

At hodie victores maximam partem dependunt Ceterum confecto bello non amicis impensas in quos insumpsere sed victis imputant, exiguntque eo nomine partim pecuniam quam in similes bellorum usus reservant, partim praedia quae sint ipsis apud eos perpetua, non exigui census. Huiusmodi reditus nunc apud multas gentes habent, qui variis ex causis paulatim nati, supra septingenta ducatorum millia in singulos annos excrevere, in quos e suis civibus aliquos emittunt quaestorum nomine, qui magnifice vivant, personamque magnatum illic prae se ferant. At multum tamen superest quod inferatur aerario, nisi malint eidem genti credere, quod saepe tantisper faciunt quoad uti necesse sit, vixque accidit umquam ut totam reposcant. Ex his praediis partem assignant illis qui ipsorum hortatu tale discrimen adeunt quale ante monstravi.

Si quis princeps, armis adversus eos sumptis, eorum dicionem paret invadere, magnis ilico viribus extra suos fines occurrunt, nam neque temere in suis terris bellum gerunt, neque ulla necessitas tanta est ut eos cogat aliena auxilia in insulam suam admittere.

Truces made with the enemy they observe so religiously that Truces they will not break them even if provoked. They do not ravage the enemy's territory or burn his crops; indeed, so far as possible, they avoid any trampling of the fields by men or horses, thinking they may use the grain themselves. Unless he is a spy, they injure no unarmed man. Cities that are surrendered to them they keep intact; even after storming a place, they do not plunder it, but put to death the men who prevented surrender, enslave the other defenders, and do no harm to civilians. If they find any inhabitants who recommended surrender, they give them a share in the property of the condemned. What is left they divide among their auxiliaries; for themselves, they never take any booty.

After a war is ended they collect the cost of it, not from the allies But nowadays the
victors pay most
of the expenses for whose sake they undertook it, but from the conquered. They take as indemnity not only money, which they set aside to finance future wars, but also landed estates, from which they may enjoy forever a substantial annual income. They now have revenues of this sort in many different countries, acquired little by little in various ways, which have mounted to over seven hundred thousand ducats[113] a year. As managers of these estates, they send abroad some of their citizens to serve as collectors of revenue. Though they live on the properties in great style and conduct themselves like magnates, plenty of income is still left over to be put into the treasury, unless they lend it to the conquered nation. They often do the latter until they need the money, and it rarely happens that they call in the entire debt. They give some of the estates to those who have taken great risks at their instigation, as I mentioned before.

If any prince takes up arms and prepares to invade their land, they immediately send a powerful force to encounter him outside their own borders. For they don't like to wage war on their own soil, nor is any necessity so great as to bring them to allow foreign auxiliaries onto their island.

---

ones. Their reliance on archery links them with the English – though their skill in shooting arrows from horseback recalls the ancient Parthians and Scythians. The 'machines' are presumably like Roman *ballistae, arietes, scorpiones* (stone-throwers, battering rams, dart-hurlers); but the emphasis on their portability probably reflects contemporary experience with cannon, which were terribly hard to drag over the muddy routes of the time.

[113] Gold coins of this name were minted by several European countries. Four ducats of Burgundy, Venice or Hungary were roughly equivalent to an English pound; and the pound itself was worth several hundred times its value today.

DE RELIGIONIBUS UTOPIENSIUM

Religiones sunt non per insulam modo, verum singulas etiam urbes variae, aliis solem, lunam aliis, aliis aliud errantium siderum dei vice venerantibus. Sunt quibus homo quispiam cuius olim aut virtus aut gloria enituit non pro deo tantum sed pro summo etiam deo suspici- 5 tur. At multo maxima pars eademque longe prudentior nihil horum sed unum quoddam numen putant, incognitum, aeternum, immensum, inexplicabile, quod supra mentis humanae captum sit per mundum hunc universum virtute non mole diffusum; hunc parentem vocant. Origines, auctus, progressus, vices, finesque rerum 10 omnium huic acceptos uni referunt, nec divinos honores alii praeterea ulli applicant.

Quin ceteris quoque omnibus quamquam diversa credentibus hoc tamen cum istis convenit quod esse quidem unum censent summum, cui et universitatis opificium et providentia debeatur, 15 eumque communiter omnes patria lingua Mythram appellant, sed eo dissentiunt quod idem alius apud alios habetur, autumante quoque, quicquid id sit quod ipse summum ducit, eandem illam prorsus esse naturam cuius unius numini ac maiestati rerum omnium summa omnium consensu gentium tribuitur. Ceterum 20 paulatim omnes ab ea superstitionum varietate desciscunt, atque in unam illam coalescunt religionem quae reliquas ratione videtur antecellere. Neque dubium est quin ceterae iam pridem evanuissent nisi quicquid improsperum cuiquam inter mutandae religionis consilia fors obiecisset[54] non id accidisse casu sed caelitus immissum 25 interpretaretur timor, tamquam numine cuius relinquebatur cultus impium contra se propositum vindicante.

At posteaquam acceperunt a nobis CHRISTI nomen, doctrinam, mores, miracula, nec minus mirandam tot martyrum constantiam quorum sponte fusus sanguis tam numerosas gentes in suam sectam 30 longe lateque traduxit, non credas quam pronis in eam affectibus etiam ipsi concesserint, sive hoc secretius inspirante deo, sive quod

---

[54] *obiecisset* from the other three texts in place of 1518M's awkward if not impossible *obiecisse*.

THE RELIGIONS OF THE UTOPIANS

There are different forms of religion not only throughout the island but even within the individual cities. Some worship as a god the sun, others the moon, still others one of the planets. There are some who worship a man of past ages, conspicuous either for virtue or glory; they consider him not only a god but the supreme god. But the vast majority, and those by far the wiser ones, believe nothing of the kind: they believe in a single divinity, unknown, eternal, infinite, inexplicable, beyond the grasp of the human mind, and diffused throughout the universe, not physically, but in influence. Him they call their parent, and to him alone they attribute the origin, increase, progress, changes and ends of all things; they do not offer divine honours to any other.

Though all the others differ from this group in various particular beliefs, they agree with them in a single main head, that there is one supreme power, the maker and ruler of the universe. In their native tongue they all alike call him Mythra.[114] But the others differ from the main group in that they define this supreme power in various ways, everyone asserting that whatever he considers to be supreme is that one and only nature to whose divine majesty, by the consensus of all nations, the highest status of all is attributed. Gradually, though, they are all coming to forsake this mixture of superstitions and unite in that one religion which seems more reasonable than any of the others. And there is no doubt that the other religions would have disappeared long ago, had not whatever unlucky accident that befell anyone who was thinking of changing his religion been interpreted, out of fear, as a sign of divine anger, not chance – as if the deity who was being abandoned were avenging an insult against himself.

But after they heard from us the name of Christ, and learned of his teachings, his life,[115] his miracles and the no less marvellous constancy of the many martyrs whose blood, freely shed, has drawn so many nations far and near into their religion, you would not believe how eagerly they assented to it, either through the secret

---

[114] In ancient Persian religion, Mithra or Mithras, the spirit of light, was the supreme force of good in the universe. Recall that the Utopians' language 'resembles Persian in most respects' (p. 181), and that under the name of Mythra some of them worship the sun or other heavenly bodies.

eadem ei visa est haeresi proxima quae est apud ipsos potissima,
quamquam hoc quoque fuisse non paulum momenti crediderim,
quod CHRISTO communem suorum victum audierant placuisse,
Coenobia et apud germanissimos Christianorum conventus adhuc in usu esse.
Certe quoquo id momento accidit haud pauci nostram in religionem 5
coierunt, lymphaque sacra sunt abluti.

Verum quoniam in nobis quattuor (totidem enim dumtaxat
supereramus nam duo fatis concesserant) nemo, id quod doleo,
sacerdos erat, ceteris initiati, ea tamen adhuc sacramenta desiderant
quae apud nos non nisi sacerdotes conferunt. Intelligunt tamen opt- 10
antque ita ut nihil vehementius. Quin hoc quoque sedulo iam inter
se disputant, an sine Christiani pontificis missu quisquam e suo
numero delectus sacerdotii consequatur characterem. Et electuri
sane videbantur, verum quum ego discederem nondum elegerant.

Quin hi quoque religioni Christianae qui non assentiunt nemi- 15
nem tamen absterrent, nullum oppugnant imbutum, nisi quod unus
e nostro coetu me praesente coercitus est. Is quum recens ablutus
nobis contra suadentibus de CHRISTI cultu publice maiore studio
quam prudentia dissereret, usqueadeo coepit incalescere, ut iam
non[55] nostra modo sacra ceteris anteferret, sed reliqua protinus 20
universa damnaret. Profana ipsa, cultores impios ac sacrilegos, aet-
erno plectendos igni vociferaretur. Talia diu contionantem compre-

---

[55] *non* omitted by 1518M, N, supplied from 1516 and 1517.

inspiration of God or because Christianity seemed very like the sect that most prevails among them. But I think they were also much influenced by the fact that Christ approved of his followers' communal way of life,[115] and that among the truest groups of *Monasteries* Christians the practice still prevails. Whatever the reason, no small number of them joined our religion, and were washed in the holy waters of baptism.

By that time, two of our group had died, and among us four survivors there was, I am sorry to say, no priest. So, though they received the other sacraments, they still lack those which in our religion can be administered only by priests.[116] They do, however, understand what these are, and eagerly desire them. In fact, they dispute warmly whether a man chosen from among themselves could receive the sacerdotal character[117] without the dispatch of a Christian bishop.[118] Though they seemed about to elect such a person, they had not yet done so when I left.

Those who have not accepted Christianity make no effort to restrain others from it, nor do they criticise new converts to it. While I was there, only one of our communion was interfered with. As soon as he was baptised, he took upon himself to preach the Christian religion publicly, with more zeal than discretion. We warned him not to do so, but he began to work himself up to a pitch where he not only set our religion above the rest but roundly condemned all others as profane, leading their impious and sacrilegious followers to the hell-fires they richly deserved. After he had

[115] On the communist practice of the early Christians, see Acts 2:44–5 and 4:32–5.
[116] Of the seven sacraments, only baptism and matrimony can be conferred without a priest.
[117] In Catholic doctrine, a 'character' is 'a spiritual seal or stamp impressed on the soul by God to indicate the consecration of that soul to him in some official capacity' (George D. Smith, ed., *The Teaching of the Catholic Church*, 2nd edn (1952), p. 1030). Quoted in the note on the term at *CW*, IV, 520, where Surtz also points out that 'Consecration at the hands of a bishop was always deemed necessary, as is presupposed in More's letter to Giles' (above, p. 35).
[118] The word translated as 'bishop' – *pontifex* – clearly has its classical sense of 'high priest' when employed in connection with Utopian religion (140:5, 194:20, 230:6), and just as clearly means 'pope' in the passage of the letter to Giles where More tells of the English theologian who wants the pope to make him bishop of Utopia (34:25) and in the passage on treaty-keeping in Europe (198:7). This was, moreover, the usual sense of *pontifex* in More's time. But the word can also mean 'bishop', and we have rendered it that way here because the context seems to require it: as in the letter to Giles, the normal procedure for providing Utopia with Christian priests would involve the pope dispatching a bishop to the island. There is no reason to expect that the pope would undertake the mission himself.

Laude trahendi
sunt homines ad
religionem
hendunt ac reum non spretae religionis sed excitati in populo
tumultus agunt peraguntque, damnatum exilio multant, siquidem
hoc inter[56] antiquissima instituta numerant, ne sua cuiquam religio
fraudi sit.

Utopus enim iam inde ab initio, quum accepisset incolas ante 5
suum adventum de religionibus inter se assidue dimicasse, atque
animadvertisset eam rem, quod in commune dissidentes singulae
pro patria sectae pugnabant, occasionem praestitisse sibi vincenda-
rum omnium, adeptus victoriam in primis sanxit uti quam cuique
religionem libeat sequi liceat, ut vero alios quoque in suam traducat 10
hactenus niti possit, uti placide ac modeste suam rationibus astruat –
non ut acerbe ceteras destruat si suadendo non persuadeat, neque
vim ullam adhibeat et conviciis temperet. Petulantius hac de re con-
tendentem, exilio aut servitute mulctant.

Haec Utopus instituit, non respectu pacis modo, quam assiduo 15
certamine atque inexpiabili odio funditus vidit everti, sed quod arbi-
tratus est uti sic decerneretur ipsius etiam religionis interesse: de
qua nihil est ausus temere definire, velut incertum habens an varium
ac multiplicem expetens cultum deus aliud inspiret alii. Certe vi ac
minis exigere ut[57] quod tu verum credis idem omnibus videatur, 20
hoc vero et insolens et ineptum censuit. Tum si maxime una vera
sit, ceterae omnes vanae, facile tamen praevidit (modo cum ratione
ac modestia res agatur) futurum denique ut ipsa per se veri vis
emergat aliquando atque emineat. Sin armis et tumultu certetur, ut
sint pessimi quique maxime pervicaces, optimam ac sanctissimam 25
religionem ob vanissimas inter se superstitiones, ut segetes inter
spinas ac frutices, obrutum iri. Itaque hanc totam rem in medio
posuit, et quid credendum putaret liberum cuique reliquit, nisi quod
sancte ac severe vetuit ne quis usqueadeo ab humanae naturae

---

[56] *inter* from 1516 and 1517, in preference to *interim* as in 1518M, N.
[57] *ut* from 1517; the other texts print *&*.

been preaching in this style for a long time, they arrested him. He *Men must be* was tried on a charge, not of despising their religion, but of creating *drawn to religion by praising it* a public disorder, convicted, and sentenced to exile. For it is one of their oldest rules that no one should suffer for his religion.

Utopus had heard that before his arrival the natives were continually squabbling over religious matters, and he had observed that it was easy to conquer the whole country because the different sects were too busy fighting one another to oppose him. And so at the very beginning, after he had gained the victory, he prescribed by law that everyone may cultivate the religion of his choice, and strenuously proselytise for it too, provided he does so quietly, modestly, rationally and without insulting others. If persuasion fails, no one may resort to abuse or violence; and anyone who fights wantonly about religion is punished by exile or slavery.

Utopus laid down these rules not simply for the sake of peace, which he saw was being completely undermined by constant quarrels and implacable hatreds, but he also thought such decrees would benefit religion itself. In such matters he was not at all quick to dogmatise, because he was uncertain whether God likes diverse and manifold forms of worship and hence inspires different people with different views. On the other hand, he was quite sure that it was arrogant folly for anyone to force conformity with his own beliefs on everyone else by threats or violence.[119] He easily foresaw that if one religion is really true and the rest are false, the truth will sooner or later emerge and prevail by its own natural strength, if men will only consider the matter reasonably and moderately. But if they try to decide things by fighting and rioting, since the worst men are always the most headstrong, the best and holiest religion in the world will be crowded out by foolish superstitions, like grain choked by thorns and briars. So he left the whole matter open, allowing each person to choose what he would believe. The only exception was a solemn and strict law against anyone who should sink so far below the dignity of human nature as to think that the

---

[119] This was not the attitude More took a decade later, when he was involved in the prosecution of Protestants. In the *Dialogue Concerning Heresies*, he wrote that 'if it were now doubtful and ambiguous whether the church of Christ were in the right rule of doctrine or not, then were it very necessary to give them all good audience that could and would anything dispute on either party for or against it, to the end that if we were now in a wrong way, we might leave it and walk in some better' (*CW*, VI, 345–6). In Utopia, which has not had the Christian revelation, a high degree of religious toleration is appropriate; in England, the fact that the 'right rule of doctrine' was clearly established justified, so More believed, harsh suppression of dissenting views.

dignitate degeneret ut animas quoque interire cum corpore aut mundum temere ferri, sublata providentia, putet.

Atque ideo post hanc vitam supplicia vitiis decreta, virtuti praemia constituta credunt. Contra sentientem ne in hominum quidem ducunt numero ut qui sublimem animae suae naturam ad pecuini 5 corpusculi vilitatem deiecerit, tantum abest ut inter cives ponant quorum instituta moresque (si per metum liceat) omnes floccifacturus sit. Cui enim dubium esse potest quin is publicas patriae leges aut arte clam eludere aut vi nitatur infringere dum suae privatim cupiditati serviat, cui nullus ultra leges metus, nihil ultra corpus spei 10 superest amplius? Quamobrem sic animato nullus communicatur honos, nullus magistratus committitur, nulli publico muneri praeficitur. Ita passim velut inertis ac iacentis naturae despicitur. Ceterum nullo adficiunt supplicio, quod persuasum habeant nulli hoc in manu esse ut quicquid libet sentiat; sed nec minis adigunt ullis 15 animum ut dissimulet suum, nec fucos admittunt et mendacia, quae velut proxima fraudi mirum quam habent invisa. Verum ne pro sua disputet sententia prohibent atque id dumtaxat apud vulgus. Nam alioquin apud sacerdotes gravesque viros seorsum non sinunt modo sed hortantur quoque, confisi fore ut ea tandem vesania rationi 20 cedat.

Mira opinio de animabus brutorum   Sunt et alii, nec hi sane pauci, nempe improhibiti veluti neque ratione penitus pro se carentes neque mali, qui, vitio longe diverso, brutorum quoque aeternas esse animas opinantur, at nostris tamen neque dignitate comparandas neque ad aequam natas felicitatem. 25

Hominum enim cuncti fere tam immensam fore beatitudinem pro certo atque explorato habent ut morbum lamententur omnium, mortem vero nullius, nisi quem vident anxie e vita invitumque divelli. Nempe hoc pro pessimo habent augurio tamquam anima exspes ac male conscia occulto quopiam imminentis poenae praesa- 30 gio reformidet exitum. Ad hoc haudquaquam gratum deo eius

soul perishes with the body, or that the universe is ruled by blind chance, not divine providence.[120]

Thus they believe that after this life vices will be punished and virtue rewarded. Anyone who denies this proposition they consider not even one of the human race, since he has degraded the sublimity of his own soul to the base level of a beast's wretched body. Still less will they count him as one of their citizens, since he would openly despise all the laws and customs of society, if not prevented by fear. Who can doubt that a man who has nothing to fear but the law, and no hope of life beyond the grave, will do anything he can to evade his country's laws by craft or to break them by violence, in order to gratify his own personal greed? Therefore a person who holds such views is offered no honours, entrusted with no offices, and given no public responsibility; he is universally regarded as low and torpid. Yet they do not punish him, because they are persuaded that no one can choose to believe by a mere act of the will. They do not compel him by threats to dissemble his views, nor do they tolerate in the matter any deceit or lying, which they detest as next door to deliberate malice. They do not forbid him to argue in favour of his opinion, except that he may not do so among the common people; but in the presence of priests and other important persons, in private, they not only permit but encourage it. For they are confident that in the end his madness will yield to reason.

There are others who err the other way, in supposing that animals have immortal souls,[121] though not comparable to ours in excellence nor destined to equal felicity. In fact, there is no small number of such people, because their view is not forbidden, since it is not wholly unreasonable and wicked. *A strange opinion about the souls of animals*

Almost all the Utopians are absolutely convinced that human bliss after death will be enormous; thus they lament every individual's sickness, but mourn over a death only if they see that a person was torn from life anxiously and unwillingly. Such behaviour they take to be a very bad sign, as if the soul, despairing and conscious of guilt, dreaded death through some secret premonition of punishments to come. Besides, they suppose God can hardly be

---

[120] The Utopians regard basic truths about immortality and divine providence as attainable by natural reason and as providing the only rational sanction for the life of virtue (pp. 161–3).

[121] Some ancient philosophers – particularly the Pythagoreans, as a facet of their doctrine of the transmigration of souls – held the same view.

putant adventum fore, qui quum sit accersitus non accurrit libens, sed invitus ac detrectans pertrahitur. Hoc igitur mortis genus qui intuentur horrent, itaque defunctos maesti ac silentes efferunt, precatique propitium manibus deum uti eorum clementer infirmitatibus ignoscat, terra cadaver obruunt. Contra, quicumque alacriter 5 ac pleni bona spe decesserint hos nemo luget, sed cantu prosecuti funus, animas deo magno commendantes affectu, corpora tandem reverenter magis quam dolenter concremant, columnamque loco insculptis defuncti titulis erigunt. Domum reversi, mores actaque eius recensent nec ulla vitae pars aut saepius aut libentius quam 10 laetus tractatur interitus.

Hanc probitatis memoriam et vivis efficacissima rentur incitamenta virtutum et gratissimum defunctis cultum putant, quos interesse quoque de se sermonibus opinantur, quamquam (ut est hebes mortalium acies) invisibiles. Nam neque felicium sorti conveniat 15 libertate carere migrandi quo velint, et ingratorum fuerit prorsus abiecisse desiderium amicos invisendi suos, quibus eos dum viverent mutuus amor charitasque devinxerat, quam[58] bonis viris, ut cetera bona, adauctam post fata potius quam imminutam coniectant. Mortuos ergo versari inter viventes credunt, dictorum factorumque 20 spectatores, eoque res agendas fidentius aggrediuntur, talibus velut freti praesidibus, et ab inhonesto secreto deterret eos credita maiorum praesentia.

Auguria ceterasque superstitionis vanae divinationes, quarum apud alias gentes magna est observatio, negligunt prorsus atque 25 irrident. Miracula vero quae nullo naturae proveniunt adminiculo, velut praesentis opera testesque numinis, venerantur. Qualia et ibi frequenter exstare ferunt, et magnis interdum ac dubiis in rebus publica supplicatione certa cum fiducia procurant impetrantque.

---

[58] Taking *quam* to refer to *charitas*, we follow 1517 in this passage, in preference to the impossible *quamquam* of the other texts. *adauctam* (next line) is also from 1517, in preference to the *auctam* of 1518M, N.

well pleased with the coming of one who, when he is summoned, does not come gladly, but is dragged off reluctantly and against his will. Such a death fills the onlookers with horror, and they carry the corpse out to burial in melancholy silence. Then, after begging God to have mercy on his spirit and to pardon his infirmities, they cover the body with earth. But when someone dies blithely and full of good hope, they do not mourn for him but carry the body cheerfully away, singing and commending the dead man's soul to God. They cremate[122] him in a spirit of reverence more than of grief, and erect in that place a column on which the dead man's honours are inscribed. After they have returned home, they talk of his character and deeds, and no part of his life is mentioned more frequently or more gladly than his joyful death.

They think that this remembrance of the dead person's probity inspires the living to behave virtuously and is the most acceptable form of honour to the dead. For they think that dead people are actually present among us, and hear what we say about them, though through the dullness of human sight they remain invisible. Given their state of bliss, the dead must be able to travel freely where they please, and it would be unkind of them to cast off every desire of seeing those friends to whom in life they had been joined by mutual affection and charity. They think that after death charity, like other good qualities, is increased rather than diminished in good men; and thus they believe the dead come frequently among the living, to observe their words and acts.[123] Hence they go about their business the more confidently because of their trust in such protectors; and the belief that their forefathers are present keeps them from any secret dishonourable deed.

Fortune-telling and other vain, superstitious divinations, such as other peoples take very seriously, they have no part of and consider ridiculous. But they venerate miracles which occur without the help of nature, considering them direct and visible manifestations of the divinity. Indeed, they report that miracles often occur in their country. Sometimes in great and dangerous crises they pray publicly for a miracle, which they then anticipate with great confidence, and obtain.

[122] Cremation was standard practice in most of the ancient world, but was not used by Christians before the nineteenth century.

[123] In the *Dialogue Concerning Heresies*, More wrote of the saints that 'if their holy souls live, there will no wise man ween them worse, and of less love and charity to men that need their help, when they be now in heaven, than they had when they were here in earth ... When saints were in this world at liberty and might walk the world about, ween we that in heaven they stand tied to a post?' (*CW*, VI, 211, 213).

Gratum deo cultum putant naturae contemplationem laudemque ab ea.[59] Sunt tamen, hique haud sane pauci, qui religione ducti literas negligunt, nulli rerum cognitioni student, neque otio prorsus ulli vacant: negotiis tantum bonisque in ceteris officiis statuunt futuram post fata felicitatem promereri. Itaque alii aegrotis inserviunt, alii vias reficiunt, purgant fossas, pontes reparant, caespites, harenam, lapides effodiunt, arbores demoliuntur ac dissecant, bigisque ligna, fruges, item alia in urbes important. Nec in publicum modo sed privatim quoque ministros ac plus quam servos agunt. Nam quicquid usquam operis est asperum, difficile, sordidum, a quo plerosque labor, fastidium, desperatio deterreat, hoc illi sibi totum libentes hilaresque desumunt. Ceteris otium procurant, ipsi perpetuo in opere ac labore versantur, nec imputant tamen nec aliorum sugillant vitam nec suam efferunt. Hi quo magis sese servos exhibent, eo maiore apud omnes in honore sunt.

Vita activa — marginal note (line 4)

Eorum tamen haereses duae sunt. Altera caelibum, qui non Venere modo in totum abstinent, sed carnium esu quoque, quidam animalium etiam omnium, reiectisque penitus tamquam noxiis vitae praesentis voluptatibus, futurae dumtaxat per vigilias ac sudores inhiant, eius propediem obtinendae spe alacres interim vegetique. Altera laboris haud minus appetens coniugium praefert ut cuius nec aspernantur solacium, et opus naturae debere se et patriae liberos putant. Nullam voluptatem refugiunt quae nihil eos ab labore demoretur. Carnes quadrupedum vel eo nomine diligunt quod tali cibo se validiores ad opus quodque censeant. Hos Utopiani prudentiores at illos sanctiores reputant. Quos quod caelibatum anteferunt matrimonio, asperamque vitam placidae anteponunt, si rationibus niterentur irriderent: nunc vero quum se fateantur religione duci, suspiciunt ac reverentur. Nihil enim sollicitius observant quam ne temere quicquam ulla de religione pronuntient. Huiusmodi ergo sunt quos illi peculiari nomine sua lingua Buthrescas vocant, quod verbum Latine religiosos licet interpretari.

---

[59] As Lupton noted, '*partam* ["produced", "occasioned"], or some similar word, seems wanting'.

They think the contemplation of nature and the reverence arising from it are a kind of worship acceptable to God. There are some people, however, and not just a few of them, who from religious motives neglect literary and scientific pursuits; but none of them is the least bit idle. They are determined to earn happiness after death *The active life* only by their labours and by doing good deeds for others. Some tend the sick; others repair roads, clean ditches, rebuild bridges, dig turf, sand or stones; still others fell trees and cut them up, and transport wood, grain or other commodities into the cities by wagon. They work for private citizens as well as for the public, and work even harder than slaves. With cheerful good will they undertake any task that is so rough, hard and dirty that most people refuse to tackle it because of the toil, tedium and frustration involved. While constantly engaged in heavy labour themselves, they procure leisure for others, yet claim no credit for it. They neither criticise the way others live nor boast of their own doings. The more they put themselves in the position of slaves, the more highly they are honoured by everyone.

These people are of two sects. The first are celibates who abstain not only from sex but also from eating meat, and some from any sort of animal food whatever. They completely reject all the pleasures of this life as harmful, and look forward only to the joys of the life to come, which they hope to merit by hard labour and all-night vigils. As they hope to attain it soon, they are cheerful and active in the here and now. The other kind are just as fond of hard work, but prefer to marry. They don't despise the comforts of marriage, but think that, as they owe nature their labour, so they owe children to their country. Unless it interferes with their labour, they avoid no pleasure. They eat meat, precisely because they think it makes them stronger for any sort of heavy work. The Utopians regard the second sort as more sensible, but the first sort as holier. If they chose celibacy over marriage and a hard life over a comfortable one on grounds of reason alone, they would be laughed at; but as these people profess to be motivated by religion, the Utopians respect and revere them. On no subject are they warier of jumping to conclusions than in this matter of religion. Such, then, are the people whom in their own language they call Buthrescas, a term which can be translated as 'the religious'.[124]

---

[124] 'Buthrescas' is another Greek compound, translated in the text. The constant, selfless industry of the Buthrescas embodies the monastic ideal (though in that ideal labour is combined with contemplation and prayer).

Sacerdotes habent eximia sanctitate, eoque admodum paucos. Neque enim plus quam tredecim in singulis habent urbibus, pari templorum numero, nisi quum itur ad bellum. Tunc enim septem ex illis cum exercitu profectis totidem sufficiuntur interim. Sed illi reversi, suum quisque locum recuperat; qui supersunt hi quoad 5 decedentibus illis ordine succedant, comites interea sunt pontificis, nam unus reliquis praeficitur. Eliguntur a populo, idque ceterorum ritu magistratuum, occultis (ad studia vitanda) suffragiis: electi a suo collegio consecrantur.

Hi rebus divinis praesunt, religiones curant, ac morum velut cen- 10 sores sunt: magnoque pudori ducitur ab his quemquam tamquam vitae parum probatae accersi compellarive. Ceterum ut hortari atque admonere illorum est, ita coercere atque in facinorosos animadvertere principis atque aliorum est magistratuum, nisi quod sacris interdicunt quos improbe malos comperiunt. Nec ullum fere supplicium 15 est quod horreant magis, nam et summa percelluntur infamia et occulto religionis metu lacerantur, ne corporibus quidem diu futuris in tuto. Quippe ni properam paenitentiam sacerdotibus approbent, comprehensi impietatis poenam senatui persolvunt.

Pueritia iuventusque ab illis eruditur, nec prior literarum cura 20 quam morum ac virtutis habetur. Namque summam adhibent industriam ut bonas protinus opiniones et conservandae ipsorum reipublicae utiles teneris adhuc et sequacibus puerorum animis instillent, quae ubi pueris penitus insederint, viros per totam vitam comitantur, magnamque ad tuendum publicae rei statum (qui non nisi vitiis 25 dilabitur quae ex perversis nascuntur opinionibus) adferunt utilitatem.

Feminae sacerdotes Sacerdotibus (ni feminae sint: nam neque ille sexus excluditur, sed rarius et non nisi vidua natuque grandis eligitur) uxores sunt popularium selectissimae. 30

Their priests are of extraordinary holiness and therefore very few. In each city there are no more than thirteen, one for each church. In case of war, seven of them go out with the army, and seven substitutes are appointed to fill their places for the time being. When the regular priests come back, they all return to their former posts. Until the time when the extra priests succeed in an orderly fashion to the regular priests who have died, they serve as attendants to the high priest. For one of the priests has authority over the others. Like all other officials, priests are elected by secret popular vote, to avoid competition.[125] After election they are ordained by the college of priests.

They preside over divine worship, attend to religious matters, and act as censors of public morality; for a person to be summoned or brought before them for not living an honourable life is considered a great disgrace. As the duty of the priests is merely to counsel and advise, so correcting and punishing offenders is the duty of the governor and other officials, though the priests do exclude flagrant sinners from divine service. Hardly any punishment is more dreaded than this; the excommunicate suffers great infamy, and is secretly tortured by religious fear. Not even his body will be safe for very long, for unless he quickly convinces the priests of his repentance he will be seized and punished by the senate for impiety.

The priests do the teaching of children and young people.[126] Instruction in morality and virtue is considered no less important than learning proper. They make every effort to instil in the pupils' minds, while they are still tender and pliable, principles useful to the commonwealth. What is planted in the minds of children lives on in the minds of grown men and serves greatly to strengthen the commonwealth; its decline can always be traced to vices that arise from wrong attitudes.[127]

Women are not debarred from the priesthood, but only a widow of advanced years is ever chosen, and it doesn't happen often. The wives of the male priests are the very finest women in the whole country.[128]

Female priests

[125] They are elected from the class of scholars – whose members are nominated by the priests and elected by the syphogrants (p. 131).

[126] Surely the priests only supervise the teaching. There are but thirteen of them per city, whereas each city includes a good many thousand children.

[127] The fundamental importance of education, including especially moral education, to the health of the commonwealth is the central tenet of the Greek treatments of the ideal commonwealth. See, e.g., Plato, *Republic* IV.424D-E, 425A; Aristotle, *Politics* V.ix.11.

[128] In *The Confutation of Tyndale's Answer* (1532–3), More took the standard position that the prohibition against female priests rests on divine revelation (*CW*,

Neque enim ulli apud Utopienses magistratui maior habetur honos, usqueadeo ut si quid etiam flagitii admiserint, nulli publico iudicio subsint; deo tantum ac sibi relinquuntur. Neque enim fas putant illum quantumvis scelestum mortali manu contingere qui deo tam singulari modo velut anathema dedicatus est. Qui mos illis 5

Excommunicatio[60] facilior est observatu, quod sacerdotes et tam pauci et tanta cum cura deliguntur. Nam neque temere accidit ut qui ex bonis optimus ad tantam dignitatem solius respectu virtutis evehitur in corruptelam et vitium degeneret. Et si iam maxime contingeret, ut est mortalium natura mutabilis, tamen qua sunt paucitate nec ulla praeter 10 honorem potestate praediti, ad publicam certe perniciem nihil magni ab his momenti pertimescendum sit. Quos ideo tam raros

At apud nos atque infrequentes habent, ne dignitas ordinis quem nunc tanta *quanta turba est* veneratione prosequuntur, communicato cum multis honore, vilesceret, praesertim quum difficile putent frequentes invenire tam 15 bonos ut ei sint dignitati pares, ad quam gerendam non sufficit mediocribus esse virtutibus.

Nec eorum aestimatio apud suos maior[61] quam apud exteras etiam gentes habetur, quod inde facile patet unde etiam natum puto. Nempe decernentibus proelio copiis, seorsum illi non admodum 20 procul considunt in genibus, sacras induti vestes; tensis ad caelum

O sacerdotes palmis primum omnium pacem, proxime suis victoriam, sed neutri *nostris longe* cruentam parti, comprecantur. Vincentibus suis decurrunt in aciem *sanctiores* saevientesque in profligatos inhibent. Vidisse tantum atque appellasse praesentes ad vitam satis; diffluentium contactus vestium 25 reliquas quoque fortunas ab omni bellorum iniuria defendit. Qua ex re apud omnes undique gentes tanta illis veneratio, tantum verae maiestatis accessit, ut saepe ab hostibus non minus salutis ad cives reportarint quam ab ipsis ad hostes attulissent. Siquidem aliquando constat, inclinata suorum acie desperatis rebus, quum ipsi in fugam 30 verterentur, hostes in caedem ac praedam ruerent, interventu sacerdotum interpellatam stragem ac diremptis invicem copiis pacem

---

[60] Though the gloss appears at this place in all four early editions, its connection with the text is obscure. It would fit better at 230:15, where excommunication is in fact discussed.

[61] *maior*, following 1517, rather than *magis* (the other texts): an adjective modifying *aestimatio*, not an adverb.

No official is more honoured among the Utopians than the priest, to such an extent that even if one of them commits a crime, he is not brought to court but left to God and his own conscience. They think it wrong to lay human hands on a man, however guilty, who has been specially consecrated to God, as a holy offering, so to speak. This custom is the easier for them to observe because their priests are so few and so carefully selected. For it rarely happens that a man chosen for his goodness and raised to high dignities solely because of his moral character will fall into corruption and vice. And even if such a thing should happen, human nature being as changeable as it is, no great harm to the public is to be feared, because the priests are so few and have no power beyond that which derives from their good repute. In fact, the reason for having so few priests is to prevent the order, now so highly esteemed, from being cheapened by numbers. Besides, they think it would be hard to find many men qualified for a dignity for which merely ordinary virtues are not sufficient.

Excommunication

But what a crowd of them we have!

Their priests are not more esteemed at home than abroad – the reason for which can easily be seen, I think, from the following account. Whenever their armies join in battle, the Utopian priests are to be found, a little removed from the fray but not far, wearing their sacred vestments and down on their knees. With hands raised to heaven, they pray first of all for peace, and then for victory for their own side, but without much bloodshed on either part.[129] Should their side be victorious, they rush among the combatants and restrain the rage of their own men against the defeated. If any of the enemy see these priests and call to them, it is enough to save their lives; to touch the flowing robes of a priest will save all their property from confiscation. This custom has brought them such veneration among all peoples, and given them such genuine authority, that they have saved Utopians from the rage of the enemy as often as they have protected the enemy from Utopians. For it is well established that on some occasions, when the Utopian line had buckled, when the field was lost, and the enemy was rushing in to kill and plunder, the priests have intervened to stop the carnage and separate the armies, and an equitable peace has been devised

O priests far more holy than our own!

VIII, 260–1). Priestly celibacy, though, is a matter of ecclesiastical discipline rather than a divine decree (*ibid.*, 307).

[129] By contrast, Erasmus describes European clerics as 'often . . . very firebrands of war' (*The Education of a Christian Prince*, CWE, XXVII, 286), and his *Folly* tells of German bishops who think it dishonourable to die anywhere but on the battlefield (*CWE*, XXVII, 140).

aequis conditionibus esse compositam atque constitutam. Neque
enim umquam fuit ulla gens tam fera, crudelis ac barbara, apud quos
ipsorum corpus non sacrosanctum atque inviolabile sit habitum.

Festos celebrant initialem atque ultimum cuiusque mensis diem,
et anni item, quem in menses partiuntur circuitu lunae finitos, ut ₅
solis ambitus annum circinat. Primos quosque dies Cynemernos,
postremos ipsorum lingua Trapemernos appellant, quae vocabula
perinde sonant ac si primifesti et finifesti vocentur. Delubra visuntur egregia utpote non operosa modo sed quod erat in tanta ipsorum
paucitate necessarium, immensi etiam populi capacia. Sunt tamen ₁₀
omnia subobscura: nec id aedificandi inscitia factum sed consilio
sacerdotum ferunt, quod immodicam lucem cogitationes dispergere,
partiore ac velut dubia colligi animos et intendi religionem putant.

Quae quoniam non est ibi apud omnes eadem, et universae tamen
eius formae quamquam variae ac multiplices in divinae naturae ₁₅
cultum velut in unum finem diversa via commigrant, idcirco nihil
in templis visitur auditurve quod non quadrare ad cunctas in commune videatur. Si quod proprium sit cuiusquam sectae sacrum, id
intra domesticos quisque parietes curat; publica tali peragunt ordine
qui nulli prorsus ex privatis deroget. Itaque nulla deorum effigies ₂₀
in templo conspicitur, quo liberum cuique sit qua forma deum velit
e sua[62] religione concipere. Nullum peculiare dei nomen invocant
sed Mythrae dumtaxat, quo vocabulo cuncti in unam divinae maiestatis naturam, quaecumque sit illa, conspirant. Nullae concipiuntur
preces quas non pronuntiare quivis inoffensa sua secta possit. ₂₅

---

[62] *sua*, following 1517; other editions, *summa*.

and concluded. There was never anywhere a tribe so fierce, cruel and barbarous as not to hold their persons sacrosanct and inviolable.

The Utopians celebrate the first and last days of every month, and likewise of each year, as feast days. They divide the year into months, which they measure by the orbit of the moon, just as they measure the year itself by the course of the sun. In their language, the first days are known as the Cynemerns and the last days as the Trapemerns,[130] which is to say 'First-feasts' and 'Last-feasts'. Their churches are beautifully constructed, finely adorned, and large enough to hold a great many worshippers. This is a necessity, since churches are so few.[131] The interiors are all rather dark, not from architectural ignorance but from deliberate policy; for the priests (they say) think that in bright light thoughts will go wandering, whereas a dim light concentrates the mind and aids devotion. *Feast days observed by the Utopians*

What their churches are like

Though there are various religions in Utopia, all of them, even the most diverse, agree in the main point, which is worship of the divine nature; they are like travellers going to a single destination by different roads. So nothing is seen or heard in the churches that does not square with all the creeds. If any sect has a special rite of its own, that is celebrated in a private house; the public service is ordered by a ritual which in no way derogates from any of the private services. Therefore in the churches no images of the gods are seen, so that each person may be free to form his own image of God according to his own religion, in any shape he pleases.[132] They do not invoke God by any name except Mythra. Whatever the nature of the divine majesty may be, they all agree to refer to it by that single word, and their prayers are so phrased that anyone can say them without offending his own sect.

---

[130] More Greek compounds, literally meaning 'Dog-day' (or possibly 'Starting-day') and 'Turning-day'. A note in Lupton's edition explains that in ancient Greece the 'dog's day' was 'strictly the night between the old and new [months], when food was placed out at the cross-roads, and the barking of the dogs was taken as a sign of the approach of Hecate.' It may be relevant that Solon, the legendary lawgiver of Athens, called the last day of each month the 'Old-and-New day' (Diogenes Laertius I.58).

[131] Doubtless there are several shifts of worship, but even so the churches must be *very* large: there are thirteen of them in each city, and each city contains over 100,000 people (p. 135n.).

[132] In one way or another, Utopian religion answers or somehow satisfies many of the complaints of the religious reformers of More's time – including complaints about idolatry and superstitious practices, ecclesiastical wealth and corruption, and censorship of expression on religious matters.

Ad templum ergo in finifestis diebus vespere conveniunt, adhuc
ieiuni, acturi deo de anno menseve cuius id festum postremus dies
est prospere acto gratias. Postero die, nam is primifestus est, mane
ad templa confluitur ut insequentis anni mensisve quem ab illo aus-
picaturi festo sint faustum felicemque successum comprecentur. At ₅

in finifestis antea quam templum petunt, uxores domi ad virorum
pedes, liberi ad parentum provoluti, pecasse fatentur sese aut
admisso aliquo aut officio indiligenter obito veniamque errati pre-
cantur. Ita si qua se nubecula domesticae simultatis offuderat, tali

satisfactione discutitur uti animo puro ac sereno sacrificiis intersint, ₁₀
nam interesse turbido religio est. Eoque odii iraeve in quemquam
sibi conscii, nisi reconciliati ac defecatis affectibus, ad sacrifica non
ingerunt sese, vindictae celeris magnaeque metu.

Eo quum veniunt, viri in dextram delubri partem, feminae seorsum in sinistram commeant. Tum ita se collocant ut cuiusque ₁₅
domus masculi ante patremfamilias consideant,[63] feminarum mater-
familias agmen claudat. Ita prospicitur uti omnes omnium gestus
foris ab his observentur quorum auctoritate domi ac disciplina
reguntur. Quin hoc quoque sedulo cavent uti iunior ibi passim cum
seniore copuletur, ne pueri pueris crediti id temporis puerilibus ₂₀
transigant ineptiis in quo deberent maxime religiosum erga superos
metum, maximum ac prope unicum virtutibus incitamentum,
concipere.

Nullum animal in sacrificiis mactant, nec sanguine rentur ac caedibus divinam gaudere clementiam, qui vitam animantibus ideo est ₂₅
elargitus ut viverent. Tus incendunt et alia item odoramenta; ad
haec cereos numerosos praeferunt, non quod haec nesciant nihil ad
divinam conferre naturam, quippe ut nec ipsas hominum preces,

---

[63] As Surtz points out in the Yale *Utopia* (421–2n.), More and some of his contemporaries used non-classical *consideo* (thus *consideant*, the reading of all the early
editions) instead of the usual *consido*.

They meet in their churches, therefore, on the evening of 'Last-feast', and while still fasting they thank God for their prosperity during the month or year just ending. Next day, which is 'First-feast', they all flock to the churches in the morning to pray for prosperity and happiness in the month or year just beginning. But on the day of 'Last-feast', at home, before they go to church, wives kneel before their husbands and children before their parents, to confess their sins of commission or of negligence, and beg forgiveness for their offences. Thus if any cloud of anger or resentment has arisen in the family, it is dispersed, and they can attend the sacrifices with clear and untroubled minds – for they are too scrupulous to worship with a rankling conscience.[133] If they are aware of hatred or anger toward anyone, they do not attend the sacrifices till they have been reconciled and have cleansed their hearts, for fear of some swift and terrible punishment. *The Utopians' confession*

But among us the worst sinners try to crowd closest to the altar

As they enter the temple they separate, men going to the right side and women to the left.[134] Then they take their seats so that the males of each household are placed in front of the head of that household, while the womenfolk are directly in front of the mother of the family. In this way they ensure that all of everyone's public behaviour is supervised by the same person whose authority and discipline direct him at home. They take great care that the young are everywhere placed in the company of their elders. For if children were trusted to the care of other children, they might spend in infantile foolery the time they should devote to developing a religious fear of the gods, which is the greatest and almost the only incitement to virtue.

They slaughter no animals in their sacrifices, and do not think that a merciful God, who gave life to all creatures that they might live, will be gratified with slaughter and bloodshed. They burn incense, scatter perfumes and display a great number of candles – not that they think these practices profit the divine nature in any way, any more than human prayers do; but they like this harmless

---

[133] Cf. Christ's injunction: 'if thou bring thy gift to the altar, and there rememberest that thy brother hath ought against thee; Leave there thy gift before the altar, and go thy way; first be reconciled to thy brother, and then come and offer thy gift' (Matthew 5:23–4). The Catholic institution of confession to priests is not paralleled in Utopia. More pointed out to his daughter Margaret that 'in Greece before Christ's days they used not confession, no more the men then, than the beasts now' (*The Correspondence of Sir Thomas More*, ed. Elizabeth F. Rogers (Princeton, 1947), p. 520).

[134] Separation of the sexes in church had been customary since the early Christian centuries.

sed et innoxium colendi genus placet et his odoribus luminibusque
ac ceteris etiam caerimoniis nescio quomodo sese sentiunt homines
erigi atque in dei cultum animo alacriore consurgere.

Candidis in templo vestibus amicitur populus: sacerdos versicolores induitur[64] et opere et forma mirabiles, materia non perinde 5
pretiosa neque enim auro intextae aut raris coagmentatae lapidibus,
sed diversis avium plumis tam scite tantoque artificio laboratae sunt
ut operis pretium nullius aestimatio materiae fuerit aequatura. Ad
hoc in illis volucrum pennis plumisque et certis earum ordinibus
quibus in sacerdotis veste discriminantur, arcana quaedam dicunt 10
contineri mysteria, quorum interpretatione cognita (quae per sacr-
ificos diligenter traditur) divinorum in se beneficiorum, suaeque
vicissim pietatis in deum, ac mutui quoque inter se officii ad-
moneantur.

Quum primum sacerdos ita ornatus ex adyto sese offert, cuncti 15
protinus in terram venerabundi procumbunt, tam alto ab omni parte
silentio ut ipsa rei facies terrorem quendam velut praesentis cuiuspiam numinis incutiat. Tellure paulum morati, dato ab sacerdote
Musica signo, erigunt sese. Tum laudes deo canunt quas musicis instru-
Utopiensium mentis interstinguunt,[65] aliis magna ex parte formis quam quae 20
nostro visuntur orbe. Ex illis pleraque sicuti quae nobis in usu
sunt multum suavitate vincunt, ita quaedam nostris ne conferenda
quidem sint. Verum una in re haud dubie longo nos intervallo prae-
cellunt, quod omnis eorum musica, sive quae personatur organis
sive quam voce modulantur humana, ita naturales affectus imitatur 25
et exprimit, ita sonus accommodatur ad rem, seu deprecantis oratio
sit seu laeta, placabilis, turbida, lugubris, irata, ita rei sensum quendam melodiae forma repraesentat ut animos auditorum mirum in
modum adficiat, penetret, incendat. Sollemnes ad ultimum con-
ceptis verbis preces sacerdos pariter populusque percensent, ita 30
compositas ut quae simul cuncti recitant privatim quisque ad semet
referat.

In his deum et creationis et gubernationis et ceterorum praeterea
bonorum omnium quilibet recognoscit auctorem. Tot ob recepta
beneficia gratias agit, nominatim vero quod deo propitio in eam 35
rempublicam inciderit quae sit felicissima, eam religionem sortitus
sit quam speret esse verissimam. Qua in re si quid erret aut si quid

[64] The form *induitur* is a passive verb with a Greek accusative, or a middle form
with a direct object. The adjective *versicolores* [*vestes*] could mean that the feathers
are iridescent or multicoloured, or that the colour of the vestment changes according to various times or feasts (like the vestments of Catholic priests).
[65] Lupton and Delcourt have the correct form. The early editions print *interstingunt*.

kind of worship. They feel that sweet smells, lights and other such rituals somehow elevate the human mind and lift it with a livelier devotion towards the adoration of God.

In church the people all wear white. The priest wears robes of various colours, wonderful for their workmanship and decoration, though not made of especially costly materials. The robes have no gold embroidery nor any rare gems sewn on them, but are decorated with the feathers of different birds so skilfully woven together that the value of the handiwork far exceeds the cost of the richest materials.[135] Also, certain symbolic mysteries are hidden in the patterning of the feathers on the robes, the meaning of which is carefully taught by the priests. These messages serve to remind them of God's benefits toward them, and of the piety they owe in turn to God, as well as of their duty to one another.

As the priest in his robes appears from the vestibule, the people all fall to the ground in reverence. The stillness is so complete that the scene strikes one with awe, as if a divinity were actually present. After remaining in this posture for a little while, they rise at a signal from the priest. Then they sing hymns to the accompaniment of *Utopian music* musical instruments, most of them quite different in shape from those seen in our part of the world. Many of them produce sweeter tones than ours, but others are not even comparable. In one respect, however, they are beyond doubt far ahead of us, because all their music, both vocal and instrumental, renders and expresses natural feelings and perfectly matches the sound to the subject.[136] Whether the words of the prayer are supplicatory, cheerful, serene, troubled, mournful or angry, the music represents the meaning through the contour of the melody so admirably that it stirs up, penetrates and inflames the minds of the hearers. Finally, the priest and the people together recite certain fixed forms of prayer, so composed that what they all repeat in unison each individual can apply to himself.

In these prayers each one acknowledges God to be the creator and ruler of the universe and the author of all good things. He thanks God for the many benefits he has received, and particularly for the divine favour which placed him in the happiest of commonwealths and inspired him with religious ideas which he hopes are the truest. If he is wrong in this, and if there is some sort of society

---

[135] The choice of feathers for the vestments may reflect Vespucci's observation that the Indians' riches 'consist of variegated birds' feathers' (*Four Voyages*, p. 98).

[136] Surtz points out that Hythloday's dissatisfaction with the increasingly elaborate church music of his time was shared by many other intellectuals, including Erasmus (*CW*, IV, 555–6).

sit[66] alterutra melius et quod deus magis approbet, orare se eius bonitas efficiat hoc ut ipse cognoscat, paratum enim sequi se quaqua versus ab eo ducatur. Sin et haec reipublicae forma sit optima et sua religio rectissima, tum uti et ipsi constantiam tribuat, et ceteros mortales omnes ad eadem instituta vivendi, in eandem de deo opi- 5 nionem perducat, nisi[67] inscrutabilem eius voluntatem etiam sit quod in hac religionum varietate delectet.

Denique precatur ut facile defunctum exitu ad se recipiat, quam cito serove praefinire quidem non audere se. Quamquam, quod[68] inoffensa eius maiestate fiat, multo magis ipsi futurum cordi sit 10 difficillima morte obita ad deum pervadere quam ab eo diutius pros-perrimo vitae cursu distineri. Hac prece dicta, rursus in terram proni pauloque post erecti, discedunt pransum, et quod superest diei ludis et exercitio militaris disciplinae percurrunt.

Descripsi vobis quam potui verissime eius formam reipublicae 15 quam ego certe non optimam tantum sed solam etiam censeo quae sibi suo iure possit reipublicae vindicare vocabulum. Siquidem alibi de publico loquentes ubique commodo privatum curant, hic ubi nihil privati est, serio publicum negotium agunt. Certe utrobique merito, nam alibi, quotusquisque est qui nesciat, nisi quid seorsum 20 prospiciat sibi, quantumvis florente republica, semet tamen fame periturum, eoque necessitas urget ut sui potius quam populi, id est aliorum, habendam sibi rationem censeat. Contra hic, ubi omnia omnium sunt, nemo dubitat (curetur modo ut plena sint horrea publica) nihil quicquam privati cuiquam defuturum. Neque enim 25 maligna rerum distributio est neque inops neque mendicus ibi quis-quam, et quum nemo quicquam habeat omnes tamen divites sunt.

Nam quid ditius esse potest quam, adempta prorsus omni solici-tudine, laeto ac tranquillo animo vivere? non de suo victu trepidum, non uxoris querula flagitatione vexatum, non paupertatem filio met- 30 uentem, non de filiae dote anxium, sed de suo suorumque omnium, uxoris, filiorum, nepotum, pronepotum, abnepotum, et quam longam posterorum seriem suorum generosi praesumunt, victu esse

---

[66] sit, omitted by 1518M, N, supplied from 1516 and 1517.

[67] An emendation first proposed in 1563 inserts per after nisi, to explain the accusat-ive case of voluntatem. But it is possible to construe voluntatem as the object of delectet. Either way the syntax is strained.

[68] The relative pronoun quod ('insofar as') loosely anticipates the idea of the main clause – wishing to die sooner rather than later. The emendation quoad, proposed by Michels and Ziegler, is plausible but not necessary.

or religion more acceptable to God, he prays that God will, in his goodness, reveal it to him, for he is ready to follow wherever he leads. But if their form of society is the best and their religion the truest, then he prays that God will keep him steadfast, and bring other mortals to the same way of life and the same religious faith – unless, indeed, there is something in this variety of religions which delights his inscrutable will.

Then he prays that after an easy death God will take him to himself, how soon or late it is not for him to say. But if it please God's divine majesty, he asks to be brought to him soon, even by the hardest possible death, rather than be kept away from him longer, even by the most prosperous of earthly careers. When this prayer has been said, they prostrate themselves on the ground again; then after a little while they rise and go to lunch. The rest of the day they pass in games and military training.

Now I have described to you as accurately as I could the structure of that commonwealth which I consider not only the best but indeed the only one that can rightfully claim that name. In other places men talk all the time about the commonwealth, but what they mean is simply their own wealth; here,[137] where there is no private business, every man zealously pursues the public business. And in both places people are right to act as they do. For elsewhere, even though the commonwealth may flourish, there are very few who do not know that unless they make separate provision for themselves, they may perfectly well die of hunger. Bitter necessity, then, forces them to think that they must look out for themselves rather than for the people, that is, for other people. But here, where everything belongs to everybody, no one need fear that, so long as the public warehouses are filled, anyone will ever lack for anything for his own use. For the distribution of goods is not niggardly; no one is poor there, there are no beggars, and though no one owns anything, everyone is rich.

For what can be greater riches than to live joyfully and peacefully, free from all anxieties, and without worries about making a living? No man is bothered by his wife's querulous complaints, no man fears poverty for his son, or worries about a dowry for his daughter. Everyone can feel secure of his own livelihood and happiness, and of his whole family's as well: wife, sons, grandsons, great-grandsons, great-great-grandsons, and that whole long line of descendants that the gentry are so fond of contemplating. Indeed, even

---

[137] Hythloday speaks as if he were still in Utopia.

ac felicitate securum. Quid quod nihilo minus his prospicitur qui nunc impotes olim laboraverunt quam his qui nunc laborant.

Hic aliquis velim cum hac aequitate audeat aliarum iustitiam gentium comparare, apud quas dispeream si ullum prorsus comperio iustitiae aequitatisque vestigium. Nam quae haec iustitia est, ut nobilis quispiam aut aurifex aut faenerator aut denique alius quisquam eorum qui aut omnino nihil agunt, aut id quod agunt eius generis est ut non sit reipublicae magnopere necessarium, lautam ac splendidam vitam vel ex otio vel supervacuo negotio consequatur? quum interim mediastinus, auriga, faber, agricola tanto tamque assiduo labore quam vix iumenta sustineant, tam necessario ut sine eo ne unum quidem annum possit ulla durare respublica, victum tamen adeo malignum parant, vitam adeo miseram ducunt, ut longe potior videri possit condicio iumentorum, quibus nec tam perpetuus labor nec victus multo deterior est et ipsis etiam suavior, nec ullus interim de futuro timor. At hos et labor sterilis atque infructuosus in praesenti stimulat, et inopis recordatio senectutis occidit, quippe quibus parcior est diurna merces quam ut eidem possit diei sufficere, tantum abest ut excrescat et supersit aliquid quod cottidie queat in senectutis usum reponi.

An non haec iniqua est et ingrata respublica, quae generosis, ut vocant, et aurificibus et id genus reliquis aut otiosis aut tantum adulatoribus et inanium voluptatum artificibus, tanta munera prodigit? agricolis contra, carbonariis, mediastinis, aurigis et fabris, sine quibus nulla omnino respublica esset, nihil benigne prospicit, sed eorum florentis aetatis abusa laboribus, annis tandem ac morbo graves, omnium rerum indigos, tot vigiliarum immemor, tot ac tantorum oblita beneficiorum, miserrima morte repensat ingratissima. Quid quod ex diurno pauperum demenso divites cottidie aliquid, non modo privata fraude sed publicis etiam legibus, abradunt? Ita quod ante videbatur iniustum, optime de republica meritis pessimam referre gratiam, hoc isti depravatum etiam fecerunt, tum provulgata lege, iustitiam. Itaque omnes has quae hodie usquam florent

those who once worked but can no longer do so are cared for just as well as those who are still working.

At this point, I'd like to see anyone venture to compare this equity of the Utopians with the justice that prevails among other nations – among whom I'll be damned if I can discover the slightest trace of justice or fairness. What kind of justice is it when a noble-man, a goldsmith,[138] a moneylender, or someone else who makes his living by doing either nothing at all or something completely useless to the commonwealth, gets to live a life of luxury and grand-eur, while in the meantime a labourer, a carter or a carpenter or a farmer works so hard and so constantly that even beasts of burden would scarcely endure it? Although this work of theirs is so necessary that no commonwealth could survive for a year without it, they earn so meagre a living and lead such miserable lives that beasts would really seem to be better off. Beasts do not have to work every minute, and their food is not much worse; in fact they like it better, and besides, they do not have to worry about their future. But workingmen must not only sweat without reward or gain in the present but agonise over the prospect of a penniless old age. Their daily wage is inadequate even for present needs, so there is no possible chance of their saving today for their declining years.

Now isn't this an unjust and ungrateful commonwealth? It lav-ishes rich rewards on so-called gentry, goldsmiths and the rest of that crew, who don't work at all or are mere parasites, purveyors of empty pleasures. And yet it makes no proper provision for the welfare of farmers and colliers, labourers, carters and carpenters, without whom the commonwealth would simply cease to exist. After society has taken the labour of their best years, when they are worn out by age, sickness and utter destitution, then the thankless commonwealth, forgetting all their sleepless nights and services, throws them out to die a miserable death. What is worse, the rich constantly try to grind out of the poor part of their daily wages, not only by private swindling but by public laws. Before, it appeared to be unjust that people who deserve most from the commonwealth should receive least. But now, by promulgating law, they have transmuted this perversion into justice.[139] When I consider and turn

---

[138] In addition to being the creators of objects which are, from the Utopian point of view, worthless, goldsmiths often functioned as bankers. As the inclusion of moneylenders in this list suggests, the idea that lending money at interest consti-tuted sinful usury remained strong in More's time – though the sentence also makes it clear that the practice was firmly established.

[139] Russell Ames suggests that there is a particular reference to legislation of recent Parliaments, completed in 1515, 'which re-enacted the old statutes against labor-

respublicas animo intuenti ac versanti mihi nihil, sic me amet deus,
Haec adnota,
lector occurrit aliud quam quaedam conspiratio divitum, de suis commodis reipublicae nomine tituloque tractantium. Comminiscun-
turque et excogitant omnes modos atque artes quibus quae malis
artibus ipsi congesserunt, ea primum ut absque perdendi metu 5
retineant, post hoc ut pauperum omnium opera ac laboribus[69] quam
minimo sibi redimant, eisque abutantur. Haec machinamenta, ubi
semel divites publico nomine, hoc est etiam pauperum, decreverunt
observari, iam leges fiunt.

At homines deterrimi, cum inexplebili cupiditate quae fuerant 10
omnibus suffectura ea omnia inter se partiverint, quam longe tamen
ab Utopiensium reipublicae felicitate absunt! e qua, cum ipso usu
sublata penitus omni aviditate pecuniae, quanta moles molestiarum
recisa, quanta scelerum seges radicitus evulsa est! Quis enim nescit
fraudes, furta, rapinas, rixas, tumultus, iurgia, seditiones, caedes, 15
proditiones, veneficia, cottidianis vindicata potius quam refrenata
suppliciis, interempta pecunia, commori? ad haec metum, sollicitu-
dinem, curas, labores, vigilias, eodem momento quo pecunia perit-
uras. Quin paupertas ipsa, quae sola pecuniis visa est indigere, pecunia prorsus undique sublata, protinus etiam ipsa decresceret. 20

Id quo fiat illustrius, revolve in animo tecum annum aliquem
sterilem atque infecundum in quo multa hominum millia fames
abstulerit. Contendo plane in fine illius penuriae, excussis divitum
horreis, tantum frugum potuisse reperiri, quantum si fuisset inter
eos distributum quos macies ac tabes absumpsit, illam caeli solique 25
parcitatem nemo omnino sensisset. Tam facile victus parari posset,
nisi beata illa pecunia, quae praeclare scilicet inventa est ut aditus ad
victum per eam patesceret, sola nobis ad victum viam intercluderet.
Sentiunt ista, non dubito, etiam divites, nec ignorant quanto potior
esset illa condicio nulla re necessaria carere quam multis abundare 30
superfluis, tam numerosis eripi malis quam magnis obsideri divitiis.
Neque mihi quidem dubitare subit quin vel sui cuiusque commodi

---

[69] As Lupton notes, *opera* and *laboribus* (where we would expect accusative forms)
seem to be ablative by attraction to the following *eisque*.

over in my mind the various commonwealths flourishing today, so
help me God, I can see in them nothing but a conspiracy of the *Reader, note well!*
rich, who are advancing their own interests under the name and
title of the commonwealth.[140] They invent ways and means to keep,
with no fear of losing it, whatever they have piled up by sharp
practice, and then they scheme to oppress the poor by buying their
toil and labour as cheaply as possible. These devices become law as
soon as the rich, speaking for the commonwealth – which, of
course, includes the poor as well – say they must be observed.

And yet when these insatiably greedy and evil men have divided
among themselves all the goods which would have sufficed for the
entire people, how far they remain from the happiness of the Utopian republic, which has abolished not only money but with it greed!
What a mass of trouble was cut away by that one step! What a
thicket of crimes was uprooted! Everyone knows that if money
were abolished, fraud, theft, robbery, quarrels, brawls, altercations,
seditions, murders, treasons, poisonings and a whole set of crimes
which are avenged but not prevented by the hangman would at
once die out. At the very moment when money disappeared, so
would fear, anxiety, worry, toil and sleepless nights. Even poverty,
the one condition which has always seemed to need money, would
immediately decline if money were entirely abolished.

Consider, if you will, this example. Take a barren year of failed
harvests, when many thousands of people have been carried off by
famine. If at the end of the scarcity the barns of the rich were
searched, I dare assert that enough grain would be found in them
to have kept all those who died of starvation and disease from even
realising that a shortage ever existed – if only it had been divided
among them. So easily might people get the necessities of life if that
blessed money, that marvellous invention which is supposed to
provide access to what we need to live, were not in fact the only
barrier to our getting it. Even the rich, I'm sure, understand this.
They must know that it's better to have enough of what we really
need than an abundance of superfluities, much better to escape from
our many present troubles than to be burdened with great masses
of wealth. And in fact I have no doubt that every man's perception
of where his true interest lies, along with the authority of Christ

ers while removing clauses unfavorable to employers' (*Citizen Thomas More and
His Utopia* (Princeton, 1949), p. 128).
[140] Many readers have seen an allusion here to the judgement of St Augustine: 'if
justice is left out, what are kingdoms but great robber bands?' (*De civitate Dei*
IV.iv).

ratio vel CHRISTI servatoris auctoritas (qui neque pro tanta sapientia potuit ignorare quid optimum esset, neque qua erat bonitate id consulere quod non optimum sciret) totum orbem facile in huius *Mire dictum* reipublicae leges iamdudum traxisset, nisi una tantum belua, omnium princeps parensque pestium, superbia, reluctaretur.   5

Haec non suis commodis prosperitatem, sed ex alienis metitur incommodis. Haec ne dea quidem fieri vellet, nullis relictis miseris quibus imperare atque insultare possit, quorum miseriis praefulgeat ipsius comparata felicitas, quorum suis explicatis opibus angat atque incendat inopiam. Haec averni serpens, mortalium pererrans pec- 10 tora, ne meliorem vitae capessant viam, velut remora retrahit ac remoratur.

Quae quoniam pressius hominibus infixa est quam ut facile possit evelli, hanc reipublicae formam, quam omnibus libenter optarim, Utopiensibus saltem contigisse gaudeo, qui ea vitae sunt instituta 15 secuti quibus reipublicae fundamenta iecerunt non modo felicissime verumetiam, quantum humana praesagiri coniectura contigit, aeternum duratura. Exstirpatis enim domi cum ceteris vitiis ambitionis et factionum radicibus, nihil impendet periculi ne domestico discidio laboretur, quae res[70] una multarum urbium egregie munitas opes 20 pessumdedit. At salva domi concordia et salubribus institutis, non omnium finitimorum invidia principum (quae saepius id iam olim semper reverberata tentavit) concutere illud imperium aut commovere queat.

Haec ubi Raphael recensuit, quamquam haud pauca mihi succurreb- 25 ant quae in eius populi moribus legibusque perquam absurde videbantur instituta, non solum de belli gerendi ratione et rebus divinis ac religione, aliisque insuper eorum institutis, sed in eo quoque ipso maxime quod maximum totius institutionis fundamentum est, vita scilicet victuque communi sine ullo pecuniae commercio, qua una 30 re funditus evertitur omnis nobilitas, magnificentia, splendor, maiestas, vera (ut publica est opinio) decora atque ornamenta reipu-

---

[70] *res*, following 1517; the other texts omit. It seems needed to justify *quae* and *una*. Compare Sallust, *Bellum Iugurthinum* XLII.4: 'Quae res plerumque magnas civitatis pessum dedit'.

authority of Christ our Saviour (whose wisdom could not fail to recognise the best, and whose goodness would not fail to counsel it), would long ago have brought the whole world to adopt the laws of this commonwealth, were it not for one single monster, the prime plague and begetter of all others – I mean Pride. *A striking phrase*

Pride measures her prosperity not by what she has but by what others lack. Pride would not deign even to be made a goddess if there were no wretches for her to sneer at and domineer over. Her good fortune is dazzling only by contrast with the miseries of others; she displays her riches to torment and tantalise the poverty of others. Pride is a serpent from hell that twines itself around the hearts of men, acting like a suckfish[141] to draw and hold them back from choosing a better way of life.

Pride is too deeply fixed in human nature to be easily plucked out. So I am glad that the Utopians at least have been lucky enough to achieve this republic which I wish all mankind would imitate. Through the plan of living which they have adopted, they have laid the foundations of a commonwealth that is not only very happy but also, so far as human prescience can tell, likely to last forever. Now that they have torn up the seeds of ambition and faction at home, along with most other vices, they are in no danger from internal strife, which alone has destroyed the prosperity of many cities that seemed eminently secure. As long as they preserve harmony at home, and keep their institutions healthy, they can never be overcome or even shaken by all the envious princes of neighbouring countries, who have often attempted their ruin, but always in vain.

When Raphael had finished his story, I was left thinking that not a few of the laws and customs he had described as existing among the Utopians were really absurd. These included their methods of waging war, their religious practices, as well as other customs of theirs; but my chief objection was to the basis of their whole system, that is, their communal living and their moneyless economy. This one thing alone utterly subverts all the nobility, magnificence, splendour and majesty which (in the popular view) are the true ornaments and glory of any commonwealth.[142] But I knew that

---

[141] The remora has a suction plate atop its head, by which it attaches itself to the underbelly of larger fish or the hulls of ships. Impressed by the tenacity of its grip, the ancients fabled that it could impede ships in their course.

[142] The view of 'More' is consistent with the Aristotelian position of his earlier speech against communism (p. 105). Aristotle insists on the connection between

blicae, tamen, quoniam defessum narrando sciebam, neque mihi
satis exploratum erat possetne ferre ut contra suam sententiam sen-
tiretur, praesertim quod recordabar eo nomine quosdam ab illo
reprehensos quasi vererentur ne non satis putarentur sapere nisi
aliquid invenirent in quo vellicare aliorum inventa possent, idcirco
et illorum institutione et ipsius oratione laudata, manu apprehend-
ens intro cenatum duco, praefatus tamen aliud nobis tempus eisdem
de rebus altius cogitandi atque uberius cum eo conferendi fore.
Quod utinam aliquando contingeret.

Interea, quemadmodum haud possum omnibus assentiri quae
dicta sunt, alioqui ab homine citra controversiam eruditissimo simul
et rerum humanarum peritissimo, ita facile confiteor permulta esse
in Utopiensium republica quae in nostris civitatibus optarim verius
quam sperarim.

SECUNDI LIBRI FINIS.

SERMONIS POMERIDIANI
RAPHAELIS HYTHLODAEI,
DE LEGIBUS ET INSTITUTIS UTOPIENSIS
INSULAE PAUCIS ADHUC COGNITAE,
PER CLARISSIMUM ET ERUDITISSIMUM VIRUM
D. THOMAM MORUM
CIVEM ET VICECOMITEM LONDINENSEM,
FINIS.

Raphael was tired with talking, and I was not sure he could take contradiction in these matters, particularly when I recalled that he had reproached certain people who were afraid they might not appear knowing enough unless they found something to criticise in the ideas of others. So with praise for their way of life and his account of it, I took him by the hand and led him in to supper. But first I said that we would find some other time for thinking of these matters more deeply, and for talking them over in more detail. Would that this would happen some day!

Meantime, while I can hardly agree with everything he said (though he is a man of unquestionable learning and enormous experience of human affairs), yet I freely confess that in the Utopian commonwealth there are very many features that in our own societies I would wish rather than expect to see.[143]

END OF BOOK II.

THE END OF THE AFTERNOON DISCOURSE OF RAPHAEL HYTHLODAY ON THE LAWS AND INSTITUTIONS OF THE ISLAND OF UTOPIA, HITHERTO KNOWN TO BUT FEW, AS RECORDED BY THE MOST DISTINGUISHED AND LEARNED MAN, MASTER THOMAS MORE, CITIZEN AND UNDERSHERIFF OF LONDON.

---

nobility and wealth (*Politics* IV.viii.9, V.i.7), defines magnificence as 'suitable expenditure on a great scale' (*Nicomachean Ethics* IV.ii.1), and in general stresses the necessary connection between money and the exercise of virtue. These views were influential in the Renaissance, when, for example, the writers of advice books for rulers regarded magnificence and majesty as among the most important princely virtues. See Felix Gilbert, 'The humanist concept of the prince and *The Prince* of Machiavelli', *The Journal of Modern History*, 11 (1939), 449–83. In both books of *Utopia*, however, Hythloday's remarks have suggested a radically opposed conception of the 'ornaments and glory' of a commonwealth. For an overview of the critical disputes about the thrust of the present passage, see Thomas I. White, '*Festivitas, utilitas, et opes*: The concluding irony and philosophical purpose of Thomas More's *Utopia*', *Albion*, 10 (1978), 135–50.

[143] In *De re publica*, Cicero says that Plato 'created a State of a kind that is to be desired rather than hoped for [*civitatemque optandam magis quam sperandam*] – one of the smallest size, not such as to be actually possible, but in which it might be possible to see the workings of his theory of the State' (II.xxx.52). With the exception of the 'Dream of Scipio', Cicero's dialogue was lost until 1820, but More may possibly have seen this passage quoted by another writer. (It is not, however, among the numerous quotations from the work in Augustine's *De civitate Dei*.)

HIERONYMUS BUSLIDIUS THOMAE MORO S.D.[1]

Non sat fuit, ornatissime More, olim omnem curam, operam, studium intulisse in rem et commodum singulorum, nisi vel ea (quae
tua pietas et liberalitas est) conferres in universum, ratus hoc tuum
(qualecumque foret) beneficium, eo maiorem hinc mereri favorem, 5
venari gratiam, aucupari gloriam, quanto illud et latius propagatum
et in plures distributum, pluribus esset profuturum. Quod etsi alias
semper praestare contenderis, tamen id maxime es nuper mira
felicitate assecutus, scilicet pomeridiano illo sermone abs te in literas
relato, quem de recte et bene constituta (ab omnibus expetenda) 10
Utopiensium republica edidisti.

In cuius pulcherrimi instituti felici descriptione nihil est in quo
vel summa eruditio vel absoluta rerum humanarum peritia desider-
ari possit. Quando ea quidem ambo in illo tanta paritate et aequabili
congressu concurrunt ut, neutro alteri herbam porrigente, 15
utrumque aequo Marte de gloria contendat. Tam siquidem multifa-
ria polles doctrina, rursum tam multa eaque certa rerum peritia ut
prorsus expertus adfirmes quicquid scripseris, doctissime scribas
quicquid adfirmandum destinaveris. Mira profecto raraque felicitas,
ac plane eo rarior quo magis ipsa sese invidens plurimis non praebet 20
nisi raris, maxime eis qui sicut candore velint, ita eruditione sciant,
fide queant, auctoritate possint, tam pie, recte, provide in commune
consulere sicut tu iam facis probe, qui quod non solum tibi verumetiam toti te genitum orbi exsistimas, operae pretium duxeris hoc
tuo pulcherrimo merito vel totum ipsum orbem demereri. 25

---

[1] This and the two following items appeared as prefatory materials in the 1516
edition. For the editions of 1517 and 1518, they were moved to the back of the
book.

JEROME BUSLEYDEN TO THOMAS MORE, GREETINGS[1]

For you, my most distinguished friend More, it was not enough to have devoted all your care, labour and energy to the interest and advantage of individuals: such is your goodness and liberality that you must bestow them on the public at large. You saw that this service of yours, however great it might be, would deserve more favour, gain more gratitude, and aim at greater glory, the more widely it was diffused, the more people shared in it and were benefited by it. This is what you've always tried to do on other occasions, and now with remarkable felicity you've attained it again – I mean by that afternoon's discussion which you have written down and published, about the right and proper constitution (which everyone must long for) of the Utopian republic.

It is a delightful description of a wonderful establishment, replete with profound erudition and a consummate knowledge of human affairs. Both qualities meet in this work so equally and so congenially that neither yields to the other, but both contend on an even footing. You enjoy such a wide range of learning and such profound experience that whatever you write comes from full experience, and whatever you decide to say carries a full weight of learning.[2] A rare and wonderful happiness! And all the more remarkable in that it withdraws itself from the multitude and imparts itself only to the few – to such, above all, as have the candour to wish, the erudition to understand, the trustworthiness to put into practice and the authority to judge in the common interest as honourably, accurately and practically as you do now. For you do not consider yourself born for yourself alone, but for the whole world; and so by this splendid work you have thought it worth your while to place the whole world in your debt.

---

[1] On Busleyden, see p. 25n. His letter came directly to Erasmus, who had solicited it, with a covering note making it clear that Busleyden wrote out of esteem for Erasmus (CWE, IV, 483). Like Budé (pp. 7–19), the wealthy Busleyden singles out Utopian communism for special praise.

[2] 'More' praises Hythloday, and Hythloday praises Cardinal Morton, in very similar terms (pp. 53, 55).

Quod praestare alia ratione neque rectius neque melius potuisses quam ipsis mortalibus ratione pollentibus eam reipublicae ideam, eam morum formulam absolutissimumque simulacrum praescribere, quo nullo[2] umquam in orbe visum sit, vel salubrius institutum, vel magis absolutum, vel quod magis expetendum videatur, utpote 5 multo quidem praestante atque longo post se intervallo relinquente tot celebratissimas tantopere decantatas Lacedaemoniorum, Atheniensium, Romanorum respublicas. Quae si eisdem essent auspiciis auspicatae, eisdem (quibus haec tua respublica) institutis, legibus, decretis, moribus moderatae, profecto hae nondum labefactatae et 10 solo aequatae, iam proh dolor citra spem omnem instaurationis extinctae iacerent. Sed contra, incolumes adhuc, beatae, felices, fortunatissimae[3] agerent, interim rerum dominae, suum late imperium terra marique sortitae.

Quarum quidem rerumpublicarum tu miserandam miseratus 15 sortem ne aliae itidem (quae hodie rerum potitae summum tenent) parem sustinerent vicem prospicere voluisti, scilicet hac tua absolutissima republica, quae non tam in condendis legibus quam vel probatissimis magistratibus formandis maxime elaboravit. Nec id quidem ab re, quando alioqui sine illis omnes (vel optimae) leges, 20 si Platoni credimus, mortuae censerentur. Praesertim ad quorum magistratuum simulacrum, probitatis specimen, exemplar morum, iustitiae imaginem, totus status et rectus tenor cuiusvis absolutae reipublicae sit effingendus. In quo in primis concurrant prudentia in optimatibus, fortitudo in militibus, temperantia in singulis, iusti- 25 tia in omnibus.

Quibus quum tua (quam tantopere celebras) respublica sit tam pulcherrime, ut liquet, composita, non mirum si hinc veniat non solum multis timenda sed et cunctis gentibus veneranda, simul omnibus saeculis praedicanda. Idque eo magis quod in ea omnis 30 proprietatis contentione sublata, nulli sit quippiam proprii, ceterum in rem ipsam communem communia sunt omnibus omnia, adeo ut omnis res, quaevis actio seu publica seu privata non ad multorum cupiditatem, non ad paucorum libidinem spectet, sed ad unam iustitiam, aequabilitatem, communionem sustinendam (quantulacumque 35 sit) tota referatur. Quo illa integre relata, omnis materies, fax et

---

[2] An emendation to *nullum* was proposed by Lupton.
[3] For *fortunatissimae* (1516, 1517), 1518M, N substitute *fortunatissime*. Both readings are possible, but there seems no compelling reason to break the established parallelism.

You could hardly have accomplished this end more effectually and correctly than by setting before rational men this pattern of a commonwealth, this model and perfect image of proper conduct. And the world has never seen a model more perfect than yours, more soundly established or fully executed or more desirable. It surpasses and leaves far behind the many celebrated commonwealths of which so much has been said, those of Sparta, Athens and Rome. Had they been founded under the same auspices as your commonwealth and governed by the same institutions, laws, regulations and customs, certainly they would not now be fallen, levelled to the ground and extinguished – alas! – beyond all hope of rebirth. On the contrary, they would now be intact, fortunate and prosperous, leading a happy existence – mistresses of the world, besides, and dividing a far-flung empire, by land and by sea.

Feeling pity for the pitiable fate of these commonwealths, you feared lest others, which now hold supreme power, should undergo the same fate; so you drew the portrait of a perfect commonwealth, one which devoted its energies less to setting up laws than to forming the very best men to administer them. And in this they were absolutely right; for without good rulers, even the best laws (if we take Plato's word for it)[3] would be nothing but dead letters. It is according to the pattern of such rulers as these – models of probity, specimens of good conduct, images of justice – that the whole existence and proper character of any commonwealth should be imagined. What is needed is prudence in the rulers, courage in the military, temperance in the private citizenry and justice in all.[4]

Since the nation you praise so lavishly is clearly formed on these principles, no wonder if it seems not only a challenge to many nations but an object of reverence to all peoples and an achievement to be celebrated among future generations. Its great strength lies in the fact that all squabbles over private property are removed, and no one has anything of his own. Instead, everyone has everything in common for the sake of the common good, and thus every action and each decision, whether public or private, trifling or important, is not directed by the greed of the many or the lusts of the few, but is aimed solely at upholding one uniform rule of justice, equality and community solidarity. Where the common good is fully respected, there is necessarily a clean sweep of everything that

---

[3] E.g., *Laws* VI.751B–C.

[4] Prudence (or wisdom), courage, temperance and justice are the four cardinal virtues of Greek and Roman ethics. Busleyden's remark summarises the main argument of Book IV of the *Republic* (especially 427D–434C).

fomes ambitus, luxus, invidientiae, iniuriae facessat necesse est. In
quae nonnumquam aut privata rerum possessio aut ardens habendi
sitis, omniumque miserrima rerum ambitio, mortales (vel
reluctantes) protrudit, maximo suo, idque incomparabili, malo,
quando hinc saepenumero dissensiones animorum, motus armo- 5
rum, et bella plus quam civilia derepente oriantur, quibus non
solum florentissimus status beatissimarum rerumpublicarum
funditus pessumdatur, verum illarum olim parta gloria, acti tri-
umphi, clara tropaea, totiesque opima spolia, devictis hostibus
relata, penitus obliterantur. 10

Quod si in his haec nostra pagina minorem forte ac velim fidem
fecerit, certe in promptu aderunt testes ad quos te relegem locuplet-
issimi, videlicet tot et tantae olim vastatae urbes, dirutae civitates,
prostratae respublicae, incensi et consumpti vici, quorum uti hodie
vix ullae tantae calamitatis reliquiae aut vestigia visuntur, ita nec 15
nomina illorum ulla quantumvis vetus et longe deducta historia sat
probe tenet.

Quas quidem insignes clades, vastationes, eversiones, ceterasque
belli calamitates nostrae (si quae sint) respublicae facile evaserint,
modo ad unam Utopiensium reipublicae normam sese adamussim 20
componentes ab ea ne transversum quidem, ut aiunt, unguem reced-
ant. Quod sic demum praestantes, tandem re ipsa cumulatissime
agnoscent quantum hoc tuum in se collatum beneficium profuerit,
maxime quo accedente didicerint suam rempublicam salvam, incolumem, triumphantem servare, proinde tantum tibi suo praesentis- 25
simo servatori debiturae quantum is haud iniuria promeretur qui
non tantum aliquem e republica civem sed vel ipsam totam rempublicam servarit.

Interea, vale, ac feliciter perge nonnihil usque meditari, agere,
elaborare quod in rempublicam collatum illi perpetuitatem, tibi 30
immortalitatem addat. Vale, doctissime et idem humanissime More,
tuae Britanniae ac nostri huius orbis decus.

Ex aedibus nostris Mechliniae. M.D.XVI.

might serve as torch, kindling or fuel for ambition, luxury, envy and injustice. These are vices into which men are sometimes pushed against their will, and to their own immense and incomparable loss, by private property or lust for gain or that most miserable of passions, ambition. From these sources there frequently spring up mental quarrels, martial clashes and wars worse than civil,[5] which not only completely destroy the flourishing state of supremely happy republics but cause their previous glories, their past triumphs, rich prizes and proud spoils taken from defeated enemies to be utterly obliterated.

If my thoughts on this point should be less than absolutely convincing, only consider the swarm of perfectly reliable witnesses I can call to my support – I mean the many great cities destroyed in times past, the states crushed, the republics beaten down, the villages fired and consumed. Today not only are there scarcely any remains or vestiges of those great calamities – not even the names of the places are reliably preserved by any history, however far back it reaches.

Such terrible downfalls, devastations, disasters and other calamities of war our commonwealths (if we have any) could easily escape if they would only adapt themselves exactly to the Utopian pattern not swerving from it, as people say, by a hair's breadth. If they act so, the result will fully convince them how much they have profited by the service you have done them; especially since in this way they will have learned to keep their republic healthy, unharmed and victorious. Their debt to you, their most ready and willing saviour, will be no less than what is rightly owed to a man who has saved not just one citizen of a country, but the entire country itself.

Farewell for now. May you continue to prosper, ever contriving, carrying out and completing new plans which will bring long life to the commonwealth, and to yourself immortality. Farewell, most learned and humane More, supreme ornament of your Britain and of this world of ours.

From my house at Mechlin, 1516

---

[5] 'Wars worse than civil' ('Bella plus quam civilia', as in Busleyden's Latin) is the opening phrase of Lucan's *Pharsalia*, an epic poem on the civil war between Pompey and Caesar.

GERARDUS NOVIOMAGUS DE UTOPIA

Dulcia, lector, amas? Sunt hic dulcissima quaeque.
   Utile si quaeris, nil legis utilius.
Sive utrumque voles, utroque haec insula abundat
   Quo linguam exornes,[4] quo doceas animum.   5
Hic fontes aperit recti pravique disertus
   Morus, Londini gloria prima sui.

CORNELIUS GRAPHEUS AD LECTOREM

Vis nova monstra, novo dudum nunc orbe reperto?
   Vivendi varia vis ratione modos?   10
Vis qui virtutum fontes? Vis unde malorum
   Principia? et quantum rebus inane latet?
Haec lege, quae vario Morus dedit ille colore,
   Morus Londinae nobilitatis honos.

---

[4] The verse pattern requires *exornes* (1516, 1517) rather than *ornes* (1518M, N).

GERARD GELDENHOUWER ON UTOPIA[6]

If pleasure you seek, good reader, it's here;
If profit, no book is more suited to teach;
If both – on this island, both will appear
To sharpen at once both your thoughts and your speech:
  Here the springs both of good and of ill are set forth
  By More, London's star of incomparable worth.

CORNELIS DE SCHRIJVER TO THE READER[7]

You seek new monsters from the world new-found?
New ways of life, drawing on different springs?
The source of human virtue? The profound
Evil abyss? The void beneath all things?
  Read here what's traced by More's ingenious pen,
  More, London's pride, and Britain's first of men.

---

[6] The Dutch humanist Geldenhouwer (1482–1542) assisted the printer Dirk Martens
in the production of many books, including the first edition of *Utopia*.
[7] De Schrijver (c. 1482–1558), a Latin poet of wide reputation, settled in Antwerp
by 1515, where he became a close associate of Peter Giles.

BEATUS RHENANUS
BILIBALDO PIRCHEIMERO,
MAXIMILIANI CAESARIS A CONSILIO,
ET SENATORI NURENBERGENSI S.D.[1]

... Ceterum quemadmodum hi lusus MORI ingenium ostendunt, [5]
et insignem eruditionem, sic iudicium nimirum acre, quod de rebus
habet, ex UTOPIA cumulatissime eluxerit. De qua paucis obiter
meminero, quod hanc accuratissimus in literis BUDAEUS, incom-
parabilis ille melioris eruditionis antistes, et ingens, atque adeo
unicum Galliarum decus, ita ut decebat, luculenta praefatione lauda- [10]
vit. Habet ea hoc genus decreta, qualia nec apud Platonem, nec
apud Aristotelem, aut etiam Iustiniani vestri Pandectas sit reperire.
Et docet minus forsan philosophice quam illi, sed magis Christiane.
Quamquam (audi per Musas bellam historiam) cum hic nuper in
quodam gravium aliquot virorum consessu, Utopiae mentio orta [15]
fuisset, et illam ego laudibus veherem, negabat quidam pinguis plus
habendum MORO gratiae, quam actuario cuipiam scribae, qui in
curia aliorum sententias dumtaxat enotet, doryphorematis[2] ritu
(quod aiunt) interim assidendo, nihil ipse censens, quod diceret ea
omnia ex Hythlodaei ore excepta, et a MORO tantum in literas [20]
missa. Proinde MORUM nullo laudandum alioqui nomine, nisi
quod haec commode retulisset. Et non deerant, qui hominis iudicio
velut rectissime sentientis album adicerent calculum. Ἆρα οὐ σὺ
τουτονὶ τοῦ Μώρου χαριεντισμὸν δέχῃ, τοιούτους ἄνδρας οὐ
τοὺς τυχόντας ἀλλὰ τοὺς δοκίμους παρὰ τοῖς πολλοῖς, καὶ ταῦτα [25]
θεολόγους πλανήσαντος ...

Basileae, VII Cal. Martias. ANNO M.D.XVIII.

---

[1] This letter does not appear in 1516 or 1517. In 1518M, N, it comes after *Utopia*,
just preceding the *Epigrammata*.
[2] From Greek δορυφόρος, 'spear-bearer' (here equals 'quill-driver').

BEATUS RHENANUS[1] TO WILLIBALD PIRCKHEIMER, COUNCILLOR TO THE EMPEROR MAXIMILIAN AND CITY COUNCILLOR OF NUREMBERG, GREETINGS

... Well, just as these toys[2] serve to display More's wit and notable erudition, so the keenness of his judgement in practical affairs comes brilliantly clear in *Utopia*. Of that, I need say only a few words in passing, because the book has already been praised as it deserves in a splendid preface by that most rigorous of scholars Budé, who is an incomparable exponent of the higher learning, as well as a giant, even unique, genius of French letters. More's book contains principles of a sort not to be found in Plato, Aristotle, or even in the Pandects of your Justinian.[3] Its teachings are perhaps less philosophical than those others, but they are more Christian. And yet (if you'd like to hear, with the favour of the Muses, a good story), when the subject of *Utopia* came up here lately in a gathering of various important men, and when I praised it, one foolish fellow said More deserved no more credit than a paid scribe, who simply writes down what other people say after the fashion of a pen-pusher (so they call him), who may sit in a meeting, but expresses no ideas of his own. Everything in the book, he said, came from the mouth of Hythloday; all More did was write it down. And for that More deserved no more credit than attaches to making a good transcript. And there was no lack of those who gave this simpleton high marks as a man of shrewd insights. *Now, don't you admire the sly wit of More, who can bamboozle men like these, not just ordinary dolts but men of standing and trained theologians at that?* ...

Basel, 23 February 1518

[1] The son of a Rheinau butcher named Bild, Beatus Rhenanus (1485–1547), like other humanists, took a new Latin name to go with his classical learning. Under this cheerful sobriquet, he assisted Erasmus in the publication of many of his works, in addition to pursuing scholarly enterprises of his own. He supervised the printing of the 1518 editions of *Utopia* (below, p. 272), which also included epigrams by More, William Lily and Erasmus, and supplied this dedicatory epistle, of which we print only the part dealing with *Utopia*. The addressee, Willibald Pirckheimer (1470–1530), was a Nuremberg patrician distinguished both as a man of affairs and as a scholar.   [2] I.e., the epigrams.
[3] The Pandects or Digests of Roman law were compiled under the Emperor Justinian in the sixth century AD. 'Your' Justinian because of Pirckheimer's legal studies and practice.

IOANNES PALUDANUS CASSILETENSIS
M. PETRO AEGIDIO D.S.[1]

Utopiam Mori tui simulque epigrammata legi, nec satis scio maiore-
ne cum voluptate an admiratione. Felicem Britanniam quae nunc
eiusmodi floreat ingeniis ut cum ipsa possint antiquitate certare. 5
Nos stupidos ac plus quam plumbeos, si ne tam vicinis quidem
exemplis ad eam laudem capessendam expergefieri possumus.
αἰσχρὸν σιωπᾶν, inquit Aristoteles, loquente Isocrate. At nobis
turpe sit lucris tantum ac voluptatibus vacare cum apud ultimos
orbis Britannos, favore benignitateque principum, sic vigeat erudi- 10
tio. Quamquam haec laus Graecorum et Italorum paene fuit propria, tamen habet et Hispania veterum aliquot splendida nomina
quibus se iactat. Habet Anacharsides suos effera Scythia, habet
suum Dania Saxonem, habet suum Gallia Budaeum. Tot habet Germania literis celebres viros, tam multos eosque insignes habet 15
Anglia. Nam quid de ceteris coniectandum est si tantum praestat
Morus primum iuvenis, deinde publicis ac domesticis negotiis adeo
distractus, postremo quidvis profitens citius quam literas? Et soli
nobis sat beati videmur, si probe prospectum sit cuticulae et arcae.
Quin ipsi quoque excusso veterno ad hoc pulcherrimum certamen 20
accingimur, in quo nec vinci turpe sit et vincere pulcherrimum.

---

[1] This letter and the accompanying poem appear in 1516 and 1517, but not in 1518M
or N.

JEAN DESMAREZ OF CASSEL TO MASTER PETER GILES, GREETINGS[1]

I have read the *Utopia* of your friend More, along with his *Epigrams* – whether with more pleasure or admiration, I do not know. How happy is Britain, which now blossoms forth with talents of such eminence that they rival those of antiquity! And how lumpish are we,[2] duller than lead, if we cannot be roused to compete for the same sort of praise by examples so near at hand. 'It is shameful to keep silent', says Aristotle, 'while Isocrates still speaks'.[3] We should feel disgraced to devote ourselves only to pleasure-seeking and money-making, when the British, who live at the ends of the earth, are bringing forth, thanks to the favour and generosity of their princes, learning in such profusion. Although the Greeks and Italians used to have almost a monopoly of good learning, Spain too has some eminent names among the ancients of whom she boasts; Scythia, savage though she is, has her Anacharsis;[4] Denmark her Saxo Grammaticus; France her Budé. Germany has many men famous for learning, England has very many, and those among the most distinguished. For what must we think of the others, if More is so outstanding – and this despite his youth, the distraction of his many other public and private concerns,[5] and the fact that literature is far from being his primary vocation? Only we, of all people, seem satisfied to scratch our skins and stuff our moneybags. Indeed, even we are shaking off our torpor and preparing to take part in this glorious contest, in which it is no shame to be beaten and

---

[1] Desmarez (d. 1526) was public orator and professor at the University of Louvain. His letter and poem (p. 265) appeared among the prefatory materials in the editions of 1516 and 1517. Erasmus was not deterred by his long friendship with Desmarez from authorising Beatus Rhenanus to omit both productions from the 1518 editions (*CWE*, V, 229).

[2] I.e., we of the Low Countries.

[3] The remark, which is attributed to Aristotle by Quintilian (III.i.14), paraphrases a line in Euripides' lost play *Philoctetes*. Isocrates was the pre-eminent orator of Aristotle's time.

[4] Anacharsis (fl. sixth century BC) was a Scythian sage, famed less for his wisdom than for the fact that, among the Scythians, any sage was conspicuous. Saxo Grammaticus (fl. thirteenth century) wrote *Gesta Danorum*, a history of his native land.

[5] This phrase, which seems to be adapted from a very similar one in Giles's letter to Busleyden (p. 27), is one of several indications of the derivative nature of Desmarez' letter.

Provocant huc tot undique exempla, provocat huc optimus princeps Carolus penes quem nulli rei amplius est premium quam eruditae virtuti, provocat huc unicus ille rerum bonarum omnium Maecenas Ioannes Sylvagius Borgondiae Cancellarius.

Maiorem in modum te rogo, doctissime Petre Aegidi, ut cum 5 primum licebit Utopiam evulgandam cures quod quicquid ad rempublicam bene instituendam pertinet in hac velut in speculo liceat cernere. Utinam fiat ut quemadmodum illi nostram religionem accipere coeperunt, ita nos ab illis administrandae reipublicae rationem mutuemur. Id fortasse facile fieret si theologorum 10 aliquot insignes et invicti in eam insulam se conferant, Christi fidem iam suppullulantem[2] provecturi, simulque eius gentis mores et instituta ad nos deportaturi.

Multum debet Utopia Hythlodaeo per quem innotuit indigna quae nesciretur, plus eruditissimo Moro, cuius penicillo nobis tam 15 scite depicta est. Porro quod utrique debetur[3] gratiae, eius non minima pars tibi secanda est, qui et illius sermonem et huius scriptum in lucem emiseris, non mediocri delectamento futurum omnibus, maiori fructui si modo diligenter expenderint singula.

Meum animum sic excitavit Utopia ut iam olim a Musis desuetus 20 denuo Musas lacessiverim, quam feliciter tu iudicabis.

Bene vale, Petre Aegidi candidissime, bonorum studiorum et fautor et mysta.

Louanii ex aedibus nostris Calen. Decemb.

---

[2] For the non-classical verb *suppullulare*, R. E. Latham (*Revised Medieval Latin Word-List from British and Irish Sources* (1965)) gives the meaning (dated 1523) 'to spring up secretly'. But the context in the present passage suggests that the prefix *sub-* has another meaning here: 'to come *from below*', 'to sprout *up*'.

[3] For *debetur*, 1516 appears to print *debentur* (as *debētur* – but the supposed bar may actually be the rough bottom of a *p* in the preceding line). The editor of the 1672 edition sought the same sort of regularity by changing the next word, *gratiae*, to *gratia*. But the idea of dividing thanks is very strong here, and *gratiae* could be a partitive genitive.

splendid to be victorious. Many examples provoke us to it, on all sides; so does our admirable Prince Charles,[6] who rewards nothing more generously than learning combined with virtue, while the great Maecenas and patron of all good pursuits, Jean Le Sauvage,[7] Chancellor of Burgundy, also urges us forward.

Let me warmly encourage you, most learned Peter Giles, to have *Utopia* published as soon as possible; in it can be seen, as in a mirror, everything that relates to the proper establishment of a commonwealth. I could wish that, just as the Utopians have begun to accept our religion, we might adopt their system of ordering the commonwealth. Perhaps the change might easily be made if a number of distinguished and persuasive theologians were sent to that island; they would invigorate the faith of Christ, which is already springing up there, and then bring back to us their customs and institutions.

Utopia owes a great debt to Hythloday for making known this land which ought not to have remained obscure; it owes an even greater debt to the most learned More, whose skilful pencil has drawn it for us so vividly. In addition to both of them, not the least part of the thanks must be shared with you, who will make public both Hythloday's conversation and More's report of it – to the no small delight of future readers, and their even greater profit, if they weigh the details prudently.

Utopia has so stirred my spirit that, though long a stranger to the Muses, I have invoked them anew[8] – with what success you must be the judge.

Farewell, most courteous Peter Giles, you who are both practitioner and patron of good letters.

From my house at Louvain, 1 December [1516]

---

6 Prince Charles of Castile.
7 Le Sauvage (1455/7–1518) held several key offices under the young Charles V. He was one of the statesmen whose response to *Utopia* More told Erasmus he was particularly eager to know (*Selected Letters*, p. 80).
8 I.e., in the poem overleaf.

*Eiusdem Ioannis Paludani rhetoris Louaniensis
in novam insulam Utopiam carmen*

Fortes Roma dedit, dedit et laudata disertos
    Graecia, frugales incluta Sparta dedit.
Massilia integros dedit, at Germania duros.   5
    Comes ac lepidos Attica terra dedit.
Gallia clara pios quondam dedit, Africa cautos.
    Munificos olim terra Britanna dedit.
Virtutum et aliis aliarum exempla petuntur
    Gentibus, et quod huic desit, huic superat.   10
Una semel totam summam totius honesti
    Insula terrigenis Utopiana dedit.

Poem on the New Island of Utopia by the Same John Desmarez,
Public Orator at Louvain

The men of Rome were brave; the lofty Greeks
Famous for eloquence; Sparta's men were strict;
The Germans, tough; the honest Marseillais
Noted for probity; urbane and witty men
Flourished in Attica; Africans were deep.
France bred religious saints; the British men
Were world-wide famous for munificence.

   The virtues have their special homes; what here
Abounds is somewhere else in short supply.
Only one isle, Utopia, displays to men
The sum of all the virtues in one place.

THOMAS MORUS PETRO AEGIDIO SUO S.P.D.[1]

Impendio me, charissime Petre, delectavit hominis illius acutissimi censura quam nosti, qui in Utopiam nostram usus est hoc dilemmate: si res ut vera prodita est, video ibi quaedam subabsurda; sin ficta tum in nonnullis exactum illud Mori iudicium requiro. 5 Huic ego, mi Petre, viro quisquis is fuit (quem et doctum suspicor et amicum video) multas magnas habeo gratias. Tantum etenim mihi iudicio hoc suo tam ingenuo quantum nescio an quisquam alius ab edito libello gratificatus est. Nam primum sive mei studio sive ipsius operis illectus, non laboris videtur fuisse pertaesus quominus totum 10 perlegeret, neque id quidem perfunctorie ac praecipitanter quomodo sacerdotes horarias preces solent (videlicet hi qui solent), sed ita sensim ac sedulo ut interim singula sollerter expenderit. Deinde, notatis quibusdam idque etiam parce, declarat cetera se non temere sed iudicio comprobasse. Postremo his ipsis verbis quibus me sugil- 15 lat tantum tamen attribuit laudis quantum non hi qui de industria laudavere. Indicat enim facile quam sentiat de me magnifice qui, si quid non satis exactum legerit, ibi queritur spe se sua destitui, quum mihi interim supra spem accidat si vel e multis aliqua saltem edere non prorsus absurda possim. 20

Quamquam (ut ipse quoque vicissim non minus ingenue agam cum illo) non video cur sibi tam oculatus et quod Graeci dicunt ὀξυδερκής videri debeat qui aut subabsurda quaedam in Utopiensium institutis deprehenderit, aut me in republica formanda quaedam non satis utiliter excogitasse, quasi alibi nihil usquam gentium 25 sit absurdi, aut quisquam umquam philosophorum omnium rempublicam, principem, aut domum denique privatam sic ordinaverit ut nihil instituerit quod praestet immutari. Qua in re (nisi sancta esset apud me praestantissimorum virorum consecrata vetustate memoria) possem profecto e singulis aliqua proferre in quibus damnan- 30 dis universorum calculos essem haud dubie relaturus.

---

[1] This second letter of More to Giles appears only in the 1517 edition, where it immediately follows the text of Book II.

THOMAS MORE TO HIS FRIEND PETER GILES, WARMEST GREETINGS

My dear Peter, I was absolutely delighted with the judgement of that very sharp fellow[1] you recall, who posed this dilemma regarding my *Utopia*: if the story is offered as fact (says he) then I see a number of absurdities in it; but if it is fiction, then I think More's usual good judgement is wanting in some matters. I'm very much obliged to this man, whoever he may be (I suspect he is learned, and I see he's a friend). His frank judgement gratified me more than any other reaction I've seen since my book appeared. First of all, led on by fondness either for me or for the work itself, he did not give up in the middle, but read my book all the way through. And he didn't read carelessly or quickly, as priests read the divine office – those who read it at all – but slowly and carefully in order to consider the different points thoughtfully. Then, having selected certain elements to criticise, and not very many of them, he says that he approves, not rashly but deliberately, of all the rest. Finally, he implies in his very words of criticism higher praise than those who set out to compliment the book on purpose. For he shows clearly how well he thinks of me when he expresses disappointment in a passage that is not as precise as it should be – whereas I would think myself lucky if I had been able to set down just a few things out of many that were not altogether absurd.

Still, if I in my turn can deal as frankly with him as he with me, I don't see why he should think himself so acute (or, as the Greeks say, so 'sharp-sighted') just because he has noted some absurdities in the institutions of the Utopians, or caught me putting forth some not sufficiently practical ideas about the constitution of a republic. Aren't there any absurdities elsewhere in the world? And did any one of all the philosophers who have offered a pattern of a society, a ruler, or a private household set down everything so well that nothing ought to be changed? Actually, if it weren't for the great respect I retain for certain highly distinguished names, I could easily produce from each of them a number of notions which I can hardly doubt would be universally condemned as absurd.

---

[1] The identity of this sharp fellow is unknown – if indeed More didn't invent him.

Iam quum dubitet verane res an commenticia sit, hic vero exactum ipsius iudicium requiro. Neque tamen inficias eo si de republica scribere decrevissem, ac mihi tamen venisset in mentem talis fabula,[2] non fuisse fortassis abhorriturum ab ea fictione qua velut melle circumlitum suaviuscule influeret in animos verum. At certe sic temperassem tamen ut si vulgi abuti ignoratione vellem, litteratioribus saltem aliqua praefixissem vestigia quibus institutum nostrum facile pervestigarent. Itaque si nihil aliud ac nomina saltem principis, fluminis, urbis, insulae posuissem talia quae peritiores admonere possent insulam nusquam esse, urbem evanidam, sine aqua fluvium, sine populo esse principem, quod neque factu fuisset difficile et multo fuisset lepidius quam quod ego feci, qui nisi me fides coegisset historiae, non sum tam stupidus ut barbaris illis uti nominibus et nihil significantibus, Utopiae, Anydri, Amauroti, Ademi voluissem.[3]

Ceterum, mi Aegidi, quandoquidem aliquos esse video tam cautos ut quae nos homines simplices et creduli Hythlodaeo referente perscripsimus, ea homines circumspecti ac sagaces aegre adducuntur ut credant. Ne pariter mea fides apud eos cum historiae fide periclitari possit, gaudeo licere mihi pro meo partu dicere quod Terentiana Mysis ait de Glycerii puero qui, ne supposititius haberetur, dis pol, inquit, habeo gratias quod pariundo aliquot adfuere liberae. Etenim hoc mihi quoque accidit perquam commode quod Raphael non mihi modo ac tibi illa sed multis praeterea honestissimis viris atque gravissimis, nescio an plura adhuc et maiora, certe neque pauciora narravit neque minora quam nobis.

Quod si ne his quidem increduli isti credant, Hythlodaeum adeant ipsum licet, neque enim adhuc mortuus est. Accepi modo e quibusdam recens e Lusitania venientibus calendis Martiis proximis tam incolumem ac vegetum fuisse hominem quam umquam alias. Exiscitentur[4] ergo ab ipso verum, aut questionibus si libet exsculpant, modo mihi intelligant operam tantum meam, non alienam etiam fidem esse praestandam. Vale, mi charissime Petre, cum uxore lepidissima et scita filiola, quibus uxor mea longam praecatur salutem.

---

[2] The reading of 1517, the only copy-text for this letter, is *fabulae*. But the syntax requires *fabula*.

[3] The *si*-clause (begun in line 8) is never completed by a main clause.

[4] *Exiscitentur*, Surtz's emendation of 1517's *Exiscentur*, is presumably More's coinage from *ex* plus *sciscitor*.

But when he questions whether the book is fact or fiction, I find *his* usual good judgement wanting. I do not deny that if I had decided to write of a commonwealth, and a tale of this sort had come to my mind, I might not have shrunk from a fiction through which the truth, like medicine smeared with honey, might enter the mind a little more pleasantly. But I would certainly have softened the fiction a little, so that, while imposing on vulgar ignorance, I gave hints to the more learned which would enable them to see what I was about. Thus, if I had merely given such names to the governor, the river, the city and the island as would indicate to the knowing reader that the island was nowhere, the city a phantom, the river waterless and the governor without a people,[2] it wouldn't have been hard to do, and would have been far more clever than what I actually did. If the veracity of a historian had not actually required me to do so, I am not so stupid as to have preferred those barbarous and meaningless names of Utopia, Anyder, Amaurot and Ademus.

But I see, my dear Giles, some men are so suspicious that in their circumspect sagacity they can hardly be brought to believe what we simple-minded and credulous fellows wrote down of Hythloday's story. Lest my personal credibility among these people be shaken, not to speak of my reputation as a historian, I am glad I can say of my brainchild what Mysis, in Terence's play, says about Glycerium's boy, to keep him from being thought a changeling: 'By all the gods, I am glad that some ladies of rank were present at his birth.'[3] Similarly, it's my good fortune that Raphael told his story, not just to you and me, but to a great many other men, of the utmost gravity and unquestioned probity. I don't know whether he told them more and greater things, but I'm sure he told them no fewer and no less important things than he told us.

But if the doubters are not satisfied even with these witnesses, let them consult Hythloday himself, for he is still alive. I recently heard from some travellers out of Portugal that on the first day of last March he was still healthy and vigorous as ever. And so let them ask him for the truth, or let them dig it out of him with their questions. I only want them to understand that I answer only for my own work, not for anyone else's credibility. Farewell to you, my dear Peter, to your charming wife and clever little daughter – to all, my wife sends her very best wishes.

---

[2] This is of course precisely what the names mean.
[3] *Andria* IV.iv; ll. 770-1.

APPENDIX
THE EARLY EDITIONS AND THE
CHOICE OF COPY-TEXT

Five editions of *Utopia* are known to have been published during
More's lifetime.[1] The fifth, which is appended to *Luciani opuscula*
(Florence, 1519), closely follows the third and has no independent
value. The relations of the first four – Louvain, 1516; Paris, 1517;
Basel, March and November 1518 – are complex, and each of these
editions contains significant unique readings. Like Lupton and
Surtz (who was responsible for the text in the Yale edition), we
have taken the third edition as our copy-text. Our reasons for this
choice will become clear if we give a brief account of these four
editions and the events surrounding their publication.[2]

1516

The first edition was based on More's manuscript, which he sent
to Erasmus on 3 September 1516: 'I send you my book on Nowhere
. . . it has a preface addressed to my friend Pieter [i.e., Peter Giles].
Well, you must do what you can for it. I know from experience
that you need no urging' (*CWE*, IV, 66). More thus committed
his book to Erasmus' hands and Erasmus' judgement, doubtless in
accordance with a prior agreement: Erasmus had been in England
for most of August, departing little more than a week before the
date of this letter. From Antwerp, Erasmus reported on 2 October

---

[1] Two others are reported by J.G.T. Graesse, *Trésor de livres rares et précieux*
(Milan, 1950), IV, 603: Vienna, 1519 and Basel, 1520. But, as Surtz points out, of
these 'no extant copies (if they were ever printed) have been found' (*CW*, IV,
cxc).

[2] The following discussion touches on all the facts that, in our judgement, bear on
the question of the relations among the early editions. For fuller treatments
(including collations), see *CW*, IV, clxxxiii–cxc, and Prévost's edition, pp. 215–
40. Parts of Prévost's treatment are highly speculative. See also the important
reviews of the Yale edition by Arthur Barker (*Essential Articles for the Study of
Thomas More*, pp. 215–28; originally published in *JEGP*, 65 (1966), 318–30) and
Clarence H. Miller (*English Language Notes*, 3 (1965–6), 303–9). Apart from the
early editions themselves and Richard Pace's *De Fructu Qui Ex Doctrina Percipitur*, all the relevant sixteenth-century documents are included in Erasmus'
Correspondence.

that Giles was delighted with the book (*CWE*, IV, 93). On 12 November, a letter to Erasmus from Gerard Geldenhouwer in Louvain announced that Dirk Martens of that city had undertaken to print it (*CWE*, IV, 125). *Utopia* evidently appeared in December. Jean Desmarez' commendatory letter (above, pp. 260–3) is dated 1 December. On 15 December, More was impatiently awaiting the book (*CWE*, IV, 171). On 4 January 1517, Lord Mountjoy thanked Erasmus for a copy of it (*CWE*, IV, 177).

The book as printed differed considerably from More's manuscript. First, at More's urging (*CWE*, IV, 79), Erasmus had collected commendations from various humanists, and one from the scholar-statesman Jérôme de Busleyden. These, together with some samples of Utopian language and literature and a map of the new island, bolster the printed version. Second, Erasmus or Giles or both (see above, p. 27n.) had added a series of marginal glosses. Finally, one set of circumstances raises the possibility that Erasmus (and Giles?) made a few changes in the text of the work. In their letters of September and October, More and Erasmus always refer to the book by a Latin title, 'Nusquama'. But Geldenhouwer's letter calls it 'Utopia' (which must therefore be the name the manuscript bore when Erasmus passed it to him), and in the printed version the former title has given way to this Graecism.[3] Conformably, in the printed version all proper nouns associated with the new island are Greek in origin. But the fact that this was not always the case is manifest in the appearance at one point of a Latin name for the principal city of Utopia: 'In senatu Mentirano ... ' (144:31). (In subsequent editions 'Mentirano' becomes 'Amaurotico'.) These circumstances may be thought to suggest that some at least of the Graecisms are due not to More but to his editor(s).

1517

From Antwerp on 1 March 1517, and again on 8 March, Erasmus asked More for a corrected copy of the printed book, with a view to sending it to either Paris or Basel (whichever More should prefer) for a second edition (*CWE*, IV, 270–1, 274). Precisely what happened in response to this repeated request is impossible to determine. Erasmus was in London briefly in April 1517. It seems very

---

[3] All subsequent letters of More and Erasmus that refer to the book also call it 'Utopia'. The earliest of these is More's letter of *c.* 4 December to Erasmus (*CWE*, IV, 163).

likely that, as Prévost surmises (p. 225), the two friends discussed at that time plans for a new edition or editions. Be that as it may, on 15 September, Thomas Lupset, who (in Paris as a student) had just completed work as proof corrector for Thomas Linacre's translation of Galen's *De sanitate tuenda*, informed Erasmus that he was 'now concerned with the second edition of More's *Utopia*, which I hope to finish at the end of this month' (*CWE*, V, 125–6). This edition, printed by Gilles de Gourmont, presumably appeared soon after, though in fact the earliest known reference to it appears to be in a letter of Erasmus to More of 5 March 1518 (see below).

The Paris edition corrects numerous errors in the Louvain edition and embodies other changes from it (see *CW*, IV, clxxxvi–clxxxvii); and More's involvement in the project seems established by the fact that 1517 includes his second letter to Giles (above, pp. 264–7), which comments wryly on readers' responses to the first edition (cf. *CW*, IV, 569). Unfortunately, the new edition was badly printed. In his letter of 5 March 1518, Erasmus (in Louvain) wrote to More that he had 'at last seen the Paris print of your *Utopia*, but it is full of mistakes' (*CWE*, V, 329). This is a fair enough statement. Gourmont evidently did not wait for Lupset to correct the proofs, and even the list of errata that Lupset or someone else compiled for the edition is grossly incomplete.

1518 March

To whatever extent Erasmus may have been involved in the Paris edition, he apparently returned to the continent at the end of April 1517 with the intention of shepherding a new edition of *Utopia* through the press of Johann Froben in Basel. On 30 May, from Antwerp, he informed More that he had sent a copy of *Utopia* to Basel (*CWE*, IV, 368; cf. V, 12). At Erasmus' request, the humanist Beatus Rhenanus agreed to oversee the production of the edition (*CWE*, V, 2; cf. V, 82). Despite their efforts, however, the book was uncommonly long in press. On 6 December, Erasmus observed to Rhenanus that Froben seemed 'to have lost interest' in the project – though in the same letter he gives Rhenanus advice about how to handle the prefatory materials in the edition (*CWE*, V, 229). His letter of 5 March 1518 to More reports that 'Those people in Basel are very apologetic about your *Utopia*, which was delayed for the elegant preface provided by Budé. They have now had it and have set to work' (*CWE*, V, 326). And in fact the book, which

also contained More's and Erasmus' *Epigrammata*, appeared (according to its colophon) the same month.

The nature of More's involvement in this edition, and of its relation to 1517, is unclear. 1518M was certainly based on 1516 rather than 1517, for it reproduces errors found in the former but corrected in the latter.[4] It also reprints from 1516 some prefatory materials omitted from 1517. And though 1518M includes almost all the substantive changes that 1517 makes to 1516, in three passages it corrects 1516 *differently* from the way the same passage is corrected in 1517; moreover, in about a dozen places only 1517 has the correct reading.[5] It would seem, then, that the first Basel edition was based on a corrected copy of 1516, distinct from that underlying 1517 but closely similar to it.[6]

There is one small piece of external support for the view that 1518M was based on a copy of 1516 corrected by the author: Richard Pace's claim that More changed the *i* to *y* in *considero* when he was correcting *Utopia* (above, p. xxxix). Since in fact both Basel editions (unlike 1517) incorporate the change that Pace mentions, as well as other parallel ones, it seems reasonable to suppose that Pace had seen a copy of 1516 corrected by More, which Erasmus forwarded to Basel.

1518 November

The last of the four significant early editions was also published by Froben, in November of 1518.[7] 1518N is 'a complete and close resetting of the March edition', which includes a few small changes from that edition (*CW*, IV, cxc). Of More's modern editors, only Prévost, who prints a facsimile of 1518N as his Latin text, claims

---

[4] The most striking of these occurs in a marginal gloss on p. 78, 'Ut servat decorum in narratione'. As Surtz observes, 'In the 1516 edition ... there is an obscure mark after "narratione" which the compositor of the 1518ᵐ edition reads as a question mark. The latter does not appear in *1517* (or in *1518ⁿ*)' (*CW*, IV, 347). Miller (p. 308) calls attention to four other errors common to 1516 and 1518M but not found in 1517; Barker (p. 220) adds another.

[5] On these matters, see Miller, p. 309.

[6] It is also possible that 1518M was *corrected*, not very carefully, from a copy of 1517. Cf. Barker, p. 220. Surtz observes that the version of Budé's letter in 1518M was, 'to judge from the text', set from 1517 rather than from a manuscript copy (*CW*, IV, clxxxvi).

[7] Like 1518M, this volume also included More's and Erasmus' *Epigrammata*. The two parts of the book have separate colophons: these date the printing of *Utopia* as November and that of the *Epigrammata* as December – so that the volume is referred to as 1518D in the Yale edition of More's Latin poems (*CW*, III, Part II).

that it embodies new authorial changes. This claim rests heavily on one conspicuous emendation in 1518N, in which Hythloday's reference to 'Mea . . . oratio' (98:7) is changed to 'Meus . . . sermo'. Prévost writes that this change 'met en relief le passage de la forme littéraire originelle du "discours" à celle du "dialogue", le livre premier composé après le discours' (p. 237). But Hythloday's reference is not to the *sermo* of Book I as a whole but to his speech – an *oratio in genere deliberativo* – in the imaginary council meeting he has just recounted (90:16–94:16). (Note, too, that Hythloday had earlier referred to his speech in the *first* imaginary council meeting as an 'oratio' (86:28).) Thus there is no reason to think that More would have preferred *sermo* to *oratio* in the phrase that 1518N emends – and, if he had, presumably he would also have changed the *second* occurrence of *oratio*, a few lines farther along (98:16).[8]

Copy-text

Which of the four early printings should be made the basis of a critical edition? Surtz (like Lupton) chose 1518M, on the ground that it is 'the last edition in which More is likely to have had a direct hand' (*CW*, IV, clxxxvii; Lupton, p. ix). For the same reason, Prévost chose 1518N as the basis of his edition.[9] This latter choice is indefensible (at least on this ground), since in fact there is no real evidence of More's involvement in 1518N. But neither is the choice of 1518M inescapably correct. In the first place, More's involvement in 1518M is not altogether certain. Second, 1517 has at least as good a claim, perhaps a better one, to authorial involvement as 1518M – and it may quite possibly embody *later* authorial views than 1518M. We know that Erasmus had sent a copy of 1516 to Basel by 30 May 1517; Lupset's copy surely did not go to the printer before 31 July 1517 (the date of Budé's letter). If we assume that both copies were corrected by More, these dates suggest that Lupset's copy may possibly have left the author's hands later than the one Erasmus shipped to Basel.[10]

---

[8] There is also a rather strong piece of indirect evidence against the view that 1518N embodies corrections by More. As we noted earlier, 1518N, like 1518M, also included the *Epigrammata*. For *this* part of the volume, it is abundantly clear that More made no corrections. He was in fact highly dissatisfied with it and made extensive corrections and revisions to a copy of it, which in turn formed the basis of the third edition of the *Epigrammata*, published by Froben in 1520. See *CW*, III, Part II, 5–9.

[9] Delcourt's text is constructed by treating 1516, 1517, and 1518M 'comme trois manuscrits' (p. 26), with the first and third having greater authority than the second. [10] Cf. Miller, pp. 308–9.

Moreover, even if we grant that both 1517 and 1518M embody authorial corrections, it is not obvious that either of them is the proper basis of a critical edition. In such cases, bibliographical theory suggests that the first edition should be the copy-text, although it should be corrected wherever later editions embody changes that can plausibly be attributed to the author.[11] This position is based on a distinction between the 'substantives' (the actual words) of a text and its 'accidentals' (such matters as punctuation, spelling and capitalisation). Studies of book production in the hand-press era suggest that in revised editions authorial corrections to substantives were usually respected. Accidentals, however, were normally regarded as the province of the printer, and each printing house (indeed each compositor) exercised, with whatever degree of consistency, independent preferences in this area. Where a series of editions embodying authorial corrections derives from a first edition based on the author's manuscript, then, one normally expects to find that each successive edition is closer, on the whole, to the author's intentions in substantives but farther from these intentions (as they were embodied in the manuscript) in accidentals. Thus the nearest approximation to the book as the author intended it is a text that follows the first edition in accidentals (except where these are obviously wrong) and emends the substantives of that edition by later editions wherever their variants appear to represent authorial corrections. Applying this argument to *Utopia*, one would conclude that 1516 is the proper copy-text.

But whether or not these theoretical considerations should determine the choice of copy-text for a strict critical edition of *Utopia*, they have little force in the case of a text like ours: since our edition – with its thoroughgoing repunctuation and regularised spelling – does not respect accidentals, a theory of copy-text founded on accidentals has scant relevance to our enterprise. What in fact does determine the issue for us (as for Lupton and Surtz) is that there is good reason for believing that 1518M is, all things considered, closer to More's intentions and aspirations for *Utopia* than either of its predecessors. 1518M is a more substantial, better-printed volume than 1516 or 1517; it also has a fuller set of commendatory letters, poems and other ancillary materials than either

[11] See W. W. Greg, 'The rationale of copy-text', in *Collected Papers*, ed. J. C. Maxwell (Oxford, 1966), pp. 374–91; Fredson Bowers, 'Current theories of copy-text, with an illustration from Dryden', in *Bibliography and Textual Criticism: English and American Literature, 1700 to the Present*, ed. O. M. Black, Jr., and Warner Barnes (Chicago, 1969), pp. 59–72; Philip Gaskell, *A New Introduction to Bibliography* (Oxford, 1972), pp. 338–43.

of the earlier editions. And More's trusted associate Erasmus made considerable efforts to ensure that 1518M was handled with care, by seeing to it that Beatus Rhenanus, a scholar of education and tastes similar to Erasmus' own and More's, was put in charge of the project, and by insisting both to Rhenanus and to Froben that careful work on the book was of the greatest importance (*CWE*, V, 12, 75, 229). More wrote *Utopia*, but to a non-trivial extent the published book – so heavily dependent on Giles's and Erasmus' work as editors, agents, publicists and commentators, and buttressed by the commendatory, and sometimes interpretative, letters and poems of a number of other humanists – was a corporate product of Erasmus' humanist circle. There seems little doubt that their corporate aims – which More surely shared – were most fully realised in the Froben editions, or that the first of these, as the last edition in which either More or Erasmus appears to have had a hand, should be the basis for our text.

WORKS CITED

Abbreviations: *CW* = Yale *Complete Works of St. Thomas More*; *CWE* = Toronto *Collected Works of Erasmus*; LCL = Loeb Classical Library; *EA* = Sylvester and Marc'hadour, ed., *Essential Articles for the Study of Thomas More*; *JEGP* = *Journal of English and Germanic Philology*. Greek and Roman classics are listed only if they are quoted (rather than merely referred to) in the Introduction or notes. Place of publication is London unless otherwise specified.

Adams, Robert P. *The Better Part of Valor: More, Erasmus, Colet, and Vives, on Humanism, War, and Peace, 1496–1535*. Seattle, 1962.

Allen, Don Cameron. 'The rehabilitation of Epicurus and his theory of pleasure in the early Renaissance'. *Studies in Philology*, 41 (1944), 1–15.

Allen, John W. *A History of Political Thought in the Sixteenth Century*. 1928; rpt 1957.

Ames, Russell. *Citizen Thomas More and His Utopia*. Princeton, 1949.

Aristotle. *The Nicomachean Ethics*. Ed. and trans. H. Rackham. Rev. edn. LCL. London and Cambridge, Mass., 1934.

——. *The Politics of Aristotle*. Trans. Ernest Barker. Oxford, 1948.

Augustine, St. *The City of God against the Pagans [De civitate Dei]*. Ed. and trans. George E. McCracken *et al.* LCL. 7 vols. London and Cambridge, Mass., 1957–72.

Baker-Smith, Dominic. *More's 'Utopia'*. Unwin Critical Library. London and New York, 1991.

Barker, Arthur. '*Clavis Moreana*: The Yale edition of Thomas More'. In *EA*, pp. 215–28. Originally publ. *JEGP*, 65 (1966), 318–30.

Baron, Hans. *The Crisis of the Early Italian Renaissance*. Rev. one-vol. edn. Princeton, 1966.

Bietenholz, Peter G., and Thomas B. Deutscher, ed. *Contemporaries of Erasmus: A Biographical Register of the Renaissance and Reformation*. 3 vols. Toronto, Buffalo and London, 1985–7.

Bolchazy, Ladislaus J. *A Concordance to the 'Utopia' of St. Thomas More and A Frequency Word List*. Hildesheim and New York, 1978.

Bowers, Fredson. 'Current theories of copy-text, with an illustration from Dryden'. In *Bibliography and Textual Criticism: English and American Literature, 1700 to the Present*. Ed. O. M. Black, Jr., and Warner Barnes. Chicago, 1969.

de Brie, Germain. *Antimorus*. In More, *Latin Poems*. CW, Vol. III, Part II (below).

Burgess, Theodore C. 'Epideictic literature'. *University of Chicago Studies in Classical Philology*, 3 (1902), 89–261.

Cappelli, Adriano. *Dizionario di abbreviature latine ed italiane*. 6th edn. Milan, 1961.

Carlyle, R. W., and A. J. Carlyle. *A History of Mediaeval Political Theory in the West*. 3rd edn. 6 vols. 1903–36.

Chambers, R. W. *Thomas More*. 1935.

Cicero. *De finibus bonorum et malorum*. Ed. and trans. H. Rackham. 2nd edn. LCL. London and Cambridge, Mass., 1931.

——. *De inventione*. Ed. and trans. H. M. Hubbell. LCL. London and Cambridge, Mass., 1949.

——. *De legibus*. Ed. and trans. C. W. Keyes. LCL. London and Cambridge, Mass., 1928.

——. *De natura deorum*; *Academica*. Ed. and trans. H. Rackham. LCL. London and New York, 1933.

——. *De officiis*. Ed. and trans. Walter Miller. LCL. London and Cambridge, Mass., 1913.

——. *De oratore*. Ed. and trans. E. W. Sutton and H. Rackham. LCL. 2 vols. London and Cambridge, Mass., 1942.

——. *De re publica*. Ed. and trans. C. W. Keyes. LCL. London and Cambridge, Mass., 1928.

——. *De senectute*; *De amicitia*; *De divinatione*. Ed. and trans. William A. Falconer. LCL. London and New York, 1923.

——. *The Letters to His Friends* [*Epistulae ad familiares*]. Ed. and trans. W. G. Williams. LCL. 3 vols. London and Cambridge, Mass., 1927.

——. *Orator*. Ed. and trans. H. M. Hubbell. LCL. London and Cambridge, Mass., 1952.

Colie, Rosalie L. *Paradoxia Epidemica: The Renaissance Tradition of Paradox*. Princeton, 1966.

Cummins, J. S. 'Pox and paranoia in Renaissance Europe'. *History Today*, 38 (August 1988), 28–35.

Demetrius. *On Style*. Ed. and trans. W. Rhys Roberts. LCL. The volume also includes Aristotle, *The Poetics*, and Longinus, *On the Sublime*, ed. and trans. W. Hamilton Fyfe. London and New York, 1927.

Diogenes Laertius. *Lives of Eminent Philosophers*. Ed. and trans. R. D. Hicks. LCL. 2 vols. London and New York, 1925.

Elton, G. R. 'The real Thomas More?' In *Reformation Principle and Practice*. Ed. Peter N. Brooks. 1980.

——. 'Thomas More, Councillor (1517–1529)'. In *St. Thomas More: Action and Contemplation*. Ed. Richard S. Sylvester. New Haven and London, 1972.

Erasmus, Desiderius. *Adages* IiI to IvIoo. Trans. Margaret Mann Phillips, annotated by R. A. B. Mynors. CWE, Vol. XXXI. Toronto, Buffalo and London, 1982.

——. *Adages* IIi1 to IIvi100. Trans. and annotated by R. A. B. Mynors. *CWE*, Vol. XXXIII. Toronto, Buffalo and London, 1991.

——. *The Colloquies of Erasmus*. Trans. Craig R. Thompson. Chicago, 1965.

——. *The Correspondence of Erasmus*. Vols. III and IV. Trans. R. A. B. Mynors and D. F. S. Thomson, annotated by James K. McConica. *CWE*. Toronto, Buffalo and London, 1976, 1977.

——. *The Correspondence of Erasmus*. Vol. V. Trans. R. A. B. Mynors and D. F. S. Thomson, annotated by Peter G. Bietenholz. *CWE*. Toronto, Buffalo and London, 1979.

——. *The Correspondence of Erasmus*. Vol. VII. Trans. R. A. B. Mynors, annotated by Peter G. Bietenholz. *CWE*. Toronto, Buffalo and London, 1987.

——. *The Education of a Christian Prince*. Trans. and annotated by Neil M. Cheshire and Michael J. Heath. In *CWE*, Vol. XXVII. Ed. A. H. T. Levi. Toronto, Buffalo and London, 1986.

——. *Praise of Folly*. Trans. and annotated by Betty Radice. In *CWE*, Vol. XXVII. Ed A. H. T. Levi. Toronto, Buffalo and London, 1986.

Fox, Alistair. *Thomas More: History and Providence*. New Haven and London, 1983.

——. *'Utopia': An Elusive Vision*. Twayne's Masterwork Studies. New York, 1993.

Gaskell, Philip. *A New Introduction to Bibliography*. Oxford, 1972.

Gibson, R. W., and J. Max Patrick. *St. Thomas More: A Preliminary Bibliography of His Works and of Moreana to the Year 1750*. New Haven and London, 1961.

Gilbert, Felix. 'The humanist concept of the prince and *The Prince* of Machiavelli'. *The Journal of Modern History*, 11 (1939), 449–83.

Goodey, Brian R. 'Mapping "Utopia": A comment on the geography of Sir Thomas More'. *The Geographical Review*, 60 (1970), 15–30.

Graesse, J. G. T. *Trésor de livres rares et précieux*. Milan, 1950.

Greenblatt, Stephen. *Renaissance Self-fashioning from More to Shakespeare*. Chicago and London, 1980.

Greg, W. W. 'The rationale of copy-text'. In *Collected Papers*. Ed. J. C. Maxwell. Oxford, 1966.

Guy, J. A. *The Public Career of Sir Thomas More*. New Haven and London, 1980.

Harpsfield, Nicholas. *The Life and Death of Sir Thomas Moore*. Ed. E. V. Hitchcock. Early English Text Society, Original Series, No. 186. 1932.

Harrison, William. *The Description of England*. Ed. Georges Edelen. Ithaca, 1968.

Heimann, David, and Richard Kay. *The Elements of Abbreviation in Medieval Latin Paleography*. Lawrence, Kansas, 1982.

Herodotus. [*The Histories*.] Ed. and trans. A. D. Godley. LCL. 4 vols. London and Cambridge, Mass., 1921–5.

Hexter, J. H. *More's 'Utopia': The Biography of an Idea*. Princeton, 1952; rpt with an epilogue, New York, 1965.

Holinshed, Raphael. *Holinshed's Chronicles [of] England, Scotland, and Ireland*. 6 vols. 1807; rpt New York, 1965.

Kautsky, Karl. *Thomas More and His Utopia*. Trans. H. J. Stenning. 1927 (first German edn. 1888); rpt with a foreword by Russell Ames, New York, 1959.

Keen, Ralph, and Constance Smith. 'Updating an updating: Some additions and revisions to: Constance Smith, *An Updating of R. W. Gibson's "St. Thomas More: A Preliminary Bibliography"*'. *Moreana*, 25, No. 97 (1988), 137–40.

Kenyon, Timothy. *Utopian Communism and Political Thought in Early Modern England*. 1989.

Kristeller, Paul Oskar. *Renaissance Thought and Its Sources*. Ed. Michael Mooney. New York, 1979.

——. *Renaissance Thought: The Classic, Scholastic, and Humanist Strains*. New York, 1961.

——. 'Thomas More as a Renaissance humanist'. *Moreana*, No. 65–6 (1980), 5–22.

Latham, R. E. *Dictionary of Medieval Latin from British Sources*. 4 fasc. to date. 1975–.

——. *Revised Medieval Latin Word-List From British and Irish Sources*. 1965.

Lewis, Charlton T., and Charles Short. *A Latin Dictionary*. 'Founded on Andrews' Edition of Freund's Latin Dictionary, Revised, Enlarged and in Great Part Rewritten'. Oxford, 1879, with reprintings to 1966.

Logan, George M. *The Meaning of More's 'Utopia'*. Princeton, 1983.

Lucan. *The Civil War [Pharsalia]*. Ed. and trans. J. D. Duff. LCL. London and New York, 1928.

Lucian. [*Works*.] Ed. and trans. A. M. Harmon *et al.* LCL. 8 vols. London and Cambridge, Mass., 1913–67.

McCutcheon, Elizabeth. 'Denying the contrary: More's use of litotes in the *Utopia*'. In *EA*, pp. 263–74. Originally publ. *Moreana*, No. 31–2 (1971), 107–21.

——. *My Dear Peter: The 'Ars Poetica' and Hermeneutics for More's 'Utopia'*. Angers, 1983.

McKerrow, Ronald B. *An Introduction to Bibliography for Literary Students*. Oxford, 1927.

Machiavelli, Niccolò. *The Prince*. In *The Chief Works and Others*. Trans. Allan Gilbert. 3 vols. Durham, N.C., 1958.

Manuel, Frank E., and Fritzie P. Manuel. *Utopian Thought in the Western World*. Cambridge, Mass., 1979.

Marc'hadour, Germain. 'More's first wife . . . Jane? or Joan?' *Moreana*, 29, No. 109 (1992), 3–22.

Marius, Richard. *Thomas More*. New York, 1984.

Martial. *Epigrams*. Ed. and trans. Walter C. A. Ker. Rev. edn. LCL. 2 vols. London and Cambridge, Mass., 1968.

Martz, Louis L. *Thomas More: The Search for the Inner Man*. New Haven and London, 1990.

Menander Rhetor. Treatise on Epideictic. In *Rhetores Graeci*. Ed. Christianus Walz. 9 vols. Osnabrück, 1968; originally publ. 1832–6. IX, 127–330.

Mermel, Jerry. 'Preparations for a politic life: Sir Thomas More's entry into the king's service'. *Journal of Medieval and Renaissance Studies*, 7 (1977), 53–66.

Miller, Clarence H. 'The English translation in the Yale *Utopia*: Some corrections'. *Moreana*, No. 9 (1966), 57–64.

——. Review of *Utopia*, ed. Surtz and Hexter. *English Language Notes*, 3 (1965–6), 303–9.

——. 'Style and meaning in More's *Utopia*: Hythloday's sentences and diction'. In *Acta Conventus Neo-Latini Hafniensis: Proceedings*, ed. Rhoda Schnur *et al.* (Binghamton, N.Y., 1994).

Monsuez, R. 'Le latin de Thomas More dans *Utopia*'. *Annales publiées trimestriellement par La Faculté des Lettres et Sciences Humaines de Toulouse*, Nouvelle Série, Tome 2, Fasc. 1, janvier, 1966. *Caliban*, 3 (1966), 35–78.

More, St Thomas. *The Answer to a Poisoned Book*. Ed. Stephen M. Foley and Clarence H. Miller. *CW*, Vol. XI. New Haven and London, 1985.

——. *The Confutation of Tyndale's Answer*. Ed. L. A. Schuster, R. C. Marius, J. P. Lusardi and R. J. Schoeck. *CW*, Vol. VIII. New Haven and London, 1973.

——. *The Correspondence of Sir Thomas More*. Ed. Elizabeth F. Rogers. Princeton, 1947.

——. *De Tristitia Christi*. Ed. Clarence H. Miller. *CW*, Vol. XIV. New Haven and London, 1976.

——. *A Dialogue Concerning Heresies*. Ed. T. M. C. Lawler, G. Marc'hadour and R. C. Marius. *CW*, Vol. VI. New Haven and London, 1981.

——. *A Dialogue of Comfort against Tribulation*. Ed. Louis L. Martz and Frank Manley. *CW*, Vol. XII. New Haven and London, 1976.

——. *The English Works of Sir Thomas More*. Ed. W. E. Campbell, annotated by A. W. Reed. 2 vols. London and New York, 1931.

——. *The Four Last Things*. In *The English Works*, ed. Campbell and Reed. I, 457–99.

——. *A Fruitful, Pleasant and Witty Work called Utopia*. Trans. Ralph Robinson. Scolar Press Facsimile of the 2nd (1556) edn. Menston, 1970.

——. *The History of King Richard III*. Ed. Richard S. Sylvester. *CW*, Vol. II. New Haven and London, 1963.

——. *Latin Poems*. Ed. Clarence H. Miller, Leicester Bradner, Charles A.

Lynch and Revilo P. Oliver. *CW*, Vol. III, Part II. New Haven and London, 1984.

——. 'Letter to Martin Dorp'. In *In Defense of Humanism*. Ed. Daniel Kinney. *CW*, Vol. XV. New Haven and London, 1986.

——. *Responsio ad Lutherum*. Ed. John M. Headley, trans. Sr. Scholastica Mandeville. *CW*, Vol. V. New Haven and London, 1969.

——. *Selected Letters*. Ed. Elizabeth F. Rogers. *CW*, Modernized Series. New Haven and London, 1961.

——. *Translations of Lucian*. Ed. Craig R. Thompson. *CW*, Vol. III, Part I. New Haven and London, 1974.

——. *A Treatise upon the Passion*. Ed. Garry E. Haupt. *CW*, Vol. XIII. New Haven and London, 1976.

——. *Utopia* [1516]. Louvain: Dirk Martens; rpt Scolar Press Facsimile, Leeds, 1966.

——. *Utopia* [1517]. Paris: Gilles de Gourmont.

——. *Utopia* [1518 March]. Basel: Johann Froben.

——. *Utopia* [1518 November]. Basel: Johann Froben; rpt as the text in Prévost's edn (below).

——. *Utopia* [1548]. Louvain: Servatius Sassenus.

——. *Utopia* [1563]. In *Lucubrations* [Latin Works]. Basel: Episcopius.

——. *Utopia* [1565-6]. In *Omnia . . . Latina opera*. Louvain: Bogard and Zangrius, 1565 and 1566. (Identical editions were published by both Bogard and Zangrius in 1565, and reprinted in 1566.)

——. *Utopia* [1672]. Helmstedt: Johann Heitmuller.

——. *Utopia*. Ed. J. H. Lupton. With the Robinson translation. Oxford, 1895.

——. *Utopia*. Ed. V. Michels and T. Ziegler. Berlin, 1895.

——. *Utopia*. Ed. Edward Surtz, SJ, and J. H. Hexter. *CW*, Vol. IV. New Haven and London, 1965.

——. *L'Utopie*. Ed. and trans. Marie Delcourt. Paris, 1983; text originally publ. 1936; translation originally publ. 1950.

——. *L'Utopie de Thomas More*. Ed. and trans. André Prévost. Paris, 1978.

——. *The Workes of Sir Thomas More Knyght, sometyme Lorde Chauncellour of England, wrytten by him in the Englysh tonge*. Introduction by K. J. Wilson. Scolar Press Facsimile of the 1557 edition. 2 vols. 1978.

Nagel, Alan F. 'Lies and the limitable inane: Contradiction in More's *Utopia*'. *Renaissance Quarterly*, 26 (1973), 173–80.

Pace, Richard. *De Fructu Qui Ex Doctrina Percipitur*. Ed. and trans. Frank Manley and Richard S. Sylvester. New York, 1967.

Parks, G. R. 'More's Utopia and geography'. *JEGP*, 37 (1938), 224–36.

Pietro Martire d'Anghiera. *De Orbe Novo: The Eight Decades of Peter Martyr D'Anghera*. Trans. Francis A. MacNutt. 2 vols. New York and London, 1912; rpt New York, 1970.

Plato. *Epistles*. Ed. and trans. R. G. Bury. LCL. London and Cambridge, Mass., 1929.

——. *The Laws*. Trans. Trevor J. Saunders. Harmondsworth, 1970; rpt with minor revisions, 1975.

——. *Philebus*. Ed. and trans. H. N. Fowler. LCL. London and Cambridge, Mass., 1925.

——. *The Republic*. Trans. H. D. P. Lee. 2nd edn. Harmondsworth, 1974.

Plutarch. *Lives*. Ed. and trans. Bernadotte Perrin. LCL. 11 vols. New York and London, 1914–26.

——. *Moralia*. Ed. and trans. Frank Cole Babbitt *et al*. 17 vols. London and Cambridge, Mass., 1927–76.

Pocock, J. G. A. *The Machiavellian Moment: Florentine Political Thought and the Atlantic Republican Tradition*. Princeton, 1975.

Quintilian. *Institutio oratoria*. Ed. and trans. H. E. Butler. LCL. 4 vols. London and Cambridge, Mass., 1921–2.

Rabelais, François. *Gargantua and Pantagruel*. Trans. Sir Thomas Urquhart and Peter le Motteux. The World's Classics. 1934.

Roper, William. *The Life of Sir Thomas More*. In *Two Early Tudor Lives*. Ed. Richard S. Sylvester and Davis P. Harding. New Haven and London, 1962.

Sallust. [*Works*.] Ed. and trans. J. C. Rolfe. Rev. edn. LCL. London and Cambridge, Mass., 1931.

Schmitt, Charles B., *et al.*, ed. *The Cambridge History of Renaissance Philosophy*. Cambridge, 1988.

Schoeck, R. J. 'More, Plutarch, and King Agis: Spartan history and the meaning of *Utopia*'. In *EA*, pp. 275–80. Originally publ. *Philological Quarterly*, 35 (1956), 366–75.

Seneca. *Ad Lucilium Epistulae Morales*. Ed. and trans. Richard M. Gummere. LCL. 3 vols. London and Cambridge, Mass., 1917.

——. *Dialogi* [*Moral Essays*]. Ed. and trans. John W. Basore. LCL. 3 vols. London and Cambridge, Mass., 1928–35.

Skinner, Quentin. *The Foundations of Modern Political Thought*. 2 vols. Cambridge, 1978.

——. 'Sir Thomas More's *Utopia* and the language of Renaissance humanism'. In *The Languages of Political Theory in Early-Modern Europe*. Ed. Anthony Pagden. Cambridge, 1987.

Smith, Constance. *An Updating of R. W. Gibson's 'St. Thomas More: A Preliminary Bibliography'*. Sixteenth Century Bibliography, No. 20. St Louis, 1981.

Smith, George D., ed. *The Teaching of the Catholic Church*. 2nd edn. 1952.

Stapleton, Thomas. *The Life and Illustrious Martyrdom of Sir Thomas More*. Trans. Philip E. Hallett, ed. E. E. Reynolds. 1966.

Starnes, Colin. *The New Republic: A Commentary on Book 1 of More's 'Utopia' Showing Its Relation to Plato's 'Republic'*. Waterloo, Ontario, 1990.

——. *The Statutes of the Realm*. Vol. 3. 1822.

Surtz, Edward L., SJ. 'Aspects of More's Latin style in *Utopia*'. *Studies in the Renaissance*, 14 (1967), 93–109.

——. 'Interpretations of *Utopia*'. *Catholic Historical Review*, 38 (1952), 156–74.

——. *The Praise of Pleasure: Philosophy, Education, and Communism in More's Utopia*. Cambridge, Mass., 1957.

——. *The Praise of Wisdom: A Commentary on the Religious and Moral Problems and Backgrounds of St. Thomas More's 'Utopia'*. Chicago, 1957.

Sylvester, R. S., and G. P. Marc'hadour, ed. *Essential Articles for the Study of Thomas More [EA]*. Hamden, Conn., 1977.

Tacitus. *Agricola; Germania; Dialogus*. First two works ed. and trans. Maurice Hutton, the third by W. Peterson; rev., respectively, R. M. Ogilvie, E. H. Warmington and M. Winterbottom. LCL. London and Cambridge, Mass., 1970.

Thesaurus linguae Latinae. 10 vols. to date. Leipzig, 1900–.

Thomas Aquinas, St. *Sententia libri politicorum*. In *Opera omnia*. Rome, 1882–. Vol. XLVIII, A 67–A 205.

Thompson, James W., and Saul K. Padover. *Secret Diplomacy*. 2nd edn. New York, 1963.

Valla, Lorenzo. *On Pleasure; De voluptate*. Trans. A. Kent Hieatt and Maristella de Panizza Lorch, introduction by Maristella de Panizza Lorch. New York, 1977.

Vegetius. *Epitoma rei militaris*. Ed. C. Lang. Leipzig, 1885.

Vespucci, Amerigo. *The Four Voyages of Amerigo Vespucci [Quattuor Americi Vespucci navigationes]*. In Martin Walseemüller, *Cosmographiae Introductio*. Ann Arbor, 1966 (University Microfilms); rpt from US Catholic Historical Society Monograph IV, 1907.

——. *Mundus Novus: Letter to Pietro di Medici*. Trans. George Tyler Northup. London and Princeton, 1916.

White, Thomas I. 'Aristotle and *Utopia*'. *Renaissance Quarterly*, 29 (1976), 635–75.

——. '*Festivitas, utilitas, et opes*: The concluding irony and philosophical purpose of Thomas More's *Utopia*'. *Albion*, 10 (1978), 135–50.

——. 'Pride and the public good: Thomas More's use of Plato in *Utopia*'. *Journal of the History of Philosophy*, 20 (1982), 329–54.

Wilson, N. G. 'The name Hythlodaeus'. *Moreana*, 29, No. 110 (1992), 33.

Wind, Edgar. *Pagan Mysteries in the Renaissance*. Rev. edn. New York, 1968.

INDEX

Utopian ideas, attitudes, customs and institutions are indexed under 'Utopia (the country)'.

The editorial introduction and appendix have been indexed. In the case of *Utopia* itself, the translation, rather than the Latin text, has been indexed, but names included in notes to the Latin text have been indexed.

Where an indexed item is referred to both in a passage of the translation and in a note to the same passage, only the page number is given. But when an indexed item occurs in a passage of the translation and also in a note attached to a different passage on the same page, the reference consists of the page number 'and n.' When an indexed item occurs in more than one note on the same page, this is shown by the suffix 'nn.' added to the page number.